The Dime Novel
in Chidren's Literature

Also by Vicki Anderson
and from McFarland

Fiction Sequels for Readers 10 to 16: An Annotated Bibliography of Books in Succession, 2d ed. (1998)

Sequels in Children's Literature: An Annotated Bibliography of Books in Succession or with Shared Themes and Characters, K–6 (1998)

Cultures Outside the United States in Fiction: A Guide to 2,875 Books for Librarians and Teachers, K–9 (1994)

Immigrants in the United States in Fiction: A Guide to 705 Books for Librarians and Teachers, K–9 (1994)

Native Americans in Fiction: A Guide to 765 Books for Librarians and Teachers, K–9 (1994)

Fiction Index for Readers 10 to 16: Subject Access to Over 8200 Books (1960–1990) (1992)

The Dime Novel in Children's Literature

Vicki Anderson

McFarland & Company, Inc., Publishers
Jefferson, North Carolina, and London

LIBRARY OF CONGRESS CATALOGUING-IN-PUBLICATION DATA

Anderson, Vicki, 1928–
The dime novel in children's literature / Vicki Anderson.
p. cm.
Includes bibliographical references and index.

ISBN 0-7864-1843-5 (softcover : 50# alkaline paper) ∞

1. Dime novels—History and criticism. 2. Popular literature—United States—History and criticism. 3. Children's stories, American—History and criticism. 4. Children—Books and reading—United States. 5. Dime novels—Publishing—United States. 6. American fiction—History and criticism. I. Title.
PS374.D5A53 2005
813'.4099282—dc22 2004019460

British Library cataloguing data are available

On the cover: Illustrative elements reassembled from the cover of the specially shaped "toy book" *Nursery Ditties* (mid–19th century)

Manufactured in the United States of America

McFarland & Company, Inc., Publishers
Box 611, Jefferson, North Carolina 28640
www.mcfarlandpub.com

Table of Contents

Introduction

From about the middle of the nineteenth century to the early twentieth century many people were reading what came to be known as the dime novel. These publications were often identified as sensational literature and were recognizable by their format, content and color.

The size was identified as pocket size, that is, five by eight inches. Although some books ran as long as one hundred pages, more commonly they had fewer. They usually had woodcut illustrations on their paper covers and were printed on poor-quality, thin paper. It was these covers, especially the orange color used by Beadle and Company, that immediately identified the dime novel. It was a true trademark. In time the term *dime novel* came to include any action-packed text selling for between five and twenty-five cents.

Distribution was dependent on recognizability at the newsstands and then later through mail-order subscriptions. These novels were almost always turned into continuing series and vice versa, so recognizability was also important for that reason. One needed to spot the various installments at once. Beadle's *Frontier Series* and the *Deadwood Dick Library* are examples of this technique. This sales approach helped the potential reader know that the book contained the exciting text that he had come to expect. The faithful readers wanted familiar scenes, well-known characters and similar action—in other words, a book that was almost identical to the last one in terms of action, people and setting.

One of the most popular subjects of these early dime novels was America's frontier days, which at the time meant anything from western New York to the Mississippi River and sometimes even a bit farther west. One of the earliest and very popular titles was *Seth Jones of New Hampshire, or, the Captives of the Frontier* by Edward Ellis, a prolific writer.

The narrative was told in predictable plot formulas about pure innocence, helpless women, law enforcers who were not always heroes and "noblemen" who were the true heroes. There were exciting chases, terrorizing captures and sensational rescues. The readers looked for stories about the capture of and rescue by heroines and heroes, of powerless older men, helpless children and "maidens in distress." There were stories of people who, when identities were finally disclosed, turned out to be lost relatives, lovers or kidnapped children.

The dime novelist eliminated all questionable events by the end of the tale; the closing chapter typically contained a number of "logical" revelations, and this abruptly revealed information guaranteed that all of the aforementioned plot made complete noble and ethical, if not always logical, sense.

These dime novels, especially the frontier stories, were considered quite violent, so people living in "civilized" cities with modern conveniences could vicariously experience the excitement of living in the "uncivilized" West. This had appeal because of the growing urbanization of the Eastern cities. People were looking for escape from the dull routine of urban life to the unexplored and dangerous life of the New Frontier.

The widespread reading of the dime novel coincided with the advance of the social sciences in the United States, including scientific criminology and penology, which were most often used in finding the cause of crime. Reading could lead to either virtue or crime. Therefore, guided or controlled reading took on an important role.

"It is not unknown to find counterfeiting and even murder springing from bad reading.... A child of ten ... held up another and robbed him of three dollars. The robber had read dime novels from the age of seven. He was particularly interested in Jesse James, and knew more of him than of Washington." Thomas Travis wrote this in 1908 in *The Young Malefactor: A Study in Juvenile Delinquency, Its Causes and Treatment*. The view that lurid literature had serious antisocial effects was widespread in the late nineteenth and early twentieth centuries. To many American literary and educational establishments, these dime novels, with their supposed sensational writing, violent characters, intricate plots, changing identities and confusion of right and wrong, gave serious and improper messages to the day's suggestible youth and were therefore severely criticized. The moral leaders of the day wanted literature to reflect idealistic family life, whereas the dime novels were seen to portray violence and crime. This criticism is analogous to today's criticism of both moving pictures and television programming.

Serious writers scorned this hack literature as many today scorn the popular, original, paperback romances that flood the supermarkets and newsstands. Fiction books that people assumed gave answers to social questions were not encouraged, especially if the social questions were controversial. But, in any age, the social questions of the day are bound to come out in the current literature, whether intended or not. Except in pure fantasy, the issues of the day almost have to be revealed in the literary works of the time. It is for this reason, among others, that the literature of any age is an important part of history even if the literary critics of the time found it unacceptable.

These books therefore conveyed the standards of the day concerning social attitudes and problems even though they consciously didn't address social issues. Most of these revealing ideas were certainly not intentional on the part of the authors, but one writes what one knows, and the everyday standards of the people is what one knows.

Although dime novels were popular mainly in the eighteenth and nineteenth centuries, they had many forerunners, as we shall see in the next few chapters. Some of these were the story papers, chapbooks, broadsides and the numerous abridged versions of classic tales. The serial book, with fresh chapters in every new publication, was also popular. Authors such as Edward S. Ellis and W. Bert Foster wrote fiction for these serial books. This kept the reader coming back for the next installment. It ensured the printer a constant clientele. This trend then continued with the publication of pulp magazines, comic books and today's paperback books.

The majority of children's books are bought by adults, and they are almost always written by adults. This was also true in the past, and it is not surprising that then, as now, it was largely the adult world that was reflected in children's books. Books that were bought were those the grown-ups thought the child *should* read; later, toward the end of the nineteenth century, that sentence would become "what the grown-ups thought the child *liked* to read."

While surveying the development of books that children read, we should also investigate the changing attitudes toward childhood over the same periods. The study of the origins of and influences on children's literature help us to understand the trends that led from the early chapbooks to modern offerings of reading material for children, Why, for example, were early books not specifically written for children? What impact did the miniature books of the John Newbery era have on the popular acceptance of literature for children? How did the modern school texts derive from religious manuals? Why did the literary series spring into such prominence in the second quarter of the nineteenth century?

The various aspects of the social history of different epochs are fascinating. The occupations and avocations, the manners and morals, the thought processes, the attitudes of parents and writers toward the young—these are reflected in children's books, including the nonliterary ones.

These early books tell us a great deal about many other facets of early American life and thought. They reflect the cultural nationalism with their sincere efforts at ideological teachings—in personal morality and ethics, in humanitarian reform and political thought. This book provides glimpses into American and British life up to 1900 and a bit beyond. And although the nineteenth century saw much hack writing, it was also a time of great American children's literary works: Washington Irving's "The Legend of Sleepy Hollow" (1820); Nathaniel Hawthorne's *Wonder-Book for Boys and Girls* (1853); Sarah Joseph Hale's "Mary's Lamb" (1830); Lydia Maria Child's "The New England Boy's Song" (1845) ("Over the river and through the woods…); Louisa May Alcott's *Little Women* (1868); and Howard Pyle's *Men of Iron* (1892) stand out.

I agree with the great book collector A. S. W. Rosenbach that "more than any other class of literature they [children's books] reflect the minds of the generation that produced them. Hence no greater guide to the history and development of any country can be found than its juvenile literature."

This book shows what written material was read by children, as best as can be determined. The selections chosen as examples are representative of the children's literature written and published during these developmental periods. They are not representative of what was best from a literary standpoint. In most cases not a lot of good material was published in these different periods. Therefore, the poorly written was well represented, and this material served as examples of children's reading for generations.

What this literature has given us is an in-depth look at what adults wanted for and from the children of that time and what their future plans for children revealed about their own attitudes toward maturing youngsters.

Although this book is not intended as a history of children's reading, it is helpful to trace the early writings as a background to what eventually became the dime novel and thereafter the basis of today's paperback books. Some of the books mentioned were meant for instruction, while others reflected those that were used for leisure reading. Some of the books of instruction have been included because of their somewhat special significance, but fiction reading is the main thrust of this book. However, one needs to note that instruction books often came in the form of fiction. The books mentioned here symbolize and represent the many important trends in these periods of development of children's literature—what and why children read—rather than set forth the significant literary works among these nonliterary books. Some readers may regret the omission of their own favorites.

Most of the examples have been selected from the collections of the Library of Congress. Some are familiar, some rare, some famous, some nearly forgotten. Taken together, all provide insight into what literate and well-intended adults felt would be best for young minds and for passing on to the future.

The pages that follow provide a sampling of the works produced in America and England for young readers. The examples also show that, from the earliest time, there existed both American productions and reissued British works. The British writings were sometimes changed to give an American look to the works. Later in the nineteenth century, however, more American books and magazines for children began to deal only with specific American subjects: the Westward movement and development; changing attitudes toward Native Americans, African Americans and immigrants; the growth of large cities and industries; plus the impact of the Civil War boom and the following depression.

It was clearly not a one-way development; in the eighteenth century, English children's books frequently appeared in the United States with little or no change, while, in the nineteenth century, many American children's books were published in England for the British market. For example, Samuel G. Goodrich, under the name Peter Parley, wrote a series of very successful informational books in the 1820s and 1830s with the intention of eliminating the British background from books for children. In his Peter Parley books he wrote about American people of the real world. Throughout this publishing period, in the English-speaking world, books crossed the ocean in both directions, and the same works were read and appreciated on each side of the Atlantic.

Enduring literature also traveled across the Atlantic in both directions: *Alice in Wonderland* found ready acceptance in America; *Little Men* was published in London before it was in Boston because its American author, Louisa May Alcott, was visiting England at that time.

The emphasis here is on aspects of the books themselves, and this approach should appeal more to the general reader, art historian or bibliophile than the professional educators. I discuss the contents of these books, plus their authors, publishers, and illustrators.

The movement that created special collections of children's books, housed in specially created children's rooms in public libraries and supervised by specially trained librarians, was very much part of the effort to counter the dangerous challenge of trash literature and to provide an attractive alternative to the lurid nickel-and-dime juveniles that were so popular in the late-nineteenth century. Because of the poor reputation of the dime novel, it has largely been neglected until recently, with only a few scholars making extensive use of this material for studies in popular culture. What nobody can deny, however, is that these books sold a tremendous number of copies and thus had an influence far beyond their literary merit.

Dime novels are important historical and literary material. As interested researchers read and learn more about the development of children's literature they need to know more about these inexpensive reading materials of the day. It is also important to remember that it was not all male dominated, since females were also readers of the dime novel (e.g., romances, fantasies). They, too, were audiences for these novels.

Books do not exist in a vacuum but are shaped by the world around them. This is particularly true of those books intended to instruct the young. Past attitudes toward children, the natural world, ethics and God, foreigners and servants: There is plenty of social history to be gleaned by looking at early children's books.

"England could have been reconstructed entirely from its children's books," writes Paul Hazard, and there is truth in the statement as well as obvious exaggeration. Because the record is so long and so rich and because over a long period of time almost all major writers have addressed themselves to children or written about them or been taken over by them, we have a literature with a continuous record not only of childhood but also of society as a whole and—what is more important—of the ideals and standards that this generation wished to impart to the children of the next generation.

One book cannot accomplish everything, and even encyclopedias have their shortcomings. It has been necessary again and again to be reminded of what the original purpose was—to make a study from a critical point of view of the worth, the kind, and the power of those contributions to children's literature which have given that literature its now acknowledged place in civilization today. It is obvious that a book of this kind, aimed at the general reader, cannot do more than reveal a portion of the vast amount of existing material. The subject of each chapter is itself worthy of a book, and I hope from my small beginnings others will produce works of greater depth within their own special fields. Notes in the text have been kept to a minimum, but for the benefit of students of early children's books, several short bibliographies, lists of appropriate books, and other items of interest to the researcher have been included.

We are lucky today that the Library of Congress collected this "trash" literature at the time of publication and later; otherwise, we would be unable to evaluate this material, which was an important part of the literature of the Americas. Today we can look at this literature with an open mind and see its role in the development of literature, especially children's literature. The library's contribution to today's research in popular culture studies, literature and publishing history is unparalleled.

Short History

Books for children, written with a predetermined purpose, have been around for about four hundred years; children's books, written with an attempt to interest the child, for less than two hundred years; and children's literature, which is well written and where the child is pictured realistically and sympathetically, has existed less than a hundred years; therefore, real children's literature is quite young in the world of printing. Fiction books, those that don't necessarily teach, were, for the most part, not available to children until the nineteenth century. It was only then that fictional literature—written specifically for children and meant to appeal to their sense of pleasure—began to appear.

The earliest books for children could be divided into two kinds: those that taught social "niceties" and those that taught "the wages of sin." The division reflected the different futures ahead for the children concerned. For the child whose expectations lay in the professional or clerical field (and for much of the Middle Ages these were one and the same), the primer was the most important book. He would be well drilled in his duty to his superiors and in social behavior. He was to be taught all that was considered necessary for the well-born, medieval child to know.

On the other hand, a young child who was conceived in sin and therefore "naturally evil" stood most in need of the attention of those concerned with the welfare of souls. It was this source, therefore, that produced the earliest books written specifically for children's salvation. The first influences on literature for children appears as a result of this Puritan conviction that every child was conceived in sin and must therefore be made aware of himself as the product of evil. He needed to be made sacred, usually best done by dying early, in order to redeem himself, or else meet his just rewards in hell.

Two other basic themes also run through the early development of children's literature: entertainment and didacticism. The first one was encouraged by William Caxton, the first English printer, who offered tales from the oral tradition in the fifteenth century. These tales continued to appear in printed form as cheap booklets, called *chapbooks*, and were sold by peddlers. They appeared in collections and retellings by scholars and artists such as Charles Perrault in 1607 and Jakob and Wilhelm Grimm in the 1820s.

The second theme, at its height in the seventeenth century with the growth of Puritanism, was religious training and moral admonition. The Puritans, in their concern for the child's immortal soul, thought of children as quite different from adults and in need of saving. Didacticism was the basis of all their writings. All writers of these serious, moral stories were sincere and were determined to offer ethical lessons. Almost all juvenile fiction up until about the mid–1800s was much the same: just simple stories, always emphasizing virtuous, stereotypical characters who live their chaste lives with reputable, predictable behavior. However, all the authors claimed that they wrote about reality. These writings, intended as models for virtuous living, were, as they themselves claimed, "true to nature ... and the conditions of ordinary life."

In general, the books that colonial children read were written by religious persons or ministers, and their contents dealt with piety, deathbed scenes, sin and precocious religious happenings. The first book for children to be published in the United States appeared in 1646. Written by John Cotton, its full title is *Milk for Babes: Drawn Out of the Breasts of Both Testaments, Chiefly for the Spiritual Nourishment of Boston Babes in Either England, but May Be of Like Use to Any Children.*

Before 1700 virtually no children's books existed as we now understand that term. The earliest ones were William Caxton's translation of *History of Troy* (1473) and Caxton's *Book of Curtesye* (1477). Caxton was the first printer in England and the editor of the very books which John Locke prescribed for children: *Aesop's Fables* (1484) and the *History of Reynard the Fox* (1481), but Caxton intended none of these for children. The fables emphasized mortal men and their follies, and *Reynard the Fox* was a satire that ridiculed unjust rulers in the guise of animals (Orwell's *Animal Farm*?). Although they were intended for adults they were read by many youngsters with great interest. *Aesop's Fables* and *Reynard the Fox* also circulated in chapbook form. However, true adventure, traditional romance and fanciful imagination rarely appeared in children's literature.

Next came the *De Civilitate Morum Puerilium* of Erasmus (1531), dealing with the subject of manners. It was translated into English by Robert Whittington in 1532 under the title *A Lytil Booke of Good Manners for Children*. It was printed by Wynken de Worde.

Then came the important *Orbis Sensualium Pictus* of John Amos

Comenius (1592–1670), published in Germany in 1657 and translated into English one year later. It was a remarkable production for its time—an encyclopedia with illustrations, including a picture alphabet in which letters were identified with the sounds of various animals. This encyclopedia, made up mostly of pictures, addresses children specifically and was designed to encourage their curiosity and a larger view of the world. The subjects covered in this book were as varied as it was possible to do at the time. This basic book was reproduced in many variations over the years. It was reprinted, reedited and pirated in hundreds of editions even as late as the nineteenth century. It was translated into many different languages, including English. It excited everyone's concept of education through entertainment and subordinated plain text to illustration. Because of this publication, Comenius was asked to help revitalize the elementary school system in Hungary.

What he found there was a system so poorly organized that the students were ignorant of even the most basic information. He determined that what was needed was a book with pictures to clarify the text. Even though Comenius was basically interested in teaching Latin to these students, he believed that observation was a key to learning and that the reaction to the senses, especially sight, must be understood before the printed word could be meaningful. Even the least motivated students could follow the simple text and clear pictures. He used common occupations and their basic tools as a model, using Latin names since this was really a Latin textbook. The book contained pictures of working people seen by children everywhere, on the streets, in the shops, and in the fields. This was attractive to young children because it linked what they saw with their eyes into words to explain what they saw. Thus we have the first concept of what is known today as children's picture books.

A further trend was the rediscovery of fables and fairy tales. *Aesop's Fables* had first been translated and printed in English by Caxton in 1484. These, like La Fontaine's *Fables* (1668–1694), were not necessarily meant as reading material for children, but people have always believed that children will enjoy these fables, legends and tales, which were primarily written by and published for adults.

At the end of the 1600s, then, most of the children who read, if they read anything at all, amused themselves with chapbooks and broadsheets—all of which would have been rejected by John Locke as "perfectly useless Trumpery." For those who read no "real" books, in spite of John Locke, there were still tales "of Spirites and Goblins."

Then came the traditional fairy tales of Perrault around 1697, with English translations appearing around 1720. Perrault's *Tales of Mother Goose* (1697) was the first fairy-tale book especially written and published for children.

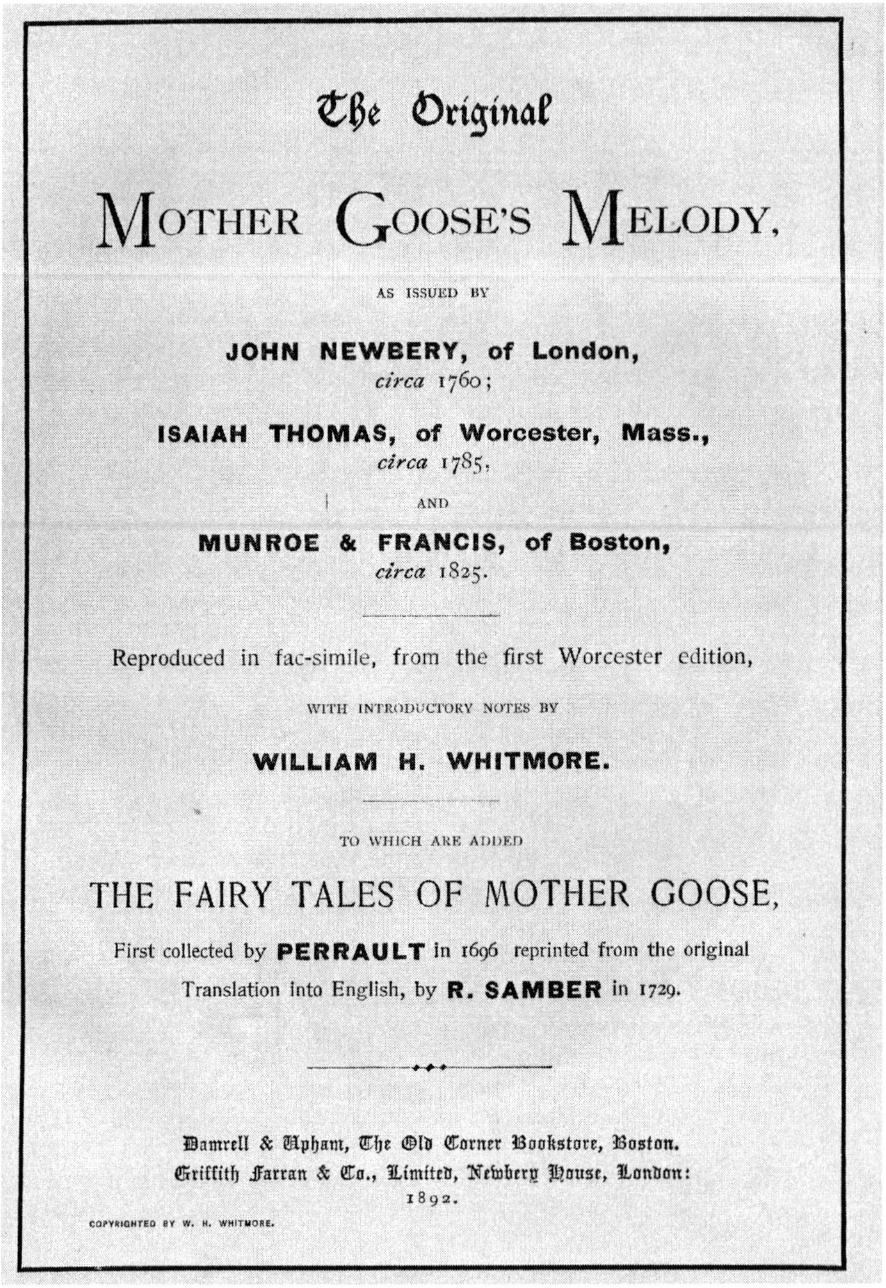

The Original

MOTHER GOOSE'S MELODY,

AS ISSUED BY

JOHN NEWBERY, of London,
circa 1760;

ISAIAH THOMAS, of Worcester, Mass.,
circa 1785,

AND

MUNROE & FRANCIS, of Boston,
circa 1825.

Reproduced in fac-simile, from the first Worcester edition,

WITH INTRODUCTORY NOTES BY

WILLIAM H. WHITMORE.

TO WHICH ARE ADDED

THE FAIRY TALES OF MOTHER GOOSE,

First collected by **PERRAULT** in 1696 reprinted from the original
Translation into English, by **R. SAMBER** in 1729.

Damrell & Upham, The Old Corner Bookstore, Boston.
Griffith Farran & Co., Limited, Newbery House, London:
1892.

COPYRIGHTED BY W. H. WHITMORE.

The Original Mother Goose's Melody: A facsimile of the 1785 Isaiah Thomas edition printed in Boston by Damrell and Upham. 117 pages; 44 pages of Preface. Pages 45–67 contain the original Mother Goose melodies; pages 71–78 contain a biography of Charles Perrault; pages 79–117 contain eight fairy tales.

This was followed by *Pilgrim's Progress* by John Bunyan. Although first published in 1678, this book is often referred to as the first children's book. It was often read to youngsters by family members and is mentioned in many children's books (e.g., *Little Women*). It, too, was not written for children but was read by them because nothing else was available.

Fortunately, by the beginning of the eighteenth century, there came a lightening of the harsh Puritan fare in children's literature. In 1715 Isaac Watts published *Divine Songs; Attempted in Easy Language for the Use of Children.* While still keeping the required moral and religious intent, Watts wrote his songs in simple words with simple verse forms and showed a sympathetic understanding of childish failings; moreover, he based his examples on the everyday world of the child's experience: family squabbles, the busy bee, the whole world of home, street and field.

By the eighteenth century there was plenty of inexpensive printed material available for everyone. Early schoolbooks were plentiful and readily available. The earliest were the hornbooks, the battledores, the primers and others.

The first "book" the child was allowed to handle without assistance was the hornbook, first published as early as 1540. We know that John Webb was licensed to print the hornbook in 1587, and that in 1609, when Thomas Dekker issued his *Gulls Hornbook*, that type of primer must have been fairly common.

A different sort of schoolbook was the battledore. Benjamin Collins, a printer from Salisbury, claimed for himself the honor of inventing this new type of schoolbook in 1770.

However, although at the beginning of the eighteenth century there was little written for children that they might read for pure pleasure, two publications were about to be published which would soon pass into the juvenile repertory. These were *Robinson Crusoe* (1719), written by Daniel Defoe, and *Gulliver's Travels* (1726), written by Jonathan Swift. Because few children's books were available, these books, though originally written for adults, were soon adopted by youngsters, as *Pilgrim's Progress* (1684) and *Baron Munchausen's Travels* (1785) had been earlier.

The outlook for juvenile literature was about to further improve, however, for in 1744 bookseller and publisher John Newbery issued the first of several books intended to entertain children: *A Little Pretty Pocket-Book, Intended for the Instruction and Amusement of Little Master Tommy and Pretty Miss Polly, with an Agreeable Letter to Read from Jack the Giant Killer, also a Ball and a Pincushion the Use of Which Will Infallibly Make Tommy a Good Boy and Polly a Good Girl.*

Newbery was among the first to consider publishing specifically for children and to issue books for pleasurable home reading rather than for school. From then on publishing houses became fully aware of the need to provide reading matter for children, though there was still little attempt to adapt it for different age groups. Nor was it thought necessary to consider what children might like or to be always greatly concerned about the way in which the books were produced. This reflected a change in the society's attitude in general and in the interest in children's literature in particular. These books contained animal's stories, traditional fables and religious hymns. By the end of the nineteenth century these books always appeared in bookstores around Christmas time, and parents bought at least one of these books for their children or grandchildren.

However, while the dime novels were becoming increasingly popular, crusading reformers and temperance societies wrote many, many pious and sentimental tracts, published by the American Sunday School Union in Philadelphia and by other tract societies in Boston and New York. Sunday school libraries sprang up to deal with these moral works, to inform and "brainwash" sensitive young minds with decency; at the same time their actual aim was to increase attendance at Sunday school. They were concerned with Sabbath breaking, the evils of drunkenness, swearing, breaking laws, gambling, the history of the Bible, happy poverty, the lives of poor and pious people, the various commandments, the broad and narrow paths, and short popular sermons.

The Religious Tract Society in England was founded in 1799, and the American Tract Society was founded in 1814. These tract societies started to print many pious books for children. They all issued similar types of moral and religious pamphlets, ranging from a minimum of four pages to a maximum of twenty-four pages, frequently with a woodcut on the first page, which served both as a cover and the title page. There was no humor or laughter in these early stories; some might have a bit of lightheartedness but that, too, was checked. Emotions, if mentioned at all, were restrained expressions; joy was offset with grief; anger was offset with acceptance, and so on.

Another factor that encouraged the beginning of a separate children's literature was the mechanical improvements in printing techniques and paper making. As technology advanced, better and cheaper paper was available, and the field of publishing took advantage of it.

In 1817 Thomas Gilpen made a paper-making machine (the Fourdrinier). This provided larger sheets of paper, which in turn could be used by the new steam-rolling presses. Paper making was being experimented with by several printers. Rag was not yet used, and poor quality paper was produced cheaply. Rag paper was later manufactured by William Orr in 1854. It was three-fourths rag and one-fourth wood fiber. These changes in paper making and printing machines made it possible to produce cheap books, which were purchased by the new, urban, working class of people looking for a way to better their social standing and for cheap entertainment. Publishers, realizing that children made up a new and somewhat undiscriminating book market, were quick to take advantage of this fact. Having chosen an enticing title and having available some spare woodcut blocks which might be relevant for a juvenile book, a publisher would commission a story or series of tales to be woven around these illustrations. As a result illustrations of different proportions might be used in the same story, while on other occasions it was clear that the pictures were carved by different people. Sometimes the inclusion of a picture was obviously forced and had little to do with the text. These books, a smidgen better than the early chapbooks, found their way to America. In America publishers were still printing 3½" × 2½" books with eight to thirty-five pages. They usually had color covers that were drawn freehand with brushes or with stencil overlays, because color printing was not yet in use in America and wouldn't be until about the 1870s. Until the 1870s the pictures on the dime novel covers were black and white.

After the illustrator gave the publisher a finished drawing, the drawing would be reproduced by one of three black-and-white printing processes: a relief process known as *wood engraving* and two photomechanical processes known as *line blocks* and *half-tone blocks*. Wood engraving involves the cutting of a picture in relief on a hard, end-grain block of wood with a tool called a *burin*. The engraver cuts away the parts of the block that correspond to the area in the drawing which are to remain white, or uninked. The uncut, raised area receives the ink when the block is run through the press and thus appears black in the finished print.

In line blocks the artist's drawing would be photographed. The negative would be exposed onto a zinc plate covered with light-sensitive gelatin. The sensitized area is covered with a wax resist; the rest of the plate is etched, so that the line drawing appears in relief.

In the half-tone method the image is developed from a photographic negative with a screen placed between the negative and the resulting image. The screen causes the light to be transmitted as dots; small dots create a light area; larger dots create a darker area.

As the technology of color reproduction advanced, color was becoming the norm. Chromoxylography was an early development and used red, yellow and blue to produce many different hues. Color half-tones are like the black-and-white relief method except that primary colors are applied as dots; the density of the color is determined by the size of the dots.

About 1825 Mahlon Day and Samuel Wood were the chief publishers in the New York City children's book trade. Wood, who had founded his shop about twenty years earlier, ran the larger and longer-lasting firm. Together, they probably published more children's books than did all of their competitors combined: Solomon King, Daniel Cooledge, N. B. Holmes and Kiggins, and Kellogg. For years Wood and Day followed very industriously in one another's footsteps, hiring from the same group of illustrators (Alexander Anderson was one) and publishing similar lists of moral subjects, classroom texts, natural and religious histories and cautionary tales. Although both considered instruction the main purpose of their children's books, they also took amusement seriously. Both let the illustrations of a book entertain but entrusted the child's education largely to the printed word.

An elaborate, thirty-two page, illustrated *History of Dick Whittington and His Cat* was published by Jacob Johnson in Philadelphia in 1802. Around 1835 Turner and Fisher of New York and Philadelphia brought out a twenty-four-page chapbook on *The History of Jack the Giant Killer*, which contained all of his wonderful exploits "Embellished with Ten Engravings." The giant's challenge of "Fe, Fi, Fo, Fum" is well known in nursery rhymes.

Although *Old Dame Trot and Her Comical Cat* was published in 1803, this story was known much earlier, perhaps as early as 1703. In 1828 Samuel King published *The Extraordinary Life and Adventures of Robin Hood*, a thirty-two-page chapbook with a colored frontispiece. Then, in 1830 he published *The Seven Champions of Christendom*, which had forty-eight pages and a color title page. W. Borradaile, also of New York, published a "Robin Hood" in 1823.

The earliest example of an alphabet printed in book form in England was that of Petyt in 1538 "BAC [*sic*] bothe in Latyn and Englysshe," and, between 1702 and 1712, under the initials of "T. W.," a book appeared which linked the alphabet firmly to the traditional theme of "A was an Archer," and so on (Think of Kate Greenaway's *A Apple Pie* [1886]).

These ABC books intended to provide religious training. Of these the *New England Primer* (1687) with its famous "In Adam's Fall/We Sinned All" and other verses of Isaac Watts had a widespread influence.

The first booklist to be offered to potential buyers was the often-quoted one of John Newbery, issued when he came to London from Reading in 1744. This is the generally accepted starting point for writers on English children's books, but because there is not a lot of solid evidence, it is best to think of this as an arbitrary date.

In Britain around 1840 toy books were produced. These were colored and were strictly for entertainment. About this same time books of cries heard in London and New York were being produced.

By the 1850s the publishers of what were first called *penny parts* (*penny dreadfuls*) came along. These publishers saw a need for escape reading among the poor working class who had learned to read. In 1867 the American Sunday School Union published *The Pretty Village*, an attractive story

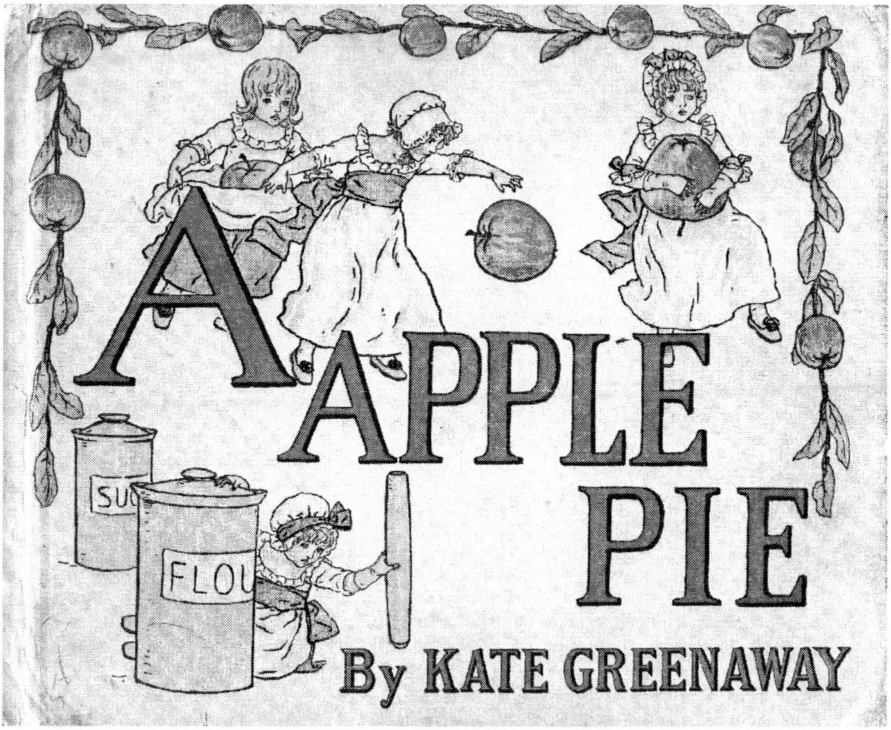

A Apple Pie: **The rhyme of "A Apple Pie" is old, and reference was made to it as early as 1671. In this book there is no rhyme for *I*. In the 1671 version by John Eachard there was no rhyme for *I* or *J*.**

with a gentler approach than the earlier, deeply religious messages. In contrast, there appeared the blood-and-thunder, dime novel school of writing for boys. America's dime novels were probably based on the English "shilling shockers," or penny dreadfuls, which were exciting, poorly developed, horror stories. However, some people believe that English authors helped start the American dime novels when American authors began pirating English stories; these American novels then spread back to England and became known as penny dreadfuls or shilling shockers. If the United States had anything to do with popularizing this questionable literature among England's readers, England got her revenge. Our "yellow journalism"—now known as the tabloids—was unknown in the United States until an American publisher got the idea from London. And so it goes.

The adult view of children and their reading material has changed substantially many times over the past three hundred years or so. Whatever these differences might be, however, there are two assumptions common to all modern views of childhood. The first is that children need

The Doings of the Alphabet: **Replica of the original. The text of the letters is in rhyme; there are pictures for all letters except *X*, *Y*, and *Z*.**

to be separated to some degree from adult life until they have been educated or have matured in some significant way. The second is that adults have something of value to teach children, so that the nurturing, training and education of children should be the responsibility of mature, educated adults.

What these assumptions mean in practical terms is that modern, middle-class children should be managed, directed, organized and defined by adults for the good of the child and of society as a whole. Management of childhood implies the restriction of children, usually by separating them from some aspect of society and by curtailing their access to some kinds of knowledge, experience and resources—including books.

In England these ideas were incorporated by Thomas Day in his *History of Sandford and Merton, 1783–1789*, a work which William Darton, a publisher, calls "Rousseau for the English." Tom Merton, a young rich boy, and Harry Sandford, son of a farmer, have a tutor called Mr. Barlow, who teaches moral behavior, contrasting the selfishness of the rich with the honesty of the poor.

Next came true nonfiction writers—Noah Webster, Caleb Bingham, and Sarah Hale—whose desire to indoctrinate the young with a sense of morality produced spellers, histories, poetry, geographies and biographies of identifiable heroes. A growing interest in natural history resulted in the production of many little books about birds, animals, fish and insects. *The History of the Robins* by Mrs. Trimmer is an example of this natural history trend.

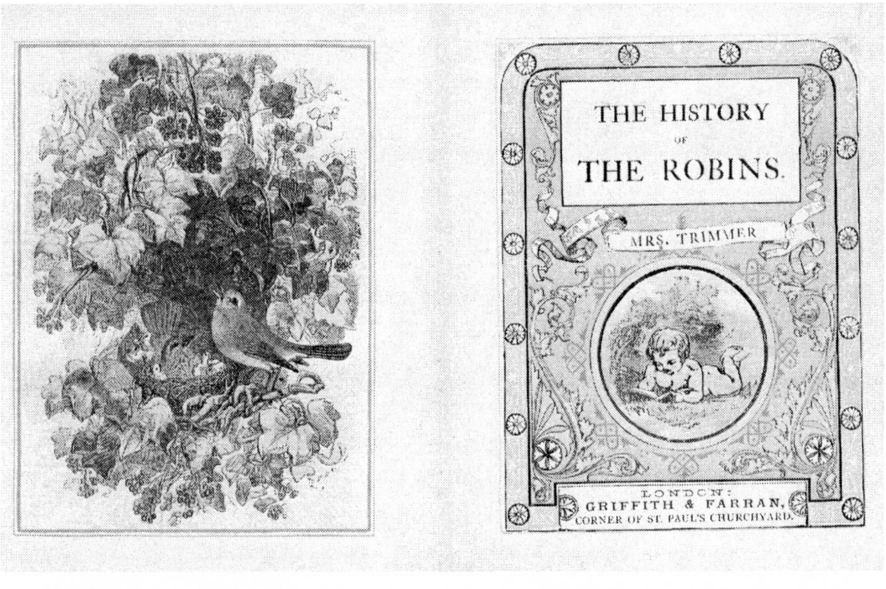

The History of the Robins: **A reissue of Favourite Library; with a color illustrated title page by Edmond Evans. This is Trimmer's best-known children's book. It has 125 pages plus 16 pages of the publisher's other books. This is volume three of eleven.**

The desire to teach only practical information gave rise to a shift in emphasis in the mid-eighteenth century with the spread of John Locke's "instruction through play." Locke stated, "There may be Dice and Playthings, with the letters on them, to teach Children the Alphabet by playing."

In 1863, one of the Beadle and Co. printers, George Munro, set out on his own and quickly started a successful series called *Munro's Ten Cent Novels*. In 1867, Robert DeWitt built up his small publishing business and offered to the reading public the first of 1,118 dime novels that would be published in the next ten years. In 1870 Norman Munro, George's brother, entered the publishing field. Still, the greatest success is attributed to three relative latecomers: Frank Tousey, Francis Street and Francis Smith.

After the decline of the true dime novel there arose comic books, big little books and pulp fiction. It should also be noted that there appeared a new literature that, although meant for a sophisticated adult readership, would later evolve into the lower-class chapbook, often in adulterated, greatly shortened form. Versions of them also appeared in popular chapbook form, joining that substratum of literature, from which at a later date, with a change in children's reading patterns, they would reemerge as traditional tales.

In fact, the first dime novels—for example *Malaeska* and *Seth Jones*—were really historical romances made to resemble Sir Walter Scott's *Ivanhoe* or James Fenimore Cooper's *Leather Stocking* books. As the dime novel grew in popularity, accurate history became lost in the more legendary-type stories like those of Frank and Jesse James.

Broadsides

Before dime novels became commonplace reading material, there were various kinds of broadsides. *Broadsides* with ballads or folk music are also sometimes referred to as *broadsheets*, *ballad sheets*, *stall ballads* or *slip songs*.

Early collections of songs and ballads in chapbooks, also known as *gurlands*, appeared as early as 1584 in England when Richard Jones printed *A Handefull of Pleaseant Delites*, which contains the ballad "Greensleeves." The term was later applied to individual poems and songs. They were sold at stalls in town markets and cities, hence the name stall sheets.

Folk music is a rural tradition in which songs are passed down by word of mouth. In the sixteenth century printed folk music became popular. Words to popular songs were printed on sheets of paper and were known as broadsides. They originally had no music, but the users were informed that the words could be sung to a popular tune known at the time. The sheets were often adorned with woodcuts. In size most broadsides ranged from approximately 13" × 16" to over five feet long.

Early broadsides rarely contained any definite illustrations, though some had decorative borders. Later ones sometimes used a "stock" illustration from a wood or copper engraving that represented an available product or service.

Later still, carefully detailed engraved illustrations of specific stores, factories or products graced some broadsides. A wide variety of type faces was used at different times and by different printers. People pasted the sheets on walls, log books and any other convenient area to learn them. When the song was familiar to them they discarded it or pasted another song over the first one.

Broadsides definitely fit the definition of "ephemeral" items: They were meant to serve their informational purpose and then be discarded. Today, because of their intended temporary use, historic broadsides are scarce, often with only one or a handful of copies of any example surviving. There was some criticism about these broadsides since the scholars of the time said there was a difference between traditional ballads and these broadsides, which had "bad representations of the original."

Broadsides were posted prominently where they would be seen by many people. They served to spread information especially before newspapers and other mass media became affordable and widely available. Manuscripts of ballads were offered for sale even before the invention of printing.

Before the printing press, broadsides were written by hand; before folk songs were written by hand there was a centuries-old tradition of minstrels and folk singers. As these declined and the printing press became more common, folk music transmission was channeled into broadsides. This success of the broadside, which could be bought cheaply on street corners, seems to have contributed to the decline of the professional minstrel, who by Elizabeth I's reign was legally classed with vagabonds. In 1520 a bookseller in Oxford sold more than 190 ballads. In an era before literacy was common, their popularity was extraordinary.

In 1556 England began requiring printers to be licensed by the Stationers' Company in London. The following year the Stationers' Company required the legal registration of printed ballads at four pence each. This continued through 1709, and the company's records contain over three thousand entries.

Technically the term *broadside* does not refer solely to folk music. Broadsides could also be handbills, proclamations, advertisements, and so on. True broadsides were sheets of paper that were printed on only one side, sometimes illustrated with one or more woodcuts or engravings. They generally contained a ballad or some other ephemeral material. Early broadsides were printed in black-letter print and are therefore called black-letter ballads. About 1700 black-letter typeset was replaced by roman type. Broadsides in roman type are called white-letter ballads.

Sometimes these sheets of printed material, using both sides for printing, were called broadsides, but since authentic broadsides were often also used as posters—an important feature of a true broadside—by using both sides for printed material, these sheets could no longer be called broadsides. Thus this double-printed material should be known as single-sheet printing and should be in a class by itself. The term "broadsheet" was often used in place of broadside for this type of material but now is more strictly applied to sheets printed on both sides.

Broadsheets were commonly folded twice or more to make small pamphlets and were sometimes called chapbooks, the dime novel of their day. The popularity of chapbooks reached its height in the eighteenth century. Chapmen were the peddlers who traveled between towns selling ballads and chapbooks.

One of the earliest printed ballads, the "Lytel Gest of Robyne Hode," was issued by Wynkyn de Worde at the end of the fifteenth or the beginning of the sixteenth century in the form of a pamphlet. The true broadside ballad began to be popular a little later in the sixteenth century and was soon widely distributed in the political and religious turmoil of Henry VIII's reign.

Broadsides had been used in Europe since the early days of moveable type to make announcements, promote locations of merchandise, and publicize news and political events. American ones appeared by the middle of the seventeenth century once the printing industry began to be established in the colonies.

In America, after the Civil War, with advances in printing technologies and color lithography, as well as the increased competition among brand-named products, many advertising signs that were displayed outdoors began to become larger and more colorful than the one- or two-color, smaller broadsides. Broadsides still served a purpose for local advertisers because they were cheap to design and print and appropriate to reach prospective consumers in remote areas. However, the larger, more colorful "billboards" began to overshadow them for advertising purposes just before 1900.

The earliest broadside in the United States was the "Present State of the New English Affairs." In 1689 Samuel Green of Cambridge, Massachusetts, put out a single 8" × 4½" sheet printed in two columns. Its purpose was "to prevent false reports," according to Isaiah Thomas. Broadsides used dark black letters and were printed lengthwise down sheets of paper in two rows, sometimes with woodcut illustrations. Later broadsides were printed on two sheets, side by side. That produced a four-column paper which could be folded in half to a more convenient size. As is mentioned in the chapter on chapbooks, *Children in the Wood* (sometimes under the title *Babes in the Wood*) was released as a broadside before it became a chapbook.

As a broadside ballad "Children in the Wood" (1597), or "The Norfolk Gentleman's Last Will and Testament," as it was also known, was widely read in both England (where this format was almost as old as printing itself) and the United States. It became part of the oral tradition of both countries.

In the same time period that chapbooks were being distributed by peddlers, between 1725 and 1825, hawkers (chapmen in England and colporteurs in France) provided a method of distributing the broadsides from publishers to readers. Distribution was done by having the ballad singers, also known as chanteurs, first purchase them in bundles at wholesale prices from the printer. These buyer/sellers could be roughly compared to the newsboys in early America, except instead of "crying" their news headlines these ballad singers sang their songs in the streets and thereby sold the broadsides. However, these broadsides were also bought by the traditional peddlers, or "flying stationers." Among their wares of ribbons, laces, threads and other ephemeral material, of which there were hundreds of odds and ends, one could find bundles of broadsides.

These broadsides, with their black-lettered text, were found everywhere from the crowded streets of the cities to the countryside, brought by the lone peddlers who went from farmhouse to farmhouse with their wares. These broadside papers were widely distributed, until the competition of new, commercially printed material signaled the end of the ballad broadsides. For many years, however, this form was important reading matter on the streets of all English and American towns.

In America, where English traditional ballads often survived intact among rural communities, many local broadside ballads were printed, especially concerning the Revolutionary War (e.g., "Hail, Columbia" and "American Bravery"). It is on these broadsides, some of which are extant today, that some of the old ballads are found in their entirety. Some short folk songs such as "Dame Durden," "The Derby Ram" and "Richard of Tauton Dean" are found on these original broadsides. Today these can be found only in the catalogs of dealers in old books. For example, a broadside printed by Wynkyn de Worde was recently sold at auction; it was popular during the reign of Henry VIII.

Broadsides are hard to classify because they not only popularized songs, ballads and poetry, which were very important selling points at this time and place, but sometimes the material was satire, political commentary, everyday news, wedding announcements, death notifications, funeral descriptions, scripture verses, protest statements, the last words of a convict, descriptions of the latest murder and other crimes, revelations about the latest catastrophe (whether local or national) or any of the interesting news of the time.

However, even the broadside ballads were based on recent events, especially crimes. Their subject matter—scandals, murders, monstrous births and strange animals, religious and political commentary, bawdy tales—resembles that of some modern tabloids. The titles of some of the broadsides found in one seventeenth-century collection gives some idea of their character: "Murder upon Murder, Committed by Thomas Sherwood"; "Newes from Hereford"; or a "Wonderful and Terrible Earthquake."

As one can see, the broadside covered the fields that the later newspapers used as selling points. The big difference is that for the most part the broadsides were in verse, often set to music and sung by the balladeers. This printed material was sometimes read aloud and supplemented with illustrations. This approach helped make this material popular and helped children learn to read. These "books" made a half-hearted attempt to include the usual didactic material but in general were not meant to be serious reading material.

The seventeenth century saw a tremendous popularity of broadsides, but this was not to last. By the eighteenth century the broadsides began to decline and were replaced by newspapers. Newspapers included stock exchange news, scandals, and the material usually carried by the broadsides. The newspapers also contained advertisements, which the broadsides didn't always do. The newspaper, with its news and information, was more acceptable to the genteel class while the broadside was news for the common people. After all, the broadside was printed on poor-grade paper which was getting poorer, not better, its size had decreased (10" × 7"), and it had inferior wood-block illustrations which, because of repeated use and bad handling, became worse. Since the printers used whatever was at hand, their intention was hard to decipher, and finally the printers' machines themselves began to show signs of deterioration. So the life of the broadside, which started as a folk ballad paper in the 1500s, began to fall from favor in the 1830s.

The popularity of singing itself declined as singing was discouraged in public houses, and laws were passed restricting noise on the street. Although it is commonly believed that the broadside was killed by the newspaper, there are those who believe that it died a natural death because people lost their interest in ballads, so it disappeared without significant notice, except by those who honor traditional things.

As a closing comment a new book (2002), *The Best of Broadside, 1962–1988* (Smithsonian Folkways Recordings, $69.99) is available. It represents the radical 1960s, but it is described as "a mimeographed newsletter full of protest songs." Sounds like the old broadsides with protest news and ballads.

Chapbooks

Before dime novels became popular reading material, there were, along with the chapbooks, the severely abridged classic tales and a bit later the fictional series stories. A so-called *chapbook* was any piece of printed matter that was distributed and sold by chapmen in all inhabited areas in America's early days.

The term *chapmen* comes from the Anglo Saxon word *ceapman* ("trade" + "man"). However, many believe that it derives from "cheap" or "cheapen." Still others believe it is a combination of *ceap*, meaning to barter or deal in business, hence cheap. In general, the term *chapbook* refers to the cheaply produced literature distributed by peddlers, but it is not an iron-clad definition, especially in America, where it is hard to tell the difference between a true chapbook, a child's book and a pamphlet.

No one knows for sure whether these books were meant for the young or for the unsophisticated, especially those that exhibit the typical chapbook form, many of which still survive.

The contents differ from earlier material meant for children by having amusing and entertaining stories rather than only religious or instructive material. This definition excludes other books, such as primers, spelling books, and catechisms. It also excludes the more expensive books with engraving and colored plates.

These loosely termed books were small, poorly printed pieces of literature. They might have as few as four pages or as many as twenty, and sometimes more. They were also small in size (about 5½" × 3½"). As a rule they were of very poor quality not only in paper and printing but also in type and illustrations. They were usually printed on one sheet of

Opposite—Child's Painting Books, **made in Germany. An example of one kind of chapbook. Ten pages folded to 5½" × 3½". One page had colored illustrations; the opposite page of an identical illustration is to be colored.**

CHILD'S PAINTING BOOKS.

paper and then folded into four, eight or sixteen pages. A lot of these had hand-colored covers to make them look respectable.

By the end of the eighteenth century chapbooks became a standard 4" × 2½" and contained sixteen pages. The quality of chapbooks varied greatly. Some printers did a creditable job, and the output was acceptable. They specialized in good books for children, including well-executed woodcuts, some of which were colored. They kept the emphasis on the story line and made sure that the grammar and spelling were correct.

Other printers, because of lack of space and other considerations, reduced the story to mere plot; drama and the high points of a good story were lost in the cutting; grammar and spelling were minor considerations; little or no regard was given to artistic talent. The main goal was to put out more and more stories to be sold regardless of the quality of writing.

Because of this expensive, limited space, sometimes the stories and entries were greatly shortened. Sometimes this was done by changing the size of the type and sometimes by cutting the text. And, of course, if the text was too short for the number of pages, the size of the type was increased.

The editors printed any material they could find and sold it in seriously shortened versions. The material had no literary value, and the grammar was not a point of interest, but what remained of the story was the action with high adventure on almost every page.

The pages were printed black on white, but the covers were usually made of colored paper (and, in the case of Beadle and Adams, in orange) and were of better quality than the interior pages. Sometimes they were bound with leather or other material, but these were of poor quality and were replaced by a more durable paper. Some of the books were printed on "sugarbag" paper or Dutch paper wrappers. The back cover generally carried an advertisement. Originally, Dutch paper was a handmade paper produced in Holland. The expression "Dutch" may stem from the fact that in Holland handmade or imitation handmade paper is still called "Hollandsch papier," which does not necessarily mean paper made by hand in Holland.

The woodcut illustrations and engravings depicted moralistic tales, but because illustrations were hard to come by and were therefore also expensive, they were used over and over again regardless of their connection to the story.

At times in the nineteenth century some printers issued chapbooks with no cover at all and no stitching; they were just a sheet of folded and uncut paper. These pieces of "literature" were meant to teach children to read and keep them amused. The contents were the traditional stories, advice to the lovelorn, jokes, riddles and humor, and the normal smattering of the strange and exotic.

For almost four centuries chapbooks were the principal form of popular literature in Europe. They were later, of course, introduced into America. Even though badly written and crudely illustrated, these chapbooks were very popular, and children loved them. Regardless of all the shortcoming these books had, they were very popular because they were the only literature available to people who had little money for luxuries. They provided reading material to children who would otherwise not get any.

However, this coarseness eventually led to the downfall of the chapbook. Parents started to react against these badly written, poorly illustrated, shallow books for their children. Still, from about 1770 on into the 1880s this is what the early American children read. These chapbooks, with child appeal, sold for a penny each. The price was the same whether sold by the traveling chapmen or sold in the bookstore, if there was a bookstore in town. Some of the newer chapbooks were not so religious. They were not the usual catechisms whose subjects were piety, death, the perils of sin and other uninspiring material. Rather, they were somewhat amusing and were meant to entertain rather than instruct. Samples of this type of book are *Aesop's Fables* and *Reynard the Fox*. They were not expensive books and had nicely engraved pictures, usually colored, and were a step above the earlier chapbooks.

Peddling was a common method of distributing many small, needed items to the inhabited new world. Peddlers traveled on foot, horseback and by wagon and boat. Their mainstay was printed material, mainly religious. They carried primers (the *New England Primer* was a best seller; some six million copies were sold), catechisms, bibles, and psalm books. These chapmen and hawkers pushed little paper-covered books in with the miscellaneous materials that they peddled about the countryside. A bit later they began to carry spelling and grammar books. These were followed by the romances, which became quite popular, but religious materials were still the best sellers.

At the time it was believed that at least five hundred of these chapmen traveled throughout this country, but they were even more popular in England.

One of the best known of these chapmen was Parson Mason Locke Weems. In the years between 1795 and 1825 he traveled between New York and Georgia peddling his own written pamphlets. Although he also sold other items, his main ware was histories, bibles, sermons and other religious material. Because of the title pages and the contents of his writing, they, too, are classified as chapbooks. (As an aside, Weems is often attributed with creating the story about George Washington and the cherry tree.)

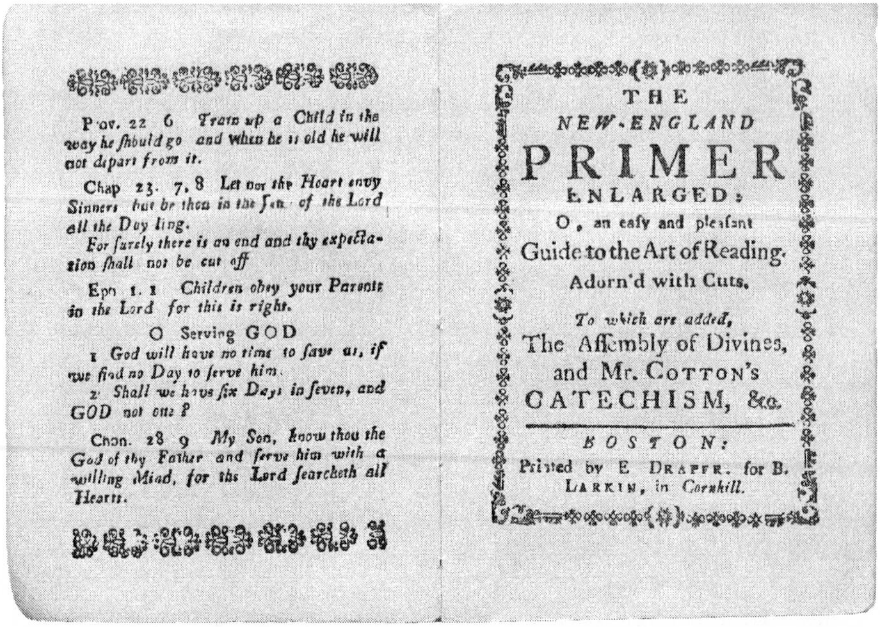

Prov. 22 6 Train up a Child in the way he ſhould go and when he is old he will not depart from it.

Chap 23. 7, 8 Let not thy Heart envy Sinners but be thou in the Fear of the Lord all the Day long.

For ſurely there is an end and thy expectation ſhall not be cut off

Eph 1. 1 Children obey your Parents in the Lord for this is right.

O Serving GOD

1 God will have no time to ſave us, if we find no Day to ſerve him.

2 Shall we have ſix Days in ſeven, and GOD not one?

Chron. 28 9 My Son, know thou the God of thy Father and ſerve him with a willing Mind, for the Lord ſearcheth all Hearts.

THE
NEW-ENGLAND
PRIMER
ENLARGED:
Or, an eaſy and pleaſant
Guide to the Art of Reading.
Adorn'd with Cuts.
To which are added,
The Aſſembly of Divines,
and Mr. COTTON's
CATECHISM, &c.
BOSTON:
Printed by E. DRAPER, for B.
LARKIN, in Cornhill.

The New England Primer: **Facsimile of the 1785 edition; size: 3″ × 4¼″.**

Another chapbook writer and peddler who deserves to be mentioned is Chapman Whitcomb, who was a teacher who needed to supplement his income and wrote his own chapbooks from 1796 to 1813. Many of his tracts were religious and moral in nature but also contained the usual Indian captures. He also wrote biography, geography and adventure books, which were printed by C. Prentiss of Leominster, Massachusetts.

Before we discuss these books, we should mention the books supplied by the Catnach family of England, especially John and his son James. There, between 1770 and 1815, the Catnach family had a printing business known as the Seven Dials. They were responsible for printing "gallows literature." They also circulated specialized ballads, street songs and sensational sheets. The latter covered murders and confessions. From 1769 to 1841 they printed the *Boys of England*, a weekly magazine that sold for a penny a copy from November 1866 until June 1899, edited, after the first nine numbers, by E. J. Brett. The first Jack Harkaway stories by Bracebridge Hemyng appeared in July 1871. "Sixteen String Jack" made his first appearance in September 1863. Because at the time newspapers were expensive, these papers served to publicize scandalous stories such as "The Execution of William Cordere, the Murderer of Marie Martin." However, they were also the producers of many chapbooks, most of which were intended for children. These were very didactic and did not have the entertaining and amusing entries that other cheaply printed tracts had. Many of them were reprints of children's stories already in circulation. They were not very popular with young readers, and, had the Catnachs added some lightness to their "street literature," they might have had even more success in their printing endeavors.

These sheets of printing were sold to chapmen for pennies; then James Catnach (1769–1813) paid his employees pennies, and each week he carried the profits (more than pennies) to the Bank of England. James Catnach Senior was a printer who had a close association with William Davidson; Thomas Bewick, the famous engraver, once worked for him. He worked in both Alnwick and Newcastle. When he retired he left James Junior his presses, a supply of type and some woodcuts. With this start James Junior set himself up as a jobbing printer. His stock in trade was street papers, song sheets, ballads and penny stories. Many of these were intended for children and sold for very little for small editions, a bit more for slightly larger books and still more for a large publication.

James Junior was a printer with the foresight to see the possibilities of printing little books for children. Forget the moral tales but give the youngsters something to have some fun with. They could still learn the alphabet but do it through rhymes and other light material. These could have been classified as pop culture books; these were books that were not usually critiqued by literary reviewers; they were marketed directly to children, who then asked for them in school, libraries and at home. They were "fad books."

This printing house had many titles, including *Cinderella*, *Cock Robin*, *Jack Spratt*, *Moll Flanders*, *Mother Goose*, *Simple Simon*, *Tom Hickathrift*, and many more.

W. S. Fortey was the last owner of the Catnach presses, but he went out of business in the 1880s, and the day of the chapbook was over; then came the penny dreadfuls and the dime novels.

Another writer who contributed to the success of chapbooks was George Mogridge. His work was published by the Religious Tract Society, but it appeared under other imprints. He would not be well known for his mediocre writing if it were not for the fact that he produced his works as chapbooks, like the ones he remembered as a young reader himself. His writings had no enduring quality but were preferable to some of the other writings of the time. However, because he was such a prolific writer, he deserves a mention in any discussion of chapbooks. He wrote under the name, among others, of Peter Parley, because the Parley name became common property in Britain just as Mother Goose did. These Parley stories bear no resemblance to the original Peter Parley stories.

His best-known work appeared under the name Old Humphrey. However, most of his work was printed anonymously.

In 1744 John Newbery changed the world of literature for children. He actually published stories meant for children to read and enjoy. These books, more than the early chapbooks, found their way to America. In America publishers were still printing 3½" × 2½" books with eight to thirty-five pages. They usually had colored covers. These covers were drawn freehand with brushes or with stencil overlays. They had several small drawings on the inside pages; the subject matter was moral lessons having to do with kindness, goodness, and industry as opposed to meanness, evilness and sloth.

Then came a change from these sober little books as they were replaced with *Jack the Giant Killer*, *Jack and Jill* and other children's stories. Woodcuts were used to illustrate the pages, and then books went on to become gilt edged, larger sized, and better printed. These appeared around Christmas time, and every child received at least one of these "nice" books by the end of the nineteenth century. The books contained animals' stories, traditional fables and religious hymns. A new feature now was the inclusion of folk and fairy tales as well as nursery rhymes. Examples of these are *Jack and the Bean Stalk* and the *Friar and the Boy*, a story involving a boy, his cruel stepmother and a kind friar. It was twenty-four pages long and was printed in 1767 by A. Barday, a business in Boston. Another was *The Children in the Woods*. This one is about how a wicked uncle murdered two children because of an inheritance. The uncle himself did not do the dirty deed but hired two scoundrels to do it for him. This story was very popular during both the eighteenth and nineteenth centuries. It was just as well known in England as it was in America, and it evolved from an oral tradition. Many different versions of this story exist. The later versions were longer, and the main characters were given different personas.

Children in the Wood was first a broadside ballad, then subsequently a chapbook and later a pantomime subject, with the alternative title *Babes in the Wood* or sometimes *The Norfolk Gentleman's Last Will and Testament*, published by Thomas and John Fleet. It was printed in 1770. They were also the publishers of *The Most Delightful History of the King and the Cobbler* in 1771.

Another popular book was *The Prodigal Daughter, or the Disobedient Lady Reclaimed* (1771). Isaiah Thomas was the printer, who later went on to become a very well-known publisher of books for children. The book contained sixteen pages and had six different woodcuts to illustrate the story. This version was in verse. The sad story tells of a young girl's death. Then when she returns from the grave she tells tales about what is like to be "on the other side." She was the daughter of a wealthy land owner but was not spoiled by her parents. However, she was proud and disobedient and bargained with the devil.

Mother Goose's Melody is thought to be the first American printing of Newbery's English publication as pirated by Isaiah Thomas; among other works pirated by Thomas from Newbery are *Nurse Truelove's New Year's Gift* (ca. 1755); *Little Pretty Pocket-Book* (1787); *Be Merry and Wise; or the Cream of Jests* (ca. 1786). These stories were all abridgments of the English editions. Editions of this book can still be found both in the United States and Britain. It was also issued in broadside editions as well as chapbooks.

Many chapbooks were being published both in England and the United States. They contained nursery rhymes such as "Mother Hubbard," "Cock Robin," "Dame Trot," "Jack Sprat" and "Tom, the Piper's Son." Most of these were written in verse, with a rough woodcut for each poem. "Dame Trot" was one of the better-known characters that appeared in chapbooks for children. Although "Old Dame Trot and Her Comical Cat" was published in 1803, the dame, her cat and their antics were known and talked about at least one hundred years earlier. These chapbooks survived into the twentieth century.

Between 1795 and 1800 Hannah More wrote a series of short stories meant for Sunday school students. They were called "Repository Tracts" and were meant to be suitable reading for the young children and early teens, who because they were from poor families had not yet learned to read, and these readings would keep these young people away from the chapbooks.

Because Hannah More knew that in order to capture and keep the attention of these young children, the tracts must be appealing to them. Her answer was to make them appear as chapbooks, that is, they were printed on cheap paper, had rough woodcuts, and had the same format as the chapbooks. These tracts were later printed on better quality paper, had better woodcuts and were bound into volumes and were sold to well-to-do children.

Many of the chapbooks that were distributed were imported from England, but about 1750 Fowle and Draper, who were Boston printers, began printing chapbooks, which they supplied to the chapmen. However, there is no indication of how many were American and how many were imported.

Thomas Fleet and Isaiah Thomas were two of the publishers that put out copies of chapbooks between 1737 and 1741. Some of Fleet's woodcuts were done by Pompey Fleet, who was actually Fleet's black slave.

Andrew Steuart printed chapbooks between 1760 and 1765 in Philadelphia, but he too imported some books from England. Although

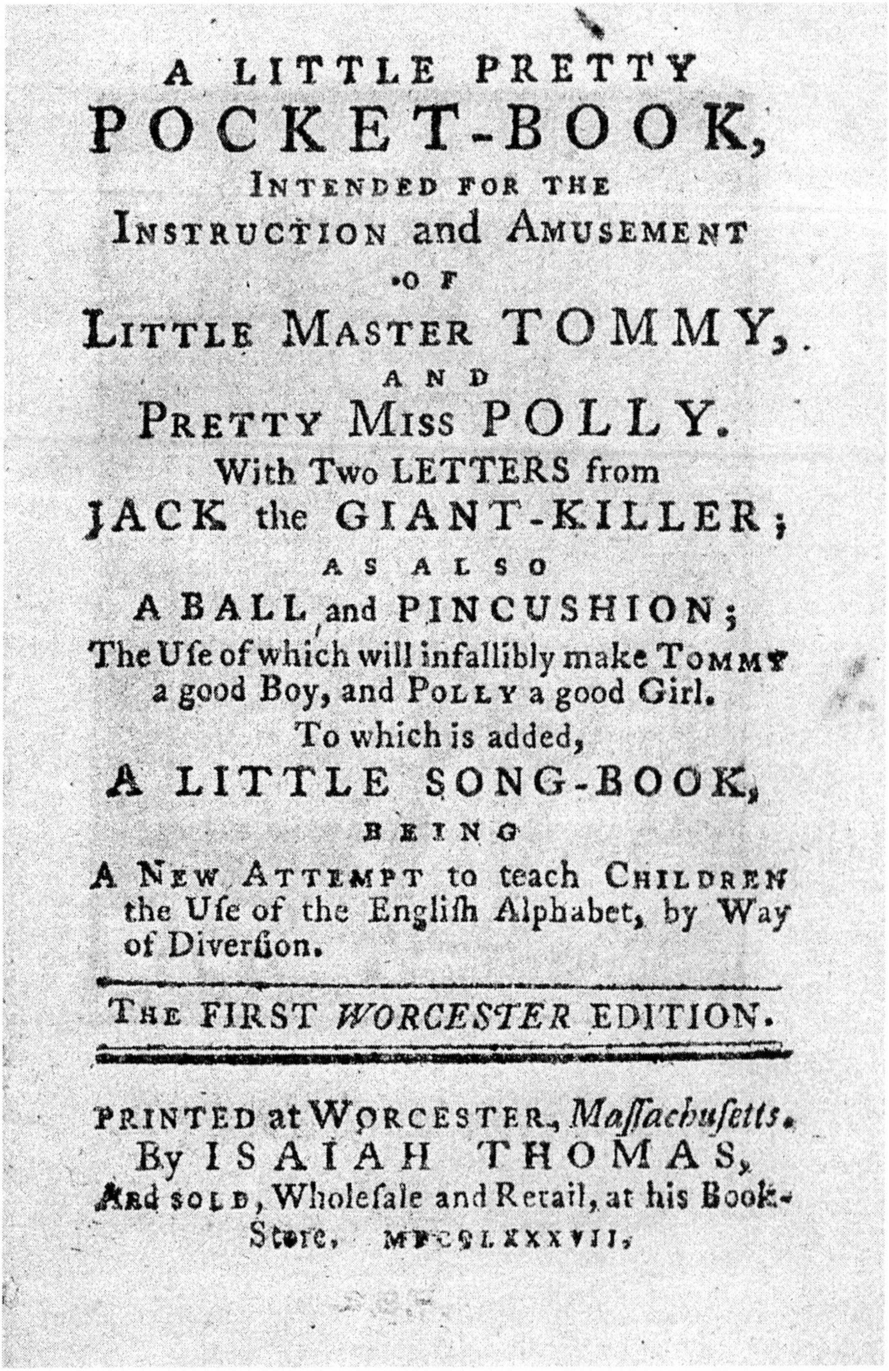

A LITTLE PRETTY
POCKET-BOOK,
INTENDED FOR THE
INSTRUCTION and AMUSEMENT
OF
LITTLE MASTER TOMMY,
AND
PRETTY MISS POLLY.
With Two LETTERS from
JACK the GIANT-KILLER;
AS ALSO
A BALL and PINCUSHION;
The Uſe of which will infallibly make TOMMY
a good Boy, and POLLY a good Girl.
To which is added,
A LITTLE SONG-BOOK,
BEING
A NEW ATTEMPT to teach CHILDREN
the Uſe of the Engliſh Alphabet, by Way
of Diverſion.

THE FIRST *WORCESTER* EDITION.

PRINTED at WORCESTER, *Maſſachuſetts*.
By ISAIAH THOMAS,
And SOLD, Wholeſale and Retail, at his Book-
Store. MDCCLXXXVII.

most of the printers issuing chapbooks were in New York, Philadelphia and Boston, there were some smaller important presses such as J. Green in New London, Connecticut. Cox and Berrt, noted booksellers, sold *Little Books for the Instruction and Amusement of All Good Boys and Girls* in 1772. In 1786 *The Death and Burial of Cock Robin* and *The House That Jack Built* were published by W. Spotswood of Philadelphia.

A very famous book, *Dick Whittington and His Cat,* was published in 1779 by Walters and Normal, also of Philadelphia. Then in 1802 Jacob Johnson, again from Philadelphia, published *The History of Whittington and His Cat,* a rather fancy, thirty-two page book. Dick Whittington was in reality the mayor of London in the years 1397, 1406 and 1419.

In the story Dick Whittington was an orphaned waif with an unusual cat that made him wealthy. It is believed that this tale first appeared as a play, but this is not provable. It certainly did become material for ballads and the popular chapbooks. Some of them were based on the "fact" that Whittington thought that the streets of London were paved with gold and he was going to get his share of it. Some were based on the "fact" that Whittington's attic residence had a colony of rats and the cat helped get rid of them. Others were based on the "fact" that Whittington made friends with his master's daughter, Mistress Alice Fitzwarren. He was accepted as an equal and later married Alice.

In 1807 Carlos C. Darling printed a typical twelve-page chapbook, with blue (not orange) covers. The *Devil and Doctor Faustus* was copied straight from an English chapbook.

William Wiliams, who is by now a well-known printer, advertised "8,000 Chap Books, sixty kinds" and "27,000 toy books, 33 kinds." In America many titles came from England even though they were printed in America. There were also those which were strictly American. Many of the American themes were about Native American kidnappings, that is, the terror felt by captives while in the hands of their captors told after their escape. This theme is one that appeals to youngsters.

Between 1820 and 1830 a printer and bookseller of children's books from New York, Solomon King, published many books meant to amuse, not instruct. In 1828 he published *The Extraordinary Life and Adventures of Robin Hood.* It was a thirty-two page book done in some color. Very few of his books survive to this day, but we know about them from the advertising found in the remaining books, most of which were found in the New York City Public Library.

About 1869 the company of Bailey and Noyes in Portland, Maine,

Opposite—A Little Pretty Pocket-Book: **Facsimile of the first American edition by Isaiah Thomas of Worchester, Mass., 1787. First published by John Newbery in 1744. No copy of that edition survived. Size 4" × 2½"; 122 pages.**

published a series of chapbooks for children. There were twelve books in the series. These were the usual 3½" × 2½" in size, but the book pages were colored blue, pink, yellow, purple and brown. They contained sixteen pages, and some of the contents were *The Shephard Boy* and *Little Frank's Almanac.* They were embellished with woodcuts of everyday objects in the area: farm animals and buildings. These chapbooks survived into the twentieth century.

Even after the Revolutionary War many chapbook titles were still being published and continued until about the 1870s. It was then that the popular literature for the entertainment for children was overtaken by the penny dreadfuls in England and the dime novel in America. These penny dreadfuls were widely read by children although they were considered to be unacceptable "literature." It was feared they would have a deleterious effect on impressionable minds. This is as true today as it was in the eighteenth century. The interest went from printed form to comic strips, movies and television.

For just a few coins it was possible to buy such books as *Jack the Ripper* and *The Crippen Horror.* Other titles that were available were the so-called nonfiction titles such as *Ventriloquism*, *Six Months in a Convent* and *Dreams and Their Interpretations.*

As a reaction to these sensational chapbooks, a new breed of writers, the ones who wrote moral tales, evolved. One of America's well-known authors of these stories was Josiah Priest. He started as a historian of the American West but wrote many stories about Native American captivities. Some of his early stories still survive.

Chapbooks and toy books were often interchanged. Many people classify toy books as chapbooks for children that were sold for a penny by peddlers or even by book sellers in towns and villages. Many of these were imports from England. Some of the titles among this group are *The Cries of London*, *History of Tom Jones*, and *The History of Pamela.*

Mahlon Day, a printer, bookseller and publisher who was in business from 1821 to 1836, produced many children's chapbooks along with other books for children. Most of these books tended toward the standard themes of piety and virtue. Mahlon Day's books were usually illustrated, and some of these in color. Day called his printed books "toys" from the term "toy books," which was used in England for some of these chapbooks.

Chapbooks were never as popular in America as they were in England, so the role they played in the development of children's literature is limited. However, in the hundred years from 1725 to 1825 chapbooks and broadsides were distributed throughout America by the peddlers that supplied all of the needs of rural families. They flourished until the onset of the affordable newspaper.

So for two centuries chapbooks were the reading material that children enjoyed even though they were originally intended for adults. But the size and content had an instant appeal to children. Before the late eighteenth century chapbooks were written for adults and did not have children in mind.

Some chapbook material still endures today, such as *Robin Hood*, *Simple Simon*, *Jack the Giant Killer* and others. They are as popular today as they were when first published.

Street Cries

The first books for children, associated with the occupations or trades, were probably books of common street cries. These had been around for a long time, and though they were not meant as children's reading matter, they were used as such. This genre was extremely long lived.

European artists, especially the French, who were fascinated by these cries and their criers, started to draw pictures of them and their wares and to record their chants, rhymes and songs. They were generally printed on broadsheets and became the forerunners of the street criers of the seventeenth and eighteenth centuries. Sometimes the criers were pictured as street merchants, sometimes as exotic traders and sometimes as unsavory characters; the illustrations ran the gamut from popular prints to fine engravings. In 1840, Pellerin and Cie of Epinal, France, produced a street-cry ABC book; street-cry board games also appeared at about this time in France.

Although cries and occupation books were quite common in the eighteenth and nineteenth centuries, these trade books can be traced back to the seventeenth century's *Orbis Sensualium Pictus* of the Moravian writer Comenius, who is discussed in the chapter titled Short History. Although he was a teacher of Latin he appreciated the importance of pictures in helping the child's memory.

Orbis Sensualium Pictus was first published in Nuremberg and was early translated into a number of languages including English. Among other aspects of life he included the various trades and their tools—all of course with their Latin names. With this picture book of the occupations that could be seen in the streets, the stores or the fields, we have the first in a long line of "jack-of-all-trades" books—a title often given to those publications which explained in detail the trades or occupations to young readers.

Some of these cries, used by the mobile tradesman with his traditional wares, used the framework of the earlier alphabet books. In some literary circles these illustrated cries books were the forerunners of the larger, brightly colored, quality paper-bound, picture books. There were two types: those that were meant to instruct, and those that just offered information and let the readers and listeners do with it what they chose. The traditional cry of the street vendor was given first, then a little poem or sentence about the vendor which could be either humorous or didactic, followed by an illustration which could be flattering, unattractive or humorous. Whatever the approach, these cries gave historians and curators a look at the social conditions of the times.

In general these traditional cries were offered to the buying public sometimes in prose and sometimes in verse. They contained illustrations that attempted to be either amusing or true, whether provable or not. Their value was weighed by the truth and detail of the trades and occupations; services were explained; the uses of various tools were clarified, and means of advertising and distribution were described.

SCISSORS to GRIND!

Jingle, jingle goes the bell
Any razors or Scissors,
  Or Penknives to grind!
I'll engage that my work
  Shall be done to your mind

The illustration shows a man with a grindstone on a wheelbarrow; his foot works the wheel while his hands hold the scissors to the stone.

In some cases, as in the *Cries of York*, and in America the *Cries of Philadelphia*, there was a definite attempt to associate the cries with particular areas, but generally the wandering trader and his characteristic call could be recognized in many parts of the country.

No Cries are sure of such renown
As those of famous London town

Marcellus Laroom offered *Cryes of the City of London* in 1687. It is the model for all future cries books. It stayed in print until about 1760; then later it reappeared with current trends. The final edition went out of print in 1821, but it was reproduced by the Stanford University Press in 1990 with the title *The Criers and Hawkers of London* (engravings and drawings by Marcellus Laroom; edited by Sean Shesgreen).

Of all the folios produced by Laroom only about thirty survive. This important work details the work life of street vendors in seventeenth- and eighteenth-century London: those that flourished and those that declined; what these hawkers cried; what services they offered and what they charged for these offerings.

Timothy Ticklecheek (pseudonym) wrote *The Cries of London* (Youth's Pocket Library #3; London: John Fairborn, 1797). It was subtitled "displaying the manners, customs and characters of various people who traverse London streets with articles to sell, to which is added some pretty poetry applicable to each character, intended to amuse and instruct all good children, with London and the country contrasted, embellished with thirteen elegant copper plate prints."

Cries of London was called out by vendors of food and other commodities and by people offering their various wares and services. There were certain words and phrases that were used to sell either food items or a particular ware or service. The offerings were varied: eels, fresh herrings, hot chestnuts, muffins, strawberries and the newest, printed ballads. In 1820 John Harris issued *Sam Syntax's Description of the Cries of London.*

A type of book very similar to those about cries was one which took a subject and elaborated on its significance, such as the life history of a particular commodity: a loaf of bread, a bucket of coal, or a cup of tea. These books, which had many illustrations with little text, could, if brought up to date, be enjoyed by children today since they offer information in an attractive way, frequently in poetry. This was the intent of books like *The Cries of New York* (1820) or *Aunt Busy Bee's New London Cries*, published by Dean and Son in 1852. However, far too few writers for children could stop at clever information; they felt compelled to include some sort of lesson for the children:

> Old shoes. Old Hats. Come little dear
> To hear me cry, you need not fear,
> There's difference great between us two.
> I always cry, but seldom you.
> And you cry tears, I should suppose,
> While I cry nothing but old clothes.

Although printed collections of cries began to appear in numbers in the late-seventeenth century, this one was identified as a poem of the fifteenth century:

> Hot pescodes, one began to cry
> Strabery rype, and cherryes in the ryse
> One had me come here and by some spyce

The cries consisted of illustrations of the various street sellers with their cries printed beneath and often a descriptive verse for each one.

Illustrations were perhaps less important in books of cries than in those on trades, for in the former, the main information was given in the words of the cry itself. Not only were the words traditional, but also were the tones in which they were called or sung. No doubt many children finally found out from one of these books exactly what the crier was really saying, although it must always have been quite obvious what was being sold.

> Jingle, jingle, jingle, goes a parcel of bells,
> Baskets, Wooden Bowls
> Of well chosen wood,
> For a kitchen utensil
> You'll find very good.

These vendors sold kitchen supplies and in return took old iron, copper and pewter. Their wares were hung on their wagons, and their cries called attention to the best articles. The street crier announced his wares: new milk, radishes, hot corn, potatoes, matches, strawberries, fuel, fish, rags, old shoes to mend or knives to grind were much like today's radio or television ads. The familiarity of street cries to the young is brought out in a passage which occurs in *London Melodies* in 1812. In this publication, reference is made to the way in which children imitated the cries.

Francis Newbery, nephew of John Newbery, published *The Cries of London*. The printers Kendrew of York and Rusher of Banbury adapted the cries under the titles *The Cries of York* and the *Cries of Banbury and London*.

The cries became a stock subject for illustrated books as early as the seventeenth century. Becoming very popular in the 1840s they were taken up in Britain with gusto by Crane and Caldecott in the 1870s and 1880s.

In America *The Cries of London* first appeared as direct reprints from England (in 1786 Isaiah Thomas published it at Worcester), but then the cries of American cities: New York, Philadelphia, and Boston appeared. The *Cries of New York* (1808) was the first American edition of cries. It contained twenty-six cries. It had been called "the first distinctly American picture book." Then *The New York Cries in Rhyme* (printed by Mahlon Day in 1826) came out.

MATS! MATS!

> Buy a Mat! Buy a Mat!
> Here's excellent Mats,
> Made of oakum all o'er,
> So nice and so proper,
> To keep a clean floor.

This is accompanied by a picture of a blind man and his young son. It is important to see how the mats are carried (in the manner of a sandwich board) and to understand that any honest business was not to be looked down upon. In 1810 the *Cries of Philadelphia* by John Bouvier for Johnson and Warnerin made its appearance. Next came the *Boston Cries*, based also on the *Cries of London*. These works are an indication of the popularity of cries books on both sides of the Atlantic, and here too an attempt has been made to appeal to local identity.

Fine Ripe Water Melons, Musk
Melons, any Melons today?

> The melons brought to this market are from the state of New Jersey, in which they grow in the greatest abundance. They are considered, from their cooling qualities, to be very useful both to the sick and the healthy. They are sold so cheap, as to be within the reach of almost every person.

There is an illustration of a horse and cart carrying melons, with a man and woman purchasing them.

Isaiah Thomas published the first American edition of a book of cries at Worchester in 1786; this was his version of *Cries of London*. The following year Young and McCulloch of Philadelphia advertised *The Moving Market; or, Philadelphia Cries*, a book that, in spite of its pretense of local origins, was probably pirated from a British book of London cries. Samuel Wood's *Cries of New York*, described by the editors of the 1931 Harbor Press reprint as the "first distinctly American picture book," came out in New York City in 1808. Wood's *Cries of Philadelphia*, published two years later, consisted mainly of his original New York cries, with a few Philadelphia cries added to it. There were at least eight editions of Wood's *New York Cries* between 1808 and 1822, and many other new or, more often, pirated cries were printed at Boston, Albany, New Haven and elsewhere.

Mahlon Day's collection of street cries first went to press around 1825 (*New York Street Cries in Rhyme*). A book with original woodcut illustrations, verse cries and rather sobering paragraphs of facts and morals, Day's offering combined the main features of numerous other chapbooks of the time. It was among the more popular of all American books of street cries.

McLoughton was the publisher for most of these books. This publishing company was established in 1828 and later became McLoughton Brothers. The company claimed to be "the first American publisher to issue children's books illustrated in color." The McLoughton Brothers employed many artists to illustrate their books, including Thomas Nast, Howard Pyle and Palmer Cox. Unfortunately, at the time, most of their work was unsigned and appeared as anonymous art work.

The street cries of the cities also became subjects for many story papers and chapbooks.

Hornbooks and Battledores

Hornbooks

A hornbook was not really a book at all but a small wooden paddle upon which was mounted a sheet of paper containing, among other material, the alphabet, in both lower- and upper-case letters. It is for this reason that they are sometimes referred to as ABC books. However, they contained more than the alphabet; there were religious tracts, usually The Lord's Prayer, and various letter combinations.

Sometimes lesson sheets were pasted on these wooden paddles. Their main purpose was to teach children the alphabet and religious lessons and thereby help them learn to read. These sheets of paper needed protection and were covered with thin slices of horn (thus the name hornbook). This paper and horn were fixed to the wooden paddle with narrow strips of brass held on by small nails. The size was consistently 2¾" × 5". These were the forerunners of the cheaper battledores, which are covered later in this chapter.

The cow or ox horns were soaked for weeks in cold water. Then the bony core was separated from the rest of the horn. The outer part of the horn was heated first in hot water and then over an open fire. After the heating process the horn could be easily molded and cut. The horn was cut along its length to make the sheets. It was reheated and pressed flat between the plates of a special machine. This was done very carefully because they could easily split.

Horn is made of many layers; after the flattening process the horn could be peeled away. These layers were then cleaned, scraped and polished. Then they were trimmed to the right size for the hornbooks. The earliest horn books had a hole bored through the handlelike projection, where a piece of string could be pulled through and tied to the student's belt to prevent them from being lost. Later the projection gradually became more elongated. Some ended with handles long enough to enable scholars to use them as makeshift bats on the playground—a forerunner of the bat and ball games that evolved into the English game of cricket.

A. W. Tuer wrote that hornbooks came into existence in the middle of the fifteenth century. His description states that a hornbook was a piece of board usually of oak, about 5" × 9" with a handle. One side had the alphabet, nine numbers and The Lord's Prayer. On the other side was a picture. Sandra Brant in her book *Small Folk* talked about the hornbook as scrimshaw, a material sometimes used to make hornbooks. These were the earliest implement used for children's education. In eighteenth-century nursery schools, the hornbook was used for instruction.

In the early nineteenth century as dame schools, nursery schools and summer schools evolved, the hornbook evolved, too. Brant's description shows the hornbook as consisting of a single sheet of paper containing ABCs and so on protected by a piece of horn and mounted on wood or leather tablets. The dame, of a dame school, "pointed to the ABCs with her knitting needle, led her brood in recitation of the hornbook's alphabet, syllabaries and The Lord's Prayer. The scrimshaw hornbook illustrated in her book was elaborately carved and a real work of art. In order for a

Physical Hornbook (facsimile)

child to have this type of hornbook the family had to have money to spare. It was only a few fortunate children who had these works of art. Most hornbooks were simple schoolbooks, not masterpieces of decorative art. The hornbook is also described in detail in *The Water Babies* (1863), a children's classic by Charles Kingsley.

Tablets of various kinds have been used to teach children the alphabet from the earliest civilizations, for example, the Roman tabella, on which wax was smeared and then scored with a stylus. A manuscript from about 1400 in the British Library mentions school children being taught by "a bok ... naylyd on a brede [breath] of tre [tree, i.e., wood]." There is an early portrayal of a hornbook in an illustration to Margarita Philosophica by Gregorius Reisch, published in 1503. There is an ivory hornbook that was carved out of a thin piece of ivory. It has both the upper- and lowercase alphabet. A small, decorative frame was carved around the edges. This hornbook measures 2" × 3½".

Kunst und Lehrbuchlein (*Book of Art and Instruction for Young People*), published by Sigmund Feterabend in Germany in 1578, is said to contain the first printed pictures of a young scholar using a hornbook. The German alphabet changed over the last hundred years. The W, V, J and Y were the most noticeable of these changes. This is one of the reasons why today Germans have trouble deciphering old German documents. Also at one time fancy script was banned in all German publications.

In an 1899 book, *Child Life in Colonial Days* by Alice M. Earle, Matthew Prior tells in rhyme of a hornbook, common enough in England, which must have proven eminently satisfactory to the student:

> To master John the English maid
> A horn book give of gingerbread;
> And that the child may learn the better
> As he can name, he eats the letter.

In England at some fairs and in bakeries, gingerbread hornbooks were made and sold even though they were criticized by the moralists of the day:

> No liquorice learning to thy babes extend
> But still ...
> All the letters are digested,
> Hateful ignorance detested.

In New England can also be found "cookey moulds," which were made of heavy wood incised with the alphabet, were of ancient Dutch manufacture, and had been used for making "kocckje" hornbooks. The true hornbook was common by Shakespeare's time and was referred to in *Love's Labour's Lost* (v.1: "Yes, yes, he teaches boys the Horn book").

The hornbook was often known as the Criss-cross-row or Chris-cross, which was either a reference to the cross at the top of it or to a device which had preceded it, in which the letters of the alphabet were strung crosswise on a wire.

Battledores

Battledores, introduced in the middle of the eighteenth century, were flimsy wooden or cardboard tablets, sometimes with gilt-edged Dutch paper on one side, superseding the hornbook in England as well as the United States as a way to teach children to read. They were shaped like the hornbooks, that is, a rectangle with a handle, but because they were made of cheaper wood or even cardboard they were not the works of art some old hornbooks were.

To obtain sufficient stiffness to bear knocking about, the battledore was printed on a double fold of stiff cardboard, with an extra piece lapping over one edge in the old pocket-book fashion. Even though most battledores had handles and looked like the old hornbooks, some were rounded like rackets, and some had no handles. These battledores, without the handles, evolved into multipaged tablets and, again, different from

A Battledore, to Instruct and Amuse: A facsimile of an original battledore owned by the Boston Public Library. Published by the Horn Book, Inc., Boston. This example, from the mid–18th century, was merely folded cardboard, without handles.

the hornbooks, contained some woodcuts. They also differed because they did not contain any religious tracts. Even though the name "battledore" leads one to believe that they were used in games, as were some of the earlier hornbooks, they were never actually used that way because of their flimsy construction.

These "books" did not have a horn covering although some of them were covered with a coat of varnish. A sheet of paper was pasted on one side, and if there was no gilt-edged paper on the other side, it had woodcuts or sometimes a rhyme or two. Actually, battledores were simply small pieces of cardboard folded twice to make a booklet. The size was 4" × 6½". They, too, featured the alphabet and some of the other subjects contained in the older hornbooks. Sometimes they were printed and sometimes engraved, but, different from the horn books, they contained entertaining material along with instruction. Battledores were a popular form of textbook as late as 1840, but children still got most of their reading from books intended for adults. The earliest battledores were covered with light-colored, gilt-embossed Dutch paper—the most famous of these paper makers were Marx Leonhardt Kauffmann and Paul Hinzberg.

The invention of these battledores was claimed by the Salisbury bookseller Benjamin Collins, business associate of John Newbery, who began to manufacture a royal battledore in association with Newbery in 1746. This information is still preserved in his account books. Between 1770 and 1780, Collins sold over one hundred thousand battledores, which cost him three pounds ten per thousand, and he sold them at twelve shillings per gross. The selling price was two pence.

Other specimens were sold under such titles as *The British Battledore*, *The Infant's Battledore* and *The New Improved Battledore*. Clifton Johnson, in *Old Time Schools and Schoolbooks* (1963), says that the battledore was issued in 1746 as a different sort of school book. A "battledore boy" was a boy learning his letters. However, it is accepted that battledores appeared as early as the end of the eighteenth century and could still be found as late as the middle of the nineteenth century. They changed little in style over the years, and accurate dating of these battledores is mostly guesswork unless a specific date sign was evident. The term *battledore* was at times applied indiscriminately to the hornbook and to other reading and spelling books.

There is a most interesting hornbook named *The British Battledore* in the British Museum as well as a little book of six pages dated 1835, containing the alphabet, Arabic and Roman numerals and words of two or three syllables, titled *The Battledore, or First Book for Children*.

By 1860 or so the hornbook was fast going out of fashion and would soon be only a memory, and so would its later variant, the more perishable, though less clumsy, battledore.

Toy Books

At the same time as the small chapbook versions of the alphabet were circulating, a move had already begun toward the type of book that would later be known as the toy book. This was usually a square book about 10" × 10", frequently printed on one side of the page only, and containing about eight leaves. The covers were of paper; a more expensive toy book could be found covered in linen. Within this general description there were many variations. Some books had text on the inside covers only; others had it below the illustrations; yet others alternated the textual and illustrative material.

To qualify as a toy book, the item should be printed in color, and the text should be pleasing and whimsical, not instructive. However, some of the cheaper toy books did try to be a learning tool. And, of course, these definitions also did not include primers, spelling books, catechisms or the more expensive printed books with engraved, colored plates.

One popular type of toy book was simply a picture book showing various men at work, one trade for each letter of the alphabet. *Aunt Busy Bee's New London Cries* (Dean and Son, 1852) was a typical hand-colored, wood-engraved toy book containing small scenes with descriptive verses below the illustrations. (See the chapter on cries for more on this type of publication.) Many of them were not strictly books from which to learn the alphabet, though perhaps they were read aloud and decorated with attractive, matching pictures; some of the books may have helped in this basic learning task. As with similar books, the alphabet was merely used as a framework for the subject at hand.

Thomas Dean and Son was the first company to issue these toy books. These were picture books for children that were colored. The subject matter of these books was coincidental; the use of color was the selling point. Most of the brief text was traditional-type stories. In 1858 Thomas Dean advertised about 200 titles, the most famous of which was *Dame Wiggins of Lee and Her Seven Wonderful Cats* (1823).

Nursery Ditties: **A specially designed, shaped "toy" book. 6" × 3"; 10 pages.**

Easy-to-read, pictorial books of poor quality continued to be issued by Thomas Dean and Son throughout the century, widening in scope to include not only toy books, but also movable books, plays and other amusing literature. The firm of Thomas Dean and Son turned their attention early to the toy book trade because of their ability to make extensive use of lithography and the newly discovered method of chromolithography. These methods were used extensively for adding color to the illustrations in their children's books.

From about 1840 onward the Dean Company all but established a monopoly in the trade of all forms of toy, movable and flap books. They set up a separate department of talented artists to put into action the complicated, exacting method of stiff paper levers which made the pictures in their books convert into different and unexpected scenes with one pull of a tab. John Harris also published what were classified as toy books; among his titles are *Lion's Masquerade* (1807); *Peacock at Home* (1807); and *Whittington and His Cat* (1825).

Edmond Evans, a printer, had been publishing a series of colored, illustrated books for children and the general reading public since the mid–1800s. In the world of children's books his books and published works were not particularly outstanding. Although he had been experimenting with printing in color since early in the 1850s, it wasn't until 1856 that he perfected the process of color printing from wood blocks. After that Evans became known as the master of color printing. At this time, even though other printers had been experimenting with color, he not only perfected it but he also had a stroke of good luck. His name became famous, and his books for boys and girls achieved success when he began to produce the series of toy books by Walter Crane about 1865. In collaboration with artists Kate Greenaway, Randolph Caldecott and Walter Crane, he issued his most successful toy books. Evans was introduced to Walter Crane in 1863, but it took two years before work began on the toy books to be published by George Routledge. Crane did three toy books for Evans, printed by Warne and then followed with two more for Routledge in 1865: *A Railroad Alphabet* and *A Farmyard Alphabet*. Steadily the toy books became more lavish, decorated in rich colors. The contemporary edited text was usually plainer in style than the old fairy tales.

Routledge's toy books were very popular in the second half of the nineteenth century, and he rarely attempted anything more than very general information, if even that. *The Shilling Alphabet: Trade of London* was printed in color by the Leighton Brothers and published as a toy book in 1869. It was certainly not meant to teach the alphabet since the accompanying rhymes would have been too difficult for an early learner. It was simply a picture book showing various tradesmen at work and intended to give pleasure rather than instruct.

In 1873, a further series of Walter Crane toy books came out in a new *Shilling* series, and one of the tales was rated among the best, *Goody Two Shoes* (1875).

Collections of toy books were often bound and sold in one volume. Walter Crane and Randolph Caldecott designed numerous, high-quality books in this format. These were printed from wood engravings by Edmond Evans. Later Warne and Routledge publishers became competitors. Toy books needed huge print orders to keep their prices low; Routledge alleged that he would begin to make a profit on a title only if he sold more than 50,000 copies, and a first print order of 10,000 was common.

After the Routledge toy books came to an end, Crane continued to collaborate with Edmond Evans and designed three small, square picture books in a rather different style, whose charm continues to please young children today. They were *The Baby's Opera* (1877), *The Baby's Bouquet* (1879) and *The Baby's Own Aesop* (1887). These talented people were truly the first craftsmen who drew and published picture books for children and elaborated the concept of today's picture books.

In Britain the vogue of the toy book started during the early years of Queen Victoria's reign. Though these picture books made some attempt to include didactic material, it was rarely done with any serious intent. Such books found an important place in children's reading (and one which was peculiar to the English-speaking world) even if only because they were both numerous and varied. Most of the toy books were published solely to give young readers entertainment, and their popularity between about 1850 and 1890 was an indication that there was to be a change of emphasis in children's book publications.

At the same time that these entertaining publications were being issued, the market offered a parallel series of books in the same field; they followed the toy book pattern. Although the study of foreign countries would be well served by this sort of pictorial treatment, the publications by Thomas Dean or William Darton, who both specialized in early toy books, offered only the most rigid illustrations and a text that was hard to believe:

> The Prussians are a warlike race
> Yet agriculture they embrace.
> When peace forbids the sword and shield
> They cultivate the harvest field.

It has always been difficult to know whether a child's book is a chapbook, a toy book or just a plain, ordinary child's book. Should one classify as chapbooks for children such toy books as were sold for a penny or so by peddlers or by booksellers in towns and villages? Was the book just for entertainment, or was it meant to be instructive?

The influence of the toy theater, which began to appear between 1810 and 1820, created an interest in drama and home acting among young people. By the 1850s, the publishing of "juvenile drama" sheets containing characters and scenes, along with books of words (usually based upon actual stage productions) was a thriving business. Very soon publications for youngsters, including Edwin Brett's *Boys of England* (this publication is discussed in the chapter on penny dreadfuls) competed with each other in offering cheap and attractive works to young readers. Many of these dramas had their origin in pantomime or melodrama, and many were based on traditional tales and favorite stories, such as "Robinson

Crusoe" and "Robin Hood." Their circulation in this form, even though a far cry from the original novels, may have had the same stimulating effect on young imaginations as the chapbooks a century earlier. These pasteboard miniature dramas could be cut out and mounted on stiff board and used for small, amateur performances.

About this same time John Green, a children's book publisher, put out a "book" of juvenile dramas in sheet form. The earliest sheets of juvenile drama can be dated to about 1810, and they have a close relationship with the tinsel pictures of this time. A printed sheet duplicating the background of a popular play was bought, along with an envelope or small box containing a variety of colored tinsel and other materials such as the head and shoulders of the favorite actor of the period. These early juvenile dramas were sold at a penny each for plain ones or two pence for hand-colored ones, which was very reasonable at contemporary prices, although some of the more elaborate Hodgson and Company plays cost much more.

By 1830 there were a great many publishers who carried and sold juvenile drama sheets, all printed and ready to be cut and assembled, packaged in a portfolio to keep them from being torn or damaged. The *Boys of England* magazine also presented toy theaters, or sheets of juvenile drama, with the first one taken from its serial "Alone in the Pirates' Lair." This magazine was by no means as worthless as the later publications of this kind. It contained articles on gardening, sports and military matters, and an early serial was a historical story founded on "Chevy Chase." In 1871 the first Jack Harkaway story by Bracebridge Hemyng made its appearance.

Then the toy theaters stopped acquiring new plays but continued to reproduce the repertoire of the early-nineteenth-century London stage with increasing bad work, just as chapbooks had copied earlier works of literature. During the nineteenth century in Britain, toy-making books became popular. One of the most widely read was the *Philosophy of Sport* (1827), attributed to J. A. Paris. The book uses playthings and other objects to teach the basic principles of gravity, weight, motion, elasticity, and so on. Toys included a jack-in-the-box, figurines that dance, a whip and a peg top, and a peashooter.

A little later the publishing house of Hodgson and Company printed sheets of some seventy plays. These books included the original dialogue, detailed stage directions and special effects. From 1835 the publishing family of Skelt reissued many of the more popular titles at one penny or even a half penny per sheet. Skelt's had a wide distribution area. George Speaight, in his *History of the English Toy Theatre* (1969) observed that their sheets were on sale not just in London but also at news stands and stationers throughout Britain so that "a generation of boys grew up to whom the toy theater meant Skelt and the words became almost synonymous."

In 1858 Ebenezer Landells, a creative wood carver and a protégé of Thomas Bewick, who was probably England's finest wood carver, wrote *The Boy's Own Toy-Maker*. (He was also the original projector of *Punch*.) This book gives instruction in the making of model boats, equipment for archery and angling and certain types of puzzles. It also includes a section on the manufacture of paper and cardboard toys.

Miscellany

Some of the leading theaters in London had pantomimes, often known as "harlequinades," named after the scenes of the show in which the harlequin and clown play the main roles. Robert Sayer, an English print shop owner, experimented with little "turn-up" books, made of a single printed sheet, with pictures, folded into four sections. Attached to the head and foot of each fold was the picture, cut through horizontally across the center to make two flaps that could be opened up or downward. When raised, they showed another picture below, each with a few lines of verse to tell the story—finishing with the words "Turn up" or Turn down," so that another picture came into view. These harlequinades were one of the first toys in book form. Children referred to them as turn-up books.

In the United States in 1814 Samuel Wood of New York published this type of book called *Metamorphosis; or, A Transformation of Pictures*, with poetical explanations for the amusement of young persons. The explanation consisted of nine lines. Over thirty-six American editions appeared between 1787 and 1820. The "transformation" was of a three-masted schooner sailing under the American flag. The best of the animated picture books were those constructed by Lothar Meggendorfer in the 1880s and 1890s. They were a wonder of ingenuity. By using a single tab at the side or bottom of the page a child could make apes swing from trees, boats roll, houses collapse, crocodiles swallow little boys, and umbrellas open. The "works" which produced these transformations consisted of a series of interconnecting cardboard levers placed between the colored illustration on the front of the leaf and the dummy pasted behind it.

Shadows and silhouettes and books containing illusion pictures have always been popular with young people. One of the first advocates of these books was Charles Henry Bennett, who gave lots of enjoyment to children with this kind of picture book. The first of these and the most successful one was *Shadows* (1856). It was published by David Bogue of

London in a binding of picturesque, paper-covered boards. The twenty-four leaves were printed by lithography, on just one side with circular pictures showing well-known comical figures, each casting shadows on the wall behind them. Many of Bennett's children's books proved extremely popular.

Also popular in the 1860s were the illusion books. Some of the best of the ones produced for children came from J. H. Brown of Brighton. *Spectropia; or, Surprising Special Illusions* (1864) contained sixteen full-page plates of eerie pictures, hand painted in vibrant colors. If the child followed the printed directions, images were seen on ceilings and walls in complementary colors. This was due to persistency of vision and the retention of the image on the retina of the eyes. It wasn't long before children started to make their own "ghosts," but *Spectropia* proved popular for many years and was printed in several editions.

The best of the silhouette books was Karl Frolich's *Frolich's with Scissors and Pen* (1879). It was translated from the German and published by R. Worthingham of New York. Frolich was an expert silhouettist. He made a living in Germany by being able to quickly cut a sitter's portrait in profile with sharp scissors and colored paper. The first of the Frolich silhouette books appeared in Germany in 1852, and others were published later.

Many of these German toy-type books were published with the poems and stories in English, such as *Comic Actors* (1891), described as a new, movable toy book by Lothar Meggendorfer and published by H. Grevel and Co., the London agents of the Munich firm.

Penny Dreadfuls

Another type of transient reading material that early teens found exciting was the penny dreadfuls, the "bloods" of the period that were in their prime from the 1840s to the 1900s. The term "penny dreadful" is, of course, an inaccurate title. The name came to be used as a description for the sensational literature, released in weekly parts in cheap periodicals, that was popular in England in the latter half of the eighteenth century. The term "penny blood" is sometimes used. The blood types were usually used to describe the "blood and thunder" series of stories that were prevalent from the 1830s to the 1850s. The dreadful types were descriptions of the lurid adventure stories for youth that emerged in the 1860s. They generally sold for a penny or, if not a penny, at least very cheaply.

By the end of the 1860s penny fiction was aimed mostly at boys and sometimes girls, as opposed to adults. This development continued through the 1870s, and by the 1880s the new genre of rough-and-tumble adventure stories had fully emerged.

There was a term popular at the time applied to cheap, smelly cigars: the "penny stinker" (ergo, penny dreadfuls were cheap and nasty). (An interesting thought is one put forth by Ann Landers in 1998: "I checked with Sally Hopkins, then director of Hallmark's Historical Collection in Kansas City, Mo., who told me that Valentine's Day first appeared in England about the time of Queen Victoria. The first Valentine's cards were called 'Penny Dreadful' and 'Rude and Crudes' because they were insulting and obscene.")

In the days of the dreadfuls for a penny, the choice of titles was wide. They included anything that would sell, from Thomas Prest's *Varney the Vampire; or, the Feast of Blood* to plagiarized Charles Dickens stories under such titles as *Oliver Twiss*. Some of the first penny dreadfuls were collections of such stories as Prest's *Calendar of Horrors* (1836) and the early serial *Lives of the Most Notorious Highwaymen* (1836–1837).

Some of the earliest titles, such as *The Royal Rake* (1842), by Leman Rede, were satirical romances rather than true blood-and-thunder thrillers. However, the very graphic woodcuts of John Rann, alias "Sixteen String Jack," and his following, henchmen like Kit Clayton, pointed out very bloody deeds such as violent highway robberies, paving the way for the later publications which were certainly penny dreadfuls. (Incidentally, Leman Rede was the first to publish *Judy*, a magazine that competed with *Punch*. There had to be some humor in the title selection.)

By the 1850s the publishers of what were first called "penny parts" soon came to be known as penny dreadfuls. The normal penny parts had eight or sixteen pages with one black-and-white illustration, usually on the top half of the page and later on the whole front page. This was done to attract potential customers. One of the promotional aspects of this literature was the carnality of the engravings. The plates that printed these engravings came to be known as "fierce" plates. They appeared on the front cover of each issue. In the beginning there was much less uniformity and generally poor-quality workmanship. The text might be all across the page or in two columns, but the latter became the standard. The text was tightly packed into these two-columns page, and stories could actually finish at the bottom of page eight somewhere in midsentence. The next issue would take up where the previous one ended, even if it meant the next word was the one which would have followed the midsentence cut-off.

The earliest books had very crude woodcut illustrations. A few talented artists and woodcutters were once used, but they had to work too fast and for too little pay, so they didn't last long. A good many publishers just reused cuts from other sources, often mixing time frames and using images that were not appropriate to the story or woodcuts from earlier chapters.

In the beginning some of these penny dreadfuls were sold as monthly accumulations of four or five weekly installments with a decorated cover printed on colored paper; these rarely survived. Volumes of these are scarce because of the high price that was paid for waste paper during the war. Also, during the Victorian period, everything with the exception of "The Boys' Own Paper" was designated as "pernicious literature" and was banned just because it was issued in weekly editions.

Penny dreadfuls were the descendants of chapbooks and broadsides. They were usually mass produced by anonymous authors or "by the author of...," printed by anonymous printers so that in-depth research is necessary to establish the relationships between authors and publishers. Sometimes even this can't be done.

Publication details were sometimes printed up the spine of a book. This was a source of information about the publisher, his address, the price of the book and a date. This was appreciated by later bibliographers. The spines of books were also used to advertise other publications, series numbers and other information.

Many arguments were presented against penny dreadfuls, but they are the same ones we hear today about movies and television. The authors and publishers of these books, like the actors and producers of today's movies and television programs, argue in return that in the end all is well because it is only entertainment, even though this may not necessarily be so, either in the penny dreadfuls of the past or in today's "entertainment."

During this period of popularity there were penny dreadfuls with every sort of setting: historical, buccaneering, domestic, ghoulish and more. Some writers combined sensational stories of slum life and vice with schoolmasterly explanations of thieves' jargon, card sharping and socialist propaganda.

English and American writers pirated each other's works freely; relays of writers took turns at stories, and the successful escapades were spun out endlessly with little regard to the basic plot. Penny dreadfuls were poorly written, the characters were implausible, and the story line foreseeable; the language and humor were unacceptable to the general public and on the whole not considered literate. The main theme was violence, extreme adventure, crime and inhumane punishment. The plots were ones of betrayal, murder, cruel imprisonment, escapes and pursuits, lost heirs, robbers and all sorts of criminals. These bloods were full of betrayed maidens, bloody murders, highway robbers and seagoing pirates to enthrall their unsophisticated readers and to appeal to those older readers who in later life vicariously relive their youthful dreams. They also contained a crude humor, often centering on the misfortunes of non-British-speaking people of unacceptable, substandard English, but the stories themselves had great energy. These kinds of stories appealed to the impressionable youth and sold well to the undiscriminating reader. Penny dreadfuls were not at first explicitly aimed at the juvenile market, but they were enthusiastically read by the young right from the beginning. Penny dreadfuls successfully found their way into the homes of teen readers. These eight-page publications were found everywhere on the street. It was the escape literature of the day. These publications outsold the classic books found in bookstores and the contemporary books by authors who would later be known as great writers.

It was pretty well accepted that this was trash reading of the blood-and-thunder variety, in spite of the claims that these were true-life stories with well-designed plots written by middle-of-the-road, respected authors. Charles Knight was one of the publishers who produced the penny literature. It was his claim that this was popular art and that it was accepted around the world. "Of course, many readers of 'dreadfuls' balanced this kind of literature with books of finer quality," he said.

Margaret Dalziel says, "It is true that from the sixties [1860] onward 'Penny Dreadfuls' were directed toward the juvenile public but, of course, this included many adults, just as the readers of comics do today." It was the accepted belief of the day that penny dreadfuls led to crime by glorifying it. This idea was pushed by the clergy, teachers, the law community and people of the literary world. It was "common knowledge" that these books made crime seem an acceptable alternative and that the readers of these books would later lead a life of crime.

The literary people of the time believed that reading novels would arouse base passions, stifle one's imagination and make a person less humane. It would also destroy the moral fiber of anyone, including the youth. It was believed that fiction corrupts the taste for the good and can be habit forming, much as alcoholism. Also, one is liable to commit acts of violence one would not do otherwise. Even after being "cured" of this devastating habit, one will never be able to suppress the craving for this exotic excitement.

People also believed that the more of these publications that were available, the more the life of crime would accelerate. The only sensible solution was to stop the publication of these awful, tempting publications. The teachers and clergymen of the country along with the judicial members and, of course, the ever-present journalists, were always on the alert to subvert this "literature"; unfortunately, these very people almost never read these stories themselves and based their opinions on hearsay and preconceived ideas.

The British Parliament on July 1, 1868, tried to halt this cheap literature because of this belief—that there was a direct connection between the rise of juvenile crime and these immoral publications and plays. The unnatural, exciting writings were corrupting the lower-class children, who would be destined to become dishonest and worse. They were concerned with "the lamentable amount of juvenile criminality, largely attributed to the spread of cheap publications and theatrical representations of an exciting and immoral character, which corrupt the children of the lower classes, and stimulate them into courses of dishonesty and vice."

Edwin John Brett was one of the defenders of what was also called "gallows literature." His publications, called "penny packets of poison," were prevalent in the mid–1860s and probably deserved the title. The stories he published were about pirates, highwaymen and city criminals. This is evidenced by the titles: *Black Rollo, the Pirate* (1864–1865); *Red Ralph* (1856–1866); *The Dance of Death* (1865–1866); and the well-publicized *Wild Boys of London* (1864–1866) series. All of these publications came out in weekly installments, each about eight pages long containing sensational illustrations.

These penny dreadfuls displaced the chapbooks by going back to the Gothic novel and its stories of murder, horror and supernatural terrors. From these melodramatic productions, not primarily intended for youth, arose the cheap periodicals for boys. *The Boys' Own Paper* was a magazine published by the Religious Tract Society. Its purpose was to compete with these sensational and cheap penny dreadfuls. Their main goal was to keep this literature out of the hands of impressionable youth with their corrupting thoughts.

It was believed that the availability of such publications as *The Boys' Own Paper* (1879–1967) and *The Boys' Friend* would be the answer to this harmful literature. These were publications put out by religious societies and some profit-making printers. Good behavior, social niceties and patriotic stories were the main thrust of these periodicals. Because legislation could not stop the publication of the penny dreadfuls, these publishers felt the profusion of "good" literature would be an acceptable alternative. The first edition of *The Boys' Friend* had a damaging article about the "horrors" of the penny dreadfuls; among other phrases were beer-swilling writers; driveling stories; promiscuous literature and how they would lead to degradation and a life of crime. However, it can also be said that the "full of sin" Sunday school literature was just as bad for the youthful readers as were the penny dreadfuls.

Vileroy; or the Horrors of Zindorf Castle; *The Black Monk; or, The Secret of the Grey Turret*; and *The Castle Fiend* paved the way for one of publisher Edward Lloyd's most successful publications, *Varney the Vampire; or, the Feast of Blood*, by Thomas Prest. None of these titles was meant primarily for the juvenile market, but it did not take adolescents long to discover the blood-curdling excitement to be had for a penny. These publications, showing scenes of crime, murder and wickedness in minute detail should have been labeled penny dreadfuls. Popular among these penny dreadfuls was *Black Bess; or, the Knight of the Road* by Edward Viles. Dick Turpin was the fictional hero of this story. (Incidentally, Black Bess was the name of Dick's favorite horse.)The real Richard Turpin lived from 1706 to 1739. He had a criminal record as a robber, smuggler and cruel predator. Edward Viles made full use of these traits in his *Black Bess* book, which was published by E. Harrison in weekly parts for five years from the spring of 1863 to the spring of 1868 in a total of 254 installments.

However, even this paled into insignificance beside the series of "Jack Harkaway" stories written by Bracebridge Hemyng. The first of the Jack Harkaway stories appeared in *Boys of England* magazine, published by Edwin J. Brett as a penny weekly which commenced publication in

November 1866 and continued until June 1899. Jack Harkaway, who won over a thousand fist fights and made over a hundred escapes from sure death, came into existence in July of 1871, and these breath-taking exploits increased the sales of the paper to the point where the proprietor named his newly acquired premise Harkaway House. The series consisted of 800–900 episodes, which were later bound into twenty-eight volumes. Assuming that each book was read by at least two or three youths, it would have been read by over half a million youngsters.

It goes without saying that some of the "penny dreadfuls" were shocking and brutal, but to apply this name to a whole genre of literature that appealed to youngsters would be a disservice. Not all of these books were about crime and its impact on society. Some of them had the same ingredients as today's mystery or thriller books: characters who were believable, settings in unique and exciting places and incidents that could occur to anyone.

This type of literature was meant to divert the boredom of the youth of the working-class population, but they were also read by educated people with refined tastes. George W. M. Reynolds, one of the most popular writers of the penny genre, by his own admission said he was not above borrowing some of these from his hired help. Also C. A. Stonehill wrote, "It is probable that in its day more people read Thomas Prest's *First False Step; or, The Manic Father* than had ever heard of a book published in the same decade, entitled *Jane Eyre*." R. A. H. Goodyear, a writer and specialist in dreadfuls and bloods said, "I recollect reading *Blueskin* by days and balancing it with Jan Porter's *Scottish Chiefs* by night." He said he found *Broad Arrow Jack* and the *Blue Dwarf* a good deal more exciting than contemporary titles and that *Jack Harkaway's Schooldays* and *Jack Harkaway among the Brigands* were just as fine as Hawthorne's *Scarlet Letter*. As a young reader, Sir James Matthew Barrie, author of *Peter Pan*, loved the swashbuckling penny dreadfuls, as did young H. G. Wells.

The publishing house of Beadle and Adams began in 1860 to publish dime novels, the American version of the penny dreadfuls of England. It was logical to publish this material which was so popular in England. It had proved to be an excellent seller, and because of the current laws that permitted the reprinting of anything from England, this cheap fiction, available without payment to authors or illustrators, was a sure thing.

The Aldine Publication Company of England, the last publisher to print penny dreadfuls, was also printing American dime novels about Buffalo Bill, Deadwood Dick, Frank Reade, and Horatio Alger. *Gentleman Jack; or, Life on the Road* (1852) was typical of the long-running serials issued at a penny a week with "numbers 2, 3 and 4, presented gratis with No. 1."

Frank Leslie's *Boys' and Girls' Weekly* and Norman Munro's *The Boys of New York* clearly pirated their material from England's Edwin John Brett's publications.

In 1850 Emma D. E. N. Southworth, a Washington school teacher, published *The Deserted Wife*. She wrote over sixty serial novels. Her books were just as popular in Britain as they were in America.

George Lippard is another American writer of this era. His *The Quaker City; or, the Monks of Monk Hall* had twenty-seven editions. It came out in 1844.

As time went on, adapted stories about real criminals made way for tales about fictional criminals. One of the best known of the latter was *Sweeney Todd, the Demon Barber of Fleet Street. String of Pearls* (the original title of *Sweeney Todd*) by Thomas Peckett Prest (1810–1879) was published by Ritchie and Company. John Medcraft called *String of Pearls* the result of "a morbid genius with a wonderful imagination."

If G. W. M. Reynolds was the most popular writer of penny parts, the story of Sweeney Todd the Demon Barber was the most popular and enduring of this type of serial. Even to this day he is as well known in the criminal world as Burke and Hare or Jack the Ripper. Sweeney Todd has been an oft-used subject for broadcasts, films, plays, stories, and even ballet since he first appeared in 1846. *String of Pearls* was serialized in *People's Periodical* from 1846 to 1848. It was later issued in ninety-two parts from 1849 to 1850. There was an abridged version meant for young boys that appeared in Richie's Paragon Library in the late 1860s.

Charles Fox asked George Agusta Sala to rewrite Prest's novel, and it appeared in forty-eight penny parts, starting in 1878. Sala strenuously denied authorship and believed T. P. Prest to be the author. Sensational book readers are always taken in by stories of cannibalism: the idea of a person's being killed and eaten by an animal or, even more morbid, eaten by other humans. The *String of Pearls* was this kind of story. In minute detail Prest told of Sweeney Todd, a Fleet Street barber and how he cut his customers' throats and dropped his victims into the cellar of the building. There they were "processed" into pot pies. These were sold to the magistrates, lawyers and clerks of the nearby courts. After reading Sweeney Todd, one might be uncomfortable about eating anything that is ground up and cooked into pies, stews or casseroles. One might also be a bit uneasy about sitting in a barber's chair while the barber sharpens his razor and lifts your neck.

There are several theories about the origin of this tale. One of them is that it's a German legend; another is that it's actually a true-to-life murder which took place in Paris in 1800; another is that it is based on the legend of Sawney Beane, the man eater of Scotland. However, Summers

Montague claims that "there persisted a very old Fleet Street tradition (current long before 1800) that such an individual as Sweeney Todd did exist and his story is only a little exaggerated." He also adds that there was an old watchman at St. Bartholomew's Hospital who used to say that his father "had been murdered for his coin by Sweeney Todd." All of these theories played a role in Thomas Prest's (1810–1879) final story. Prest, who was the author of many penny dreadfuls, read lots of old legends and often was seen at the taverns along Fleet Street. Although Prest wrote many stage productions, many of them, including *Sweeney Todd*, were plagiarized by other playwrights, who then cashed in on their successes. George Dibdin Pitt was the writer who brought *Sweeney Todd* to the stage.

Even today *Sweeney Todd, the Demon Barber of Fleet Street* with Angela Lansbury and George Hearn went from Broadway (1979), where it won eight Tony awards, to Hollywood and then to video by Turner Home Entertainment.

The flourishing of these types of publications can be attributed to three major factors: the 1870 Education Act (basic education for one and all was becoming the cry of the day; everyone wanted to learn to read); the invention and perfection of the printing presses (i.e., power rather than hand labor and continuous feed via rotary presses; most of the credit for the improvement of presses is credited to Robert Hoe and Company of New York City); and the invention and development of paper-making machines (i.e., paper made any length and size as opposed to paper made by hand in a limited number of sizes; this invention is credited to Thomas Gilpen of Brandywine, Delaware).

Dime Novels

Synopsis

"Touch but a hair of her head and by the Lord who made me, I will bespatter that tree with your brains." "Bang! Bang! Bang! Three shots rang out on the midnight air." These exciting sentences were the essence of the dime novel, a form which was born, grew, was crippled and died in the span of about twenty-five years (but its ghost lingers on).

In the 1860s a new kind of fiction, written mostly by new authors, that was bold, frank and sometimes humorous was available to young readers. It was melodramatic in its literary style, materialistic in its handling of values, and sentimental in its view of the problems of the day. These new authors were concerned with capturing the interest of their young audiences and so paid close attention to their tastes. Their stories still contained plenty of moral advice, but they deeply buried their didacticism in adventurous tales; stories of dramatic encounters between noble youth and villains of various kinds; and stories of poor children rising meteorically in the day's accepted society. This type of fiction was indicative of a society that had grown more complex and was, therefore, less sure of its values, more aware of its problems and more willing to accept escape through sentimentality and melodrama. This new social reality, albeit sometimes badly described, appeared both in and between the lines of this new fiction.

It was also getting away from the introverted character of the hero or heroine and looking more to the world outside the self and home. The new language, both subtly symbolic and refreshingly plain, was a breakthrough in writing for young audiences. No little Peterkin needed to ask any Old Kaspar what this was all about. The battles with Native Americans, the capture of road agents and bank burglars, and the retribution which hit the villain who attempted to cheat the girl out of her patrimony told their story in language so plain that there was never any mistake in grasping it.

Moses Lawton, created by Louisa Tuthill, was typical. He was "tall, erect ... [with] an even row of well-kept teeth.... [His] expression was mild and kindly." A reader would not be likely to take tall, erect Mr. Lawson of the even, well-kept teeth for a villain or to mistake the unattractive, crooked-toothed Mr. Ferguson of the same story for the hero. The very use of these descriptions was another indication of the change in emphasis by this new generation of authors: interest in the outer person, as against the preoccupation of the earlier authors with inward character alone.

"The dimes" is a term that has no one concise meaning. There is one in the minds of the critics, mostly concerned parents and some literary reviewers; another one comes from the lips of remembering readers; and another was in the minds of those who provided books for young readers.

For the most part dime novels are known as the salmon-colored 25,000-to-30,000-word books which were issued once a month beginning around 1860 and ending just before 1880. These little pamphlets were to swell into an enormous flood of printed pages. They included swift-moving thrillers, mainly about the American Revolution, the frontier period and the Civil War. First sold in 1860 for ten cents, the books featured such real-life adventurers as Buffalo Bill and Deadwood Dick and such fictional characters as Nick Carter. The quality of the novels dropped in the 1880s, and they were eclipsed by other series, pulp magazines and comic strips in the 1890s. They were both panned and praised by both scholars and laymen, as we shall see in the ensuing pages.

Because of the belief, in the early 1880s, that there should be basic education for everyone, cheaply produced literature was a natural for publishers, who could see that certain people would not read the "best literature" of the day. It must be remembered that while the publishing of the dime novel was going on, Americans were reading, or had available to read, other literature. In September of 1869, almost the exact date of the first dime novel, Henry Wadsworth Longfellow's *The Children's Hour* was published. In 1861 the first *Elsie Dinsmore* by Martha Finley was published, and the first *Little Prudy* (by Sophie May, a pseudonym for Rebecca Clarke) was printed in 1864, followed by five other titles. *The Marble Faun* by Nathaniel Hawthorne was being favorably reviewed by the literary critics. *Mill on the Floss* by George Eliot and *Jane Eyre* by Charlotte Brontë were known among the reading public. Other great authors of the time had books on the market: Wilkie Collins, Charles Dickens, Louisa May Alcott and Charles Kingsley. Jules Verne had published his first two novels.

In actuality there was a literary standard of the time, established by the Unitarian Ladies Commission. They published, for one and all to see, in the *Unitarian Review*, these standards which they applied to acceptable books. Not all literary reviewers adhered to these standards, but they had a strong influence. The standards were not so much what good literature should be but what it should *not* be. The number-one fault to be watched for was poor execution, that is, poor style, faulty construction, jumbled events, poor characterization and stereotyped characters and incidents. While critiquing books reviewers felt that well-constructed stories were few and far between; that the English language was misused and abused; and that slang (the sure sign of poor writing) was used far too much. It appears again and again that slang is a sign of the uncultured, and it is the use of slang that is a tip-off to parents that their boys were reading sensational literature. An example of this can been seen and heard in Meredith Willson's play *The Music Man* where the singer suggests there is trouble in River City and offers as proof such sure signs of corruption as men with nicotine-stained fingers, certain vulgar words being used in conversation and dime novels hidden away in the corn crib! Familiarity with dime novels is equated with a cheapening of the language of such readers. Another fault listed by the ladies is what they called mixed character, which took in not only the true dime novels but also much of the rags-to-riches literature of the day. By mixed character they meant a book that went from childhood to adulthood too rapidly and actually became an adult novel. And, of course, the old standby, sensationalism, was to be avoided. They defined sensationalism as the exaggeration of incident, lack of proper connection between cause and effect, and the startling and often horrible character of events. In a few words, sensationalism was made up of "vulgar words and vulgar thoughts."

The Beadle Company was the largest publisher of the dime novel. The idea of publishing novels of 100 pages and selling them at ten cents apiece originated with Irwin Beadle and his editor, Orville J. Victor. The credit is usually given to the head of a firm, in this case two brothers, Irwin and Erastus Beadle, but nobody denies that Victor's contribution to the success of the house was enormous. The firm published joke books, yearbooks, almanacs and books of fun. Among these is *Jim Smilies' Frog*, the first edition in book form of Mark Twain's *Jumping Frog*. The Beadles were knowledgeable and shrewd businessmen. They saw a need for cheap novels, but they knew they had to sell in volume in order to make a profit. Even though these original dime novels were written and published in order to give "in cheap and wholesome form" an idealistic and fantasized, interesting and exciting picture of American life, it must be said of these novels that for the most part the better ones were American and not British adaptations; they were certainly published to make money.

The name Ann Sophia Winterbotham Stephens must be recognized. This lady, who is described as "highly respectable," is the author who began this type of story, whose general name, the dime novel, was to become a synonym for a literary pestilence. This endearing lady wrote the first in a long line of books which, in the opinion of many, were directly responsible for the moral downfall of hundreds of young men. *Malaeska, the Indian Wife of the White Hunter*, by A. S. W. Stephens, was published in the summer of 1860 and was the first of the Beadle dime novels. "After her father killed her White husband Malaeska took her child to her father-in-law in New York. She was prevented by him from revealing her relationship and returned to her tribe alone. Years later she returned, met her son as he was about to wed and told him of his Indian blood. He killed himself and she died."

Another early novel published by Beadle was *The Privateers' Cruise and the Bride of Pomfret Hall*, by Harry Cavendish. As the hero's name is the same as that of the author it is safe to conclude that this is the first of the pseudonyms which were to be used so much in the history of the dime novel. It was an age when the fictitious name was part of the equipment of half of the authors.

Except for the authors mentioned in this book, who were the crème de la crème of the genre, most authors received very little money, and some, if the publisher could get away with it, got nothing at all. You will recall in *Little Women* (by Louisa May Alcott), that Jo's first sale was of this sort, and although she did not sell to Beadle it is likely that at the time publishers sought material at the cheapest rate possible. Thus, for a first-time author this could be only name exposure, not money.

The use of the newly invented, rotary printing press made volume printing both possible and profitable. The publishers were employing "sweat shop" labor techniques to keep expenses down. Very small percentages were given to news agents whose stands and stores handled these books.

Edward Ellis, who wrote under at least six pseudonyms, is one of Beadle's best-known writers, and *Seth Jones* is one of the most successful series books. It was another Beadle little orange pamphlet with a full-length drawing of the hero on the cover and repeated on the frontispiece, another testimony of the literary judgment and business instinct of the Beadles. The book sold 6,000 copies immediately and 400,000–500,000 copies before the end. It was translated into six foreign languages. The author wrote more than 70 novels for juveniles and more than a dozen series of juvenile stories comprising about 150 volumes. His *Deerfoot* series was one of his most popular achievements.

A standing order of the American News Company, a company that carried the Beadle novels, was for 60,000 copies of each story as each new one appeared. A second edition was usually called for within a week. Some of the popular novels, such as *Seth Jones*, went through ten or twelve editions. The price of the novel was low, but the profit for the publisher was high because of the cheap labor, the pittance paid the authors, the cheap paper and the volume of sales. Many dime novels sold hundreds of thousands of copies; some sold millions. These books were light and easily carried in the pocket and promptly became an inseparable part of the clothing of any boy of the period. It is often pointed out that they could be read in school concealed from the teacher by a textbook or in church hidden in a hymn book or in the presence of one's parents camouflaged behind some permitted magazine.

Alfred F. Goldsmith, a book dealer and Walt Whitmans' bibliographer, says "that he procured a large copy of Henry Wadsworth Longfellow's *Tales of a Wayside Inn*. He tore out the leaves and when [his] parents' eyes were on him used this hollow sham to conceal the copy of *Old Cap Collier* which he was actually reading." Booth Tarkington says "that he was forbidden by his parents to read dime novels but that he managed to do so constantly concealing them inside a copy of an approved book." It should be remembered that Tarkington's Penrod was engaged, at his first appearance, in trying to write a dime novel.

In sheer numbers these books of adventure constituted some of the largest groups of children's books of the era. If concern for their influence can be accepted as testimony to their popularity, they were also among the most in demand.

Samuel Hopkins Adams says, "Dime novels? Of course they were taboo, strictly so. To be a devotee of this type of reading was as bad as smoking the surreptitious cigarette or going to a leg show of the Black Crook variety. Brought up a minister's son, albeit, a very liberal minister, I was not supposed to know anything about that sort of literature. But I can recall reading circles gathered in the barn on rainy days when some adventurous spirit of the Third Ward crowd would produce one of these thrillers and read from it while the rest of us shoved for favored positions near him where we could see the illustrations."

So, one can see in this new freedom in children's books that many authors, at least in the eyes of some people, went much too far. The great outcry of the time was sensationalism. Sensationalism defined here was the author's use of wild sequences of exciting but improbable incidents to cover an otherwise rather insubstantial story. Deservedly or not, much of the hue and cry was directed at one particular author: William T. Adams, who wrote for children under the pen name of Oliver Optic. He was the prototype of these new authors, and much of the criticism was aimed at him and his books, which, of course, was a sure indication of his popularity and success. In the literary world it was not always the number of copies sold or the remuneration received for your stories that made you a legend but the profusion of attacks on your writing that served as a testimonial to your success.

Adams was born in Massachusetts in 1822 and had a public school education plus two years of private tutoring. For twenty years he was a teacher and then principal in the Boston public school system. Adams began writing juvenile novels about 1855 and continued very successfully until nearly the end of the century. He was one of the most prolific American writers, producing as many as four adventure books for boys each year and a few books for girls and editing a magazine for young people. After a few books of fiction for children, Adams discovered a rich vein of popularity in the form of the series stories. In his lifetime he produced many: the *Great Western* series; the *Lake Shore* series; the *Yacht Club* series and many others, most of them written after the 1860s. One of the earlier single stories, however, an 1854 juvenile novel titled *Poor and Proud*, was the early model for many of the upcoming stories of success and achievement and exhibited the basic pattern for the themes and attitudes which emerged in children's fiction of the period. The poor but genteel child is given an opportunity to display the solid virtues of hard work, perseverance, courage, cheerfulness and pleasing manners in pursuit of a decent living, but real success comes not through laborious application but through making a favorable impression on some wealthy person or through sheer luck. In all cases the central character does not so much achieve material success as qualify for it.

Thus Adams and others wrote the American dream story over and over in the fictional biographies of young people who closed the gap between poverty and wealth. They insisted that their heroes and heroines be genteel whatever their initial poverty, well bred however straitened in circumstances and socially equal to the best that American opportunity could offer. The reviewers at the time of publication were favorable to Adams at first, but then became critical as he became more popular. They said that *Poor and Proud* was a lively tale especially in comparison with stories of earlier years. It was meant to appeal as much to young audiences as to their parents. As the title indicated the major lesson of the tale dwelt with the right and wrong kinds of pride. It was possible to be poor and proud, the story taught, but pride must not be allowed to keep those who are poor from any sort of work which can support them.

Here are some other reviews of Adam's books: *Our Standard Bearer*, a brightly written book, full of information and attractive to his boy readers; *Bear and Forbear*, Oliver Optic's books are always great favorites with the young people. This is quite as interesting as the rest of the series. *Shamrock and Thistle*: The style is somewhat inflated, and it has a general tone of boyish exaggeration throughout; approved because of fairness exhibited by him in speaking of Ireland. *Vine and Olive* has too much slang, despite useful information. Later, from the *Nation*, we have this: "If we could have our way the sale of them should stop immediately and entirely." However, this same reviewer said earlier that the *Yankee Middy* was clear and interesting, superior to most books for the same class of readers; *Work and Win* was lightly criticized for having its moral in the preface and therefore could be missed. However, with *Seek and Find* the criticism began in earnest. The book was said to be a lively but improbable story, the characters were not real people, and there was nothing in it either improving or elevating.

Louisa May Alcott, in her August 1875 installment of *Eight Cousins*, dropped a bombshell. For in this portion of the story Alcott put herself forward as a leading critic of sensational books for boys. "Mrs. Jessie and Dr. Alec had entered the room where Will and Geordie sat reading. Mrs. Jessie wasted no time in informing the boys that she disapproved of their books. 'I wish Rose would drive a bargain with Will and Geordie also for I think these books are as bad for small boys as are the cigars for the large ones,' said Mrs. Jessie, sitting down on the sofas between the readers, who politely curled up their legs to make room for her. 'I thought they were all the fashion,' answered Dr. Alec, settling in the big chair with Rose. 'So is smoking but it is harmful. The writers of these popular stories intend to do good, I have no doubt but, it seems to me, they fail because their motto is Be smart and you will be rich instead of Be honest and you will be happy.'

'Now, Mum, that's too bad. I like 'em tip top. This one is a regular screamer,' cried Will. 'They're bully books and I like to know where's the harm?' added Geordie. 'You have just shown us one of the chief evils, and that is slang,' answered their mother. 'Some of them are about first-rate boys, Mother; they go to sea and study, and sail around the world, having great larks all the way.'

'I have read about them, Geordie, and although they are better than the others, I am not satisfied with these Optical illusions, as I call them. I put it to you, boys, is it natural for a lad of fifteen to eighteen to command ships, defeat pirates, outwit smugglers and so cover themselves with glory that Admiral Farragut invites them to dinner saying "Nobel boy, you are an honor to your country?"' "

Alcott had unleashed a storm. Some of the critics scolded her, but they were gentle compared to the gentleman whose books she had called "Optical illusions." His fury knew no bounds. An editorial war ensued, which *Appleton's Journal* and *Scribners Monthly* as well as *Oliver Optic's Magazine* joined in on. Although Adams took the brunt of the attacks on sensationalism, he was by no means the only offender. The name Horatio Alger, Jr. was often coupled with his. Indeed, Alger got his start through the encouragement of Adams. Most of the criticism aimed at Adams was equally applicable to the Alger books and to those of many others. Elijah Kellogg wrote *Burying the Hatchet; or, The Young Braves of the Delaware*, a basically honest story which was not as sensational as the title would lead one to believe. The book was reviewed and said to be "an honest and in every way admirable picture of the life in the Pennsylvania frontier after Braddock's defeat." His books were "highly interesting yet eminently uplifting." Only as pieces of literature did they leave something to be desired. However, the contemporary reviewers felt that even the errors in grammar, of which Kellogg was frequently guilty, could be forgiven because the author had so much to offer his readers.

Harry Castlemon (Charles Austin Fosdick) wrote fifty-eight adventure stories. He was reviewed in the *Literary World*, which stated that *Buried Treasure* presents some "rather unwholesome company, not a little feverishly exciting incidents and a good deal of slang and coarse local dialect." But Castlemon said, "Boys don't like fine writing. What they want is adventure. The more of it there is the better fellow you are." Its chief redeeming feature and a historically interesting one is that it presented a picture of poor white life in the South. The *Independent* said it was not a desirable book for children's reading because "the romantic adventures of a bad boy are not the best reading for a good boy." There were also a number of eminent dime novelists who were not American. Mayne Reid, perhaps the best known of them all, was born in Ireland, but his wild adventure books did not compare in lasting popularity with those of the American authors. One of the least-tempered reviews printed in *Literary World* said of Reid's *Castaways* that it was a story "in which the most unreasonable incidents are thickly intermixed with a few facts of natural history." The reviewer said that the title should be taken as the proper instruction to children for treatment of the book itself.

The early writers of these dime novels were not intentionally composing sensational fiction, and the reviewers of these first novels spoke well of them. William Everette, a reviewer for the *North American Review*, said he had read about ten of these novels and, although it was uphill work, the reviews were not scathing. *Malaeska* by A. S. W. Stephens he thought was silly; *Maum Guinea* by Metta Victor (the wife of the Beadle Company's Orville J. Victor) he discussed as merely one of the many stories derived from Harriet Beecher Stowe's *Uncle Tom's Cabin*. This book supposedly was praised by President Lincoln and Henry Ward Beecher. Edward S. Ellis's *Seth Jones* and the *Trail Hunters* were "good, very good." His Native Americans were human beings. The novels, as a whole, he found to be "unobjectionable morally, whatever fault may be found with their literary style and composition. They do not even obscurely pander the vice or excite the passions." He ended by wishing Victor success.

However, throughout these two decades the reviewers fluctuated in their opinions of the sensational books. It is not clear whether this was because of the state of the art of book reviewing, especially juvenile literature, or because of the dilemma of what to do about popular, literarily poor books. There was a conscious attempt to recognize any redeeming merits, while pointing out all literary defects, and to try to understand their popularity. This unresolved problem leads one to believe that reviewing has not progressed very far in a hundred years. One still does not know what to say about literarily poor books which are tremendously popular (e.g., Judy Blume's stories, *Nancy Drew* series and *Jaws*).

It is curious, and it is documented in the writings of the time, that it was often the format that was objectionable, not necessarily the content. Much was written about the material published in hard cover, higher-priced formats and the moral content of that which was published cheaply. There needed to be clarification between cheap literature and cheaply produced literature. Why, for example, was Captain Mayne Reid's *Rifle Rangers* a righteous and proper book when bound in board covers and borrowed from Miss Cary's circulating library but a trap for the young when bound in paper and bought at Steve Fowle's newsstand for ten cents? What was it that caused Edward S. Ellis's *The Riflemen of the Miami* to be pure when it came from the shelves of the public library or the Sunday school library but suddenly be a well of poison when bought, in rather cleaner condition, at an emporium?

John Cotton Dana, librarian of the Newark Free Library, says, "Dime novels, which in my boyhood were the ones by Beadle, were forbidden, but I have a distinct recollection of disobeying my orders and reading at least a few. They were passed about, more or less among us boys. By some chance Ballantyne's *Wild Man of the West* in hard covers got into our house, and all of us boys read it, and I guess all the boys in the neighborhood. If there ever was a dime novel, that was one. It was a bound book, so it passed as reputable."

The paper-covered novels were not the only harmful reading that fell into boys' hands. There was a class of books, cloth bound and respectable looking, that told of get-rich schemes and of promotion through trickery, favoritism or accident. Their heroes progressed from newsboy to chief editor, from cabin boy to captain, from yard hand to railroad superintendent and all within a brief period without legitimate effort. Other books of the same class, feverish and unwholesome, told of lurid adventures.

Very heavy criticism of the dime novel is recorded by Frances J. Olcott, who divides bad literature into two groups. In one group he puts the thrilling tales of impossible adventure. He speaks of them as "Weak, sentimental and enervating. They are not action motivating nor are they enriched with noble ideas of right and wrong." In the other group he puts the really vicious tales whose language is unacceptable, whose standards of life are false and whose moral message is missing. Under the guise of glamour, lurid love stories and daring adventures of criminals are presented thereby "arousing emotions of murder in the breasts of young boys." It is this second type that he says constitutes the difference between the sensational dime novel and good popular fiction. He stresses that the authors of the "yellow" stories used people of low moral character and held them up as heroes oppressed by the laws and the socially accepted behavior of the day. This inspired the reader to "feel admiration for, and a desire to protect, this criminal and to follow in his path. These writers teach criminality not good citizenship." He goes on to say that these easily obtainable books of feverish adventure and evil reading will do harm to a child through his natural craving for the stories of wild adventure and for tales that excite the emotions. So let everything possible be done to keep these sensitive boys and girls, especially boys, from familiarity with crime. Do not thrust upon them from shop windows the picture-covered dime novels whose content can arouse a boy's mind-tantalizing thoughts. It is just this sort of thing that starts many an honest but romantic boy off on an open and perilous road, when a little censorship might save him years of foolish wanderings and also save the state the expense of eventually housing him in its prisons. The character of children is formed largely by the books they read or do not read. The elements of indecision throughout life can often be traced to this want of early training in books. Many a girl's sentimental or foolish marriage and many a boy's rash venture into cattle ranches can be traced to books that fed early indications of a tendency to future evils.

These ideas and those expressed by Alcott at the time and by John James Wilson in 1932—that the dime novels were the origin of all youthful crimes—is not new, and it is repeated many times. In the 1930s and 1940s it was the movies that were corrupting the youth. In the 1950s and 1960s it was television. In the 1970s and 1980s it was computer misuse. I expect the argument to go on for decades to come. There was a great deal of concern surrounding the reading for children during these years. Not everyone believed that the didactic books of the past were to be read to the exclusion of the bold, daring and exciting novels of the time. William McCormack wrote an article titled "The Dime Novel Nuisance" in a magazine called *Lend a Hand*, edited by Edward Everette Hale. Although he believed that the dime novel might create runaway boys, juvenile house breakers and body bandits, he also believed that the view of life coming from the Sunday school library was just as much to blame. "I have no patience, with the all too common philanthropy that would rob the dirty faced urchin of his Bold Eagle Bob, the Boy Buccaneer and offering in its stead Willie Russell's Sacrifice."

Edmond Pearson, who wrote a book in defense of dime novels, said that they were beneficial on the whole. A strong argument was put forth to the effect that it was better to have boys with the intellectual curiosity to at least read the dime novels than to have boys who were too dull and unmotivated to read anything at all. Most of the reviewers and literary leaders of the day agreed that there was a place for interesting and exciting books if they had some literary value and basic ethical standards.

In 1897 S. S. Green wrote a paper that was revolutionary not only for defending fiction books for the young but also for defending their reading of such authors as William Adams, Horatio Alger Jr. and others. He insisted that sensational stories had their value and were far better reading for boys than the *Police Gazette*. Dime novels should not be condemned because they have interesting plots, but because the incidents are shocking and unnatural. It is true that they have little literary merit and give incorrect pictures of life, but poor as they are they have a role in the world. Such exciting stories serve a purpose in two ways. Not only do they keep boys from worse reading (like the *Police Gazette*) but they also give young people a taste for reading. It is certainly better for some people to read these exciting stories than to be doing what they would be doing if not reading. It is certainly a benefit to such people to enable them to grow up with a love of reading, even though they will read only sensational books. However, the tastes of many people do improve. A boy begins by reading Alger books. He goes to school. His mind matures. He outgrows the books that pleased him as a boy. If girls and boys grow up with a dislike for reading or without feeling attracted to it they will never read anything. But if a love of reading has been cultivated by giving them, when young, such books as they enjoy, they will turn naturally to reading as a pleasant use of their time and will read such books as benefit them at each growing stage of intellectual development and will thus be saved from idleness and vice.

Clark agrees with this and says, "Yes, give them unlimited quantities of Jules Verne, Captain Marryat, Mayne Reid and the like. Let boys revel in Oliver Optic and Horatio Alger. This literature is false to life, tawdry in sentiment, full of impossible incidents, but let them have it, go through it and outgrow it. It will lead to something better or, if not, it is better to have a taste for even this reading than to have no taste for it at all."

The great difficulty in this matter is to see to it that every class of reader get the best books they will read and to see that good readers be kept from poor books as would be satisfied with good ones if the more exciting reading of poor books were not so readily accessible. In furnishing books to children it is evidently of no use to give them good books which they will not read. It is also of no use to give them books they will read if they are bad ones. Therefore we must have well-written books that are interesting, well-researched books that are useful and provocative books that will be read.

Dime novels began to die in the 1870s, when the first series of Beadles came to an end. They weakened again some years later when postal rates caused the change from the little book to the magazine format. They diminished further in the 1880s of too much sensationalism. They finally died out when the nickel libraries and the boys' weeklies (which were themselves dime novels in a slightly changed format) became popular. They have been killed by yellow journalism, by motion pictures, and so on.

G. S. Turner in his *Boys Will Be Boys* recounts the delightful story of a writer who disappeared, as they were apt to do, having left his hero bound to a stake with wild animals encircling him and an avalanche about to fall from above. As the deadline approaches for the next episode, several other authors try to find a means of escape for the unfortunate man, but without success. Then at the eleventh hour the missing author shows up. He takes the briefest look at the previous installment and without a moment's hesitation writes, "With one bound Jack was free."

In the 1880s, when the literary qualities of the stories had cheapened, when hacks were turning out novels at lightning speed, when the pictures on the front covers heaped horror upon horror, there was justification for the assaults. These authors are of little significance today, partly because their talents were less remarkable than their output, and partly because their books reflect a conventional idea of adventure rather than the real thing. It is unfortunate that the successive waves of immigrations and the westward thrust toward the frontier did not at the same time inspire children's books of any real merit.

Introduction

As one can see from the previous chapters the dime novel was not a new idea in the 1850s, but was the result of a long history of literary developments that started in the 1650s, or earlier. As it happened, in the 1850s there were many potential readers who previously did not have the chance to read popular fiction literature because of the expense of the hard-cover books, the lack of public libraries or the lack of this kind of literature.

Before we break down the dime novel material into several clarifying categories, the idea should be put in a general historical context by a brief account of the development and range of the American dime novel specifically. From its first issue, the dime novel was considered by the educated elite to be subliterary, and by the 1870s, the tales were universally criticized for their immoral and perverse subject matter. But in the 1850s, because of recent developments in both printing techniques and marketing practices, dime novels with their stimulating adventures of bootblacks, detectives, outlaws, pirates, and soldiers, their exciting histories, romances, wars, the West, city and rural life, were affordable, accessible and abundant.

Compulsory school law had created a demand for various kinds of reading materials, and more of the general public could read and write than ever before. In a society that had few sources of entertainment, the time was ripe for cheap novels.

Even before the 1850s this new reading generation was looking for this type of materials; the West had been opened, and the interest in this new land was high; tales of Native American warfare were exciting to city people, and these interests were exploited by the new publishers.

It was just prior to the Civil War that this cheap fiction called dime novels appeared. These books appealed to the group of readers that were being ignored by the traditional publishers. These publications contained serialized adventure tales and sold in the millions. Instead of rejoicing at the idea of millions of unlettered citizens beginning the reading habit, social critics denounced the trend and predicted disaster.

Even though the earlier dime novels were fundamentally harmless (they were primarily stories of the new West that exploited the fictitious adventures of Buffalo Bill and Deadwood Dick, urban rages-to-riches stories by Horatio Alger and the school-type stories of Frank Merriwell), they were heavily criticized by the elite.

It is impossible to understand fully the literature of any period without closely examining the society that produced it. Books for children, even those that were fiction are a statement of their time. They may not deal directly with the current social issues, but they disclose a good deal about social attitudes and contemporary thinking. This may not have been the author's initial intent at the time of writing but is a inescapable result.

There were few writers of children's fiction in any historical period that covered social questions with any seriousness, and fewer still if the social questions were controversial. However, social morés are so much a basic part of everyday life that it is almost impossible to keep them out of one's thinking and writing. Clearly, any nonfantasy fiction that was written for children between 1820 and 1860 revealed the social moral views of the day, implicitly or explicitly. Of course, this kind of literature, the kind that attempted to address the social conditions of the times, was not encouraged. But it is for this very reason that literature, regardless of its literary merit, is an important factor in the history of any period, even if it was considered objectionable at the time.

There were always books available for children to read in America, but they were often instructional literature of one kind or another. After the Revolutionary War, fictional literature for children became more acceptable but was still rare. Fiction books, which were then defined as those that did not teach moral lessons, were not easily available to children. The American production of such books was negligible; most non-school juvenile books were pirated or imported from Europe, especially England.

The rise of a truly American fictional literature, written specifically for children and meant for amusement, was almost entirely a twentieth-century phenomenon.

Over these last 300 years the adults' concerns about what their children read had changed. Once, they had believed that children ought not to be exposed to the reality of adult life until they had either been educated or had matured in what was considered important ways.

Another belief was that as adults they had an important role to play both in educating their children and in helping them mature painlessly. In terms of moral training, worldly growth and basic education, the role that responsible adults played was a valuable asset to both children and society at large.

There was also the belief that working-class people, both children and adults, should read self-help types of books that point out the value of the work ethic and that stress the importance of close-knit family life. The reading of fiction did not meet these criteria. Therefore, these dime novels were a natural target for attacks by the moralists of the day.

Because these books were read mostly by youngsters, just as the comic books of today are read mostly by youngsters, they were a public concern. Many people of the literary class, the religious sects, the teachers and other educators believed that the sensational dime novel, with its alleged violence, unclear plots, characters without acceptable personalities and story lines that muddle of the concepts of right and wrong, good and bad, rights and responsibilities, sent an improper message to their young reading audience. This meant they were bound to criticize this literature, sometimes without ever having read it themselves. Judges, teachers, clergymen, Sunday school superintendents and even police chiefs began to denounce dime novels. This was at the time, the most appropriate explanation of crime and the easiest excuse for the offender, until their place was taken by the moving pictures and later by television.

There were youngsters whose parents had shamefully neglected their children and allowed them to get into mischief and worse; these parents found it very easy to stand in a police court and place all the blame on the dime novels. The culprit for their children's misbehavior couldn't be neglect by them. It had to be the ever-evil dime novels that were being read.

Much in these novels was considered to be against good literary standards. But the characters, morals and stories found in the dime novels also offered popular ideas; the dime novel stirred up romantic images of vanishing heroes such as Western outlaws and Native Americans that modernization was doing away with. The new authors, with their serial stories of adventure and excitement, didn't do away with the old literature immediately. There were still plenty of stories containing nothing but moral lessons, and they were brought for children. However, the newer approach, with a different point of view, grew more and more popular. This was another sign that the thinking of American parents and readers was changing. American social change was moving—and moving fast.

To keep expenses down dime novel authors were poorly paid; they had to be able to write at a rapid rate to meet daily and weekly deadlines, sometimes for several serials at the same time. Although they became expert at developing exciting plots, there wasn't always time to make sure that each installment ended with its characteristic, cliff-hanging incident. The publishers could very well order a rapid end or interminable prolonging of a tale depending on how successful the story was with the reading audience. Authors borrowed plots, copied or rewrote each other's work, and pirated foreign stories just as the foreign press borrowed from the Americans.

Now, with this unprecedented success of the dime novel, writers for the first time were able to support themselves by their writing, but still only the most prolific writers kept it up for an entire career, and few seem to have made large sums of money. (As is true today, percentage-wise few novelist can make a comfortable living by fiction writing alone.) Soon there arose endless popular series for boys and girls, predecessors of the factory-like output of the Stratemeyer empire, which has reached down even to the present day. Many of these books are rare today, since they were read to pieces and then thrown away. Dime novels covered subjects that were varied; they offered adventure in far-away places, circuses, fire fighting, mystery (with detectives of every kind), railroading, sea stories (polar exploration was a favorite), sports, science fiction and fantasy, westerns and mining camps of the gold fields. Some of these series continued the trend of featuring recognizable, recurring characters.

There was also a return to virtue. Nick Carter was as good as Rollo or as an Oliver Optic boy, though not perhaps as goody-goody. He never drank, swore or smoked a cigarette. Frank Merriwell was a school and college hero. (However, Old Cap Collier, the hero in the adult dime novels, although the savior of the innocent and the terror of criminals, was himself not an ideal character. He gambled, drank, and smoked.) The firm of Street and Smith proposed to the experienced dime novelist William G. Patten (who wrote under the pen name of Bert L. Slandish) the character who became the well known Frank Merriwell. By 1895, the publishers saw a waning interest in the western sagas and an interest in a more lighthearted hero with a lighthearted name (like Jack Parkway) who should be thoroughly American and who might go through school, a military academy or college. There was to be an emphasis on athletic adventure in the narative, since there was everywhere a growing interest in college sports.

Popular fiction had a number of forerunners in the previous century—narrative tracts and chapbooks, execution broadsides and heavily abridged versions of classic stories like *Robinson Crusoe.*

Definitions

By some definitions, dime novels were cheap, paper-covered fiction; they were usually sensationalistic, featuring detective stories, westerns, outlaws, bandits, villains, lost love, damsels in distress, femmes fatales and melodramatic plots, with many written in installments with suspenseful ending chapters. Charles Bragin defines the dime novel as "briefly 'lurid literature' of the West, detectives, bandits, etc. peculiarly American, with lurid cover illustrations. Most dime novels sold for a nickel, and most ten cent books were not dime novels."

There are also other definitions of the term "dime novel." The meaning of the term has undergone many changes since Irwin P. Beadle first used it in 1860. He put this title on his paper-covered novels and called them Beadle's dime novels. However, cheap, sensational, paper-covered literature had been published by a number of other American publishers for some thirty years before that date. It was said that originally this "yellow-covered" or "yellow-back" literature, as it was known from the color of its paper wrappers, was pirated almost exclusively from the British popular fiction of the time. The term has mistakenly been used to define many inexpensive paperbacks. The first dime novels, for example, *Malaeska* and *Seth Jones*, were really historical romances that imitated the works of Sir Walter Scott or James Fenimore Cooper. In later books, as the dime novel grew in popularity, accurate history became hidden in legendary stories like those of Frank and Jesse James. So one needs to look at this definition more closely, since, for one thing, many American and British publications were issued as inexpensive paperbacks in past years. In the 1850s came Nathaniel Hawthorne's reworking of the Greek myths, *Wonder Book for Boys and Girls* (1852) and *Tanglewood Tales* (1854). From folklore motifs, Howard Pyle and Frank R. Stockton created their own tales, which are still in print and continue to delight children. Examples are *Salt and Pepper, or, Seasoning* or *Young Folk* (1886) by Pyle and *The Bee-Man of Orn* (1887) by Stockton. Additional authors are Elijah Kellogg, of the *Elm Island* series; Noah Brooks, writer of pioneer stories like *Boy Settlers* (1876); John Townsend Trowbridge, best known for his *Jack Hazard and His Fortunes* (1871); Charles A. Stephens (especially important to *The Youth's Companion*), who wrote a *Knockabout Club* series of *Travelogue Story Books* (1872) and Charles C. Coffin, whose war stories included *Boys of '76* (1876) and *Boys of '61* (1881). All of these writers were members of a company of authors who introduced various realistic pictures of life at sea, on the farm and on the battlefield, and they were widely read. *Children of the New Forest* (1847) was the last children's book to be completed by Captain Marryat and was the first, enduring, historical novel for children.

An elaborate 32-page, illustrated *History of Whittington and His Cat* was published by Jacob Johnson in Philadelphia in 1802, and Turner and Fisher of New York and Philadelphia brought out a 24-page chapbook about 1835 called *The History of Jack, the Giant Killer,* which contained the whole of his wonderful exploits. Solomon King published in 1828 *The Extraordinary Life and Adventures of Robin Hood,* a 32-page chapbook with a colored frontispiece. In 1830 he brought out, in 48 pages, also with a colored frontispiece, *The Seven Champions of Christendom,* by Richard Johnson. W. Borradaile, also of New York, published a *Robin Hood* in 1823. Although *Old Dame Trot and Her Comical Cat* was published in 1803, this story was known much earlier, perhaps one hundred years earlier. All these were first published in paper format but certainly could not be considered dime novels. Between the 1840s and the 1890s the sensational dime novels, the story papers and the cheap "libraries" were appearing in three different formats. Although the content of these three formats was alike, there were differences. The three formats overlapped, and some novels appeared in all three formats, but still the differences were there. The story papers were actually eight-page weekly newspapers. They contained serialized stories, anywhere from one to a half dozen or more, along with religious sermons, some humor, local news and some fashion articles. Their goal was to have a little something for every member of the family. (See more about story papers in the Story Paper chapter.)

The dime novels first appeared in pamphlet form, printed on cheap paper, and contained very fast-moving adventure stories, appealing mainly to young boys. The pages were printed black on white, but the covers were usually colored paper, generally orange, and were of more

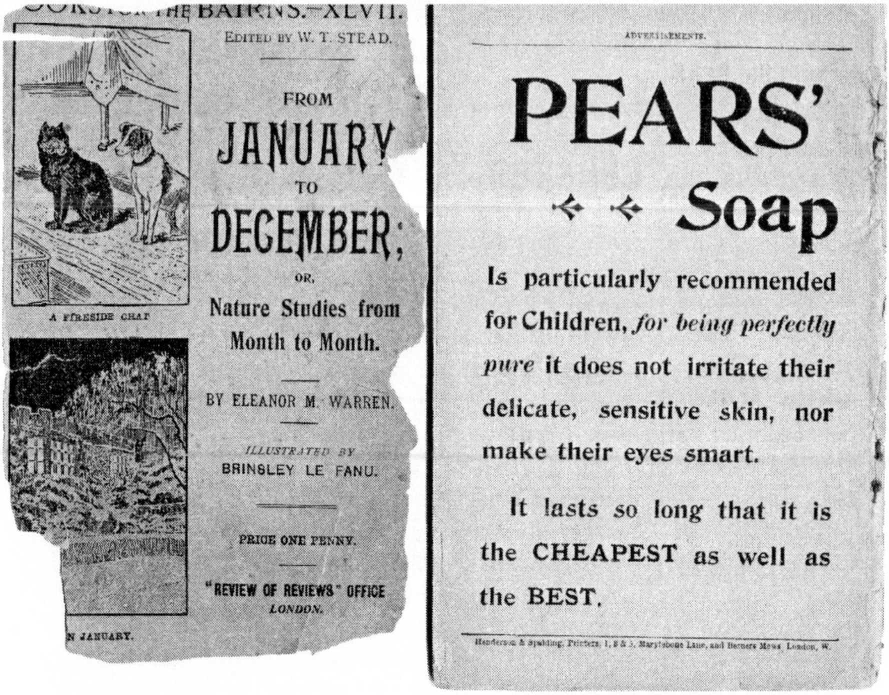

Books for the Bairns: From January to December: **"Nature Studies from Month to Month." An example of the advertising used with these publications.**

durable paper than the inside flimsy pages. Some books were leather bound, but these were of very poor quality and were discontinued; they were replaced by better-quality paper. The back cover was a profitable place to have an advertisement. Then came the cheap libraries. These were serial books selling for a dime but often even for a nickel. They were 8" × 11" in size. They ran from16 to 32 pages in two and sometimes three columns of print. It was in 1875 that a Chicago publisher, Donnelly, Lloyd and Co., issued the first copy of the Lakeside Library. It was the beginning of an avalanche of series books known as cheap libraries. These libraries were numerous; it is believed that almost 500 different series were published, whereas the dime novels numbered about 350.

The physical layout of the Beadle and Adams dime novel changed during the fifty years the company published these books, but the stories themselves remained about the same. Although the outside dimensions varied somewhat, the books were always paperbound with a woodcut on the cover that depicted some stupendous and generally bloody feat of daring. The novels were short, ranging from 30,000 to no more than 80,000 words, and they were packed from cover to cover with action. The early novels were tales predominantly about frontier life, but the later series included narratives that reflected the diverse interests of the reading public: sea voyages, mining camps, city life, detectives, scouts and cowboys. The contents of these novels were not only the reflection of the interests shared by Easterners in the adventure and romance of the West; they served also as information sources, as history, for the Eastern clientele.

The earliest books had, for the most part, very crude, woodcut illustrations. A few respectable artists and engravers were employed, but they had to work so quickly and cheaply that they produced poor-quality work.

As publication became better organized, artists learned to vary the shapes of their blocks to break up the two-column page structure into more challenging shapes. These illustrations were frequently dramatic and recall the rather stilted confrontations of the cheap, contemporary, theatrical prints. This is hardly surprising since the same artists were employed on both bloods and cheap series of theater plays.

Dime novels of this period sometimes sold for only a nickel. In the 1890s these so-called nickel weeklies began to appear with color illustrations, and shortly thereafter some stories assumed the format of the modern paperback novel. Robert Prowse, identified by his initials R. P., was responsible for many of the better-quality, colored covers and illustrations in the boys' stories from about 1860 to the end of the century, but it seems impossible to find any other information about him and his life. This is a frustrating situation that applies to all too many of the prolific authors and artists. At the beginning of the nineteenth century, the cheapest fiction was of two kinds: either one sheet folded to a small-format chapbook size of about twenty-four pages and usually dressed up for a more middle-class readership with a hand-colored frontispiece, or the larger-format domestic novel by such authors as Mary Bennett or Hannah Maria Jones, which was published in parts.

In the early days, four or five weekly installments were sometimes gathered into a monthly collection, with a decorated wrapper printed on colored paper, which rarely survived. In 1870 the main theme of the dime novel was detectives and the criminals they were after. One of the first was *The Detective's Ward; or, the Fortunes of the Bowery Girl.* This was written by "Agile Penne." It was serialized in the *Saturday Journal*, a cheap publication put out by Beadle and Adams. By this time the Beadle Publishing Company had moved from genre to genre, from pamphlets to dime novels, as the public's taste in reading changed. By the end of the nineteenth century, detective stories had become a mainstay among all cheap literature for youngsters. This stemmed almost directly from the crime theme of the early chapbooks.

Popularity

Dime novels were the main source of entertainment for the common man, giving some excitement, romance and escape, both for the city people and the rural population—the city because of the boring jobs most of them had and the rural people because they were cut off from the activities of the city. These popular books brought to attention the ideals of the times. Their colorful and exotic fictional characters told of the typical American values of patriotism, individualism, frontier virtues and belief in hard work as the road to betterment of their lives.

There is no need to look for reasons for the quick and tremendous success of the Beadle dime novels, any more than we need to wonder why America's most popular magazines are bought in such enormous numbers today. There are several reasons for the popularity of this sensational literature at this time. One is that the literacy rate was high. The 1840 census shows that 97 percent of white adults over twenty-one in the Northeast and 91 percent in the Northwest were able to read. Universal primary education for white children was standard between 1830 and 1850. This information, of course, was exploited by the easy availability of cheap literature.

Another reason for the popularity of this literature was the beginning of what we now call commuting—workers going back and forth to work by train or streetcar. This free time on board was spent in light reading. As the working population moved into the suburbs and away from the urban factory districts, people spent more time traveling and therefore more time on light reading. Another factor was the influence of the labor unions. The *Workingman's Advocate*, a national weekly publication, not only printed news of interest to working-class readers but included dime-novel, sensational reading. The *Labor Leader*, a weekly publication out of Boston and printed by the Knights of Labor, offered information about labor organizers and informed leaders of the working class about political issues. This publication also presented dime-novel fiction, especially stories with workingman heroes. It also reviewed other dime novels and other working-class fiction.

The popular dime-fiction formula has two separate patterns: the first emphasizes the traits of a character—a knight, an outlaw, a rogue. This character is featured in a series of loosely detailed personal contests. The second emphasizes the growth of one unique person, a picture of self-control and adherence to the social order. The dime novel is more of the first kind. The hero enters innumerable fist fights, rivalries for women, tests of work skills, courtroom battles and the climatic strike or election. Set against this somewhat repetitive plot of tests, contests, challenges and duels is a story of development and education, of struggling upward.

All the heroes must learn self-control, temperance, thrift and hard work. Often this education is tied to a romantic plot.

Dime novels also offered readers exciting stories of adventure and love at the lowest price the readers had ever known. It was the prohibitive price of the hard bound books that kept most people from reading. Although the price of these more literary books sounds low, compared to the salaries of the day, they were quite expensive. The dime novels were not meant for the serious reader to sit and enjoy in libraries, but were meant for young boys, for travelers on the road, for soldiers, for sailors, for brakemen on the railroads and for hunters in camps. However, no one who was aware of the popularity of these novels needed to be told that these books were confined to boys or to rude, uncultured men. These stories were enjoyed by everyone, except for a small, opinionated group of people.

The importance of the dime novel also came at the same time as the study of the social sciences in the United States. This included the belief in a scientific approach to criminology and penology, because this was a way of finding out why crime was committed. It was also believed that reading could be either a benefit or a curse, so controlling what children read was important to the morals of these children. Ideally, the working classes were expected to read stories that stressed work, family, self-improvement and similar books.

To many of America's literary and educational leaders, dime novels had sensational writing, violent characters and events, complicated plots because of changing identities, and unclear lines between right and wrong. This evaluation brought them to the conclusion that an unsuitable message was being brought to the youth, whose minds were still impressionistic; they were therefore severely criticized. Beadle and Adams responded to this criticism (which has a distinctly modern ring). Beadle and his popular writers of these books, like the actors and producers of today's movies and television programs, argued that it's acceptable because it is, after all, only entertainment, even though that may not necessarily be so, at that time and even today with our entertainment ratings of television programs and movies.

The suggested remedy was not to ban this material, but to offer cheap, wholesome literature for these new, unsophisticated readers. Throughout the century both religious societies and profit-making publishers attempted to provide this alternative. Commentators write that the most successful of these did not attempt to moralize, but tried instead to provide fiction slanted toward what they considered more desirable social behavior.

It is not true that all of this cheap literature consisted of male detective or male outlaw stories. Females were also a popular subject, and therefore a lot of this type of fiction, especially romances, was aimed at both mature women and young girls. They like to read about sudden wealth, found children, and women who achieved independence and had exciting adventures. These dime novels, appealing to both sexes, made their way to today's paperback stories of adventure, romance and other cross-sexual interests.

Pro and Con Opinions

What was the real attitude of the day toward dime novels? The dime novels were singled out for moral attack because they were read largely by young boys, just as comic books, also read by youngsters, are of greater public concern today than are yesterday's story papers, pulps or the love story "slicks." Actually, many of the dime novels appeared first in the story papers.

Booth Tarkington says that he was "forbidden by his parents to read dime novels," but he still read them by hiding the orange-covered books inside acceptable reading, such as *Pilgrim's Progress*. He did this forbidden reading while in hiding, sometimes under the piano, sometimes behind the sofa, but most often in the sawdust box in the stable. In Tarkington's *Penrod* one will remember that Penrod was trying to write a dime novel while in the sawdust box. He was never punished when caught, but he was scolded and encouraged to read history and standard works.

Robert Bridges, editor of *Scribner's Magazine*, says: "My greatest sin was Jack Parkway and his adventures. Perhaps they could not be classed as dime novels, and I was afraid that the present generation of boys would laugh at the tameness of Jack's adventures."

Percy Taxman, associate editor of the *Pictorial Review*, writes: "What a fascination the Wild and Wooly West has had for foreigners. I live in Melbourne, Australia, and long before I had reached the age of twelve I was familiar with many phases of life in America and with much of its early pioneer background, almost entirely from what I had absorbed from dime novels. Furthermore, those colorful volumes gave me an intense desire to visit the United States and meet as many of its remarkable inhabitants as possible. A country that could produce such unusually interesting men and women as those who figured in its books could not be overlooked."

Herbert Asbury, author of *Up from Methodism*, *Hayrack* and the *Gangs of New York*, says, "I read dime novels whenever I could get them as a boy, and never met with any opposition from my father. Indeed it was my recollection that he read them himself; I recall that the first ones I ever read were dog-eared and scuffed and had been around the house for many years before I came upon them and tasted their delights. My grandfather, himself a forty-niner and with several years' experience among the Indians, was always violently opposed to the novels that purported to describe life among the red-skins, for he said they were packed with lies and were unfair to the Indians. But he always read ones that dealt with life in the great cities."

Here is another's experience: Walter S. Adams, director of the Mount Wilson Observatory, says,

> I did read dime novels as a boy and usually kept them carefully concealed in the attic. This was not absolutely essential, because my father, although disapproving of them in a general way, did not consider them as works of the "Evil One," to use the current New England expression. I must have been about ten or twelve when a dime novel first fell into my eager hands, and the frenzied rapture that the poets speak of is a pale anemic thing compared with the maddened joy that the initiation into American literature brought me. The book contained pages and dealt with the glorious exploits of the noble son of the West named Deadwood Dick. A more versatile, ingenious, courageous and handsome hero has never yet appeared on my horizon. The man existed solely for the doing of good in a most picturesque manner. Dick had the good luck to possess a remarkably capable feminine partner in the thwarting of villainy named Calamity Jane. And he needed her all right, to help thwart the diabolical depredations of a cur named Pieta Dave. This inhuman wretch, by a detestable stroke of deception, captured Dick in the very first chapter, and tears of sympathy filled my eyes when I read how Dave and his gang hanged Dick, riddled his body with bullets from their six-shooters, placed his body in a sack filled with stones, and then, with ghoulish glee, the dastards hurled the whole grim package from the dizzy height of a yawning precipice into the boiling cauldron of a stream several hundred feet below. But before the end of the story it was discovered that Deadwood Dick did not die in the event but was revived by the water in the river.

John Cotton Dana, librarian of the Newark Free Library, says, "Dime novels, which in my boyhood were the ones by Beadle with yellow covers, were they not? were forbidden. But I have a distinct recollection of disobeying my orders and reading at least a few. They were passed about, more or less, among the boys."

Eugene T. Sawyer says, "Perhaps my chief inspiration was old Ned Buntline, who was really the first one to write penny dreadfuls and the inventor of the dime novel. He made Buffalo Bill famous, but he was vastly more picturesque himself than Bill or any of his other characters."

In his essays Robert Louis Stevenson, surely like many other boys, reveals a love both of reading exciting, picaresque fiction and of collecting the "penny plain," two-pence, colored sheets produced for the juvenile theater during the period. Anthony Comstock, an antivice crusader, was the chief agent of the New York Society for the Suppression of Vice. In Comstock's 1883 account of his struggles, *Traps for the Young*, he writes that "the editor of the blood and thunder story papers and cheap stories of crime ... [is] willing or unwilling [among] Satan's efficient agents to advance his kingdom by destroying the young." Comstock worried intensely that young readers would take the "pernicious" characters and stories as models for their own lives. The fact that reading figured so prominently in the moral or reform literature of the late nineteenth and early twentieth centuries is significantly indicative of the class friction of the era. The moralists believed that fiction should reinforce bourgeois ideals, especially the sentimentalized picture of sedate family life. Dime novels to them were replete with immoral violence, whether true or not, and dime novels and similar genres appealed to large numbers of the working-class public and often sold millions of copies. So the culture elite took aim at them.

Here are various comments that have been made about dime novels: "Your child is in danger of having its pure mind cursed for life." "These sure-ruin traps comprise a large variety of half-dime novels, five- and ten-cent story papers, and low-priced pamphlets for boys and girls. This class includes the silly, insipid tale, the course slangy story in the dialect of the barroom, the blood-and-thunder romance of the boarder life, and the exaggerated details of crime, real and imaginary."

F. K. Mathiews, chief librarian of the Boy Scouts of America, wrote in 1914, "I wish I could label each of these books 'Explosive! Guaranteed to Blow Your Boy's Brains Out.' [A]s some boys read such books, their imaginations are literally 'blown' and they go into life as terribly crippled as though by some material they had lost a hand or foot." This was applied to both dime novels and series books.

Brander Matthew said in 1883, "The dreadful damage wrought today in every city, town, and village of these United States by the horrible and hideous stuff set weekly before the boys and girls of America by the villainous sheets which pander greedily and viciously to the natural taste of young readers for excitement, the irreparable wrong done by these vile publications, is hidden from no one."

Also, "The saffron-backed dime novels of the late Mr. Beadle, ill famed among the ignorant, who are unaware of their ultra Puritan purity, ... began to appear in the early years of the Civil War; and when I was a boy in a dismal boarding school at Sing Sing, in the winters of 1861–1863, I reveled in their thrilling and innocuous record of innocent and imminent danger.... I make no doubt that if the dime novels of my school days had been in circulation in Shakespeare's boyhood the Bard would have joyed in them," said Brander Matthews in 1923.

On July 1, 1868, the British Parliament was concerned with "the lamentable amount of juvenile criminality, largely attributed to the spread of cheap publications and theatrical representations of an exciting and immoral character, which corrupt the children of the lower classes and stimulate them into courses of dishonesty and vice."

W. H. Bishop (in *Atlantic Monthly*, Sept. 1879) had three principal complaints: Dime novels are too widely read; they are too conspicuously displayed; and most important, they corrupt children.

The attitude of the reading public was exemplified thus: "If you find a twelve-year-old boy addicted to juveniles," said Douglas Wiggin in 1901, "you may as well give the poor creature up.... His ears will be deaf to the music of St. Paul's Epistles and the Book of Job. He will never know the Faerie Queene or the Red Cross Knight, Don Quixote, Hector or Ajax. Dante and Goethe will be sealed oracles to him until the end of time.... He drank too long and too deeply of nursery pap, and his literary appetite and digestion are both weakened beyond cure."

The debate over the morality of the dime novels produced pronouncements similar to those sometimes found today about the influence of television on children. Authors and publishers often defend themselves in the prefaces against charges of immorality; all of the stories end fittingly, although some aim merely at humor and entertainment.

Beadle Publishing House

Dime novels, sensational blood-and-thunder adventure stories in paperback form, in the main taking place on the American frontier and glorifying the virtues of American individualism, are often recognized to have been first published by Irwin Beadle.

In 1858 Erastus Beadle (1821–1894), Robert Adams (1837–1866), and Erastus's brother Irwin Beadle (1828–1882) moved to New York City from Buffalo, New York, where they had published a children's magazine, *The Youth's Casket*. Irwin, who was a printer, advertised a dime song book from this New York premise, and this was followed in 1859 by a dime cook book and other nonfiction works.

The Beadles' dime novel series began in June 1860 and was advertised as "Books for the Millions! A Dollar Book for a Dime! 128 pages complete, only Ten Cents!!" By the end of that year thirteen titles had been published, and the firm's name had been changed to Beadle and Adams. A few months later, in February 1861, Erastus Beadle established an English branch of the firm in London, and the series began to appear there as Beadle's American Library, priced at sixpence per book. Beadle, however, was not really the first publisher of paper-covered novels;

they had been published since the 1830s in slightly different formats. They were larger in size than Beadle's dime novels and were usually sold for twenty-five cents. But even twenty-five cents for reading matter was still considered expensive for most people, who were making a dollar a day, and farm labor usually earned only room and board.

However, in the year 1860 this previously little-known publishing house (Irwin P. Beadle and Co.) started to print cheap books; these were even cheaper than the old story papers. It was the popularity of these earlier story papers that encouraged Beadle to publish *Malaeska: The Indian Wife of the White Hunter*, written by Ann S. Stephens. This is now considered to be the first real dime novel. This book was very popular and sold over 300,000 copies and was translated into five different languages. Stephens had been writing for the popular magazines of the day but was now also a novel writer. When *Malaeska* was published, it was supposed to be a tale about Native American life, but the action it contained opened up the field of reading material to a new model for the dime novelist.

The first edition of *Malaeska* was published without a cover illustration. In a later edition *Malaeska* is shown as a dark-skinned woman wearing a feathered headdress. She is holding her dying husband as she reaches out to her very light-skinned son. Although this sad story about Native American life was not of the blood-and-thunder school, its style set the format for all the rest of the Beadle dime novels, that is, a pocket-sized booklet of about 25,000 words on 128 pages printed on white rag paper. It had the salmon-colored, paper cover and had a steel engraving of the main character on the cover; it also had what came to be the accepted emblem of all future publications: a ten-cent piece.

With this success the idea of publishing an entire story in a single issue was introduced, and within a short time more than 65,000 copies had been sold. The fast action, even though not well written, a whole story, all in one book for a dime, immediately attracted other publishing houses (as well as many would-be authors), and the number of dime novels made available to the American reading public in an endless stream of various editions began.

By April 1864 Beadle's dime books alone had sold more than five million copies. Between 1860 and 1897, beginning with the publication of Stephens's *Malaeska*, the house of Beadle and Adams published over 3,100 dime novels. Beadle and Adams's publishing house was based on the obvious success of action-packed stories; this brought a new look at

Opposite—Beadle's Dime, Dialogues, No. 12. Inside cover reads: "*Petite Dramas, Dress Pieces:* Contains 94 pages of text (dramas). 'Filled with original ... contributions from favorite (sources).'" The important feature is the original Beadle logo (one dime).

BEADLE'S DIME

DIALOGUES, NO. 12.

BEADLE AND COMPANY, 98 WILLIAM STREET, N. Y.

contemporary American culture. The authors of these dime novels were largely hacks, some of whom were not well known at the time but became well recognized, even today.

Edward Sylvester Ellis's *Seth Jones; or, the Captives of the Frontier* sold over 600,000 copies. Edward Wheeler, the author of the *Deadwood Dick* series, wrote at least two hundred tales, and Edward Z. C. Judson, better known as Ned Buntline, wrote over four hundred novels for several different publishing houses.

One of the best known and very popular authors was Edward S. Ellis (1840–1916), a Trenton, New Jersey, school teacher who, at the age of twenty, had a manuscript accepted by Beadle. This was *Seth Jones; or, the Captives of the Frontier* (1860). The great success of this led Beadle to give Ellis a contract for four novels a year. He later wrote for other publishing houses and used many pseudonyms. This meant that the advertising department of the firm of Beadle, if there was such a department, had decided to plunge heavily into this publication. The house had bought a manuscript (for seventy-five dollars), which it was to publish on October 1.

On that date the book appeared: *Seth Jones; or the Captives of the Frontier*, another little orange pamphlet of 123 pages, with a full-length drawing of the hero on the cover and repeated as a frontispiece. Again the strong literary judgment and stronger business knowledge of the Beadles had paid off. The book sold 60,000 copies right off the press and 4,000 or 5,000 more before the end. It was translated into a number of foreign languages, perhaps eleven.

Seth Jones was Beadle's second novel and was a definite sign of what was to come. It was one of the most successful titles in the entire Beadle collection. Following this success, at lease once a month, the Beadle Company distributed more and more of these poorly written but exciting "thrilling romances," such as *Apollo Bill, The Frontier Detective, Deadwood Dick on Deck; or, Calamity Jane, the Heroine of Whoop-Up*, and hundreds more. Because they were published by Irwin P. Beadle Company of New York, they couldn't be missed, with their orange paper covers and dark black lettering.

Besides the original dime novel series, Beadle issued books called new dime novels, pocket novels, and Beadle's Dime Library, and (from 1881) they started *The Boy's Library of Sport and Adventure*, even though young boys had always been a target.

Although Beadle and Adams published these additional, cheap paperbound books, no series succeeded like the dime novels and half-dime novels. During the 1870s and 1880s, the dime novel as literature was unequaled in mass appeal.

With Beadle's Half-Dime Library, the company started catering to the teenage readers, and that inspired other dime-novel publishers to start printing series books aimed at these younger readers. However, some still continued to appeal to adults. The difference in price seems to be the determining factor in identifying an audience: ten cents for fiction for adults, five cents for teenagers.

Most Beadle novels were about 100 pages. There were also quarto and octavo broadsheets (e.g., *The Boy's Library*) of 16 or 32 pages. The dime novels contained about 80,000 words; books in the Half-Dime Library sold at five cents and contained about half that number of words.

In 1877 Erastus Beadle introduced a new format which became very popular. This was the quarto size, a regular sheet of printing paper folded into a 16-page booklet. It ended up being approximately 8½" × 12½". Then in 1884 he introduced an octavo size, a small pamphlet with 32 pages that measured approximately 7" × 10". These formats cost the reader either five or ten cents.

In 1877, Beadle also introduced the concept of presenting a fictional hero who would appear at regular intervals as the dime novels appeared on the newsstands. Deadwood Dick was the first of these heroes. Edward L. Wheeler, author for *Boys' First-Rate Pocket Library*, introduced Deadwood Dick to the dime-novel world, appearing in Beadle's Half-Dime Library until 1897. During the early 1880s, Beadle began printing the popular stories of Buffalo Bill, a Western hero who had been introduced in three earlier Street and Smith serials. Soon Buffalo Bill was so popular that many publishing houses, including Beadle's Dime Library, Street and Smith's *New York Weekly* and Frank Tousey's *Wide Awake Library*, were offering Buffalo Bill stories. Street and Smith began a series called *Buffalo Bill Stories*, which lasted until 1912; it was followed by the *New Buffalo Bill Weekly* (1912–1919). Then the stories appeared in *Western Story Magazine*, first in dime-novel format, then in pulp magazine format. The stories were in print in the pocket-book format until 1932. Many of the tales featured such folk heroes as Davy Crockett. In general, each dime novel was complete in itself, though there were many companion stories containing further adventures of the same characters, and Beadle did print serials in its *Saturday Journal* (1870–1882) and *Banner Weekly* (1882–1897).

By April 1864 Beadle and Adams had published four million dime novels. They alone published 3,158 separate titles; sales of each title ranged from 35,000 to 80,000. Even the *North American Review* was forced to notice and comment on some of the Beadle books, which, as a rule, they never touched.

Beadle and Adams, though important, did not entirely dominate the sensational fiction genre. Their success with tales of pioneers and the frontier needed to be expanded to a wider range of fiction—romances, detective tales, working-girl stories, tales of the American Revolution, mysteries of the cities, outlaw stories—which was published in the story papers, cheap libraries and pamphlet novels mentioned earlier. From the early 1880s detective fiction began to take over as the principal subject.

Even though the publishing houses of Beadle and Adams and Street and Smith published the most successful of these story papers, dime novels and cheap libraries, they were far from the only companies to do so. Many other competitors soon appeared on the scene, and by the 1870s many sorts of cheap fiction were available. In 1863 Irwin Beadle left the firm and set up in partnership with one of his clerks, George Munro, as Irwin P. Beadle and Co.; this rival firm began to produce its own ten-cent novels.

Frank Tousey's *American Tales* started in 1863; Thomas Elliott started the *Ten-Cent Novelettes* (1863); and Robert DeWitt put out the *Ten-Cent Romances* (1867). Then Beadle and Adams issued a *Fireside Library*; George Munro, a *Seaside Library*; Norman Munro, a *Riverside Library*; and Frank Tousey published the *Five-Cent Weekly Library* (1878–1893) and the *New York Detective Library* (1883–1898), among others.

Frank Tousey, one of the more successful dime-novel publishers of the day published what came to be known as "the big six": *Pluck and Luck* (1898–1929), featuring adventure stories; *Work and Win* (1898–1925), where the sports features of Fred Fearnot appeared; *Secret Service* (1899–1928), where the adventures of the Bradys, detectives par excellence, were featured; *Liberty Boys of '76* (1901–1925), a group of 100 young men who won the war against the Britains and helped the colonies gain their independence; *Wild West Weekly* (1902–1927), where the heroic "Young Wild West" (better known as "Wild") tames the west; and *Fame and Fortune* (1905–1928), stories of boys who made money, mostly on Wall Street.

While the Williams and Gleason House had turned out titles by the dozens, the Beadle house was turning them out by the thousands. Its total sales in the course of a few years would mount into the millions.

Other firms in the past had attempted ambitious "libraries" that would presumably go on forever but actually expired with the sixth or seventh number. Irwin and Erastus Beadle contributed nothing new, except the low price of a dime—and success. They drafted the same authors who had written for the story papers. Stephens headed up the first dime-novel series; other writers from the first series included Mary Andrews Denison, long the editor of the *Boston Olive Branch*; Augustine Joseph Hickey Duganne, who had contributed to most of the story papers, including *The Flag* and the *Weekly*; and Edward S. Ellis, who had already, at the age of nineteen, written a serial for the *New York Dispatch*.

All the Beadle stories followed the good story-paper tradition, but with an extra emphasis upon the Wild West.

The Beadle Co. and its successors swept the nation, meeting the demand of adults and children for action on the Western frontier, for emphasis on the importance of the individual, for an ideal world in which everyone could achieve greatness—along with detective thrillers, such as Harlan Page Halsey's *Old Sleuth Stories* and John Russell Coryell's *Nick Carter* series.

Because Street and Smith issued the *Log Cabin Library* series (1889) and the *Nick Carter Library* (1891), it became the accepted leaders. Street and Smith began printing series paperbacks in the late 1880s. These are claimed by some to be the beginning of the dime-novel paperback, or "thick book," as they differed from the earlier pamphlet books, similar to the ones Beadle issued.

Sales of dime books increased when the Civil War broke out. These novels were distributed to all of the troops on both sides, especially the Union troops, and were said to be "the soldiers' solace and comfort in camp and campaign."

The Civil War was especially profitable for the enterprising Beadles. Their books went to the fighting front by the millions. And although many of them were given to the troops free, a great many of them were sold. The little books were sent to camps in large packages, bound up like fresh-cut firewood. They were shipped on freight cars on the new rail lines, on wagons where trains couldn't go, and on canal boats, where necessary. When these bundles arrived in camp, the army post person had to distribute them quickly, or else they would be torn away from him.

The sale of dime novels by the million was such an astonishing event, in Civil War days, that it caught the attention of the *North American Review* of Boston. On July 1864, it printed a review of "Beadle's Dime Books," which was written by William Everett. It was a conscious attempt to recognize their merits, to point out their defects and to understand their popularity. Again this was unusual for this "trash" literature.

What started as Irwin P. Beadle and Co. (1860) and then became Beadle and Co. and finally Beadle and Adams was succeeded in 1898 by M. J. Ivers and Co., which in turn was succeeded in 1908 by Westbrook and Co., which went out of business in 1937.

There exists no single, comprehensive bibliography of dime novels, Albert Johannsen's *House of Beadle and Adams* (1950) is a definitive bibliography of the Beadle and Adams publications. Charles Bergin's *Bibliography: Dime Novels 1860-1964* is another source. Don Russell's *Lives and Legends of Buffalo Bill* (1960) and *Dime Novel Roundup*, a newsletter that publishes articles, notes and biographical listings, are other resources.

Horatio Alger

While middle-class children were reading evangelical and home-based fiction, both of which were very popular in the 1850s, poorer children were reading sensational adventure stories meant mainly for working-class boys. The dime novel and the "rags-to-riches" publications were becoming widespread. Leading all these in popularity were Horatio Alger's stories of urchins adrift in New York, where if diligent and thrifty, they were "bound to rise." Among all classes of children, reading novels (fiction) was becoming more acceptable than in previous years.

Horatio Alger was a native of New England, but he had an aptitude for writing and so moved to New York, where the publishing business was centered at the time. His talent, such as it was, was directed toward the interests of young boys. Basically, he developed a formula and wrote the same story over and over again. His boy heroes, solid personifications of American democracy, and his adventures didn't stray far from the formula. (If one follows "Murder, She Wrote," as one instance, one sees this formula at work.) His first successful book and probably his best known was *Ragged Dick; or Street Life in New York* (1868). It is the typical rags-to-riches theme found in all of his books. This theme made his name known in almost every household. Even today the mention of Horatio Alger conjures up pictures of the rags-to-riches theme.

Although this first book for boys, *Ragged Dick*, appeared in 1868, by that time Alger had already published several other poorly written novels (*Paul Prescott's Charge*; *Charlie Codman's Cruise* and *Helen Ford*), but after *Ragged Dick* had found an enthusiastic audience of boys, he began to write for them only, putting out over a hundred books in series of eight or ten titles each: the *Ragged Dick* series (*Rufus and Rose*), *Luck and Pluck* series (*Luck and Pluck; or, John Oakley's Inheritance* [1869], *Tattered Tom* series (*Tattered Tom; or, the Story of a Street Arab* [1871]) and many others.

Ragged Dick is the story of an orphan boy who works as a bootblack on the streets of New York. Although he is a poor street foundling he is ambitious and honest and could respond favorably under the right influences. A kindly businessman takes an interest in Dick; he gives him good advice, buys him new clothes and encourages him to try to rise above his present station in life. Dick, on his own initiative, learns to read and write, saves some of his scant earnings and shows signs of self-improvement in terms of how he dresses and takes care of his personal hygiene. Then, as luck would have it, he rescues a child from drowning. The child's father is a rich businessman and rewards Dick with a job as a clerk, which gives him respectability.

Alger used *Ragged Dick* as an example of American democracy at

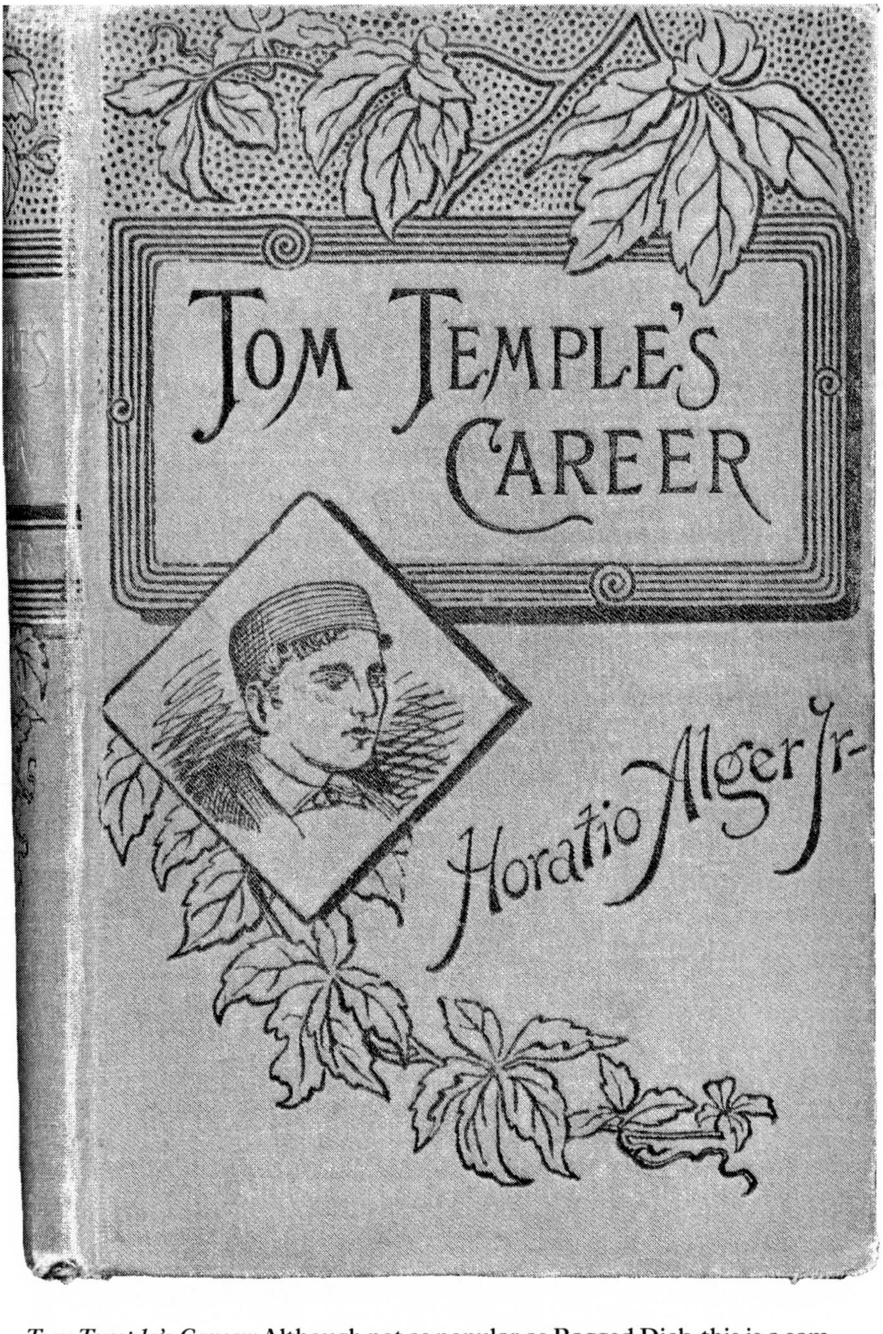

Tom Temple's Career: Although not as popular as Ragged Dick, this is a sample of Alger's work. 278 pages with 8 pages of Burt's other available books.

work. All anyone needs to rise in the middle-class world is to be honest, work hard and believe in yourself. However, if chance falls in your lap, take advantage of it. *Ragged Dick* is not a son of a wealthy entrepreneur; he does not long for money and high position; all he wants is a decent job with a chance to move ahead.

What Alger saw in a democratic society was not a society without class distinctions but one in which the class lines were breakable. His stories said that any American might climb ahead from a lowly beginning by having ambition, not being afraid of hard work, and possessing high moral standards; the books Alger wrote owed much of their popularity to the fact that American readers shared this democratic view. The stroke of luck that always pushed an Alger boy hero across class lines from low to middle seems to some of today's readers as a contradiction of the author's stated faith in hard work and clean living as the key to success. No doubt, in his own mind, Alger knew that there were occasional shortcomings in the work-ethic, reward formula, but luck for the deserving was an integral part of nineteenth-century beliefs; besides, it was an already established tenet in the Protestant faith that the intervention of providence on the side of the worthy was deserving.

The whole meaning of Alger's phenomenal success, on this point as on others, lies in the accuracy with which he reflected the popular opinion of this time. Alger's heroes want respectability even more than they want money or any particular goal or position. However, acceptance by a respectable middle class requires that these boys, who have been independent, however poor, give up their freedom and take on the mannerisms of those whose class they wish to belong to. And they do so. Not reluctantly but eagerly, these ambitious boys correct their speech, discipline themselves to keep regular hours and give up their spontaneous and spendthrift ways. They learn to fit in with the respectable class. Wanting this middle-class acceptance, they conform to middle-class standards when and where they must. So Dick, like all of Alger's heroes, exchanges some of his American-inspired independence after he meets the "patron" who can introduce him to the middle-class life he so desires. Almost at once, he adopts all of the employer's virtues. Alger regularly urged this upon his readers, making "his employer's interests his own," taking on the manners as well as the opinions of his "superiors," and exhibits a respect that borders on the servile. In theory at least, the way to the top was open to the poorest and the most uneducated immigrants if they were willing to work hard and use their native initiative. There was no assumption that the "the rich man in his castle, the poor man at his gate" were locked into place by divine will: "God made them high or lowly, and ordered their estate."

Becoming rich through hard work was not a fashionable idea at this time, but it was encouraging and legally inspiring, and its prophet, in books for young people, was Horatio Alger Jr. This concept appealed to the American public at the time: that the democratic promise was a reality. It was the popular outlook of the time, and his stories reflected, with a great deal of accuracy, this attitude.

Another irony is that even though Alger maintains that hard work, honesty and ambition are the factors one needs to rise above one's station, his literary heroes always got to move up because of a lucky break that had nothing to do with those factors. Alger's intent was to show that this "lucky break" came to those who had acceptable, moral standings. In other words goodness comes to those who are worthy. Many believe that most of these dime novel stories were moral and that their message was one of the rewards of virtuous living.

Although it seems strange to equate the rags-to-riches stories of Horatio Alger to romanticism, his stories did bring to children's literature the "romance" of childhood. Alger's literary heroes were bootblacks, match boys, newspaper carriers and peddlers of all kinds. These were street youngsters who worked to eke out a living; they lived without any outside support and lived a day-by-day existence.

These "heroes" were numerous in the 1850s. Alger, through his various plots, took these youngsters off the streets and into more respectful occupations; he did this by showing that hard work and Christian beliefs with a touch of good luck would build good character and therefore bring success. Alger did not write well, but his books suited the times. His books were read by thousands, and the Horatio Alger hero has become a symbol of the proverbial "rags to riches" story. Alger's sentimentality, like that of some other 1850s' authors, was partly an effort to elicit sympathy for the underclass. The effectiveness of the approach is shown by his 1871 book, *Phil, the Fiddler; or, Story of a Young Street Musician*, which exposed the abuses of a contract-labor system then operating in New York City; business owners were taking unfair advantage of unskilled workers. Boys who were brought from Calabria, Italy, to beg in American streets were not only exploited, but also so badly abused by their masters that many of them died.

The publication of this work brought an outcry from the public in the form of protests and meetings that culminated in the bringing of a test case to the court system. The case centered on the brutal mistreatment of a child. The New York legislators, after hearing how the system led to the wrongs suffered by these helpless youngsters, caught in a web not of their doing, passed a law preventing the cruelty to children. This law was the first of its kind in the United States. So, even though Alger's boys were not models of child behavior, they were presented as pure enough, likable enough and deserving enough to convince Americans to recognize the problems these children faced.

Beginning with *Ragged Dick* in 1868, Alger wrote more than one hundred books, mostly in series of six titles. As a writer he was insignificant, but as a social mover and shaker he was astonishing, and although his books are no longer read, his name remains an American household word.

If today the Alger success stories seem far fetched, it should be remembered that Andrew Carnagie, John D. Rockefeller, Henry Ford, Joseph Pulitzer and many others made their way to wealth from humble beginnings. Alger naturally did not think in terms of the establishments of great foundations; to him success meant simply status and respectability. His morality was commercial morality: Honesty is the best policy, but one must be aware of sharpies and never trust a stranger. Curiously, respectability and wealth, when they came, were not always the result of hard work. Assistance from a rich, kind uncle was sometimes required, and it was not unusual for Alger's heroes to be the rightful heirs to large fortunes or the recipients of generous rewards for brave deeds or to be handsomely adopted.

Not all of his heroes' successes were necessarily the acquisition of money. What these workers wanted was acceptability, steady employment, and respectability. They did not always climb swiftly to the summit; their achievements were often more modest. This is made clear in Paul, in *Paul, the Peddler* (1871) and its sequel, *Slow and Sure; or, From the Street to the Shop* (1872), who progresses only "from the street to the shop." Paul ends up as a proprietor of a men's outfitters. "At the end of two years he took a larger shop and engaged two extra clerks, prompt in his engagements, and of thorough integrity, he is likely to be even more prosperous as the years roll on." They wanted only a life away from the streets, where bad moral standards was tempting and corrupting.

In 1871 a new serial by Alger, *Tony the Tramp*, began. Alger, whose *Ragged Dick* series had made him well known, began writing serials for the *New York Weekly*, in which *Tony the Tramp* is introduced as "a story for young and old.... Parents and guardians will read it and recommend it to their children, because in many cases it will revive recollections of their own early struggles.... Each boy ... will fancy himself the hero and of course feel his blood pulse sympathetically as he puts himself in his place." What is particularly interesting about this Alger serial is that it is one of the earliest appearances of the tramp in fiction.

Alger's *Frank's Campaign*, the first of a popular series of stories set in America in which the heroes climb from poverty to wealth, was published in Boston by the Loring House. By this time series books were beginning to replace the dime novel. Again the literary people, including librarians, were against this new turn. They were against not only Alger and his series but also Martha Finley of the Elsie Dinsmore stories and her numerous sequels. These were "juvenile series … [of a] ranting, canting, hypocritical sort."

The unprecedented success of Alger's subliterary writings of the post–Civil War period drew the attention of historians who wanted to see for themselves why Alger spoke so convincingly to the American people of that time and place. Their analysis revealed many of the myths and truths of a very complex period of American history.

Although most of these street young men smoked cigarettes, gambled and participated in pan handling, Alger made them appear acceptable as worthy people while still representing the reality of life on the streets.

Ragged Dick is a good example of this use of literary license. Dick was a bootblack who lived on the street, with ragged clothes and a box for a bed. Even though he had basic bad habits he was "Noble in Character." This nobility saved him from his minor shortcomings. Dick was "not a model boy in all respects," Alger admitted, but his "sins" were no more than bad habits. "His nature was a noble one and had saved him from all mean faults." With luck and good fortune Dick moved from the streets to a better life, which, it was apparent, was what he deserved.

Alger's main goal was to inspire sympathy for these boys because they were forced to work on the streets in order to live and to support themselves and their families. To make his stories appealing and persuasive, Alger had to make his characters believable, and to do that, he had to overlook the worst aspects of the lives of street workers, including their moral corruption. Alger met this challenge with sentimentality. He agreed to some of the hazards of street life, admitting that boys might take to smoking or gambling or begging, but he evaded the "vicious knowledge" Sara Parton had accused him of.

Other Writers

Later on in the 1800s, the way in which books were publicized changed; publicity was no longer based on a popular author but on a favorite character. This allowed the publishers to use any number of anonymous writers to put out story after story at a cheaper rate than hiring a specific author. The publicity was centered on a special character, and the cover illustration identified the book by this character, not any specific author.

Old Sleuth was the first successful and longest-reigning of these characters. This biweekly series, by the Munro Publishing House, featured Old Sleuth in at least one-third of its issues. The stories were credited to "Old Sleuth" himself but were written by Harlan Page Halsey starting in 1872. The success of this character was so great that in 1885 the Old Sleuth Library began and lasted until 1905. Halsey wrote his other detective stories for the *New York Weekly* under a different pseudonym, Judson Taylor.

Nick Carter was another famous dime-novel character. In 1886 in Street and Smith's *New York Weekly*, a story titled "The Old Detective's Pupil" appeared. Nick Carter was the pupil. Then in 1891 Street and Smith, because of the popularity of the Nick Carter stories, started a new series called the *Nick Carter Library*. It contained Nick Carter stories exclusively. This was the first weekly with adventure and detective stories based on one character. These stories were to continue with several name changes: the *New Nick Carter Weekly* (1912); the *Nick Carter Stories* (1912–1915); then the *Magnet Library* and the *New Magnet Library* up until 1933.

All in all over 1,000 Nick Carter stories were written, with more than 3,000 separate issues, since many of the stories were reprinted, some of which were only slightly rewritten.

The adventures of this popular detective covered many years; the character was kept alive for the public by an ever-changing, yet easily recognized, appearance that was tailor made for the present-day reader. As a result, many detectives were given either the word "Old" as part of their name (Old Sleuth, Old Search, Old Broadbrim), suggesting a person of wisdom, or an alliterative name (Dave Dotson, Dash Dare), one that was easy to remember. Both examples had been part of the old dime-novel tradition. The name Nick Carter suggests a break with this tradition and the coming of something new.

Edward Jason, using the pseudonym Ned Buntline, was a well-known American author who wrote sensational literature with an American background. He used his own experiences and personified the hero in many of his tales. (Buntline was quite a colorful character himself. He shot a jealous husband and was nearly hanged by a lynch mob.) "He was, in fact, the first of the dime novelists, having invented the technique and brought it to perfection some twelve years before the firm of Beadle and Adams popularized the form" (*Dictionary of American Biography*). While Ned Buntline was writing his own Western stories, he met and became friends with William F. Cody, a border scout and Pony Express rider. Cody was another colorful character who also enjoyed the Wild West. Ned Buntline called his friend Buffalo Bill and wrote a long series of books which were very successful. Buffalo Bill became a folk hero and was a household name.

In 1869 *Buffalo Bill, King of the Border Men*, was published. The tale ran for a long time and was continued by Colonial Prentiss Ingraham for Beadle and Adams. Incidentally, Cody himself wrote a few dime novels:

Death Trailer, the Chief of the Scouts; or, Life and Love of a Frontier Fort (1878).

William Wallace Cook, author and editor, wrote for both Street and Smith and Tozer Publications. He at one time worked as a clerk, a ticket agent and a paymaster. In 1893 he began to write fiction books. He, like almost everyone else, used many pseudonyms. He wrote 14 Nick Carter stories, 75 Frank Merriwell ones and 176 Diamond Dick stories. He also wrote his autobiography, *The Fiction Factory*, in 1912. He was the author of *Plotto*, a basic information manual for beginning authors.

An example of the way current events helped shape dime novels can be seen through the John L. and Gentleman Jack stories published by Street and Smith and Alfred B. Tozer. Tozer's only slightly pseudonymous boxing stories about John L. started when John L. Sullivan was heavyweight champion. After Jim Corbett defeated Sullivan, the John L. stories turned around and were about the new winner, Corbett, known as Gentleman Jack (the stories were ghostwritten by Edward Stratemeyer). Both the John L. and Gentleman Jack stories contained characters and ideas taken directly from the lives of these men as well as accurate information taken from the newspapers.

The first issue of John L. was titled *John L., Jr. the Young Knocker-Outer; or, Fighting for a Fortune.* It appeared in 11 of the first 47 stories ghostwritten by Tozer. The last was *John L., Jr. in Boston; or, Fighting for $100,000.*

Louisa May Alcott used a pseudonym for her sensational fiction. This fact was discovered by Leona Rostenberg. While Rostenberg was researching at the Houghton Library, Harvard University, she found five letters, written in 1865 and 1866, from Boston publisher Elliott, Thomes and Talbot to Alcott. The pseudonym was A. M. Barnard. The name of the periodical where her thrillers appeared is *The Flag of Our Union*. The titles of three of Alcott's sensational narratives were named in the letters.

These three Alcott thrillers were published as dime novels by Elliott, Thomes and Talbot: *V. V.; or, Plots and Counterplots* by A. M. Barnard (1870) (Ten-Cent Novelette #80); *The Skeleton in the Closet* by L. M. Alcott (1867) (Ten-Cent Novelette #49); and *The Mysterious Key, and What It Opened* by L. M. Alcott (1867). *A Long, Fatal Love Chase, a Gothic Romance* was rejected in 1866 and not published until 1995. Another novel, believed to be her first, *The Inheritance*, was published later.

"Louisa May Alcott had written a dime novel! Not one but three dime novels. One of her sensational stories was published as a dime novel and two began as dime novels. An analysis of their nature and their publication may enrich the early history of the dime novel and of Miss L. M. Alcott." So says Madeleine B. Stern. Stern came across a letter from

James R. Elliott of Elliott, Thomes and Talbot: We would like more stories from you ... and if you prefer you may use the pseudonym of A. M. Barnard or any other man's name if you will."

Among American authors the best known were Oliver Optic and Harry Castlemon. These two were true dime novelists. Elijah Kellogg and J. T. Trowbridge were not considered true dime novelists. Oliver Optic, whose real name was William Taylor Adams, is a good example of dime-novel writers. In the 1850s Adams started to write novels for children. He wrote many books over a fifty-year period, changing from fiction for children to the ever more popular series books. He was the author of the Great Western series, the Lake Shore series and the Yacht Club series, among many others.

Optic wrote 116 full-length books. He edited *Oliver Optic's Magazine for Boys and Girls* from 1865 to 1875. Optic's books, in keeping with the times, were written in series, but he had a sense of the dramatic and

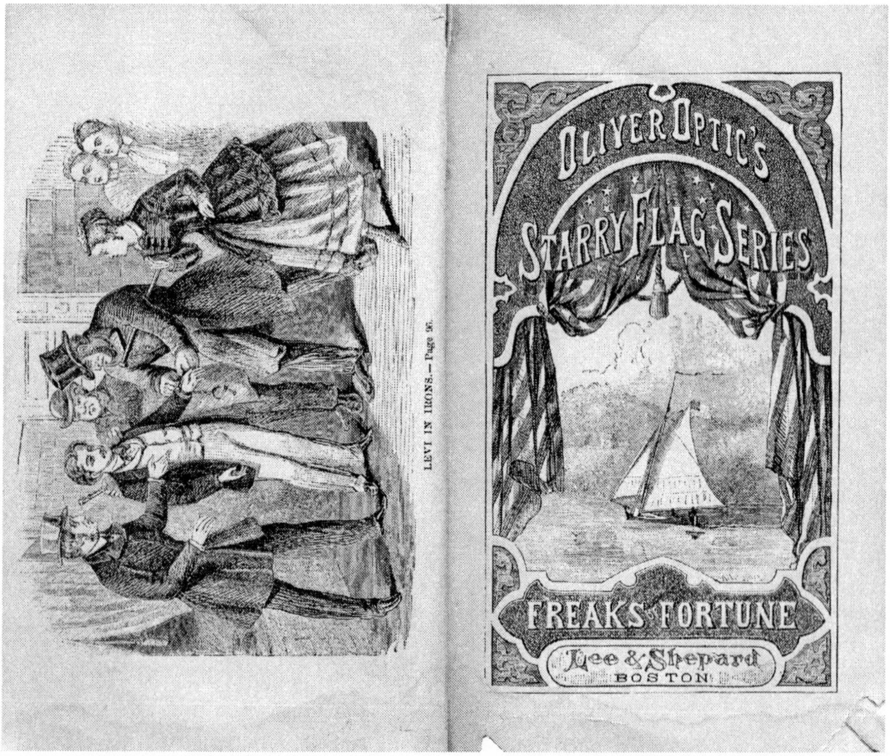

Freaks of Fortune or Half Round the World: **Number two in the six part Starry Flag Series. Also the fourth of the serial stories published in "Our Boys and Girls." 303 pages.**

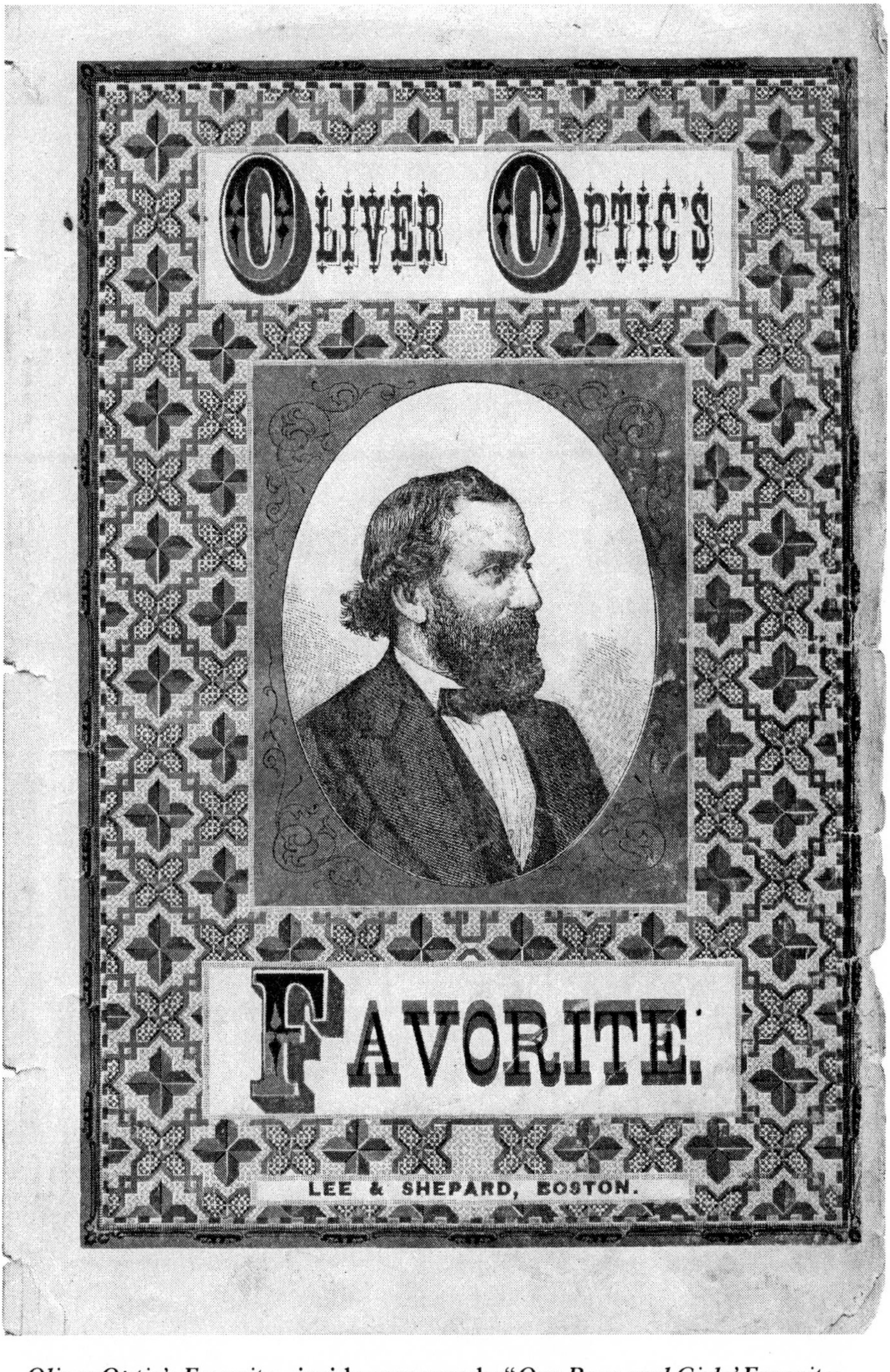

Oliver Optic's Favorite—inside cover reads: "*Our Boys and Girls' Favorite:* 'Stories of the sea, tales of wonder, records of travel, anecdotes of natural history, wonderful things, dialogues, puzzles, &c.'" 728 pages.

could make the trial of a boy falsely accused or the outcome of a boat race into scenes of excitement and suspense. His heroes were travelers in the *Boat Club* series (1854), the *Woodville* series (1861–1867), the *Army and Navy* series (1865–1894), the *Starry Flag* series (1867–1869), and many more.

The reader, along with the story's hero, went on exciting adventures to far-off places. The readers learned both geography and science as they read exciting stories. Optic's heroes were likable and ready to face any obstacle, and although Optic was a moral writer, he didn't let the moral theme interfere with his engaging stories. His books were read enthusiastically by more than one generation of youngsters.

Oliver Optic's Magazine for Boys and Girls, a semiannual periodical, began in January 1867; by 1871 it had become a monthly. It was published by Lee and Shepard and edited by Adams himself (Oliver Optic). In 1871 Lee and Shepard published *Our Boys' and Girls' Favorite*, which contained many stories and poems. The magazine was discontinued when Lee and Shepard went bankrupt in 1875. The magazine's editorial column was used to defend Oliver Optic's books for boys from attackers such as Louisa May Alcott and Edward Eggleston.

Oliver Optic wrote twice as many books as Castlemon. Castlemon and Optic are of little significance today, partly because their talents were less remarkable than their output and partly because their books reflect a conventional idea of adventure rather than the real thing.

Harry Castlemon (Charles Austin Fosdick) 1842–1915, was one of the most popular dime-novel writers, successfully rivaling G. A. Henty and Oliver Optic. He wrote over 58 books in adventure series: *Afloat and Ashore*, *Boy Trapper*, *Gunboat Club*, *Pony Express*, *Rocky Mountain*, *Rod and Gun*, and *Sportsman's Series*. He had a lively style and knew how to hold his audience. He had served in the navy during the Civil War and used these experiences in all his books. He knew very well what he was about: "Boys," he said, "don't like fine writing. What they want is adventure, and the more of it you can get into 250 pages of manuscript, the better fellow you are."

Elijah Kellogg's first and best book was *Good Old Times*. It tells of his grandfather's life as a Maine backwoodsman a hundred years earlier. Kellogg did not formally offer a moral, but his tales emphasize the importance of courage, endurance, upright living and the dignity of work. He was eagerly read; he liked and understood boys and knew many of them. Kellogg's stories have specific local color, for his characters speak in the Eastern vernacular, and his setting is recognizable as Maine.

John Townsend Trowbridge (1827–1916) drew on his own early life on the Erie Canal when he wrote *Jack Hazard and His Fortunes* (1871). This story is about a boy who runs away from his stepfather. There were

Frank on a Gunboat: Number one in the six part Gunboat Series, considered one of Castlemon's (i.e., Fosdick's) best. Based on his own experiences as a youth. 256 pages.

several sequels. This book first appeared as a serial in *Our Young Folks*. Because Trowbridge was a poet as well as a novelist, he enriched the quality of writing for young people. His characters were realistic and individualistic; their realism, not just the adventures they experienced, held the attention of the readers.

Another dime author was Edward S. Ellis, author of *Seth Jones; or, the Captives of the Frontier*, his first novel. One does not have to be very old to recall the time when that name was signed to many books. Ellis, pleased by the success of this first novel and by that of the dozens that he wrote for the same house, started a literary career which lasted until his death in 1916. He wrote more than a dozen series of juvenile stories; this made up about 150 volumes. He was a typical writer of dime novels, but he often rose far above the average in quality, and his graduation into historical writing of a respectable order also sets him apart from his fellow writers of yellow backs. To be included in "Who's Who in America" is a modest distinction for the author, but Ellis was one of those dime novelists whose name was included in this prestigious publication. The biographical dictionaries were not, as a rule, friendly to writers whose work was all in books with paper covers. Before many years had passed, however, the author of *Seth Jones* had accomplished the feat which the writers' world used to describe as "getting between boards."

In *Seth Jones* the Native Americans who capture Ina are Mohawks. Seth and the other white men call them "imps" or, in a moment of stress, "varmints." So strong a term as "devils," however, was not permitted to be said by the characters in these books. At this early stage "devils" was considered profanity, which was strictly forbidden. It is said that *Seth Jones* was one of Abraham Lincoln's favorite stories.

Ellis received $75 for *Seth Jones*. At that time, however, he had no literary reputation. Later the firm would pay him $250 for a novel of forty thousand words. It paid Stephens $250 for the right to reprint "Malaeska" in book form.

Among others who wrote this form of fiction for cash was young Louisa May Alcott. The fees were sometimes large enough (they ranged from $75 to $700 per title) to attract famous names such as Mayne Reid.

Early in the 1900s, Street and Smith offered five important series: *Brave and Bold* (1902–1911), emphasizing adventure stories; *Tip Top Weekly* (1896–1912), which had colored pictures on the cover, a new innovation; *Nick Carter Weekly* (1897–1912), featuring detective stories; *Diamond Dick Jr.* (1896–1911), a hero in an up-to-date Western; and *Buffalo Bill Stories* (1902–1912), another Western hero who was to become very popular.

A number of lesser writers were also beginning to grind out the Western fiction that was immediately popular.

William Brett, an unsuccessful minister, took up the writing of inspirational stories for boys partly on the encouragement of William T. Adams, author of the *Oliver Optic* series.

It is interesting to note that Edgar Allan Poe's early stories were first published in the dime-novel format; they were thus consigned to being thought of as second-class literature.

Samuel Wood (also a school teacher who went into another field) went into the secondhand book business. His experience led him to believe that many children's books were unsuitable for young readers, so he decided to print children's books which he himself had written or compiled. Writing cheap stories was often combined with journalism, school teaching, and working for the popular theater.

Isaac Watts (1674–1748) wrote *Hymns 1707* and *Psalms 1719*. These publications went through many editions.

Anna Aikin Barbauld is perhaps best remembered now as joint author with her brother John Aikin of *Evenings at Home*. Any child of any generation would appreciate it. Recent reprints will at least give that opportunity to the present generation of children.

Dorothy Kilner (1755–1836) wrote *The Adventures of a Pincushion, Memoirs of a Pegtop; The Good Child's Delight; History of a Great Many Little Boys and Girls*; *Familiar Dialogues*; *Holyday Present*; *Life and Perambulations of a Mouse* and *Jemima Placid*. All are in the same style, the little masters' and misses' adventures being of a simple and everyday sort, each little incident having its appropriate moral. They belong to the class of volumes covered with Dutch paper, gold trimmed and adorned with flowers in blue, pink and green, which are especially associated with the name of John Newbery.

The British writers for boys, Mayne Reid (1818–1883), Robert Michael Ballantyne (1825–1894), William Henry Giles Kingston (1814–1880), Frederick Marryat (1792–1848) and George Alfred Henty (1832–1902) were read with enthusiasm by boys in America. The American adventure tales also made their way to England. England's Aldine Publishing Company pirated and published single issues of the *New Buffalo Bill Library* (1899).

Reid's books were *The Boy Hunters: or, Adventures in Search of a White Buffalo* (1852) and *The Young Voyageurs: or the Boy Hunters in the North* (1854) among many others. He wrote a book to be released around Christmas time for twenty-some years.

Ballantyne wrote over one hundred books for boys. His first book, *The Young Fur Traders* (1856), was a great success. Some of his most popular books were *Coral Island: a Tale of the Pacific Ocean* (1858) and *Martin Rattler, or, a Boy's Adventure in the Forests of Brazil* (1858).

Kingston's best-known book is *Peter the Whaler* (1851). He also contributed *The Three Midshipmen* (1873); *Trapper's Son* (1873) and *Snow-Shoes and Canoes* (1876).

Frederick Marryat's *Masterman Ready; or, the Wreck of the Pacific* (1841) was the first adventure story specifically written for young people, particularly young boys. He also wrote *The Children of the New Forest* (1847) and *Settlers in Canada* (1844). Another well-known book by Marryat is *The Little Savage*. This book was finished by his son, Frank, after Frederick's death.

G. A. Henty, a prolific writer, wrote his first boys' book in 1871: *Out on the Pampas, or, the Young Settlers* (1871). Probably his best-known is *Beric the Briton: a Story of the Roman Invasion* (1893).

One of the first authors to produce readable fiction set in the rich environment of the young United States was James Fenimore Cooper. His bold, imaginative stories of pioneers and Native Americans broke the traditional European scene and set the stage for the future. (In 1831 Cooper wrote *The Bravo*, a book about Venice.) Cooper was the first to popularize the frontier theme for exciting reading.

At about the same time, a young Southerner, Edgar Allan Poe, migrated to the North and published "The Murders in the Rue Morgue," "The Gold Bug" and "The Purloined Letter." These short stories were somewhat of an innovation to replace the pompous, long-winded European novels. Poe's real contribution, of course, was the detective, a purely American character. However, the great American adventure was the making of America. It is unfortunate that the succeeding waves of immigrants and the westward thrust of the frontier did not at the time inspire children's books of any real merit. It was not until the War of 1812 that American authors began to write children's books with seriousness.

Subjects Covered

J. Edward Leithead researched and wrote articles that appeared in the *Dime Novel Round-Up*. His aim was to classify dime novels into specific categories. Although his work was not definitive, it did lay excellent groundwork for further study.

The series of articles called "The Anatomy of Dime Novels" (1965–1971) is a model for classifying and indexing these elusive materials.

Phillip Durham, in his article "Dime Novels: An American Heritage," classified 1,531 dime novels published by Beadle and Adams and determined the following percentages of books by subject. He found that one-half to one-third of the dime novels were about the new West and the frontier:

Subject	*Percentage of books published*
The West in general	30
Miners, mining and mining towns	10
Texas life	6
City life	6
Detectives of the city	6
Detectives of the West	5
Native American tales	5
Border life before the Civil War	4
Scouts	3
American Revolution	3
Fur trappers	2
Overland journeys	2
Southern Mississippi River	2
Colonial times	2
Mexico	1
Miscellaneous	9

The Western outlaw stories were not centered around the education and success of a self-made man, like the Horatio Alger stories, or around an interclass romance, like the Laura Jean Libby stories but around the persecution of a hero or of a defenseless person, which forces the hero into a justifiable though illegal revenge, like Joseph Badger's series of dime novels about Joaquin Murieta. These stories began in 1871, with Murieta as a minor character, a "demon incarnate." By the late 1870s and early 1880s, the acceptance of the outlaw "hero" tales had Murieta become the central character, whose violence was justified by his early persecution.

The outlaw tales dealing with the Jesse James gang made a successful appearance in 1889, when Street and Smith and Frank Tousey began publishing and distributing them, and they remained popular until strong public objection led to their suspension in 1903. Though the exact reason for the "cleanup" remains uncertain, two suggestions have been put forward. One, the outlaw stories that were most seriously attacked were the ones that appeared in nickel libraries that were meant for young boys. Tousey's *Five-Cent, Wide-Awake Library*, which offered sixty outlaw stories including the eighteen "original" Jesse James stories and at least twenty-five Claude Duval stories, was considered a boys' weekly, as was Beadle's *Half-Dime Library*, which carried the Deadwood Dick stories. Second, the James Brothers' stories and other living outlaw stories were being published while these outlaws were still at large.

Cities were used more in the later fiction than in earlier stories. The city was a place of opportunity, so many authors had their fictional characters living in a city where they supposedly had the opportunity to make good. True to reality, most stories of these spectacular rises in fortune had a city background. However, the city was also a place of wickedness, a place where temptations were always present, where morality was an almost unknown quality and ideals a rare commodity. Many of the tales with city backgrounds pictured city people as cold hearted and morally irresponsible.

William Taylor Adams's (Oliver Optic) use of a real and identifiable city as background was typical of the times. The basic theme of Adams's *Poor and Proud; or, the Fortunes of Katy Redburn* (1858) was an example of the stories of success and achievement which were plentiful in the 1860s and 1870s. A poor, but genteel, youngster has a chance to show that hard work, diligence and personal courage along with a cheerful and pleasant manner can help one to earn a decent living. Real success, however, comes about, not through those virtues, but through making a favorable impression on some wealthy person or through sheer luck. *Poor and Proud* was a good story, especially in comparison with some of his earlier stories.

Adams wrote not only for the parents but also for the youngsters in the family. It was both realistic and moral. As the title specifies, the moral of the book is both the right and wrong types of pride; that it is possible to be poor and proud but that pride must not keep the poor from any kind of work by which they can support themselves and their family. There were also throughout the story other moral lessons for the benefit of the child readers. Perhaps more so than Adams's *Poor and Proud* was *The Shadow in the House* by O. A. S. Beale. This story offers the kind of sentimentality which was once used exclusively with adults but was now seen in the readings for children. The differences between the tone and attitude in this story and those in earlier writings for children are representative. The strong emotionalism in this story offsets the popular moral of reasonableness, an approach now found to be unacceptable. Beale's solution to the conflicts presented in her stories is very sentimental, a far cry from the learning from experience and rational reflection approaches so well used in earlier stories.

Middle-class children read evangelical and home-based fiction. These books were written by religious persons or ministers, and their contents deal with piety, death-bed scenes, and sin. There is nothing resembling humor in these stories; some might have a bit of lightness, but emotions are very controlled: Joy is offset with grief, and anger is offset with acceptance.

Almost all the stories were based on the endless fight between good and evil, and although both the readers and writers of these books might have had a few moral shortcomings themselves, the heroes and heroines of these stories never did. There were spirited encounters between young men and villains of every description; there were moving stories of poor youngsters rising above their humble beginnings and succeeding in the middle-class world. There were fights, but they were always over some moral issue, and the fights were with fists, not guns.

However, between 1880 and 1900 these stories became very sensational. No longer were Daniel Boone and Kit Carson the heroes; now Deadshot Dave and the Black Avenger were the protagonists. These were drinking men who robbed trains and killed people.

Some of these books were ignored, some were read and accepted as tolerable reading material, but a great many of them were read with real interest by the youngsters. Even though these authors were aware of the need for moralistic lessons for youngsters, they paid more attention to the tastes in reading among this group. Didacticism was wearing thin because adventure stories were more satisfying. Moreover, this new fictional literature, usually written by young authors, just starting out in a career of writing and trying to sell their first stories, was lighter in style, even though still melodramatic in approach; it was more materialistic in its treatment of values and more sympathetic in the handling of problems, usually with a bit of humor. This new approach was aimed at keeping readers interested in asking for more.

When stories began to be written with boys as the main character, there were several different types of boys. There was the likable and realistic youth; there was the rather impudent Christian-type hero; there was, especially in the later weeklies, the wonders of wisdom and valor; and there were the boys who had just been up to mischief. The majority of stories for youth were now those that were commercially successful, citing again and again the deeds and daring of supermen like Jack Parkway, Sexton Blake and Deadwood Dick. Thus, as the authors wrote the American dream over and over in the fictional histories of young people who made the break between poverty and wealth, they made sure that their heroes and heroines were genteel even though they had been born into poverty; they were always well bred, however barren their early environment had been.

The later 1840s and the 1850s also saw an ever-growing emphasis on what has been called the "employee virtues"—industry, punctuality, order, and loyalty to one's employer. While industry and orderliness had always been emphasized in children's stories, earlier writers usually referred to them in terms of school lessons and domestic chores. For young readers, managing time well meant making room in their lives for both duty and pleasure; above all, it allowed them time enough to be "useful to others." Later attention to these good habits focused directly on industry and employment and came first, before individual needs or personal pleasure.

In the new fiction, only honest business people prospered; those who engaged in "sharp practices" sooner or later came to naught. The new writers so closely tied together the relationship between personal virtue and economic success that the older idea that the practice of virtue would ensure financial success came to be read in reverse: Success implied the practice of virtue.

The language of this new fictional style was different from the limited, restrained style of old; this was another sign of the changing focus on reading. The description of a young hero by his patron was representative of a new concern with outer, rather than inner, traits, perceived and dramatically described: "the burning brow, the flashing eye, and anon, the quivering lip and languid pulse." The language was no longer realistic but very symbolic. It is always easy to identify the youngster who is headed for success in any of these later stories. He is well favored, well spoken and well mannered. Somehow his background, however deprived when the story begins, has prepared him for a middle-class place in society.

All during the eighteenth century, series books were popular among children; however, when Jacob Abbott started to publish the *Rollo* books (1835) and Samuel Griswold Goodrich began his *Peter Parley* books (1827), which were two of the most popular series at the time, they were overwhelmingly successful. These books were generally not illustrated but some had steel engravings.

Juvenile literature began to take in more of the world outside the home; the new social order, regardless of how badly it was described or accounted for, appeared in, as well as between, the lines of this new approach.

A dime-novel detective story written in 1892 was motivated by the sensational murder of the Borden family. In this story the murders are not committed by the daughter, Lizzie. They are committed by counterfeiters, and Lizzie herself is quite liberally fictionalized. This publication shows how current happenings became the subjects of dime novels. This particular story was issued just two weeks after the actual murders. *Dash Dare on His Mettle* had to be written in a hurry soon after the murder, no doubt, for the author to be able to cash in on a very popular and exciting leading news story.

It was only natural for the Borden case to become the subject of a dime novel. Dime-novel plots capitalized on murder, mayhem and mystery; all of these were present in the Borden killings. In addition to the "three m's"—murder, mayhem, and mystery—the Borden case, with Lizzie herself as a possible murderer, depicted mayhem in the way the crime was committed and certainly mystery, since at that time the fact that a genteel, well-brought-up, kindly woman could commit this kind of crime was unthinkable.

Edward Stratemeyer wrote *Dash Dare on His Mettle, or Clearing Up a Double Tragedy*, which appeared in the Old Cap Collier Library.

In Stratemeyer's version of the murder Ella Canby (Lizzie) lives with her father and stepmother. Dash Dare is the investigator who finds clues about why the murder was committed. He spies on Robert Manning, a pseudodetective. As is typical of these dime novels, the action moves fast: Dash is captured, he escapes, he follows a "ghost," and he slips into an old mill, where he discovers a group of counterfeiters. He gets captured again, is left for dead and escapes again. He exposes the real murderer, Maddox; Ella is saved and all ends well. In these dime novels no matter how terrible and unseemly the criminals are, they are either dead or in jail by the end of the story. However threatened the supposedly innocent women are, they are saved just in the nick of time by the hero. The hero might have been in a fight or two and might have nearly been taken in by the unknown villain; he might even have used violence on suspected wrongdoers, but he always does it on the side of right and honor.

Since Nathaniel Hawthorne introduced Natty Bumppo, American heroes have often been people who are controversial in terms of the current laws and mores. Stratemeyer's retelling of the Borden story is representative of this rightness and of these American cultural ways and beliefs.

It is hard to avoid seeing that the more these authors of children's fiction turned their attention to the outer world, the more they were awed by what they saw, and the more they looked for artificial solutions to provide the escapism of melodrama.

Concepts of poverty and charity were also changing over this forty-year period of social change. Juvenile fiction of the 1850s revealed how far the clear lines of ethics of earlier years had changed in the face of the social complexities of the time. The duty of a Christian believer toward the poor, once so plain, was now quite unclear and complicated by a great number of current considerations. The duty to the poor did not end, but it was made more complicated by the necessity not to encourage the "idle in their idleness or the vicious in their vice." Goals were much more materialistic than they had been in earlier children's stories. The definition of success and the rewards of virtue were pictured in material terms; the hero of a typical story of the 1850s achieved economic and social success much faster than did most of his counterparts in earlier juvenile fiction. Where earlier writers liked to see their heroes economically comfortable and socially respectable, the new writers wanted them extremely successful and socially situated without par. How different the situation had become since the sketchy beginnings of readings for youth a hundred or more years earlier. It would seem that sensational literature had been developed to satisfy a new mass of undiscriminating young readers, ready and eager for vicarious excitement, if no better material could be put within their reach.

Propp Interpretation

The American dime novel offers one of the best opportunities of all popular fiction for the description and classification of a large group of books having common traits. Because the dime novel was written for popular reading, it has not been considered a serious contributor to the development of mainstream American literature. Now the current, renewed interest in the studies of this genre look at the dime novel from the point of view of literary history or sociology but not at the more formal analysis of its narrative structure. This chapter explains the codification of the traits of the dime novel and describes how these interrelate. The methodology used is a theory of generic "markers" that are based in part on the original work of Vladimir Propp and in part on a semantic theory of "scripts" or "frames" developed by contemporary linguists like Victor Raskin. Although the subject matter in this text is diverse, a system of organization is used to arrange the contents of the novels in a predictable pattern. It is through an investigation of this pattern that the dime novel, as a generic class, may be best understood.

Vladimir Propp in *Morphology of the Folktale* uses a model for the fairy tale based on a kind of sequential chain. He describes levels of steps within the narrative sequence that must occur before another step can occur. Some of the steps may be omitted in the sequence, but the steps that appear must follow a prescribed order. Propp's formulation of sequential progression has become a fundamental concept in the formal analysis of generic forms, but his influential model does not take into consideration the mechanisms, or "markers," that trigger the changes from one narrative step to another. These markers are important because they help the reader distinguish among sets of forms by limiting the meaning of certain key concepts within a specific genre.

The dime novel is described here synchronically, as a system of generic forms. A convenient schematization for the description of the dime novel formula is a three-part narrative division: the initial situation, the principal action, and the resolution.

The Initial Situation

The principal action in a dime novel is preceded by a kind of prelude that is revealed in the beginning of the tale by the narrator or is implied or revealed in the resolution of the tale. The prelude constitutes the action that takes place before the actual opening of the narrative. The prelude may be understood as a "loss" (L) sustained by the hero (H) (sometimes the loss is a secret loss known only to the hero and the reader). The concept "sustained," a marker that connects the hero and his loss, has a restrictive meaning in the tale. "Sustained" means either stolen or lost. Generally the hero loses one of two possessions, a girl or gold, but it is important to emphasize that this loss often goes unrevealed until the conclusion of the tale.

Graph 1 Prelude

The prelude may be graphed simply as

```
H————————L
(a) sustains = stolen, lost
(b) L = gold, girl
```

Graph 2 Prelude

Because of his loss, the hero becomes an "outsider" (H1). He lives like the frontiersman on the outside of civilized society, or he lives like the outlaw outside of society's law. Because he is an outcast or "loner," the hero often assumes a disguise to prevent others from learning his true identity. It is important to note here that the hero's position as outsider in the narrative is the result of a foul deed perpetrated against him; his girl has been kidnapped, his wife killed, or his gold stolen. The hero does not shun society; he is forced out. Adding this step to the graph, we have the finished prelude:

```
H————————L
         / \
        /   \
       H     H1
(c) H1 = Outsider
```

Graph 3 Prelude Complete

As an outsider, the hero displays certain physical traits that are characteristic of every dime-novel hero. Thomas D. Clark explains that the dime novel heroes "were the noble hunters who stood more than six feet tall, had coal black hair, black eyes (if not black, then cold gray ones), his limbs were hard and sinewy, he walked with a free and easy but compact grace, his hearing was superb, he could smell to perfection, sense his way about in the dark, keep his hands off the women, use a knife with dexterity and swim the Mississippi River with as much facility as the average, heavy-footed settler could jump a spring branch. Another important trait worth noting is the hero's speech; unless he is in disguise, he speaks standard Victorian English.

Early in the narrative the outsider hero encounters an "insider" who has traits similar to his own. The insider is an honorable man (HM) who is brave and resourceful, only a notch below the hero himself. The honorable man is a stalwart citizen of the community, a position he has earned through courage and hard work. The encounter between the two is generally a rescue of the insider by the hero.

H1————————HM
(d) encounter = rescue
(e) HM = insider

Graph 4 Initial Situation (Marker 1)

Because of their natural compatibility, a friendship begins, and it is revealed to the hero that the honorable man owns an important possession (X). The honorable man has come by this possession through hard work or love. The important possession is usually a girl (a daughter or fiancée), but it may also be gold or land. "Earns" means that the possession, if it is a girl, loves the honorable man, or if the possession is gold or land, it has been discovered or inherited.

earns
HM————————X
(f) earns + loves, discovered or inherited
(g) × = girl, gold, or land

Graph 5 Initial Situation (Marker 2)

The villain (V) enters the narrative by stealing the honorable man's possession. If the possession is a girl, the villain kidnaps her; if the possession is land or gold, he steals it outright, or he swindles, defrauds or blackmails the honorable man.

X————————V
(h) stolen = kidnap, rob, swindle, blackmail

Graph 6 Initial Situation (Marker 3)

Like the hero, the kidnapped heroine and nefarious villain are stock characters in the dime novel. Clark describes the heroines as "luscious maidens ... paragons of beauty and virtue." The villains were "renegade white men who trafficked with the Indians, counterfeited money, speculated in land and way laid travelers." It was not unusual for them to be pockmarked or slashed across the face with hideous knife scars. Their beards and hair were long, scraggly and greasy. Their clothes were worn and filthy, and their language was vile and profane.

The initial situation brings together the principal characters and sets the stage for the remaining action in the novel. Diagrammed, the initial situation looks like this:

```
       sustains
H————————L
          / \   encounters            earns            stolen
         H   H1←————————HM————————X————————V
```

GRAPH 7 INITIAL SITUATION COMPLETE

Two very popular texts, Edward S. Ellis's *Seth Jones* (1860) and Edward L. Wheeler's *Deadwood Dick on Deck* (1878), may illustrate more clearly the formula for the initial situation in the dime novel. In *Seth Jones*, Alfred Haverland, who was "a splendid specimen of 'nature's nobleman'" is chopping wood when the "eccentric" Seth Jones confronts him. Seth warns Alfred about a possible Indian attack. Because Seth warns the homesteader about the impending attack, Alfred befriends Seth, and they return to Alfred's family, which includes his wife and daughter, Ina. The daughter is "a beautiful creature" … rather small in stature, but graceful as a gazelle, free from the restraints which the conventionalities of life impose on those of her age. She has dark hair, gathered in a roll behind, fine expressive blue eyes, a perfect Grecian nose, thin lips and a full chin, rendering the profile perfectly straight from the forehead downward." The Haverlands plan to depart by river, but before they can make their escape, the Indians capture Ina and attack the family.

```
       sustains
H————————L
          / \   encounters            earns            stolen
         H   H1————————HM————————X————————V
             (Jones rescues
             Haverland from                        kidnapped
             certain death by
             the Indians)      (Haverland has a
                               beautiful daughter,
                               who loves her father)
H1 = Seth Jones
HM = Alfred Haverland
X = Ina
V = Indians
```

GRAPH 8 INITIAL SITUATION FOR SETH JONES.

Seth's loss forms part of the resolution of the tale, and the loss answers question like Why does Seth visit the Haverlands? Why does he help them?

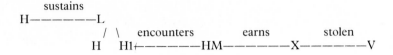

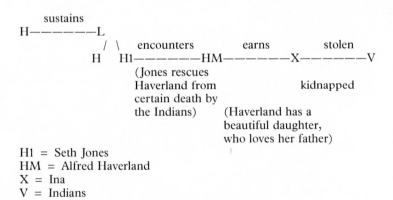

The Principal Action

After the initial situation is established, the greater part of the dime novel, the principal action, takes up the complications that develop as the hero attempts to regain the honorable man's stolen possessions. The first step of this process is the union of forces between the hero and the honorable man:

joins
H1————————HM
(i) joins = assumes responsibility for quest

GRAPH 10 PRINCIPAL ACTION (MARKER 1)

In *Seth Jones*, Seth, immediately after he saves the family from certain death, begins to search for the kidnapped Ina. At the burned-out Haverland homestead, Seth meets Everard Graham, who has come to marry Ina. Graham and Ina were betrothed in childhood, but, of course, Seth is unaware of this. With Seth in the lead, they set off to find Ina, and "the entire safety of the company rested with him [Seth]."

After the hero and honorable man join forces, they suffer a series of death threats from the villain, but it becomes obvious that the villain cannot win in a fair fight with either the hero or the honorable man.

confronts
HM————————V
(j) confronts = honorable man's or hero's superiority demonstrated

GRAPH 11 PRINCIPAL ACTION (MARKER 2)

Seth is captured by the Mohawks because of Graham's clumsiness. Seth endures torture, but he still manages to write messages on rocks to his comrades, whom he somehow knows are following. Haverland and Haldidge, a hunter whose family has been massacred by the Indians, have indeed set out upon Ina's trail. They discover Graham, who has escaped from the Indians by outrunning four of the fastest Mohawk braves, and the three men follow the Indians' trail, which is periodically punctuated with Seth's notes. Although Seth is a captive, he helps the trio overcome his Indian captors, freeing himself and Ina. In his confrontation with the bloodthirsty Mohawks, Seth clearly demonstrates his superior cunning and bravery. Because he cannot fairly defeat the hero or honorable man, the villain must turn to dirty tricks. The villain sets traps for the honorable man, and the traps always reveal the villain's treachery and deceit.

sets traps
V————————HM
(k) sets traps = villain's treachery and deceit displayed

GRAPH 12 PRINCIPAL ACTION (MARKER 3)

Although they outnumber the Haverland party ten to one, the Indians in *Seth Jones* set numerous ambushes. The Indians refuse to fight man to man because they realize their inherent inferiority.

```
      defeats
H————————V
(l) defeats = enables HM to regain lost possession
```

GRAPH 13 PRINCIPAL ACTION (MARKER 4)

When Seth detects and overcomes the last Indian ambush, he enables Haverland to return safely home with Ina.

The Resolution

The conclusion of the dime novel reunites the honorable man and his lost possession, and this union enables the hero to recover his own private loss.

```
      regains
HM————————X
(m) regains = return of gold, girl or land
```

GRAPH 14 RESOLUTION (MARKER 1)

After the return of the possession, a series of disclosures occurs. In *Seth Jones*, Haverland discovers that a new house has been built for him by the settlers; Graham reveals that he is Ina's childhood sweetheart, and they marry; Seth Jones turns out to be Eugene Morton, the lost love of Mary, Haverland's sister. This revelation is the prelude that occurs before the actual beginning of the narrative. Completing this initial first step we have:

```
     sustains
H————————L
          / \
         H   H1 (outsider)
(Mary is lost through deception of old lover)
H = Eugene Morton
H1 = Seth Jones
L = Mary Haverland
```

GRAPH 15 PRELUDE OF SETH JONES

Mary marries Seth. Seth becomes an insider, a member of the frontier community.

```
     replaces
X————————L
          / \
        H1   H (insider)
```

(n) replaces = return of hero's girl or gold

Graph 16 Resolution (Marker 2)

The completed diagram for the narrative sequences of *Seth Jones* is:

The Initial Situation

```
   sustains
H————————L
        / \
       H   H1   encounters         earns          stolen
                ————————HM————————X————————
(Mary is lost through              (Haverland has a
deception of old lover)            beautiful daughter,
                                   who loves her father)
                (Jones rescues
                Haverland
                from certain death
                by Indians)                        Kidnapped
```

H = Eugene Morton
H1 = Seth Jones
L = Mary Haverland
X = Ina
V = Indians

The Principal Action

joins	confronts	sets traps	trap broken	defeats
H1——————	HM——————	V——————	HM——————	H1——————V
(Seth leads search for Ina)	(Seth endures torture, demonstrates superiority)	(ambushes for Haverlands' party)	(Seth detects ambushes)	Seth detects final ambush; leads Haverland home)

The Resolution

```
HM————————X————————L
                  / \
                H1   H (insider)
(Haverland reunited with         (peaceful and safe return
daughter; Graham reunited        of Ina enables Seth to
with lost sweetheart)            marry Mary and become
                                 Eugene Morton, insider)
```

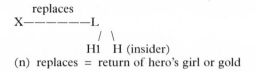

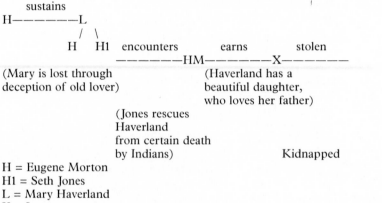

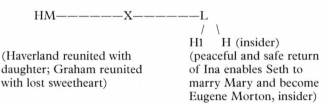

Library Research Collections

The Rare Book Room of the Library of Congress started to collect paperbound American works: the dime novels dated between 1860 and 1915, with titles and authors that would surprise many book-collecting aficionados. It was a collection of which Anthony Comstock would not have approved.

Valta Parma, Library of Congress librarian, is the far-sighted librarian who saw the value of these highly criticized pieces of literature. "What in the name of Ned Buntline do you think you're doing?" was the question asked at the time. What Parma was doing was salvaging dime novels from an atmosphere where the books, collected by the Copyright Division, were deteriorating. In time he built a collection of over 20,000 titles and in so doing saved many valuable books that would have otherwise been destroyed. It is believed that Parma read *Dime Novels; or, Following an Old Trail in Popular Literature* by Edmond Pearson, and this helped him in his decision to do this collecting.

Through copyright deposits, the Library of Congress has accumulated a dime-novel collection of nearly 40,000 titles from 280 different series. The prolific publishing houses of Beadle and Adams, Frank Tousey and Street and Smith are well represented. There is a particularly extensive run of the Seaside Library, the series founded by George Munro in 1877. Issues are recorded in a card file by publishers' series. The Seaside Library is indexed separately by author or title. Selected dime-novel series have been microfilmed. Sadly, however, many thousands of other dime novels and other Americana collections had already been lost by this time—by people who didn't see the value of this literature. We are therefore grateful to the few, interested people who saved this genre for today's scholars. Unfortunately, dime novels and paperbacks were printed on cheap, self-destructing paper. Only in the last thirty years or so did some librarians begin a well-planned action to save this pulp-type fiction.

At least two factors account for this critical neglect. On the one hand, as was mentioned, almost all dime novels written between 1860 and 1902 were printed on cheap pulp paper—a very poor medium. Thus only a relatively small number of dime novels survive today, and the majority of these are not always available to scholars; they are either in the hands of private collectors, or they are deteriorating, uncatalouged and unmicrofilmed, in the book vaults of a few major libraries. On the other hand, literary critics have, sometimes with good reason, neglected dime novels because of their mediocrity. But it was the dime novelist—working almost anonymously for large publishing houses, meeting unreasonable deadlines, and assuming that sales were the accepted measure of success—who gradually, over a period of more than fifty years, shaped the dime novel's most characteristic elements.

It was these first, large, national publishing projects that gave the American reading public "escape" literature. The function and meaning of dime novels can be summed up in one word—escape. Throughout the standard critical works of the day, these stories were defined as subliterary—as daydreams, wish fulfillment, with no other purpose than escape, even if only for a short time, from a humdrum life of work.

Dime novels depict an inside view of American life in the late-nineteenth and the early twentieth centuries. These stories brought to readers a wide range of subjects and scenes, portraying common beliefs about men and women, about minorities and ethnic groups, and just about all kinds of everyday subjects. They certainly are a bit of America's literary past. If for no other reason, these dime novels are an important part of our cultural history.

As these novels gained more success, with each issue selling in the hundreds of thousands of copies, they came to be recognized as part of our literary heritage. While disapproved of by many parents, educators and librarians of the time, they were nevertheless widely read. They told stories of adventure, detection and even some moral virtues that drew a lot of readers.

"Serious" writers looked down on "hack" material just as many writers of today ignore the popular paperback romances that one finds in supermarkets and newsstands. Because of the low reputation this literature earned in its early days, it has been unjustly neglected until recently. However, there are scholars who are making profitable use of this material for studies in popular culture. Everybody who is interested in this field knows that these books sold a vast number of copies and therefore had an influence far beyond their stated literary merit.

Among the most important aspects of dime novel research is the study of format. It is also a feature that is little discussed except in general terms. The physical appearance of an individual dime novel says much about the marketing strategy of its publisher. As part of an ongoing series, each dime novel had to say to the browser at the newsstand in its day, "Buy me." Because the Library of Congress collects "trash literature" which, when properly housed, has become a primary source for research students to study, we are in luck today. These dime novels have become important historical and literary research materials. Today the dime novel is finally being recognized as an important part of the popular fiction genre. The study of this popular fiction is now becoming more and more academically respectable.

"The papers collected here reflect the varieties of interdisciplinary research current on these literary genres. The essays put to rest any lingering doubts on the scholarly value of collecting and studying dime novels, series books and paperbacks.... It [is] clear that the study of this material is central to the understanding of American culture," says Larry E. Sullivan, former chief of the Rare Books and Special Collections Division of the Library of Congress.

The Library of Congress has one of the largest collections of dime novels in the country. Its contribution is especially important for today's students of popular culture and for the new interest in universal literacy, even library and publishing history. Although the emphasis here is on fiction studies and popular literature, dime novels had a more far-reaching impact. In fact, interest in such literature has increased with the growing study of the life of the common man and of his reading habits. Volumes of these materials are scarce.

Early in the 1900s the original dime novels became collector's items. One of the earliest and most successful collectors was Frank P. O'Brien, who later donated his collection to the New York Public Library. This collection has about fifteen hundred Beadle publications, with some original manuscripts, copyrights, personal correspondence between O'Brien and dime-novel writers, and other miscellaneous notes.

George Hess was another early collector; his large collection went to the University of Minnesota, where it has been carefully preserved and expanded. The Hess collection is now the largest, dime-novel collection in the United States. This Hess Collection contains George Munro's Seaside Library, ordinary editions in their Children's Literature Research Collections. It also contains (Norman) Munro's Library (1883–1888); Harper's Franklin Square Library (1878–1893); and Lovell's Library (1882–1889). Some of these were microfilmed and are available to the public. The Popular Culture Library at Bowling Green State University has about two thousand dime novels, story papers and nickel weeklies, especially the *Tip Top Weekly*. The Library of Congress has the second largest collection and contains many of the earliest dime novels in pristine condition, including the first edition of *Malaeska*, the first dime novel ever published.

The *Happy Hours Magazine*, the journal for the Happy Hours Brotherhood, a group of dime-novel collectors, is trying to unite all dime-book appreciators: "So in 1924 we had it all planned to start the Happy Hours Brotherhood and to publish the *Happy Hours Magazine* as the official organ.... [The] first issue [was] Jan–Feb 1925 and was published every two months.... The last number was published in 1931.... In early 1932 it became *The Dime Novel Round-Up*.... The magazine has been published on schedule for 51 years, 1931–1981." Two collectors from New England need to be mentioned because they began to publish a paper for other collectors called *Dime Novel Round-Up*. Ralph Cummings was one of the pioneers; later Edward T. Le Blanc and J. Randolph Cox took over the publication. Started in 1931 this small publication became unrivaled for information, and it is still published today.

Among examples of the best research in the dime-novel field are the writings of Albert Johannsen, Edward T. LeBlanc and J. Randolph Cox. These writers have explored the field in depth and have shown, among other things, the tremendous breadth in the subject matter of dime novels, the variety of publication formats, the different types of reader populations they addressed, the violent attacks against novels by various "reformers" and the uneasy truce between the publishers of dime novels and the "respectable" purveyors of literature to the American public.

A major attempt to sort out the literature was made in Montague Summers's massive *Gothic Bibliography* (1940), where late-eighteenth and nineteenth-century sensational literature of all kinds is listed, as well as three-volume novels. Summers attempted to assign authors and dates, but his list is not free of discrepancies and errors.

Decline of the Dime Novel

When did the downfall of the dime novel begin? What was the cause of the decline in dime novel sales?

The end of the dime novel is the result of several sideline developments in the 1890s. One, the Panic of 1893 hurt financially many small and large publishers. A number of publishers went out of business in the 1890s including Beadle and Adams, whose demise seemed to mark the end of an era. Many of the authors who were lucratively employed in writing dime novels started to write for the new pulps, the series books and the movies. Two, the International Copyright Agreement of 1890 ended the pirating of foreign fiction. This helped in making cheap pulp books and series books quite profitable. The pulps took most of the adult readers, and the series books the younger readers. Three, the Loud Bill concept changed rival postal rates from the little book to the magazine format. In 1839, Park Benjamin and Rufus Wilmot Griswold, publishers of story papers, published cheap reprints of novels in paperback form, identified them as periodicals, and distributed them at the lower postal rates. These were 50-page 5" × 8½" pamphlets. This format was copied by many other publishers and distributed in the same way until the introduction of the Loud Bill which took the cheap postal rates away from these publishers. Four, the introduction of the Sunday newspapers which were cheap and contained some of the normal dime novel material, slowed demand. Both the dime novel and the story paper formats were dying out in the face of these reasonably priced Sunday newspapers and the cheap pulp magazines. Five, the 1890s saw the beginning of the printing of the inexpensive magazines, both the slick and the pulp variety.

For over 60 years the dime novels filled the need for the low cost fiction that the public demanded, but competition arose in the attempt to give the reader more for his money and the pulp magazine was born. As early as 1888 the thick magazine *Argosy* appeared, an outgrowth of the juvenile story-paper, *The Golden Argosy*, and in 1903, the *Popular Magazine* appeared. *The Blue Book* started in 1904 under the title *The Monthly Story Magazine*, and *All-Story* magazine was brought out in 1905. These were followed in rapid succession by many others. The 32-page dime novel had passed into history. Movies, however, were the last straw. The first nickelodeon appeared in Pittsburgh in 1905. A nickel allowed the user to watch a short film that lasted about 10 minutes. Some subjects covered were fashions and current events backed up by piano music. Nickelodeons were placed in public buildings everywhere. These moving pictures on one or two reels offered more adventure than the print material could. It had appeal to viewers of all ages, so when one had a spare nickel or dime to spend on pleasure, the new moving adventure was more appealing than the book.

There were also genuine changes in both sensational fiction and working class culture that left the dime novel behind: a leftover attitude of the common people, the real producers of the culture of the nineteenth century. Readers also missed that popular dime novel detective Frank Merriwell.

Many of the now popular pulps were outgrowths of the earlier dime novels. Dime novel characters Frank Merriwell and Nick Carter now appeared in pulp magazines. In fact, these two famous characters and a number of others, including: Old King Brady, Young Wild West, Frank Reade, and Diamond Dick, and real bandits such as the James boys, spanned the change from dime novel to pulps. It is, again, difficult to make any distinctions as to when one ended and the other began. Probably none of these were, in the strictest sense, real characters in any dime novels. They belonged to the cheap libraries or the weeklies of varying titles geared toward boys.

By 1907, the *Atlantic Monthly* had published a eulogy of the dime novel: Charles M. Harvey's *The Dime Novel in American Life*. Harvey's opening paralleled that of W. H. Bishop, writing in the *Atlantic* 28 years earlier: "Are not more crimes perpetrated these days in the name of dime novels than Madame Roland ever imagined were committed in the name of liberty? It looks that way. Nearly every sort of misdemeanor into which the fantastic element enters, from train robbery to house burning, is laid to them."

So it can be inferred that dime novels first "died" in the 1870s when the first series of Beadle's novels stopped being printed and distributed.

They "died" again in the 1880s because the public was tiring of the sensationalism. They "died" again some years later when postal rates caused the change from the little book to the magazine form. They "died" once more because of the popularity of the cheap nickel libraries and the boys' weeklies, which were very like the old dime novels in a different format. They "died" when the new yellow journalism became available and they "died" at the hands of the moving pictures, and for all anyone knows, by the World War and by Prohibition.

Postal Regulations

Cheap fiction publishers were always subject to postal regulations; the first cheap books of the 1840s had reduced their price by appearing as newspapers and newspaper supplements, which had lower postal rates than books. Their demise came when the post office began to charge book rates for these supplements. Many publishers lost their business because of increased costs of distribution.

The success of these cheap publications depended on inexpensive distribution. The American News Company, in business from 1864 to 1904, was one of the most successful firms in this area. It and others had a monopoly in the field of story paper, magazine and dime novel distribution to newsstands, and other outlets for these publications. They handled the Beadle and Adams, the Street and Smith, Robert Bonner, Norman Munro and Frank Tousey publishers, among others. Those names were the unchallenged leaders.

Ainsworth Spofford, the Librarian of Congress in 1888, appeared before the United States Congress supporting legislation excluding dime novels from second class postal rates (for periodicals) and placing them in third class rates (for books). Henry Harris, Assistant Postmaster-General, also recommended this legislation.

Eugene Francis Loud, a representative from California, brought to Congress a bill to exclude all this kind of literature from second class rates. At the time, the difference between second class and third class was seven cents per pound of mail.

There was a long, harsh battle between the post office officials and the publishers of second class mail. Loud's bill lost in 1900. He said,

> This law has been so distorted and warped.... we now have a condition prevailing whereby any publication under our American sun, even to the advertisement of a private business, a dime novel, or a side show of a circus is admitted as second class matter.

In 1901 Charles Smith, Postmaster-General, excluded these libraries (the paper publications handled as newspapers) from second class mail.

Publishers' Weekly commented, "At last the Postmaster General found courage, to make the startling and revolutionary ruling—that a book was a book and not a periodical." Publishers, specifically George Munro's Seaside Library, Harper and Brothers Harper's Franklin Square Library, John Lovell's Library and Norman Munro's Library, printed libraries and mailed them under the classification of periodicals which was cheaper than shipping them as books. Even though these publications were numbered and dated, there were, for the most part, full length books. Even if the book was too long for one issue it was issued as part two with a separate number and date.

Finally, in 1904 the Supreme Court decided that these libraries "were books and not periodical publications within the meaning of the act of March, 1879." This was the conclusion the Librarian of Congress made 16 years earlier.

Series Books

Series books have been part of children's literature from the early pamphlet novels to Horatio Alger's more booklike publications to today's paperbacks like Ann Martin's *Babysitters Club* or hardcover books like Anne McCaffrey's *Dragonsong* series. Because easy-to-read adventure stories, identifiable by a singular hero or heroine, were in demand and because readers, who identified with certain heroes and heroines, wanted more of the same, series books evolved. However, series books are not often found on approved reading lists because of the misunderstandings and preconceived ideas that dominate this genre.

Like the young audiences of the early movie films, series book readers share a common history; both were targets of reformers' ardent and, for the most part, ineffective, movements to control children's leisure activities, including reading. Series books are considered, like the dime novel, to be a subculture of the literary world. Both dime novels and series books have been conveniently ignored or actively attacked. The attacks have gone on at least from the time when Louisa May Alcott singled out Oliver Optic for his supposed use of slang and sensationalism. He, along with Horatio Alger Jr. and Harry Castlemon, was among the first writers of series books for boys.

Series books emerged at about the same time as the dime novel. These entertaining books with young heroes and young villains had a great deal of exciting, improbable action. These books were also basically innocent; they contained no sex, no heavy violence, and no didactic teachings and had easy-to-understand dialogue; and while the heroes were almost always Anglo Saxons, presented as superior to all other nationalities, that was typical of the times. These stories were also excessively patriotic, another sign of the times. They were never examples which would lead young readers to a sinful and wanton life as critics predicted.

Most of the stories were based on the ongoing fight between good

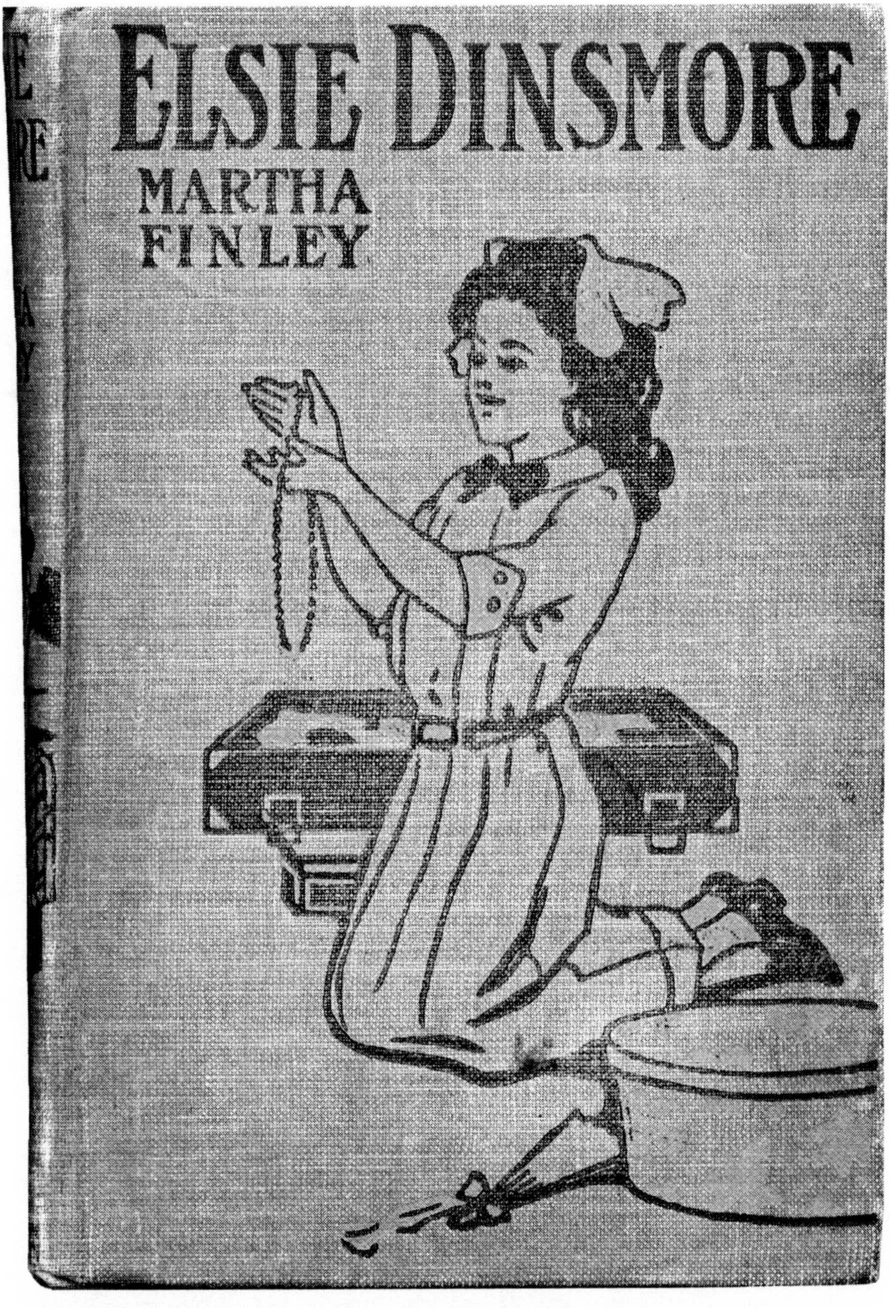

Elsie Dinsmore: This title was the first of 28 Elsie stories. 395 pages with 8 pages of advertising.

and evil, and even though the readers and writers of these books had a few moral shortcomings of their own, the heroes and heroines of these stories never did. Although these early series books were aimed at boys, there was a girl readership to be satisfied. The girls' series books were important because they tell about an entirely new female field of reading of the time. For the first time in the history of children's book publishing, girls were the subject of their own unique kind of adventure story. Appearing under collective heroine titles such as *The Motor Girls*, *The Outdoor Girls* as well as *Betty Gordon*, and *Ruth Fielding*, these books were a planned offshoot of the boys' adventure series. The series' appearance and their instant success indicate that young girls were a real reading audience in society and perhaps for the first time affected the reading process as well as the purchase of fiction books.

The market for these books grew in the late 1800s and prospered even more during the first half of twentieth century, when any number of small publishers promoted and printed thousands of children's series books. Because these books were very popular, profit-seeking publishers printed, publicized and circulated them in great numbers. They were the stock reading fare of the young people. They were bought by the millions and avidly read by responsive teens and as such were an important factor in influencing and building the ideas and attitudes of these young readers. In spite of the importance of the series books in developing the national character—and this importance has been recognized in numerous studies—there has been little critical research into the series book field itself until recent years.

Catherine Ross, professor at the University of Western Ontario, Canada, found series books to be the favorite books among young readers for the last hundred years. She also found that they were the objects of scorn by teachers and librarians.

As the offspring of the dime novel the series books were conceived by Edward Stretemeyer in the late 1890s. Aimed at the preteen and teen reader, the series included *Nancy Drew*, *Hardy Boys*, the *Bobbsey Twins* and many, many others.

The elitists were so sure that Nancy Drew would corrupt girls' minds that H. W. Wilson Company, the largest manufacturer of library supplies, refused to print the index cards for the card catalog for Nancy Drew and even published a list of nearly sixty authors who should not be circulated by libraries, all of them authors for series like *Tom Swift* and the *Bobbsey Twins*.

Along with this was the belief that fiction was useless because children learned only from facts. Here's a quote from 1850: "No part of education ... No dissipation can be worse than that intended by the perusal of exciting books of fiction ... a species of a monstrous and erroneous nature." What made series books especially evil for children was that they were "addictive." Children weren't content to read just one; they'd read the second, third, and so on.

Ross's research shows that young readers often complain about the difficulty in getting started in a new book, wading through the early chapters and characters. In a familiar series, this difficulty is averted. This "instant start"—instead of frustration—plays a large role in luring students into regular reading.

The Stratemeyer syndicate, between 1910 and 1931, produced as many as twenty-five different series simultaneously. Because the syndicate hired ghost writers, or more specifically, writers who used numerous pseudonyms to write for different publications, bibliographic information became almost impossible to verify. Even the customarily reliable *Children's Books in Print* does not bring series books together as such. Recently, because of the growing number of serial books, keeping the bibliographical information current is still a challenging task. In the single year, 1988, Grey Castle Press in Sharon, Connecticut, published seven "Nancy Drew Files" editions, from *Buried Secrets* to *White Water Terror*. Reprints of other Nancy Drew books appear in the *Nancy Drew Hardy Boy Supermystery* and the Nancy Drew Mystery Stories series. In 2002 *Listening Library* released a Nancy Drew audio book, *The Secret of the Old Clock*. However, with this growth in the number of publications and a renewed interest in series books, there are now societies devoted to the works of a single author, and these collectors are a good source of information on certain series books. There are also special collections, series book collectors and dealers, librarians and curators, and professional journals that are devoted to a single series or single author.

The early series books usually ran four to six titles each, but the later ones had more titles per series. (A list of series books and their individual titles is appended.) Most of these serials revolve around a single character. Serials were roughly comparable to today's sequels. Sequels differ in that even though the characters are the same from book to book, the story line is continuous, whereas series stories have the same characters, but each tale is not necessarily a continuation of the previous book. And although librarians and other literary people looked down on serial books, they accept the sequels of today.

The writing of these series books was somewhat different from the writing of dime novels. It took a unique knack to be able to write both the dime novel and the series books. The writers had to be more creative, more adept in the use of language and more attuned to the reading market in both genres. These authors had to develop a style that appealed to both the youth and the adults; success in the dime-novel field was not necessarily indicative of success in the series book field.

There was also a definite handicap, due to the heavy criticism of the dime novel.

It is to the credit of these authors that they gained fame in both fields. Three reviewers that did a great deal of research into dime-novel series are Albert Johannsen, Edward T. Le Blanc and J. Randolph Cox. Their investigations have shown that the dime novels and series books have more to offer the scholar of literature than has been shown so far.

The five most successful writers who wrote both dime novels and the early series books are Edward Ellis, W. Bert Foster, Harrie Irving Hancock, William Gilbert Patten and Edward Stratemeyer. Even though they were heavily criticized for both their dime novels and their series books, they made an important contribution to juvenile literature.

Edward Ellis was a noted writer of dime novels, but like so many others he also wrote for children when this trend proved profitable. Many of his children's books had a Western frontier background, such as *Ironheart, War Chief of the Iroquois* (1899) and the popular Log Cabin and Young Pioneer series. Then later, again going with the trends of the time, he started writing current topic books such as the *Flying Boys* and the *Launch Boys*.

Harrie Irving Hancock, author for the publishing houses of Frank Tousey, Norman Munro and Street and Smith, also wrote under the name of H. Irving Hancock. It was under this name that he wrote most of his series for boys. He wrote eleven different series books with the main thrust on adventure, military and sports. He also wrote over sixty boys' serials for *Golden Hours* and more than fifty hardcover books in his boys' series. His dedication to the physical health of all young men showed in his books on jiujitsu and his articles in the *Frank Manly Magazine*. He is best remembered for his nine stories about Dick Prescott and friends. They live in Gridley and go through school together. Two of them later go to West Point (a four-volume West Point series). Two others move west and become engineers (a five-volume Young Engineers series). Two others go to Annapolis (a four-volume Annapolis series). All six meet again in the Conquest of the United States series (a four-volume series).

W. Bert Foster, the third of these five outstanding authors, also wrote both dime novels and series books. The first couple of books he wrote are the famous Ruth Fielding books for the Stratemeyer syndicate. He also wrote the Grace Hill and Alice Emerson girls' books. Foster wrote many hardcover boys' series books as well. For instance, *The Frozen Ship* was part of the Clint Webb series. Then for the adults he penned the Cap'n Abe Cape Cod novels.

William George Patten was a writer of sports stories. He is best known as the author of the Frank Merriwell series. Out of the many dime novels he wrote, twenty-eight were reprinted as hardcover novels. He also wrote the sixteen-volume Big League series under the name of Bert L. Standish, the *Rex Kingdom* series using the name Gordon Braddock and the *Oakdale* series as Morgan Scott. He, like so many of these authors, wrote under many pseudonyms.

Although many of the same authors wrote different books under different names, actually these were known as the publishers' "house names." Well-known examples are the Bobbsey Twins, Tom Swift, Nancy Drew and the Hardy Boys. It's true that Mildred Wirt Benson was the author of 13 of the original stories in the Nancy Drew series, using the pseudonym Carolyn Keene. She wrote 23 of the first 30 Nancy Drew mysteries. She sold her stories for $125 each and received no royalties.

The apparent and deep-seated concern of self-appointed critic Franklin K. Mathiews was with the quality of books by William Gilbert Patten, W. Bert Foster, Edward Stratemeyer, and others, especially their sensationalism, but it seems clear that he was troubled with the dime-novel origins of these authors. However, in spite of the desperate, rancorous attacks on these writers, their dime novels and series books, there is no need to defend these authors. They were competent, interesting and vigorous writers. They wrote what their readers wanted, and they did so successfully both for the dime-novel market and the series book demand. These writings were a major factor in the development of literature for children and young adults for the next hundred years.

Story Papers

Was escape reading a legitimate pastime? Was escape reading's influence upon the many readers they reached good or bad? These are the questions that literary critics and sociologists asked when story papers began to show widespread appeal. If the mediocre story plots and poor production techniques were better, would their influence be good, or was it that they were popular because their content and substandard appearance made them "bad"?

Story papers, cheaply produced and widely distributed, needed to be gauged by the readers themselves. At the newsstands the reading public had the choice to buy and read what they wanted. They were free to choose the "better" publications over story papers if they wanted to. However, if they had done that in great numbers, the companies that published authors like Robert Bonner of the *New York Ledger* and Francis Smith, of *Bertha, the Sewing-Machine Girl: or, Death at the Wheel* (1871), would not have been as successful as they were.

Story papers were never considered literarily acceptable, but we should judge them by their social impact, not their literary value. To judge these as unacceptable is as moralizing as the practices of the ministers of early-nineteenth-century sermons. At that time, most of these critics thought that *any* reading material was sinful.

Good literature can offer escape as well as well as "trash," but over the years publishers have found that great literature seldom satisfies the general reader looking for a way to escape from the trials of everyday life. To many people who were hard working, generally poor, whose lives and jobs were monotonous, these story papers offered a wide world of adventure, mystery, love, and escape.

These early story papers were actually weekly newspapers. They contained serialized stories, along with religious sermons, humor, local news and fashion commentary. Their aim was to offer something for every member of the family. Although the early story papers were intended for adults, the publishers tried to include something for the children as well. In some issues they included a column or two devoted to children: a short moral story, a puzzle, a song or poem. The *Fireside Companion* carried a column called "Apprentices' Biographies." It contained illustrations and information about apprentices in many industries. Most of these biographies were of the Horatio Alger ilk. The *Family Story Paper* carried a section known as "For the American Boys and Girls." This section ran for the first five years of the paper's existence.

Favorite themes of these story papers was the importance of learning a good trade (the "Education of the Shop" was a regular column) and how one's personal contribution is important for American democracy. This was stressed in clever and appealing ways.

From time to time the papers printed an entire page devoted to children's interests. This page included an illustrated serial story for the boys, songs and poems for the girls and a fairy tale for the youngest children. Sometimes it included a puzzle and a section devoted to answering questions asked by children and answered by the editor. Although the answers stayed clear of behavioral problems, the questions that asked about careers and schooling were openly answered. However, as the serials became more and more popular, the children's sections were dropped. The "answers" column continued, but the longer articles were also dropped, as were other interest sections. They also encouraged confidential letters from their adult readers. Usually the letters to the editors in newspapers were from men, not women, but in the case of story papers, more women than men asked questions.

From 1845 to 1885, when they made few editorial or format changes, story papers were read by millions of people. The publishers were smart enough to know that the attraction these papers had for many Americans was the fiction, not the rest of the material. Because of this realization, the papers became more and more literary until they cut out almost all the news and built up their collection of serial stories.

The success of these papers lasted for years because there was a market for them; many people who lived in remote places were eagerly looking for reading material; they were looking for anything at all to read and were not choosy. For these reasons story papers deserve a place in the development of books and reading in America.

By today's standards, one would think that these stories would prove to be unpublishable because they were very badly written, printed even worse and were only ephemeral. However, today we still see lengthy serials, using the twin "good" and "bad" situations as a vehicle for holding the readers' attention.

Usually the story papers had black-and-white illustration on the front page, emphasizing the featured serial. It might be a single illustration

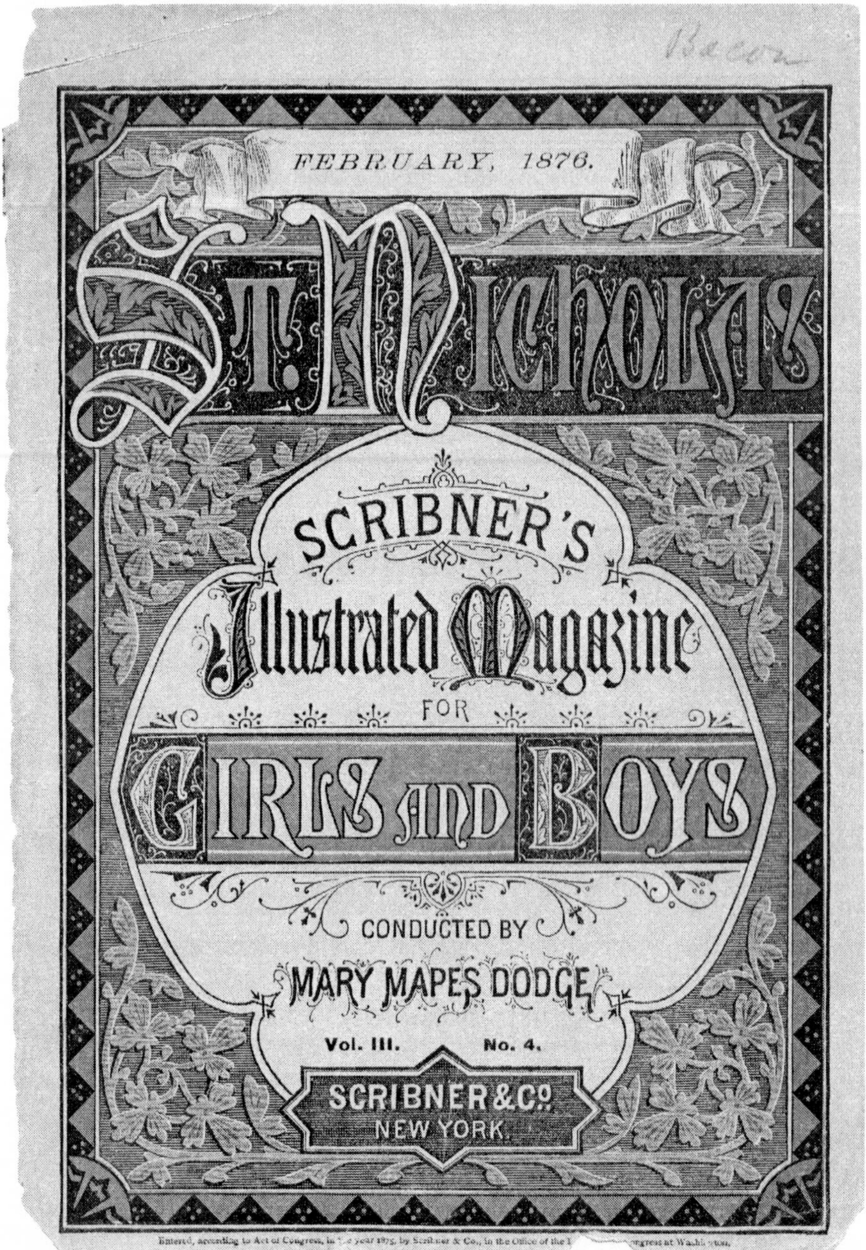

St. Nicholas Magazine: Scribner's Illustrated Magazine for Girls and Boys. This edition contained "The Boy Emigrants" by Noah Brooks. Published from 1873 until 1940.

showing a specific event taken from the book, or it could be a series of pictures showing very graphic scenes from the stories in that issue, even if these illustrations were not really indicative of the story. Their only function was to sell copies of the story paper.

In the early 1950s, a survey showed that the top-selling magazines were *Ladies' Home Journal*, *Life*, *McCall's*, *Reader's Digest*, and *Saturday Evening Post*. Just as *Life* was number one among the illustrated magazines at this time, *Harper's Weekly* and Frank Leslie's *Illustrated Newspaper* were in the forefront in their time. The survey showed that then, as now, illustrated publications were preferred by the readers—the story papers then and the highly illustrated magazines now. The contents, from the beginning, appealed to the whole family: romance for the women; adventures for the men and Alger-type success stories for the youngsters. Because of this, these story papers had a bigger circulation than the dime novels and the cheap libraries. When the reader was faced with being able to buy only one publication, the story paper was the logical choice because its offerings appealed to a greater variety of reading tastes.

In 1839 the first American story paper appeared. Park Benjamin and Rufus Griswold published the *Brother Jonathan Weekly*, a giant-sized story paper measuring 22" × 32". It was meant for the casual reader. By now most of the millions of people living in America were literate. These readers needed material that was both entertaining and cheap. Because distribution was made easier by using the railways and production was made easier by the use of the new, steam rotary press, the market was ripe for new reading material, and the story papers filled this niche. For the most part, these story papers consisted of several short stories, chapters from serial novels, and a few news items, organized in a newspaper-like format. The *New York Mercury*, the *Fireside Companion* and the *Saturday Journal* were among the earliest of these papers.

These story papers were not threatened by the dime novels. The dime novels were appealing to the market for low-priced fiction that had been encouraged by these weeklies, but they did have some impact. The story paper people who entered the field after *Saturday Night* started were large companies who already published dime novels, boys' and girls' series and anything they could get from England. This pirating included Carlyle's *French Revolution*, the New Testament and most of the books about the highwayman Claude Duval. They did take one precaution: Over each story paper serial was printed the statement "This story will not be printed in book form."

The dime novels grew in popularity in close connection with the story papers. It is nearly impossible to separate the two. Almost all the story paper serials were reissued in paper-covered booklets because the same setting of type was used for both story paper columns and the double-

The Youth's Companion: Established in 1827, it was circulated weekly until 1927, when it became a monthly. Ten cents a copy or $2.00 a year. Size is 11" × 14"; 26 pages.

columned, dime-book pages. Even in the latter half of the century, the same story, although not always the same type, served for both the story paper and the dime novel.

The *Family Story Paper* featured many detective stories, each with a different type of detective, including "Sleuth" and "Dash Dare," along with specialized detectives such as custom house detectives, shadow detectives and any kind of detective that would interest the reading public. There were Canadian detectives, Irish ones and even a female detective who was introduced as one of the "best detectives in the world."

As more and more Irish migrated into New York in the seventies and eighties, the story papers started to appeal especially to them. Not only did Irish detectives become more numerous in the criminal districts of New York City, and not only did Irish immigrants suffer heroically through appalling trials, but Ireland's own freedom became of deep concern, especially to the *Fireside Companion* and the *Family Story Paper*.

Eugene T. Sawyer, the author of the Nick Carter series and a writer for the *New York Weekly*, said that low-priced reading material was not confined to the bottom rungs of the economic or educational ladder. He had gone "into bookshops and seen bankers and capitalists gravely paying their nickels for the same tales their elevator boys read."

No one wanted to be associated with "low classness," and sensationalism was low class. The authors of these story paper serials had to add something representing "class" to their crime stories, so, scattered throughout the publications were pieces of advice to young boys not to talk to strangers, especially country boys and seemingly polite city women. There were snippets about the horrors of prostitution, the unhappiness of women in such roles and man's cruelty by using different standards for prostitutes than for himself. The papers also had short stories about licentious and mercenary villains.

The intellectual magazines could take more liberty with their style, that is, they could use colloquialisms, slang and idioms, but the story papers could not; they needed to prove to their faithful readers that they were reading real literature. This gave the writing a pompous style and is the difference between the story papers of the time and the popular literature of today. Today, even popular literature (tabloids) may use slang and colorful language with abandon, and they certainly do so.

The contrast between yesterday's story papers and today's magazines is not as great as it at first appears. The best offerings of the best magazines of today are certainly better than those offered in the story papers, but the worst stories of these papers are no worse than some of today's best sellers or earlier pulps.

The *Saturday Evening Post*, in its early editions, published many serial stories from the story papers, capitalizing on their popularity. These serial stories, appearing not only there but also in many women's magazines, were read by educated people who found them acceptable, but in the early nineteenth century, readers of the story papers were, if not laughed at, at least looked down upon.

All story plots had to have a theme of opportunity. The main character, born into one of the lower classes of society, had to take advantage of any opportunities that came his way and improved himself by the end of the story. If writers were concerned with opportunity, publishers were concerned with equality. Civil War problems were never mentioned, and race and nationality were equally proportioned in all stories, according to the population.

Did the story papers cut into the readership of the "better" publications? It is argued that it did not; it just created a new reading public, just as today the tabloids do not reduce the readership of magazines and newspapers, but have made a larger reading audience that wasn't there before. Just because the writings of Mrs. Southworth were there doesn't mean that this reading public would have picked up Nathaniel Hawthorne.

In 1856 the American economy was good and people could afford more reading material. Most Easterners took the *Tribune*, and almost everyone took at least one story paper.

In Boston the printing house of Edward, Henry and George Williams began in 1841 to publish their first story paper. It was titled *Uncle Sam* and cost three cents per copy or a year's subscription for $1.50. It was a normal-sized sheet (like today's newspaper) but only had four pages, as was the standard of the day. It had a masthead, and the front page always had a picture. The Williams publishing house was also printing Prentiss Ingraham's stories. Soon the Williams's business, at first very obscure, was issuing weekly newspapers as well as cheap books.

Because of Buffalo Bill the name Ingraham became a household word. Everyone was reading his stories although his name was interchangeable with cheap, trashy literature. The *International Magazine* spoke of Ingraham as the author of "a large number of the vilest yellow-covered novels ever printed in the country." In 1847 the Knickerbockers described him as one "who has within the last ten years written more immoral works than any other of the many penny-a-line scribblers to whom the 'cheap and nasty' school of ephemeral publications has given birth." Nonetheless, compared to some dime novels and the later pulp fiction Ingraham's stories were rather tame.

In 1840 the *American Union* appeared. It featured full-blown stories in each issue. Oliver Optic was one of the writers for this publication. He later went on to write for the weeklies and other publishing houses. At this time he and other writers who would later write for children wrote for adults.

In 1860 Beadle and Company saw a market for dime novels as the popularity of the story papers closed the market to their earlier pamphlet books. The *New York Picayune*, a humorous weekly, said in 1852, "'Yellow Kivered Books' [pamphlet books] have fallen into distaste with 'prentice' boys and love-sick damsels, since the issue of the bed blanket weeklies." In 1869 the *New York Weekly* hired Ned Buntline, who had a long and successful career with the story papers. His first story was *King of the Sea; a Tale of the Fearless and Free*, then came *The Black Avenger of the Spanish Main; or, the Fiend of Blood*. He contributed *The Volunteer; or, the Maid of Monterey* and *The Red Revenger; or, the Pirate King of the Floridas*. Many Buntline titles were self-explanatory. An extensive advertising campaign preceded his first contribution, leading to a circulation increase to 300,000.

The *New York Weekly* also published "A Thrilling Tale of the Mexican War" by Charles Averill, a writer who had previously written for Williams's. Dietrick Lager, who for a while wrote for the little Boston weeklies, dropped out of the literary world. In 1871 he was back again with "Abler Holder's Bound Boy; or, the Poor Relation"; from then on his position on the *New York Weekly* was secure. Both Ingraham and Buntline wrote Buffalo Bill stories. Although he was real (William Cody) he was depicted a bit differently both from real life and from each author's point of view. Ingraham saw him as a nonsmoker, he spoke English fairly well, never using slang or swear words. Buntline saw him as a smoker, if only occasionally; his control of the English language left something to be desired and included some colorful speech patterns. It was in 1869 that the *Weekly* announced that it had "secured the exclusive services of three of the best romance writers in America." These three were Edward S. Ellis, Ann S. Stephens and John W. Watson. (There is more information on these authors in the chapter on Dime Novels in the section "Other Writers.")

Edward Ellis was the author of the famous Seth Jones books as well as many other dime novels. The *Saturday Night* stated, "He needs no encomium from our pen. He stands first as a writer of Indian stories and has gained a reputation second only to the renowned Cooper." Even though he was a salaried employee under the name Edward Ellis he could assume as many pseudonyms as needed, and he used many.

Because the *Saturday Night* owners had specific agendas, Ellis was expected to follow the directions made by the subscription campaigns. While writing for *Saturday Night* Ellis visited Texas, St. Louis, Chicago and New York to gather material specifically for these areas. He wrote these four books under the name of E. S. St. Mox.

The story papers carried city-life stories in serial form for their young readers. Although the hardships of city life, represented by the slums, was not the best fare for children, these stories were read by young and old alike. The only thing that changed was the age of the main character. One such story, by Edward S. Ellis in *Saturday Night*, had an eight-year-old boy, high up in a tree, about to rescue a two-year-old girl from the clutches of a gorilla. The publishers advertised this story as being for both adults and children. The adult readers did not hold it against the story just because the hero and heroine were young, any more than the youngsters held it against Buffalo Bill because he was an adult.

John Watson never met the advertised "best romance writer in America." He wrote under the pseudonym of Ian Maclaren and was the author of the *Drumtochty* series.

Beadle's papers offered more stories about Native Americans than any other publisher. There was always a cadre of young boys who couldn't get enough of these frontier and sea stories. Of course there was always a definite market among America's young boys, and the Beadle organization capitalized on this. They catered to boys with articles about baseball; it also carried ads for athletic clothes with their prices. This latter enterprise came about because of the articles written by Ned Buntline, who called himself "Dashing Ned." His clothes were a sign of the "in" look among the young readers.

Not only the stories but the news and editorials were also aimed at young boys, including giving advice to mothers on how to raise these youngsters.

George Munro, who earlier worked for the Beadle house, was among the first to issue family story papers. He, in partnership with two other men, started this rival house on a combined capital of $600. This new publishing company grew to be a great "mover and shaker" in this field. Before Munro retired he was a member of the council of New York University and a generous donor to various other universities.

The demand for both story papers and dime novels put pressure on Beadle. Even though it was distributing some three thousand dime novel titles, George Munro issued stories every day of the year from his Seaside Library. These publications were delivered directly to the subscribers' homes along with the daily paper. This low-priced literature, be it dime novel or story paper, was big business, and Beadle and Adams had to compete.

Some of the story papers for boys (from the age when they began to read until their late teens) included *Boys of New York*, *Young Men of America*, *Golden Hours*, *Happy Days* and *Golden Weekly*. The stories in these papers were later reprinted in dime-novel format. (A list of these early papers is appended.) After a while most story papers were catering to boys; special serials were offered; same-age heroes were the subjects most often covered. Even though girls were readers, they were assumed to be part of the family, not individuals, as the boys were.

In 1864 Cassell's bought some paperbound manuscripts from Sylvanus Cobb, a Boston publisher. These were then published as "decently sensational" and were intended for adults. One of these stories was *Marie Bernard; or, the Felon's Daughter*, a serial by Horatio Alger. Most of the Cobb novels had the old Frederick Gleason copyrights, but these had expired some time ago. The novels were pirated by dime-novel publishing houses and by country newspapers all over America. Sometimes one of the lesser-known papers would take even a recent Cobb story and pirate it.

The idea behind the plot was to take the heroes as near to the edge of decent morality as possible, or even let them almost step over the line, but make sure you rescue them in time. Cassell also published R. L. Stevenson's *Black Arrow* (1888); *Kidnapped* (1886); and *Treasure Island* (1883).

The *People's Literary Companion* printed Revolutionary War stories by William Eyster. He also contributed stories to the dime-novel publishers. Prentiss Ingraham contributed to almost every issue during the late 1870s and early 1880s, some of them about his hero, Buffalo Bill. Ingraham also was writing weekly installment stories for Beadle plus a few short stories for Vickery's *Fireside Visitor*, an advertising sheet. Now that advertising was a stable part of the printing industry, many innovations were possible; magazines could come in different sizes, they could include color illustrations, and the contents could be aimed at a larger audience.

When Mrs. Alex McVeigh Miller had financial problems, she gave up the thought of becoming a great poet and decided to write stories for the story papers. She spent a great deal of time studying the style of the current weeklies. Instead of just reading the papers she concentrated on what these stories had that appealed to potential readers. Then she started to write, determined to ease her family's financial burden. When she finished *The Bride of the Tomb* she submitted it to the *Family Story Paper* and had greater success than she could imagine. She eventually wrote some seventy novels

The Bride of the Tomb was just what the reading public of the time wanted. It is a ghoulish story of a girl, kidnapped, wounded, and buried alive with hope of being saved later by a well-meaning friend. In the May 16, 1881, edition of the paper, part one of *The Bride of the Tomb* was on page five. The following week it was on page one. Miller had, in her terms, "achieved the first page." The previous week's lead story—a detective story by "Young Sleuth"—was found somewhere on the inside pages.

The Bride of the Tomb was on the front pages for the next two issues. When the story was about half told, the editors offered Miller a contract for her next story, "An Old Man's Darling," and promoted advertising for it. They were also bold enough to make an offer of $5,000 to any person who could write a better story.

Edgar Allan Poe wrote in the *Philadelphia Dollar Newspaper* in 1844 "The Premature Burial." There was now an interest in predeath burials.

In almost any week between the early 1880s to the 1930s in either Norman Munro's *Family Story Paper* or George Munro's *Fireside Companion*, a reader could have found one or sometimes two of Laura Jean Libbey's romances in print. (Libbey claimed that her first story was accepted in the 1870s, when she was fourteen, by Robert Bonner of *The New York Ledger*, but he told her to come back when she was eighteen.) Libbey's stories were popular because she wrote at a time when these family story papers sought feminine stories for publication; the demand was at its peak; circulation exceeded 350,000 copies per week. For only five cents a week, a reader got a sixteen-page paper with the popular series installments. Because these story papers were meant for the family, the publishers needed stories that would appeal specifically to women. Romances, whether set in an exotic foreign locale or in a small hometown or a large city like New York, were especially sought after. Even though part of Libbey's success was because of her own patience and perseverance, a large part was because of the publishing world that demanded a number of good stories for women readers.

Part of Libbey's popularity came from her ability to fulfill the regular weekly demands, but her financial success came from the lucrative contracts she negotiated. During the 1880s, because of her popularity, publishers were willing to negotiate very profitable contracts with her to write for their paper for a fixed rate per installment for a fixed number of years. Libbey was able to have a new story begin as the old one ended or sometimes have a new installment in the same issue as the last installment of the previous story. After a three-year contract to write exclusively for two papers (Bonner's *New York Ledger* for $100 per week and Norman Munro's *Family Story Paper* for $60 per week from 1887 to 1889), Libbey negotiated a three-year contract with George Munro's *Fireside Companion* starting in 1889 for $150 per installment. She renewed this contract for five more years. Then in 1897 she returned to write for *The Family Story Paper*.

She again negotiated a five-year contract for $150 per installment, an agreement which earned for her $39,000 in five years. When she was under contract with one paper, only reprints could be published by any other company, that is, publish them as if they were new, not stories which had previously been published. Also, in the 1890s she had a contract with George Munro's *Fireside Companion* for $200 a week; it was a contract to edit Munro's *New York Bazar*. This contract had a two-year renewal. It is said that Libbey earned $30,000 in three years.

After the original success of Libbey's stories, the policy of reprinting kept her stories going on and on and made her a valuable author for Street and Smith's *New York Weekly* and other publishing houses. Street and Smith's bookkeeping for the Eagle series showed a news company order for 14,855 copies for Eagle #566, a reprint in 1908 of one of Libbey's novels. What made her stories valuable for reprinting in such numbers? Beginning in the 1880s, using the theme of working-girl fiction, which had already been introduced in the older story papers, she took advantage of this interest in stories about girls working outside their homes. In the 1830s and 1840s, as girls started working in the mills, the working girl as a unique character for stories for women began to become very popular. Every fictional heroine was typically given her choice between a forced marriage and the fate that was worse than death. She in this situation often found a penknife or a long silver pin handy but always decided, after long consideration, not to use it. Only in the later, and more cynical, eighties did the heroine actually try to commit suicide. In the *Family Story Paper* they actually had a girl consider suicide simply because she was out of work and starving. Moreover, it was suggested that the poor girl could hardly be blamed for her morbid thoughts. That's why the *Family Story Paper* was regarded as immoral by some of its competitors.

The publishing houses not only issued a nonending supply of stories with working girls as main characters but also encouraged the working girls themselves to read and spread the word among their friends about these stories.

The family story papers, which had published Libbey's early stories, had been replaced later in the century by periodic magazines. In 1922 Street and Smith began *Smith's Magazine*; this monthly magazine of fiction started *Love Story Magazine*. Announcing its topic in its title, this fifteen-cent semimonthly was very successful. It reached a circulation of 100,000 within a year and 600,000 by 1929 and then shifted to weekly publications.

It was about the mid-eighties that the circulation of story papers began to decline. The *Fireside Companion*, because it was running three Old Sleuth stories at one time, had a circulation of 280,000 in 1885, but the end of this greatness was in sight. Was it the Sunday supplement that killed the story paper? Was it cheap books? Or was it the fact that this type of ephemeral material was doomed to become tiresome?

The Sunday supplement editors saw to it that their paper was flexible and, even if it did once in a while offer a serial story, was committed to being different from the story papers. The dime novels, now selling for a nickel, were still doing well among the young audience of readers. Street and Smith were still putting out dime novels.

It is said that the decline of the story paper is not as surprising as the fact that it lasted so long. People were looking for something new because the offerings of the paper was losing its allure and becoming repetitious. The reading public was ripe for something new, if not in content, then in its appearance.

Comics

Comic strips and comic books are an important part of American life. It is estimated that more than one hundred million Americans read the comics. The strips, as originally produced, were meant to be humorous and were therefore called comic strips or funnies. Through the years there has been a shift from basic, unabashed humor to human interest, adventure and social issues. Research shows that the general public, including children, read comics to satisfy their desire for action, excitement and adventure. The humorous situation in which the characters find themselves is immediately apparent. The story line is built on suspense, and the conclusion is quickly reached. Comics are easy to read: Even if the words are difficult, the pictures carry the story; the dialogue is limited and to the point. The good guys and the bad guys are easily identified. It is believed that a comic strip appearing in the *San Francisco Examiner* called "The Little Bears and Tigers," printed in 1889, was the first comic strip in America to appear regularly and was enjoyed by many newspaper readers. James Swinnerton was the artist who offered this light touch as a change from the daily news.

Later, on February 16, 1896, the first colored comic strip appeared. It was presented as a panel, drawn by Richard Felton Outcault, and appeared in the *New York World*. The title was "The Great Dog Show in M'Googan's Avenue." A funny little kid was the main character; he was dressed in yellow and soon became know as the "yellow kid." He became so popular that he appeared in another comic panel called "War Scare in Hogan's Alley." They were the first six-box cartoon series. This was the beginning of what we know today as the "funnies," appearing in all the daily and Sunday newspapers.

Just a little later on, December 12, 1897, the "Katzenjammer Kids" strip appeared in the *American Humorist*. The Katzenjammer Kids, direct descendants of Max and Moritz, were first created in the *New York Journal* in 1897, and that strip is the oldest strip still in existence. Max and

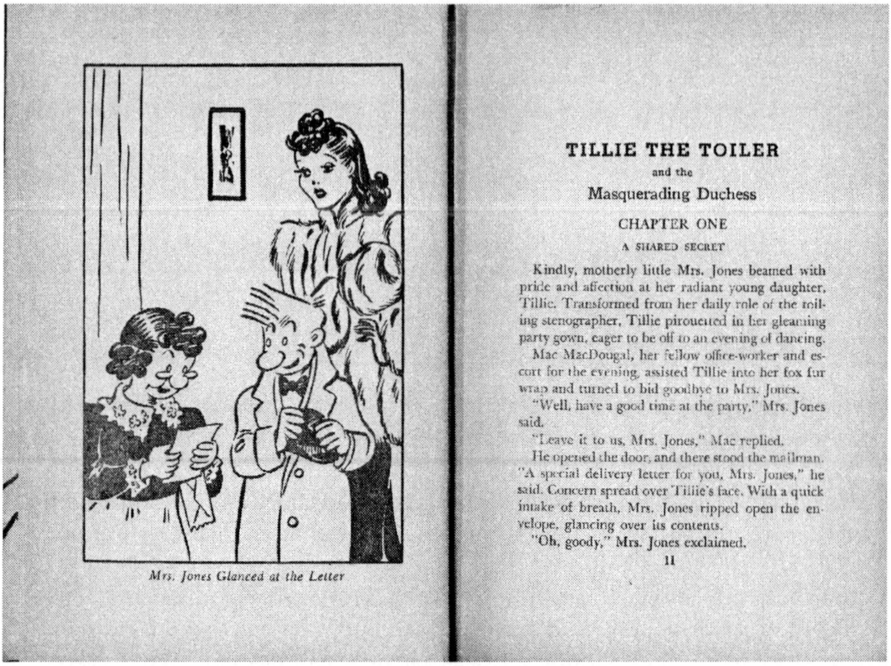

Mrs. Jones Glanced at the Letter

TILLIE THE TOILER
and the
Masquerading Duchess

CHAPTER ONE

A SHARED SECRET

Kindly, motherly little Mrs. Jones beamed with pride and affection at her radiant young daughter, Tillie. Transformed from her daily role of the toiling stenographer, Tillie pirouetted in her gleaming party gown, eager to be off to an evening of dancing.

Mac MacDougal, her fellow office-worker and escort for the evening, assisted Tillie into her fox fur wrap and turned to bid goodbye to Mrs. Jones.

"Well, have a good time at the party," Mrs. Jones said.

"Leave it to us, Mrs. Jones," Mac replied.

He opened the door, and there stood the mailman. "A special delivery letter for you, Mrs. Jones," he said. Concern spread over Tillie's face. With a quick intake of breath, Mrs. Jones ripped open the envelope, glancing over its contents.

"Oh, goody," Mrs. Jones exclaimed.

11

***Tillie the Toiler:* "Based on the famous newspaper strip by Russ Westover." This is an example of books based on popular comic strip characters. 248 pages.**

Moritz were two pranksters appearing in comic verse in Germany, created by Wilhelm Busch in 1865. Krazy Kat, often thought of as the best example of American comic strip art, was the creation of George Herriman and began appearing in 1910. Krazy Kat, Ignatz Mouse and the policeman Offisa Pupp form a triangle of unrequited love, set against a surreal background. This strip was drawn by Rudolph Dirks.

With this strip an important movement took place in the daily funnies. Now story lines were actually given some thought and were written; this meant that each panel was sequential, and an actual story evolved, moving from panel to panel very much like the format of the moving pictures. The stories had a cast of characters who appeared regularly and in identifiable outfits.

Rudolph Dirks is also credited with putting the dialogue in balloons, the balloons being in the same panel where the speech was occurring. This made the comics funnier and caused more laughter among the readers. This technique is still in use today after over one hundred years.

Other celebrated American strips of the early and mid-twentieth century include "Little Orphan Annie" (1924), "Dick Tracy" (1931),

"Li'l Abner" (1934) and "Peanuts" (1950), which includes the dog Snoopy.

Many of the popular Big Little Books published later grew out of these comic strips. There is more on this in the following chapter, Big Little Books.

Ironically, none of these artists, Rudolph Dirks, Richard Outcault and James Swinnerton is given any notable credit in the field of children's literature, including the art produced in comic strips and Big Little Books, at least it was not found in any of my research.

In 1919 the *Daily News* of Chicago offered a way for young artists and writers to succeed by giving more space to the comics in the daily newspapers. "Dick Tracy," "Little Orphan Annie" and "Moon Mullins" were the direct result of this new practice. In the 1930s the *New York Telegram* offered their readers "Alley Oop," which became very popular. Alley Oop was a cave man. He was a likable hero who had a wife and a pet stegosaurus.

There is a distinction between the comic strips in the newspapers and the comic books known more commonly as simply the comics. The comic strips were designed for whole family reading. These may have been funny or silly, romantic or fantastic, but they had been precensored and proved to be harmless. The comic book, on the other hand, is something a child may buy for himself and read alone or with other children. Even though "Archie," "Bugs Bunny," "Little Lulu," "Mickey Mouse," "Loony Tunes," and a few others may be harmless, good clean fun, and popular with children, it was still thought it would be better to bring children to better reading with a different kind of reading material which still had equal child appeal. Because by the time children reach the teenage years, these innocent comic books were being dropped while sexy romances, jungle perils and crime horrors were gaining popularity. The plots of these new comic books are basic: The hero solves any and all crimes, saves the world from an outer-space invasion or rescues the "damsel in distress." This is not totally foreign to our American culture. Our first popular novels, such as James Fenimore Cooper's popular novels, had heroes with unique personal attributes like Hawkeye the woodsman, who, with outstanding senses, saves the story's nice, innocent ladies from outside harm; he does this again and again. This is not much different from Superman, with his unique abilities, saving Lois Lane time and time again.

Today the majority of blockbuster movies are based on the same superhero mentality. The distance is not far between the heroes in *Deerslayer* and Steven Seagal. A new movie was released in 2002 called Spider-Man, a film based on forty years of Marvel comic books, and at least two more Spider-Man movies are in the works.

There is the typical American optimism in these comic book stories, too. It is an attitude in which everything is possible, including defeating a common enemy or saving the planet from an invasion of evil-looking and even more evil-thinking space beings. There are no sad or failure endings in comic-book stories, only "to be continued."

In general, comics have four characters who are repeated in most of the stories: one, the hero, pictured as very muscular, dressed in a costume revealing this all too well; two, the villain, also very physical with his own costume and attributes that correspond to the hero's; three, the female, also very physical, and the clothes she wears reveals this; and four, the minor male, who could be the hero's sidekick or son. These are personified by Robin, Kato and Billy Batson, who could become Capt. Marvel by saying "Shazam."

Wertham's article in *The Saturday Review* quotes James A. Fitzpatrick, chair of the Joint Legislative Committee of New York, as saying, "We are alarmed over the continued violence in comic books despite the industry's self-regulating code. If comic books, as the industry claims, are the folklore of today, then the codes are the fables."

Wertham's solution is: "The time has come to legislate these books off the newsstands and out of the candy stores." The article tells about the crimes committed by children that supposedly never occurred before the comic books incited children and others to try these crimes. He quotes police officers and judges who believe there is an unmistakable connection between juvenile delinquency and the eager reading of comics by youngsters. (Where have we heard all this before?) Here are some quotes from his writings: Superman has "phantasies of sadistic joy in seeing other people punished again and again." "The Batman stories are psychologically homosexual." Batman's relationship with Robin is "a wish dream of two homosexuals living together." Wonder Woman was "the lesbian counterpart of Batman."

Dr. Wertham's book, *Seduction of the Innocent* (1955), and his other articles appear to be emotional and biased. That is because he based his study on the lowest common denominator of the publications; he chose the worst and most violent among the possible offerings to analyze. They were not taken equally with the less violent and more humorous among the output.

Amy Kiste Nyberg wrote in her seal of approval: The History of the Comics Code, that the poor printing quality of the comics would "spoil a child's natural sense of color."

The United States Senate began to investigate comic books through the creation of a subcommittee in 1954. The senators were concerned about "the possible deleterious effect upon their children of certain of the media of mass communication." This subcommittee found evidence of "murder, mayhem, robbery, rape, cannibalism, carnage, necrophilia, sex, sadism, masochism and virtually every other form of crime, degeneracy, bestiality and horror." In response the senate endorsed a "voluntary" publishers' code that covered language, content, visuals and plots of comic books. Among the provisions was the stipulation that "the letters of the word 'crime' on a comics magazine shall never be appreciably greater than the other words contained in the title. The word 'crime' shall never appear alone on the cover." Furthermore, "Females shall be drawn realistically without exaggeration of any physical qualities."

To offset this opinion John Townsend, in his book *Written for Children* (1974), says, "Besides the good books, children will read the not so good ones. It is a natural and healthy instinct to react against parental taste and to forge [*sic*] for oneself. It is surprising how some of the longest and most interesting reading lists will include popular series and comic books. We expect a lot if we expect a child to read only what will engage his mind to the full. *Tom Swift* and the *Bobbsey Twins*, *Biggles* and *The Famous Five* go down easily; the ideas and vocabulary are simple for the intended age group; the plots and situations are such as the authors know from long experience will touch off a ready response." Comics can be traced back to cave drawings, Greek vases and Bayeux tapestry. The first cartoon strip in Europe was seen in the early 1800s. Rudolph Topffer, a Swiss artist, created a strip which divided stories into individual picture frames and showed the continuous narrative printed beneath the pictures. He drew these comic pictures to illustrate novels for his pupils. These were fanciful with grotesque figures which were the forerunners of today's comic strip techniques.

During the 18th century William Hogarth of England printed a series of satirical drawings telling various stories. One of them was called "A Rake's Progress." In England, *The Comic Annual*, 1830, edited by Thomas Hood, although primarily aimed at the adult market, was very popular with the young. It was full of very bad jokes, semifunny stories in which many of the characters came to pseudosad endings, and had the sort of easy-to-understand humorous illustrations enjoyed by all those with an interest in humor, not only children. Hood wrote most of his material himself, and the series continued until in 1839, when the ninth and last volume appeared. They were then all bound in pictorially printed, paper-covered boards with red morocco spines.

The first British comic to appear regularly was Ally Sloper's "Half Holiday" (1884), which was published in London by the Dalziel brothers; it featured the adventures of a hard-drinking and disreputable ne'er-do-well. It was meant to entertain boys and young men.

In May of 1890 Alfred Harmsworth, a British newspaper proprietor, launched *Comic Cuts* and *Chips*, which were intended to capture the penny dreadful market; like other early comics, they contained many one-picture jokes as well as comic strips. *Chips* featured Wearie Willie and Tired Timmy, a pair of tramps. *Chips* and *Comic Cuts* survived until 1953. *Comic Pictorial Nuggets* started in May 1892, continuing as *Nuggets* from November 1892, until it ceased publication in March 1905; the *World Comic* ran from 1892 to1908 and was followed by the famous *Chums* in September 1902.

Then came the age of the comics, possibly remembered from one's own childhood, with names like "The Magnet," "The Gem," "The Bulls-Eye," "Tiger Tim Tales," "The Champion," "Chatterbox," "Hotspur," "The Jester," "The Marvel," "Merry and Bright," "Pluck," "The Rover," "The Triumph" and the "Wild West Weekly."

American comic books are more the descendants of our own dime novel, rather than the penny dreadfuls of England. Notable heroes of this genre include "Superman" (1938) and "Batman" (1939). (Jerry Siegel and Joe Shuster, cartoonists, sold the rights to the Superman character to DC Comics for $130 in 1938!) Later, various movie cartoon figures were also featured in comic books, for example, Bugs Bunny and Tom and Jerry. Comics in Britain have generally been for either children or adults. In America there is on the whole no such division. Moreover, American comic art comes in a different format—not in the style of the British comics (a weekly, illustrated tabloid) but in syndicated newspaper strips and in comic books.

In the past there has been much criticism of comics, both strips and books, especially during the horror comic phases, but they now attract less hostility than does television and have become an attraction for collectors, who pay large sums of money for rare back issues.

The Comic Book Collection of the Library of Congress has a sizable collection of titles. They date from the 1930s to the present. It is estimated that there are about 5,500 titles. They are made available to serious researchers in the history and the social influence these publications had on American culture. Because of the tenuousness of these paper books and the value of them as collectables, this restriction is necessary. There is a microfiche collection of the five most famous comic book series: Action Comics, Adventure Comics, All Star Comics, Batman and Superman.

In 2002 a new book, Comic Book Culture, was released by Collectors Press ($49.95). So there is still interest in this genre.

Big Little Books

Big Little Books (BLB) have their roots in children's literature in the late eighteen and the early nineteen hundreds. These are small, thick books with printing on the left-hand pages and illustrations on the right side. They are small, blocky and colorful. They measure 3½" × 4½" and are at least 1½" thick. The text was usually over three hundred pages of cheap newsprint, which, of course, didn't last long in pristine condition. They had cardboard covers, usually colored. Anyone, child or adult, could follow the story either by reading the text or by following the drawings. They promised adventure, some in exotic places, excitement, heroes and heroines with spectacular escapades, scary stories and humor to each reader. Many a child learned to read and to like books because of their pleasurable experience with these books early in life. They were not just plain books because some covers were looked on as art. In fact, the text drawings themselves were considered valuable art and are collected for this feature.

The Dell Publishing Company of New York, in conjunction with Whitman Publishing Company, was one of the main printers of these books. Later Whitman became part of the Western Publishing Company. Big Little Books is the name Whitman gave these books, and although the format and names varied over the years, this name became almost a generic trademark for these books, to the point where they were often referred to as BLB, and everyone in the printing industry knew what was meant. They often came out in series, as did the earlier chapbooks. These books were especially popular during the Great Depression years, the 1930s and 1940s, but they were still being published long after this date, even though their real beginnings were in the early comics and series books.

The stories were based on many different sources: newspaper comic strip characters, current literary personalities, radio shows, fictional detectives, space stories, motion pictures and others. Goldsmith Publishing

The Adventures of Huckleberry Finn: **An authorized, abridged edition of Mark Twain's famous story. Illustrated by Henry E. Vallely. 3½ × 4½ × 1½"; 424 pages. A Better Little Book; one of the many versions of Big Little Books.**

Company of Chicago used radio characters (e.g., Eddie Cantor, Jack Pearl, and others) in a series called *Radio Stars*.

Events from history is another theme used for these books. The World Syndicate Publishing Corporation used personalities (e.g., Kit Carson, Buffalo Bill and Daniel Boone) to reflect history.

The motion picture theme was the mainstay of the Engel–van Wiseman Book Corporation. In the Five Star Library series were *Little Minister* starring Katharine Hepburn and *Robin Hood* with Douglas Fairbanks. The Lynn Publishing Company of New York also put out movie-based books in a series called Lynn Books: *Tales of Two Cities* with Ronald Coleman and *O'Shaughnessy's Boy* with Wallace Berry and Jackie Cooper. Saalfield Publishing Company's movie-based books included *It Happened One Night*; *Little Colonel*; and *Our Gang*, and they also published "Popeye" and cowboy stories. Comic-strip based books were *Betty Boop*, *Little Orphan Annie*, and *Mickey Mouse*.

Another theme of the Big Little Books was outer space. Buck Rogers and Flash Gordon were the heroes of these books. Buck was a space adventurer who went from planet to planet fighting aliens and robots. Stories of Flash Gordon with his girlfriend, Dale Arden, took place mostly in and around the planet of Mongo. Both of these heroes were the forerunner of the Star Trek shows and movies of today.

Of course, adventure was another theme followed by these books. *Terry and the Pirates* by Milton Caniff is an example of this theme. The Tarzan series, *Jungle Jim* and *Don Winslow* are others. Crime was a popular subject for Big Little Books. Here we have Dick Tracy, Charlie Chan, Ellery Queen and others. Dick Tracy was created by Chester Gould. He was the typical, hard-nosed, gun-carrying fighter. His enemies were No Face, Mrs. Prune Face, Fly Face, the Rodent and others.

Interestingly enough, Dashiell Hammett, a well-known crime writer (*Maltese Falcon*) wrote a comic-strip series called "Secret Agent X-9," which was reproduced as a Big Little Book. The illustrator was Alex Raymond. Another theme of the Big Little Book series was the raw, untamed West, always with the loyal hero winning in the end. Nothing appealed to youngsters like the old cowboy and Indian games. Tom Mix, the Clint Eastwood of the 1930s, is a good example of the Wild West protagonist. He is the classic hero who fought scoundrels, drifters and rustlers. His fellow cowboys were Gene Autry and Roy Rogers.

Western stories were also peopled with cowboys like Buck Jones and Ken Maynard. One book of interest was *Flame Boy and the Indians' Secret because* it was illustrated by a Hopi Indian: Sekakuku.

Toward the end of the Big Little Book era there was a real interest in airplanes and pilots. Therefore, Tailspin Tommy by Glenn Chaffin appeared. One title was *Tailspin Tommy: The Dirigible Flight to the North Pole*. Another airplane series hero was Smilin' Jack by Zack Mosley.

Dahlia Messick was the first (and rare) female illustrator of Big Little Books. She changed Dahlia to Dale to overcome the female stigma attached to illustrators. Her heroine, Brenda Starr, was popular. An example is *Brenda Starr and the Masked Impostor*. There were three other female illustrators, but they were not as well known. Martha Orr illustrated

Apple Mary; Juanita Bennet illustrated *Treasure Island* and Marjorie Buell illustrated *Little Lulu*.

These books were intended for preteens with their tales of Dick Tracy, Flash Gordon and Tom Mix, so BLBs were carried by every dime store, newsstand and amusement center all over America.

There were also competitors: Little Big Books, Better Little Books and Fast-Action Books, but Big Little Books was the generic name that identified these books. It appeared on the cover of Whitman's first edition of Dick Tracy. *The Adventures of Dick Tracy* came out around Christmas time in 1932, a year before the true comic book made its appearance. BLBs were most popular between the years 1932 and 1938.

During the 1920s titles included *Fairy Tales*, *Sunny Hour*, *Friendly Animal*, *Forest Friend*, *Campfire Girl*, *Sleepy Road* and *Daddy Duck*. All of these were series. The most popular series, The Boy Adventure, which included titles like *Ted Marsh* and *Buffalo Bill and Pony Express* is what made Big Little Books a household phrase.

This was the time when prohibition was the law of the land, gambling was illegal and organized crime was making the most of this situation. The field was ripe for the likes of Red Berry and Dan Dunn. In the field of adventure there were many heroes and heroines. The good people prevailed, and the "bad guys" were vanquished, but before this happened there were cliff-hanging events that took the reader from one chapter to the next. Dick Tracy and Flash Gordon were by far the most popular characters featured in these publications.

These books were a continuation of the newspaper comic strips by being reprints. The stories appearing in these first books were reworked writings taken from the popular daily newspaper comics. The publishers noted when a certain comic strip reached a popularity that was acceptable; they acquired reprint rights, hired a cartoonist to draw the characters, rewrote the text and put these works on the market as Big Little Books. They almost always altered the original drawings because they had to fit this new format. The dialogue, which had appeared in balloons in the original comic strip, needed to be removed and replaced by text.

One of the Big Little Book artists that gained recognition was Alex Raymond, who drew Flash Gordon and Jungle Jim. Henry Vallely was an artist used often, and the books he illustrated were valuable regardless of text content. Then there were the caricatures of Dick Tracy and Buck Rogers; these artists were not particularly talented, but they gave the characters an exciting demeanor one does not easily forget. As mentioned before, none of these comic strip artists—Rudolph Dirks, Richard Felton Outcault and James Swinnerton—are given any credit in the field of children's literature, at least none that I have been able to find.

The movie industry in Hollywood and the Big Little Book publishers in New York worked together to promote movies and sell books. Many of the Big Little Books contained photos upon which a movie was based. Tarzan is a good example of this. The Tarzan books were popular, and the picture of Johnny Weismuller on the cover helped both industries. What can surpass Tarzan's leaping from vine to vine, herding elephants and succeeding in his missions of mercy? Likewise, one can picture Gary Cooper riding the range, tall in the saddle, taming the Wild West; and W. C. Fields making jokes and satiric remarks as he appeared in *David Copperfield.*

The books about movie adaptation were smaller, measuring 4¼" × 1¼" and had only about 250 pages, with photographs replacing the drawings on the opposite pages. Over time, there were many changes in size and number of pages. Some of these were single titles, not part of a series. Not all Big Little Books had the text on one page with illustrations on the next page. It appears that the more literary ones had more text than pictures. The Zane Grey editions were almost all text, albeit condensed from the originals.

It is estimated that 1,100 titles of this type of book were published in the first twenty years. Originally these books sold for either five or ten cents; now, if they can be located and are in good condition, they can sell for anywhere from $20 to $1,000. The most valuable books were those with popular characters. The most famous of these are Buck Rogers, Dick Tracy, Donald Duck, Little Orphan Annie, Mickey Mouse, Popeye and Tarzan.

Pulp Fiction

The fiction pulp magazines began to appear in the 1890s and were still being distributed in the 1950s.

Pulp fiction has been defined by Henry Steeger, president of Popular Publications, this way: "Pulps were the principal entertainment vehicle for millions of Americans. They were an unflickering colored TV screen upon which the reader could spread the most glorious imagination he possessed. The athletes were stronger, the hopes were nobler, the girls were more beautiful and the palaces were more luxurious than any in existence; they were always there at any time of the day or night on dull, nongloss paper that was kind to the eyes."

Another definition is offered by Charles Beaumont, who is both a book writer and a screenwriter: "Cheaply printed, luridly illustrated, sensationally written magazines of fiction aimed at the lower and lower-middle classes. Were they any good? No. They were great.... They inspired, excited, captivated, hypnotized and, unexpectedly, instructed the restless young who have become responsible adults."

They were printed on rough woodpile paper with untrimmed edges and measured about 7" × 10". A common characteristic is their richly illustrated, colored covers.

Frank A. Munsey, a retired telegrapher who lived in Maine, wanted to start a profitable weekly magazine. By changing his former children's magazine, *The Golden Argosy*, into a tabloid-type magazine for adults, called the *Argosy*, he, hypothetically, started the pulps. As he sees it, "the story was more important than the paper it was printed on."

By using the new, high-speed production equipment he reduced costs and increased circulation; he put out a magazine that sold for a dime and contained lively and entertaining stories. These periodicals specialized in adventure, intrigue, romance, science fiction, sports and Westerns. These pulps were important in launching the careers of such writers as Raymond Chandler, Dashiell Hammett, and Ellery Queen.

They gave us Philip Marlow, Sam Spade, Nick and Nora Charles, and the Fat Man.

Street and Smith started the *Popular Magazine*, which featured work by H. G. Wells and H. Rider Haggard.

When the pulps first began to appear, they were innocent enough. It was the new postal regulation that gave them a push. This new regulation made the dime novel more expensive to mail, but did not affect the pulps, which at the time were considered periodicals. There is more about this regulation in the chapter on dime novels (Postal Regulations).

These pulps, very popular in the nineteenth century, got their name from the inexpensive paper upon which they were printed. This paper, produced from wood pulp and then chemically treated, produced a rough-textured paper that was printable.

The size of these books was 7" × 10" and ½" thick with about 130 pages. They, like the earlier chapbooks, had colorful covers, but these covers were done with less taste than those of the earlier publications. They were provocative and were meant to attract the undiscriminating reader. These covers also included some printed words that were meant to entice. (These were very much like the phrases on today's tabloids found on supermarket shelves.) The essence of pulps' appeal to potential readers was this colorful visual that grabbed a buyer's attention through the deliberate use of their dramatic, intriguing, beguiling covers. This practice sets these cheaper periodicals apart from the more expensive and tasteful "slick" magazines that used typographic design or nondramatic illustrations for cover art. The publishers of the different pulp magazines paid serious attention to this cover art. By the late 1920s, this technique of cover art was brought to a high level. The kind of art that was displayed on these colorfully painted, cunningly composed covers representing the contents of the magazine (although this was not always the case) was appealing in a, vivid, alluring way. This, in this place and time, was necessary since the bulk of magazine sales was made through newsstand outlets, where the covers could attract the reader into buying from a rack, not by annual or monthly subscriptions, where the covers could not be seen until the publication arrived.

Earl K. Bergey, a cover artist, was a master of pulp magazines' illustrative elements: the deliberately provocative, almost scandalous combination of the components of constructed pictures and words that conveyed to the potential reader a thought about the most promising drama that the book offered. This approach found a place of importance in the pulp publishing business. With other great pulp artists such as Rudolph Belarski and Raphael De Soto, Bergey created a distinctive style for Popular Library, one of the best-selling lines of pulp paperbacks. His specialty was the lush human female figure wearing suggestive ladies' garments that later became known as the "Brass Brassiere" school of art.

The same thing was at work in earlier forms of inexpensive fiction: The publishers of the cheap story papers of the late nineteenth century, for instance, used brightly colored cover illustrations to capture a purchaser's attention and his spendable money. This is an example of where you *can* tell a book by its cover.

Pulp magazines and paperback books were certainly important cultural factors; on their colorful and suggestive covers and on their pages of unfinished, rough paper, information about the conditions and circumstances that was found appealing at this time by the reading public was revealed.

These pulps, of course, received their share of both praise and condemnation. True to the literary evaluation tradition up to this time, for the most part, the people who read them, praised them; those who didn't read them pointed out their shortcomings. Byron Preiss, an author of books on pulps, gives his opinion this way: "The old American pulps were filled with adventure, ambitious plots, and taut dramatic stories. At times they were also filled with hack writing, racism, sexism, and titillation. They were products of their times, and, as such, remain an accurate portrait of tastes and attitudes of America in the first forty years of the nineteenth century."

Competition among the many pulp fiction publishers was fierce. Each company did whatever it took to sell its wares. The newsstands were filled with garishly pictured, generally poorly written stories, and the public was willing to spend its scarce and hard-earned money for this material. Each publisher tried to outdo the others in gimmicks to stimulate buying. The publishers had lots of titles to sell, so they put on advertising campaigns full of adjectives that proclaimed the excellence of these books. They made the poorest stories sound like the best and most startling ever offered.

The pulp publishers then began to aim their stories at specific audiences. There were Western pulps, detective pulps, science fiction pulps and romance pulps. The Great Depression made people want escape reading. They needed hard-hitting, action-packed adventure stories. The pulp detective story filled this need. There was violence in these stories, but it was directed at evil and presented in such a way that no one was upset because the culprits were "done in." The good guys were good and admired, and the bad guys were bad and deserved what they got.

Because there was now a trend toward detective stories, the old Western heroes, such as Deadwood Dick, turned detective (e.g., *Deadwood Dick as Detective; a Story of the Great Carbonate Region*, which was still written by Edward L. Wheeler, who created him in the first place). Prentiss

Ingraham, the ghost writer for Buffalo Bill, was also turning to crime fiction, and then Buffalo Bill became a pseudodetective.

A new term was making itself known in this new detective literary world. "Sleuth" and "sleuth-hound" (it is thought that this term comes from the old Norse "sloo" tracker.) In one of Munro's dime novels the name "Old Sleuth" was given to one of his detectives. Later, in 1882, in the *Boys of New York* weekly there was a story called "Young Sleuth, the Detective." By the 1890s detective stories equaled the number of Westerns that the publishing houses were producing. Titles like *Kid Keen in New York; or, The Western Wonder on an Eastern Case*, by Howard M. Boynton, and *The Cafe Detective; or, Roy Kennedy's Big Score*, by Percy Preston, appeared. Then came the period of specialized detectives: the post office detective, the revenue detective and the hotel detective. As yet the idea of a highly personalized detective had not been created, but Nick Carter was soon to appear—in 1886.

The pulp magazine was one of the reasons for the downfall of the dime novel, even though many pulps were direct descendants of these very dime novels. Characters like Frank Merriwell, famous in the dime-novel field, and Nick Carter, a newcomer, also began to appear in pulp magazines. Along with the long-running and popular dime novels and pulp fiction there were series books characters such as the Hardy Boys and Nancy Drew. This issuing of boys' and girls' series books was another cause of the downfall of the dime novel. The pulps took most of the adult, dime-novel readers, and the series books took the younger readers.

Why then did these pulps also die out? Although they lasted into the 1950s, they had been fading for a while. The very early movies were one cause of the downfall. Nickelodeons (a movie theater which cost a nickel) sprang up in stores and centers all over America.

The one- and sometimes two-reel "movies" they offered presented a visual adventure to young and old alike, and, when the decision had to be made between spending a nickel for a dime novel or attending a movie house, the movies won out.

The movies also capitalized on the pulps. James Cagney, a cocky tough guy, and Edward G. Robinson, a gang lord, appeared and were very popular. Jean Harlow was a brassy prostitute who really was a good person. All these owe their appearance to the basic stories in the pulp fiction books. Even though television has many programs dealing with police and criminals, the sales of detective stories for young readers is still significant.

With the oncoming demise of the dime novels, many of the writers who made a good living writing weekly stories followed their readership to the pulps, the series books and then the movies. Then came World War II, and the resulting paper shortage (paper was the mainstay of the pulps) was certainly another reason. Then after the war the American people wanted a different kind of entertainment and more pleasurable pastimes. They were tired of the war and its necessary shortages and looked forward to more abundant purchases that were becoming available. Their literary interests turned toward slick, glossy, and definitely more elegant publications.

The Library of Congress's pulp fiction collection has about 15,000 titles taken from about 300 pulp magazines with all different subjects available. The Serial and Government Publications Division has recently microfilmed these magazines but has kept the very valuable colored covers intact. Special precautions were taken to preserve them because of the highly acidic nature of the inside pages.

Black Mask, *Weird Tales* and *Amazing Stories* are kept in the Rare Book and Special Collections Division because these titles were exceptionally popular. (One of *Black Mask Magazine*'s founders was H. L. Mencken.) The pulp magazine collection consists of approximately 8,500 issues of pulp magazines, ranging from the early days of *Argosy* through the heyday of *Astounding*, *Thrilling*, *Romances* and *Popular Detective*, through the last days of the pulps in the 1950s. The collection is particularly strong in the nonspecialty titles such as *Argosy*, *Short Stories* and *Blue Book* and in the science-fiction pulps, such as *Fantastic Story Quarterly*, *Startling Stories*, *Amazing*, *Wonder Stories* and *Weird Tales*.

Conclusion

While researching material for this book I looked at a great number of early children's books and works about children's books and their reading, but I know that I have just touched the tip of the iceberg.

Many of the kinds of books covered in this publication are still read today—the alphabet book, the easy-reading book for beginners, the Biblical tales, the animal stories and so on. However, just as we are now aware that these books are by no means the whole extent of children's reading, so it is important to bear in mind that large areas of children's literature have not been touched, and those that are mentioned here are merely a smattering of all that is available.

There is a great deal of extant information about the developmental stages of children's literature. Each chapter here is only a start for more in-depth research. Thus this book is not an end but a beginning.

Many stages were gone through before a distinct genre of literature for children came about. It is impossible to try to pinpoint any real beginning, but one can detect trends and see signs of things to come; these lead to indications of the beginning of something new.

Literary periods, like any historical era, have a way of merging indistinguishably into one another. As author Agnes Repplier has so aptly said, "Nothing is so hard to deal with as a period. Nothing is so unmanageable as a date; people will be born a few years too early; they will live a few years too long. Events will happen out of time. The closely linked decades refuse to be separated." For example, horn books were in use for some three hundred years before they were recognized as literature indicators; chapbooks, especially characteristic of the eighteenth century, came into existence earlier than that and were still being printed in the nineteenth century.

We are lucky today that the Library of Congress has collected, classified and stored some of this "trash" literature. Otherwise, we would be unable to evaluate this material, which was an important part of the literature of the Americas. Today we can look at these works with an open mind and see their role in the development of literature, especially children's. The library's contribution to today's research in popular culture studies, literature and publishing history is unparalleled. Scholars also should not think that all of the cheap literature of the past was made up of male detective or male outlaw stories. Females made up a large part of the reading public, and much of this fiction, especially from the story paper romances, was aimed at women, including young girls. They, as much as the males of the day, were attracted to the popular fantasies of sudden wealth, mistaken identities, women shaking off the chains of marital bondage, and other adventures. The dime novel for both sexes evolved into the original paperback fiction of our age with both violent adventures and romance fiction.

Beadle and Adams published *Belles and Beaux* in 1874; *Girls of Today: A Mirror of Romance* in 1875 and the *Weekly Library* from 1879 to 1886. George Munro published *New York Monthly Fashion Bazaar* from 1879 to 1885 and the Sweetheart Series from 1898 to 1903. Norman Munro published *The Family Story Paper* from 1873 to 1921 and the *New York Weekly Story Teller* from 1875 to 1877. Street and Smith published the Bertha Clay Library from 1900 to 1932; the Love Story Library from 1926 to 1932 and the New Romance Library from 1907 to 1917.

The study of "popular fiction" is now becoming respectable. But, because much has been overlooked in both social and literary history, only a few dedicated librarians and book collectors have saved this literature for today's scholars. Unfortunately, because publishers have always printed dime novels, pulp fiction and other "nonliterary" works on cheap, self-destructing paper, a lot of these original publications have seriously deteriorated or are already lost forever. These titles are now not available for scholar research. Only in the past few years have some librarians begun a systematic program to save this ephemeral fiction.

Today's researchers of American history, popular culture or early American popular fiction can now study this cultural phenomenon. Merle Curti wrote in *The Yale Review*: "Reading dime novels today can give you insight into the 1800s. The student of social and intellectual history who tries to understand the transit of ideas from the more favored to the less favored must examine dime novels."

During the 1920s the early dime novels became collectors' items. George Hess, whose collection went to the University of Minnesota, was an important collector. The collection has been carefully preserved and expanded, and it is now the largest, dime-novel collection in the United States.

The Library of Congress has the second largest collection, and it contains many of the earliest dime novels in pristine condition, including a first edition of *Malaeska*, the first dime novel ever published.

The Library of Congress, as one of the largest collectors of dime novels in the country, has become one of the few research libraries that systematically collects fiction published in paperback form: the dime novels of today.

In 1925 two collectors in New England, Edward LeBlanc and Ralph Cummings, began a newsletter for their fellow collectors. In 1931 their small publication became *Dime Novel Round-Up*; it is still published today, with J. Randolph Cox as editor.

The chapters presented here reflect the varieties of interdisciplinary research necessary. The available, but scattered, material should convince scholars that collecting and studying such literature is valuable and necessary. Accurate dating of these materials is difficult if not impossible. There are factors one can follow in order to estimate a date: style of type, types of wood carvings, and other construction methods. However, these guides are not dependable since some printers used any old type, any old woodcuts and any construction methods that were cheap and semidurable. There were also any number of different editions of many books. For instance, for some children's books, such as *The Divine and Moral Songs of Isaac Watts* and the poems of Ann and Jane Taylor, there have been many editions, both British and American, since their initial publication. For other books, such as Louisa May Alcott's *Little Women*, there are many modern editions in print and more to come, I'm sure. The whole question of editions is therefore complicated, and so I made no attempt to discover or list all of the earlier editions or to include all that may be in print at the present time.

Dime novels furnish an intimate picture of American life in the latter part of the nineteenth century and the early years of the twentieth. Their stories bring readers into contact with a wide range of subjects and scenes, portraying attitudes about women and men, about minorities and ethnic groups and about everyday matters. They preserve a bit of America's past. For these reasons, the dime novels are an important part of our cultural history.

It has been suggested that Horatio Alger was not a true dime novelist, but a copier using the dime-novel format to introduce reforms dealing with the working class's reading habits and culture. He had a great deal of success with the Ragged Dick stories. They were published in the respectable juvenile magazine, *Student and Schoolmate*, and were fairly well received by reviewers who saw them as an alternative to the real dime-novel fictions; his following stories, published in Street and Smith's *New York Weekly*, were not as successful and were looked down upon both by the genteel culture he represented and the sensation-loving public for whom he wrote.

Important changes can be seen in the movement of the dime novel detective and in the appearance of Frank Merriwell in the 1890s. Although no separate chapter focuses exclusively on the dime-novel detective, this genre dominated the arena of both dime novels and then pulp fiction. The process by which stories of city life, of the Molly Maguirs, of hobos and of criminals all became stories of detectives has a different and contradictory political meaning. At times, detectives substituted for outlaw heroes, much as G-men were to replace gangsters in the movies of the Great Depression and tales of class conflict were turned into crime stories. The reasons for and meaning of these changes in sensational type fiction can be understood only with an in-depth study of the pulp fiction of the early-twentieth century and of its relation to the new developing film industry and the new working class of immigrant laborers from Eastern and Southern Europe and the share-cropping South.

However, this research also highlights the dime novel's deliberate evasion of race. Looking at it from this point of view, the dime novel was a failure. The dime-novel industry was largely isolated from African American audiences and African American writers; also, no narrative plots were developed that could tell a racial story, as the few accounts of race studies in the dime novels show. J. B. Dobkin searched through 8,000 nickel library serials that appeared between 1879 and 1910 and found "no black hero figure,' about fifty African American characters important to the story line and the total disappearance of African American characters after 1906 and 1907. Initially, what he and other researchers found were conventional, negative stereotypes. One exception is an African American detective in several stories like *Old Cap Collier's Black Tom, the Negro Detective; or, Solving a Thompson Street Mystery* and Ingraham's *Darkie Dan, the Colored Detective; or, The Mississippi Mystery*. Black Tom sets a detective story in the neighborhood of New York's African American community: Black Tom, the detective, was a mysterious individual who "came and went into and out of the Negro quarters of the city, like a phantom." However, when the African American detective solves the mystery of the white woman's corpse found in the African American part of town and helps a poor white woman garment worker to get her rightful inheritance, it is discovered that he is really a white detective in disguise.

Though the discriminating reader might interpret this as a metaphorical disguise—the detective is both Black and White—the text does not lead one to believe this. In the stories about working girls who end up inheriting a fortune, the lady always states that she is still a working girl, or in the stories where the nobleman ends by recalling his days as a miner the proudest and best of his life, the White detective is clearly an impersonator, as the story ends. "Nick Miller received much praise for his wonderful work, and his clever impersonations of the mysterious individual known a Black Tom, the Negro detective."

Prentiss Ingraham's Darkie Dan is a Black detective hero, but the narrative about this African American figure is the reconstruction of slavery. Set in the South, Dan stays with his master after emancipation, and his detective work is in service to his white master and the master's family.

Even though in 1900, the *Bookman* announced "The Extinction of the Dime Novel," this was not entirely accurate. True, some dime novel publishers went out of business, including the well-known and successful Beadle and Adams; still, this inexpensive, sensational literature went on long after 1900. As with all previous literary trends the story papers and the dime novel were declining as new formats and new themes were being introduced. The newspapers, the pulp fiction publications and the motion picture industry played a role in the changes of literary styles.

By 1907 the *Atlantic Monthly* had published a eulogy of the dime novel, Charles M. Harvey's "The Dime Novel in American Life." Harvey's opening parallels that of W. H. Bishop, who wrote in the *Atlantic* 28 years earlier, "Are not more crimes perpetrated these days in the name of the dime novels than Madame Roland ever imagined were committed in the name of liberty? It looks that way. Nearly every sort of misdemeanor in which the fantastic element enters, from train robbery to house burning, is laid to them."

Appendix A: Chronology of the Dime Novel and Related Works, 1860–1902

This list of important events in the relevant years points out the number of literarily acceptable books that were being published during the same period that Beadle, Tousey and Street and Smith were publishing their dime novels.

1860 First dime novel published in numbered series by Irwin P. Beadle & Co.: *Malaeska, the Indian Wife of a White Hunter* sells 300,000 copies in the first year. *Seth Jones; or the Captives of the Frontier* sells 450,000 copies in the first year. Between 1860 and 1874, 321 novels appear in Beadle's dime novels.

1861 Orville Victor becomes the editor for Beadle publications and remains a powerful influence until 1868; known for his moral and literary standards.

1862 Theodore Winthrop publishes *John Brent, a Western Romance*, set in the Rockies.

1863 In April, William Bullock of Pittsburgh patents the continuous-roll printing press, which prints paper on both sides.
The first appearance of Munro's dime novels.

1864 A. K. Loring publishes Horatio Alger, Jr.'s, *Frank's Campaign; or What Boys Can Do on the Farm for Their Camp*, the first of this house's thirty-six publications.

1865 Mark Twain publishes "The Celebrated Jumping Frog of Calaveras County."
Lewis Carroll publishes *Alice's Adventures in Wonderland.*
Mary Mapes Dodge publishes *Hans Brinker, or the Silver Skates.*

1866 Beadle & Co. publishes a shortened version of Twain's story of the jumping frog as Jim Smiley's *Frog in the Dime Book of Fun.*

1867 Munro begins publishing *The New York Fireside Companion* as a family paper.
deWitt releases his *Ten Cent Romances* and Irwin Beadle's *Six Penny Tales.*

1868 Beadle and Co. establishes Frank Starr and Co. as a subsidiary.
Loring publishes Alger's *Ragged Dick; or, Street Life in New York*, which cements the rags-to-riches paradigm.

1869 Ned Buntline (Edward Judson) publishes the first Buffalo Bill dime novel: *Buffalo Bill, King of the Border Men*, in Street & Smith's *New York Weekly*. The front page woodcut, supposedly modeled on Judson himself, established the buckskinned, knife-wielding image of William Cody.

1870 Beadle enters the field of the story paper with the *Saturday Star/Saturday Journal*, printing novels that would be published subsequently as books in one of the firm's series.

1871 Edward Eggleston publishes *The Hoosier School-Master*, which sells 500,000 copies.

1872 Beadle and Co. becomes Beadle & Adams.
The first dime novel detective appears in *Old Sleuth, the Detective; or, the Bay Ridge Mystery* in Munro's *New York Fireside Companion.*

1873 Mary Mapes Dodge founds *St. Nicholas Magazine* for children.

1874 In western cities like Deadwood, the likes of Billy the Kid and Calamity Jane gain national attention.

1875 Norman Munro, having departed from his brother's firm in 1873, begins publishing *The Boys Own Story Teller*, a series of novels with adolescent heroes.

1876 The Pictorial Printing Company begins publishing the Nickel Library, the first 32-page, octavo, five-cent serial devoted to frontier adventures. The format dominated the field until the close of the century.

1877 Beadle and Adams introduce the Half Dime Library, intended for boys, and the Fireside Library, intended for family reading.
Frank Tousey begins publication of *New York Boys Weekly* and *The Young Men of America*, both with full-page color illustrations.

1878 Buffalo Bill appears in Frank Tousey's Wide Awake Library.

1879 A bill changing the postal rates of library books and periodicals. Second-class mail matters. *Postal Act* of March 3, 1879, commonly known as the Loud Postal Bill.
Beadle and Adams begin publishing the Waverly Library of Romances for "young ladies."

1880 The American News Company, 1864–1969, with 32 regional branches, distributes all the leading novel serials, story papers, and libraries, doing a profitable business and achieving a virtual monopoly.

1881 Joel Chandler Harris publishes *Uncle Remus: His Songs and His Sayings.*

1882 Frank Tousey begins publishing the series New York Detective Library.

1883 Munro transforms *The Boys Own Story Teller* into *Our Boys of New York*, a nickel, biweekly magazine that runs serialized novels and draws the ire of reformers who believe that the adolescent criminal heroes will lead the readers to ruin.

1884 On August 26, Ottomar Megenthaler of Baltimore, Maryland, patents the linotype, automatic typesetting machine.

1885 William Dean Howells publishes *The Rise of Silas Lapham.*

1886 Henry James publishes *The Bostonians* and *The Princess Casamassima.*

1887 Joseph Kirkland publishes *Zury: The Meanest Man in Spring County.* In 1888 *The McVeys*, a sequel, is published.

1888 Edward Bellamy publishes *Looking Backward*, a best-selling technological utopia that inspires the creation of Bellamy societies throughout the country.

1889 Street and Smith enter the dime-novel market with the Log Cabin Library and the Nugget Library. They publish more than forty different novel series, among them the Nick Carter Library. They soon command the field.

1890 Jacob Riis publishes *How the Other Half Lives.*
William James publishes *Principles of Psychology.*
William Dean Howells publishes *A Hazard of New Fortunes.*

1891 Street and Smith enter the field of science fiction with Philip Reader's *Tom Edition Jr. and His Air Yacht.*

1892 Mary Hallock Foote achieves national attention with *The Chosen Valley*, a Western written from a woman's point of view.

1893 Stephen Crane publishes *Maggie: A Girl of the Streets.*

1894 John Muir publishes *The Mountains of California.*

1895 Stephen Crane publishes *The Red Badge of Courage.*

1896 Street and Smith begins publication of *Tip Top Weekly*, which soon achieves a circulation of one million.

1897 Richard H. Davis publishes the best-selling *Soldiers of Fortune.*

1898 Assets of Beadle & Adams are purchased by M. J. Ivers & Co.

1899 Kate Chopin publishes *The Awakening.*
Charles Chesnut publishes *The Conjure Woman.*

1900 Theodore Dreiser publishes *Sister Carrie.*
L. Frank Baum publishes *The Wonderful Wizard of Oz.*

1901 Booker T. Washington publishes *Up from Slavery.*
Charles Chesnut publishes *The Marrow of Tradition.*
Frank Norris publishes *The Octopus.*

1902 Frank Tousey furthers his command of the juvenile field of story papers and libraries by introducing several more publications, including Frank Reade's *Weekly* and the *Wild West Weekly.*

Appendix B: Annotated Bibliography of Dime Novels

Abbott, Jacob. *Handie.*
Handie Level is a white, teenaged carpenter. He and Rainbow become friends.

_____. *Rainbow's Journey.* 1860.
Rainbow and Handie go to Three Pines Farm and catch a thief.

_____. *Selling Lucky.* 1860.
Rainbow is in Boston and experiences racism. Rainbow's kindness and admirable qualities are described.

_____. *Stories of Rainbow and Lucky.*
Rainbow, 14, is an African American. He is intelligent and hard working.

_____. *Three Pines.* 1860.
Rainbow examines the relations between himself and his white friend Handie and the neighbors.

_____. *Up the River.*
Rainbow takes a job delivering mail to other post offices and overcomes some racism.

Abbott, Rosa. *Pinks and Blues; or, the Orphan Asylum.* Boston: Lee and Shepard, 1870.
A story of two girls on a country roadside.

Adams, Captain "Bruin." *Black Spy; or, the Yellowstone Trail.* New York: Beadle's Dime Novels, 1873.
An Indian story of the upper Missouri River.

Adams, J. F. C. *Fighting Trapper; or, Kit Carson to the Rescue.* New York: Beadle's Dime Library, 1879.
Another Kit Carson story, this time by J. F. C. Adams. Many other writers wrote about Carson.

Adomeit, Ruth E. *Aunt Rose and Her Nieces.* Boston: American Tract Society, 1862.

Aiken, Albert W. *Kit Carson, King of Guides; or, Mountain Paths and Prairie Trails.* New York: Beadle's Boys Library, 1882.
Carson is headed for the headwaters of the Little Colorado River. He fights Mangas Colorado. Big Foot Wallace appears in this story.

_____. *Red Arrow, the Wolf Demon; or, the Queen of the Kanawha.* New York: Beadle's Saturday Journal, Nov. 12, 1870–Feb. 18, 1871.
This story takes place in an Ohio Valley settlement in 1780. Girty, Kenton and Boone appear in the tale.

_____ and Davenport, Frances Helen. *Ambitious Girl; or, She Would Be an Actress.* New York: Beadle and Adams, 1887.

This story has been attributed to several authors, but the real claim is Albert W. Aiken. The action takes place in the village of Cold Snake, New Jersey.

Aiken, George L. *Kit Carson's Bride; or, the Flower of the Apaches.* New York: Munro's Ten Cent Novels, N.D.

Ainsworth, William Harrison. *Dick Turpin, the Notorious Highwayman.* New York: Norman Munro, 1871–1879.

A story of the life and adventures of Dick Turpin, a burglar, murderer and robber. The real Dick Turpin was a housebreaker, sheep stealer and highwayman; he was hanged for these crimes. He lived under the name John Lamer. He made characters in several books including Edward Viles's *Black Bess; or, the Knight of the Road.* Black Bess was Turpin's horse.

_____. *Jack Sheppard.* New York: Norman Munro, 1839.

Sheppard has been made the unworthy hero of many dime novels. In truth he was merely a vulgar scoundrel who did not hesitate to rob his only true friend.

_____. *Rookwood.* London: Bentley, 1834.

In this book Ainsworth says Turpin rides Black Bess from London to York without a break, but it is believed that another highwayman, Swift Nick, performed this feat. This book created the legend of Dick Turpin.

Alcott, Louisa May. *Behind a Mask; or, a Woman's Power.* New York: Morrow, 1975.

This book contains "Abbot's Ghost," a story about a haunted abbey; the "Mysterious Key," a tale of death and confused identity and "Pauline's Passion and Punishment."

_____. *Double Life.* Boston: Little Brown, 1988.

This book contains "Ariel," a tale on an enchanted island; "A Pair of Eyes," a story about a woman with intense mesmeric powers; "Fate of the Forests," a story of prophetic powers and the murderous Kali cult; "Taming a Tartar," a swashbuckling adventure story and "A Double Tragedy," a murder mystery.

_____. *Long, Fatal Love Chase.* Thorndike, Maine: Thorndike Press, 1996.

An Englishwoman falls for an older man who takes her to France, where she discovers he is already married. When she leaves him, he pursues her and confines her to a lunatic asylum in Germany, but she escapes. This novel was written in 1866 and was rejected by the publisher as too sensational.

_____. *Mysterious Key, and What It Opened.* Boston: Elliott, Thomes and Talbot, 1867.

Paul, an Englishman, lives in the Trevlyn house. He is looking for proof to solve a mystery. He disappears and reappears as Paolo. He disappears again and joins the Italian Revolution. The mysterious key in the title is a silver key that opens a tomb where a missing paper is found.

_____. *Skeleton in the Closet.* Boston: Elliott, Thomes and Talbot, 1867.

Madame Arnhim, a widow, has a lover, Gustave Novaire, who is jealous. The mystery of Madame's past (the skeleton in the closet) unravels. The mystery is resolved when the skeleton in the closet is exhumed.

_____. *V.V.; or, Plots and Counterplots.* Boston: Thomes and Talbot, 1870.

V.V., Virginie Varens, is a dancer who has many different disguises. She becomes a widow when her cousin Victor kills her new husband, Allan Douglass. Chapter names tell of the story's intrigue: Won and Lost; Earl's Mystery; The Iron Ring; A Shred of Lace; and more.

Alger, Horatio. *Luke Larkin's Luck; or, the Fortune of a Plucky Princeton Athlete.* New Jersey: Nautilus, June 15, 1907.

_____. *Struggling Upward; or, Luke Larkin's Luck.* New Jersey: Nautilus, 1890.

Relates the adventures of Luke Larkin, a poor boy who perseveres against many odds and gains success.

_____. *Tom the Bootblack; or, The Road to Success.* New York: Burt, 1889.

_____. *Tony, the Tramp.* New York: Beadle and Adams, 1876.

_____. *Young Salesman*. New York: Hurst and Co., 1894.

Anon. *Children in the Woods*. Various editions, 1597, 1711, 1879, 1972.

"Being a true relation of the inhuman murder of two children." A broadside ballad.

Anon. *Devil and Doctor Faustus*. Montpelier, Vt.: Carlos C. Darling, 1807.

"Containing the history of the wicked life and horrid death of Doctor John Faustus: and shewing how he sold himself to the Devil, to have power for twenty-four years to do what he pleased: also the strange things done by him and Mephistopheles with an account how the Devil came to him at the end of twenty-four years and tore him to pieces." This was copied in its entirety from the English chapbook.

Anon. *Friar and the Boy; or, the Young Piper's Pleasant Pastime*. Boston: A. Barclay, 1767.

"Containing the witty adventures betwixt the Friar and boy in relation to his step mother, whom he fairly fitted for her unmerciful cruelty."

Anon. *Prodigal Daughter; or, a Strange and Wonderful Relation*. Boston: Isaiah Thomas, 1771.

A long moral story with a trance and a vision: "shewing how a gentleman of great estate in Bristol had a proud and disobedient daughter, who, because her parents would not support her in all her extravagance, bargained with the devil to poison them, how an angel informed her parents of her design, how she lay in a trance for four days, and when she was put in the grave, she came to life again and related the wonderful things she saw in the other world."

Anon. *Riddle Book*. Mass.: J. Metcalf, 1828.

A chapbook of riddles with woodcuts and the answers to the riddles.

Anon. *Riddle Book—Book for the Entertainment of Boys and Girls*. New Haven: Sidney's Press, 1826.

A chapbook of riddles in the form of poems, with illustrations.

Anon. *Undutiful Daughter; or, the Devonshire Wonder*. Philadelphia: Andrew Steuart, 1771.

A sordid tale told in verse.

Appleton, Victor. *Astral Fortress*. New York: Stratemeyer, Edward, 1981.

When Tom Swift and his crew jump back from the Alpha Centauri system through hyperspace to Earth's galaxy, they are captured by their arch enemy David Luna and taken prisoner aboard his astral fortress.

#5 of Tom Swift series

Armstrong, Frank P. *Metamora, the Forest King*. New York: Beadle's Dime Novels, 1870.

An Indian story of Plymouth town in colonial days during King Philip's war in 1675.

Avallone, Michael (Nick Carter). *Run, Spy, Run*. Los Angeles: Award Books, 1964.

Nick Carter was introduced in 1886. In this story he is not a detective but a spy with the code name N3, Killmaster, very like James Bond. It was published anonymously. It was the beginning of the long-running series (261 titles) of Nick Carter.

Badger, Joseph E. *Big George, the Giant of the Gulch; or, the Five Outlaw Brothers*. New York: Beadle's Dime Library, 1880.

Life in the gold diggings in 1852.

_____. *Black John, the Road-Agent; or, the Prairie Sink*. New York: Beadle's Dime Novels, 1873.

Outlaws and Kickapoos in Kansas during the bad old days of the early settlements.

_____. *Border Renegade; or, the Lily of the Silver Lake*. New York: Beadle's Dime Library, Feb. 27, 1872.

Attacks on early Michigan settlers by roving bands of Delaware Indians led by the infamous George Girty, brother of the more notorious Simon Girty.

_____. *Caribou Zip; or, the Forest Brothers*. New York: Beadle's Dime Novels, 1874.

A story of the great Pontiac War in 1763.

Joseph Brant, with scouts and others, is mentioned in this Native American tale.

_____. *Dusty Dick; or, Old Toby Castor's Great Campaign.* New York: Beadle's Dime Novels, 1872.
A companion story to *Mountain Kate.* It covers the troubles with the Sioux in Minnesota.

_____. *Forest Princess; or, the Kickapoo Captives.* New York: Beadle's Dime Novels, 1871.
A sequel to *Mad Ranger.* An attack by Kickapoos in Indiana. Two scouts aid General Samuel Hopkins in putting down the outbreak.

_____. *Girl Captain; or, the Reprisal of Blood.* New York: Beadle's Dime Novels, 1873.
A story of Revolutionary War days in the Carolinas, the swamp region and its people. It tells of "cowboys" and "skinners."

_____. *Joaquin, the Saddle King.* New York: Beadle and Adams, 1881.
A story of Joaquin Murieta in the early days of California.

_____. *Little Thunderbolt; or, the Rangers of the Carolinas.* New York: Beadle's Dime Novels, 1873.
A story of the Carolinas during Revolutionary War days.

_____. *Mad Ranger; or, Hunters of the Wabash.* New York: Beadle's Dime Novels, 1877.
A tale of Tecumseh's time.

_____. *Masked Guide; or, the Road Agents of the Plains.* New York: Beadle's Dime Novels, 1870.
In the Black Hills of Kansas there are bandits, Native Americans, scouts, villains and more.

_____. *Mountain Kate; or, Love in the Trapping-Grounds.* New York: Beadle's Dime Novels, 1879.

_____. *Mustang Sam; or, the Mad Rider of the Plains.* New York: Beadle's Dime Novels, 1874.
A story of the gold seekers in the Sierra de Chuska, New Mexico–Arizona.

_____. *Night-Hawk Kit; or, Daughter of the Ranch.* New York: Beadle's Dime Novels, 1871.
A story of the "Night Hawk" gang of outlaws on the Brazos River in Texas.

_____. *Outlaw Ranger; or, the Old Hunter's Last Trail.* New York: Beadle's Dime Novels, 1872.
A story about Devil Davis's gang of outlaws. There are vigilantes, woodsmen and others in northwestern Missouri.

_____. *Pirate of the Placers; or, Joaquin's Death Hunt.* New York: Beadle's Dime Novels, 1882.

_____. *Red Dan, the Ranger; or, the League of Three.* New York: Beadle's Dime Novels, 1872.
A story of exciting times in North and South Carolina. Steed Bonnet is one of the characters.

_____. *Redlaw Half-Breed; or, the Tangled Trail.* New York: Beadle's Dime Novels, 1870.
A story of counterfeiters, cattle and horse thieves and a vigilance committee in Kansas.

_____. *Three-Fingered Jack, the Road Agent of the Rockies; or, Boy Miner of Hard Luck.* New York: Beadle's Dime Novels, 1878.

Ballantyne, Robert Michael. *Coral Island.* Edinburgh: Thomas Nelson and Sons, 1858.
A story of three people shipwrecked on a South Sea island. The *Gorilla Hunters* (1861) is a sequel.

_____. *Gorilla Hunters.* Philadelphia: Porter and Coates, 186?.
A story that takes place in the wilds of Africa.

_____. *Hudson's Bay; or, Every-Day Life in the Wilds of North America.* Boston: Phillips, Sampson and Co., 1859.
This is considered Ballantyne's best work and was widely influential. Based on letters he sent to his mother while he was away for six years.

_____. *Martin Rattler; or, a Boy's Ad-*

venture in the Forests of Brazil. London: J. M. Dent and Sons, 1860.

An adventure in the forests of Brazil which teaches geography and history.

_____. *Young Fur Traders.* 1856.

Barker, Colin A. *Golden Belt; or, the Carib's Pledge.* New York: Beadle and Adams, 1860.

A tale of the tropics in early Spanish days and of the wedding of a Spaniard with a Carib maid.

Barrett, John E. *Love and Labor; or, The Master Workman's Vow.* New York: New York Weekly, 1884.

Beale, O. A. S. *Shadow in the House.*

Belknap, Boynton. *Lew Wetzel, the Scout; or, the Captives of the Wilderness.* New York: Starr's American Novels, 1869.

One of Edward Ellis's pseudonyms. Kentucky rangers and Native Americans in the Ohio Valley after the Battle of Chillicothe.

Bird, Robert. *Nick of the Woods; or, the Jibbenainosay: A Tale of Kentucky.* Philadelphia: Carey, Lea and Banchard, 1837.

Bird's work appeared in George Munro's *Fireside Companion.* He wrote about life in early America.

Bishop, Bertha Thorne. *Broker's Ward; or, Blanche Ratcliff's Trials.* New York: Frank Starr Co., 1870.

Blake, Lillie D. U. *Forced Vows; or, A Revengeful Woman's Fate.* New York: Frank Starr Co., 1870.

Zella Dangerfield and her brother, a New Orleans Spaniard, try to ruin Blanche Grafton.

Blount, Margaret. *Dangerous Woman; or, The Broken Troth.* New York: Frank Starr Co., 1870.

A love story that takes place in and around London.

_____. *Maniac Bride; or, The Dead Secret of Hollow Ash Hall.* New York: Frank Starr Co., 1870.

Takes place in a haunted house in England. Another example of gothic horror stories.

_____. *Rejected Wife; or, A Broken Life.* New York: Frank Starr Co., 1870.

Bowen, James L. *Brave Heart; or, the Lost Heirs of Lanwick.* New York: Beadle and Adams, 1867.

A Native American tale in Ohio. Also in retrospect twenty years earlier in England.

_____. *First Trail; or, the Forest Foundling.* New York: Beadle's Dime Novels, 1870.

_____. *Maid of Wyoming; or, the Contest of the Clans.* New York: Beadle's Dime Novels, 1866.

This story takes place in Wyoming Valley, Pennsylvania. Attempts of pioneers from Connecticut to establish a colony in 1769.

_____. *Mohegan Maid; or, The Stranger of the Settlement.* New York: Beadle's Dime Novels, 1867.

A story of King Philip's war. It takes place in Connecticut and covers trouble with Native Americans.

_____. *Red Rider; or, the White Queen of the Apaches.* New York: Beadle's Dime Novels, 1869.

Prospectors from Texas attempt to develop silver deposits in southwestern New Mexico. They are hampered by Apaches.

_____. *Red Skin's Pledge; or, the Double Plot.* New York: Beadle's Dime Novels, 1868.

A tale of horse thieves among the Creek Indians and bad men in Alabama after the War of 1812.

_____. *Simple Phil; or, the Pineville Massacre.* New York: Beadle and Adams, 1866.

Perils of early settlers in Pineville on the Ohio frontier. A Native American foray, several women are captured and a search for the captives.

_____. *Three Indian-Hunters; or, the Maidens of Idaho.* New York: Beadle and Adams, 1867.

Brushes with Native Americans on the western plains in 1865, in one of the territories of the time.

Bowman, James F. *Island Home; or, The Young Castaways.* Boston: Gould and Lincoln, 1852.
Written under the pseudonym of Christopher Romaunt.

Boynton, Howard M. *Cadet-Detective; or, the Mystery at West Point.* New York: Beadle's Dime Novels, 1893.
West Point in 1889. A detective posing as a cadet captures a thief who stole $20,000 in gold.

_____. *Cadet-Detective's Hot Hustle; or, West Point Rogues.* New York: Beadle's Dime Novels, 1896.

Braddon, Paul. *Daniel Boone, the Hero of Kentucky.* New York: Frank Tousey's Wide Awake Library. Nov. 11, 1893.

Bretty, Edwin John. *Young Harkaway and His Boy Tinker Among the Turks.* London: Boys of England Office, 1876.
Publisher of Jack Harkaway's *School Days* (1871), the first in this long series.

Brooks, Noah. *Boy Emigrants.* New York: Scribner's, 1903.

_____. *Boy Settlers; or, Early Times in Kansas.* New York: Scribner, 1891.
American journalist and editor; wrote several books of historical fiction describing America in the mid-nineteenth century. This story describes pioneer life in America. Another book was *The Boy Emigrants* (1876).

Buntline, Ned. *Black Avenger of the Spanish Main; or, the Fiend of Blood: A Thrilling Tale of the Buccaneer Times.* Boston: F. Gleason, 1847.

_____. *Luona's Oath; or, the Curse Fulfilled.* New York: Frank Starr Co., 1870.

_____. *Old Sib Cone, the Mountain Trapper.* New York: Starr's American Novels, 1876.
A tale of an emigrant train and trappers in the Western plains in 1841.

_____. *Planter's Ward; or, A Woman's Love and a Woman's Hate.* New York: Frank Starr Co., 1871.

_____. *Red Revenger; or, The Pirate King of the Floridas: A Romance of the Gulf and Its Islands.* Boston: F. Gleason, 1847.

_____. *Secret Vow; or, the Power of Woman's Hate.* New York: Frank Starr Co., 1871.

_____. *True as Steel; or, the Faithful Sister.* New York: Frank Starr Co., 1871.

_____. *Wronged Daughter; or, a Wife's Intrigue.* New York: Frank Starr Co., 1870.
New York City life, in which not all that glitters is gold. A sad story of a sailor, his sister and his father, whose second marriage causes trouble.

Burr, Dangerfield. *Buffalo Bill, the Buckskin King; or, Wild Nell, the Amazon of the West.* New York: Beadle's Dime Library, April 21, 1880.
Buffalo Bill is at the headwaters of the Republican River to help out Lord Varian Elphistone.

"By a celebrated author." *Great Spy System; or, Nick Carter's Promise to the President.* New York: Street and Smith, 1907.

"By a celebrated author." *Nick Carter, Detective: The Solution of a Remarkable Case.* New York: Street and Smith, N.D.
This case baffled the shrewdest detectives on the regular force and had practically been abandoned when Nick Carter took hold of it.

Caldwell, J. R. *Privateer's Bride; or, the Channel Scud.* New York: Beadle's Dime Novels, 1877.
An adventure story of a privateer in the war with England.

Carleton, Latham C. *Hunters; or, Life on the Mountain and Prairie.* New York: Beadle's Ten Cent Novels, 1863.
Another pseudonym of Edward Ellis. It

is estimated that he used around thirty different names. This is one of the Western adventure stories.

Carr, Nick. *America's Secret Service Ace: Operator 5*. California: Borgo Press, 1874.

Carson, Lewis W. (Albert Aiken). *White Slayer, the Avenger; or, the Doomed Red-Skins*. New York: Starr's American Novels, April 19, 1870.

The White Avenger is a man whose home is burned and his wife and children are killed by Native Americans. A white girl captive is rescued.

Carter, Nicholas (Dey, Marmaduke). *Kid Curry's Last Stand; or, Nick Carter in Dangerous Surroundings*. New York: Street and Smith, 1907.

He wrote under the name of Marmaduke Dey; he also used "A Celebrated Author" and "Author of Nick Carter." One example of the many, many Nick Carter stories.

Castlemon, Harry (Charles Austin Fosdick). *Boy Traders; or, the Sportsman's Club Among the Boers*. Philadelphia: Porter and Coates, 1877.

Castlemon's real name is Charles Austin Fosdick. Under this pseudonym he wrote many stories for boys from the post–Civil War period until the early twentieth century. Other titles are *Boy Trapper*; *Don Gordon's Shooting Box*; *Frank Nelson in the Forecastle*.

_____. *Buried Treasure*. Philadelphia: Porter & Coates, 1871.

_____. *Frank on a Gun-Boat*. Philadelphia: John C. Winston, 1864.

Fosdick wrote more than sixty adventure stories. He himself fought on a gunboat during the Civil War. The hero is Frank Nelson, who appears in many books. He got the youth of America away from the Rollo books.

Cavendish, Harry. *Black Rover; a Tale of Land and Sea*. New York: Beadle's Dime Novels, 1869.

Black Rover is a pirate. He kidnaps the daughter of a Cuban Spaniard in the Caribbean Sea, but he is captured and killed; the daughter is recovered.

_____. *Privateer Cruise and the Bride of Pomfret Hall; a Sea Tale of '76*. New York: Beadle and Adams, 1860.

A story, apparently by an American writer, of privateering during the Revolutionary War. The style is much like that of the English authors of the early nineteenth century. It is told in the first person.

_____. *Reefer of '76; or, the Cruise of the Fire-Fly*. New York: Beadle's Dime Novels, 1860.

A sea story of 1776 to 1779. Paul Jones is introduced as one of the characters.

Chandler, Raymond. *Big Sleep*. New York: Knopf, 1939.

Chandler's career was given a boost with the pulp publications. He wrote for the *Black Mask*, a periodical. His most productive years were from 1933 to 1959. *Big Sleep* was made into a movie in 1946.

Clark, C. Dunning. *Graybeard, the Sorcerer; or, the Recluse of Mount Royale*. New York: Beadle's Dime Novels, 1871.

A story of the military occupation by the French of Montreal, Canada, in early colonial times.

_____. *Mute Chief; or, the Witch of Cherry Valley*. New York: Beadle's Dime Novels, 1871.

This story covers the massacre of November 10, 1778, in Cherry Valley, New York, by Tories and Native Americans. The massacre was led by Walter Butler.

_____. *Pale-Face Squaw; or, the Last Arrow*. New York: Beadle's Dime Novels, 1869.

This tale takes place in colonial times in Jamestown, Virginia.

_____. *Prairie Trappers; or, the Child of the Brigade*. New York: Beadle and Adams, 1868.

A Native American treasure tale of the Black Hills. Conflicts between the Hudson's Bay Company and the Northwest Fur Company.

_____. *Sumter's Scouts; or, the Riders of the Catawba*. New York: Beadle's Dime Novels, 1867.

A story of the struggle for independence in South Carolina.

_____. *Tim, the Scout; or, Caught in His Own Toils.* New York: Beadle and Adams, 1867.
Tecumseh's brother, the Prophet, on the Tippecanoe River in Indiana is the theme of this story.

Claxton, Sara. *Secret Marriage; or, a Duchess in Spite of Herself.* New York: Beadle and Adams, 1879.
A story that takes place in England, resplendent with dukes, barons and other royalty.

Cody, William F. *Death Trailer, the Chief of the Scouts; or, Life and Love of a Frontier Fort.* 1878.

Coffin, Charles Carleton. *Boys of '76.* New York: Harper, 1876/1904.
Coffin wrote many history-type books for children.

Collier, Old Cap. *Black Tom, the Negro Detective; or, Solving the Thompson Street Mystery.* New York: Old Cap. Collier Library, 1893.
Black Tom, a detective, is a mysterious individual who "came and went into and out of the Negro quarters of the city, like a phantom." When he solves the mystery of a white woman's corpse and helps a poor white woman garment worker get her rightful inheritance, it is discovered that he is really a white detective in disguise.

_____. *Old Cap Collier; or, "Piping" the New Haven Mystery.* New York: Munro's Ten Cent Novels, 1883.
The first Old Cap tale. His gift to this genre was his ability to assume disguises.

Comstock, Captain. *Kill-Bar, the Guide; or, the Long Trail.* New York: Starr's American Novels, 1869.
A story about the Cherokee and fighting in Georgia. Kill-Bar is an alias for Davy Crockett.

Coomes, Oil. *Foghorn Phil, the King of the Border; or, the Secret Foe.* New York: Beadle's Dime Novels, 1874.
Powder River and the Big Horn country, Native Americans, traders, hunters, bad men, and so on, in 1870.

Coryell, John Russell. *Great Enigma; or, Nick Carter's Tripe Puzzle.* New York: Street and Smith, 1892.

_____. *Old Detective's Pupil; or, the Mysterious Crime of Madison Square.* New York: Street and Smith, 1886.
Coryell wrote under many pseudonyms including Nick Carter. This is one of his better-known books.

Cowdrick, J. C. *Silver-Mask, the Man of Mystery; or, the Cross of the Golden Keys.* New York: Beadle's Half Dime Library, June 17, 1884.
Road agents and miners in "Golden Egg," a mining town in New Mexico, Billy the Kid is featured in this story.

Daly, Jim (Edward Stratemeyer). *Gentleman Jack; or, from Student to Pugilist.* New York: Five Cent Library, 1892.

_____ (Edward Stratemeyer). *Gentleman Jack's Big Hit; or, Downing the Prize Ring Fakirs.* New York: Five Cent Library, 1893.

_____. (Edward Stratemeyer). *Gentleman Jack's Debut; or, the Ring Champion of the Stage.* New York: Five Cent Library, 1893.

_____. (Edward Stratemeyer). *Gentleman Jack's Soft Mark; or, Knocked Out in Three Rounds.* New York: Five Cent Library, 1893.

Dearborn, Andrew. *Scarred Eagle; or Moorooine, the Sporting Fawn.* New York: Beadle and Adams, 1870.
A story of the siege of the fort at Detroit during Pontiac's war.

Denison, Mary Andrews. *Grandmother Normandy.* Boston: Lathrop and Co., 1886.

_____. *Prisoner of La Vintresse; or, the Fortunes of a Cuban Heiress.* New York: Beadle's Dime Novels, 1860.
Life in Cuba and New York in the middle of the nineteenth century.

Dexter, Will. *Antelope Abe, the Boy Guide; or, the Forest Bride.* New York: Beadle and Adams, 1872.

A tale of Native Americans in Southwestern Iowa in pioneer days.

_____. *Young Mustanger; or, the Red Terror of Texas*. New York: Beadle and Adams, 1872.

A Native American tale of San Saba, Texas.

Duff, Paul James. *Crimson Love*. Chicago: n.p., 1895.

Tom Freeman, editor of the Chicago Gang, gets into and out of trouble. Not well written but an example of early pulp publishing.

_____. *Woman's Duplicity*. Chicago: Nile Publishing Co., 1891.

Vincent Ashley woos both Mary Henley and Mary Sillery. A rather silly story about male/female relations.

Duganne, Augustine Joseph Hickey. *Bravo's Daughter; or, the Troy of Carolina*. New York: E. Winchester, 1850.

Set in South Carolina during the Revolutionary War.

Edwards, Eleanor Lee. *Betrayed Bride; or, Wedded but Not Won*. New York: Frank Starr Co., 1869.

Two orphans married to the wrong men jump into a river in New England and supposedly drown but find their way to London on a ship that later is set afire.

Edwards, Julia. *Beautiful but Poor*. New York: Street and Smith, 1890.

Written under one of Stratemeyer's many pseudonyms.

Ellis, Edward Sylvester. *Bill Biddon, Trapper; or, Life in the North-West*. New York: Beadle's Dime Novels, 1860.

The life of hunters and trappers in the 1850s, while traveling through Missouri, Kansas and Nebraska. They are headed for the headwaters of the Yellowstone River.

_____. *Frontier Angel; or, a Romance of Kentucky Rangers' Life*. New York: Beadle's Dime Novels, 1861.

A story of flatboating in northern Kentucky and southern Ohio. In this, as in other stories, well-known historical characters appear.

_____. *Irona; or, Life on the Old Southwest Border*. New York: Beadle's Dime Novels, 1861.

Life in Texas, including a trip by flatboat up the Rio Grande River past Austin and then overland to the mountains.

_____. *Nathan Todd; or, the Fate of the Sioux' Captive*. New York: Beadle's Dime Novels, 1861.

A sequel to Bill Bidden. A Native American and trapper tale of the Northwest.

_____. *Prairie Rangers*. New York: Beadle's Dime Novels, 1866.

Life and adventure in the Nebraska Territory, the far Northwest and California in 1850.

_____. *Prairie Trail; or, Tim Button, the Trapper*. New York: Beadle and Adams, 1867.

A chase on horseback, after a bank robber, across the plains from New York, through Native American country, to California.

_____. *Rescue*. New York: Beadle and Adams, 1866.

A sequel to *Prairie Rangers*. Adventures in San Francisco and New Mexico with the same characters as in *Prairie Rangers*.

_____. *Seth Jones, of New Hampshire; or, the Captives of the Frontier*. New York: Beadle's Dime Novels, 1860.

One of the first and most successful Beadle novels. Was Seth in actuality a cultured man named Eugene Morton, who dressed in buckskins, affected the western speech patterns of the frontiersman and rescued the heroine?

_____. *Steam Man of the Prairies*. New York: Beadle's Dime Novels, 1868.

An inventive St. Louis boy and his iron man among the Native Americans of the prairies to the west.

Emerald, John. *Crested Serpent; or, the White Tiger of the Tropics*. New York: Beadle's Dime Novels, 1874.

A story of Mexico during the reign of Maximilian.

Emerson, Edwin. *Mad Horseman; or, the Prairie Tournament*. New York: Beadle's New Dime Novels, 1877.

Emmett, George. *Young Tom's School-days.* London: Hogarth House, 1870.
British publisher of boys' story papers. Written to compete successfully with Edwin Brett's *Jack Harkaway's School Days.*

Enton, Harry. *Monarch of the Moon; or, Frank Reade, Jr.'s, Exploits in Africa with His Electric "Thunderer."* New York: Frank Tousey, 1897.

Eyster, William. *Cedar Swamp; or, Wild Nat's Brigade.* New York: Beadle's Dime Novels, 1860.
This is one of the many dime novels Eyster wrote based on the Revolutionary War. He wrote both dime novels and series books. they were printed by People's Literary Companion.

Fable, Edmund. *Billy the Kid, the New Mexico Outlaw; or, the Bold Bandit of the West!* Denver: Denver Publication Co., 1881.
Billy was in real life William H. Bonney with several aliases. He was first in prison for petty thieving but became a fugitive, murderer and cattle rustler.

Fleming, May Agnes. *Midnight Queen; or, a Tale of Illusion, Delusion and Mystery.* New York: Frank Starr Co., 1870.
A romance of London during the great plague of 1666.

_____. *Twin Sisters; or, the Wronged Wife's Hate.* New York: Frank Starr Co., 1869.
Under the title "Hazelwood" this novel appeared as a serial in the *New York Mercury.* The story takes place in several different locales: New York City, St. Croix, Canada and England.

Fosdick, Charles Austin. *Elam Storm, the Wolfer; or, the Lost Nugget.* Philadelphia: Porter and Coates, 1895.

_____. *House Boat Boys.* Philadelphia: Porter and Coates, 1895.

_____. *Mystery of the Lost River Canyon.* Philadelphia: Porter and Coates, 1896.

_____. *Oscar in Africa.* Philadelphia: Porter and Coates, 1894.

_____. *Sailor in Spite of Himself.* Philadelphia: Porter and Coates, 1898.

_____. *Sportsman's Club Afloat.* Philadelphia: Porter and Coates, 1902.

_____. *Steel Horse; or, the Rambles of a Bicycle.* Philadelphia: Porter and Coates, 1888.

_____. *Young Game Warden.* Philadelphia: Porter and Coates, 1896.

Foster, W. Bert. *Lost Galleon of Dubloon Island.* Philadelphia: Penn Pub. Co., 1901.
Foster wrote under seven different pseudonyms. He wrote both dime novels and series books. An island adventure story.

Gleason, George. *Tippy the Texas; or, the Young Champion.* New York: Beadle's Dime Novels, 1874.
A story of New Mexico in 1846 and Mexico in 1848.

Goodrich, Samuel. *Two Doves and the Owl.* 1819.
A book with illustrations of monkeys climbing over a placid camel observed by a man in a tricolored hat. A type of nature book.

_____. *Vagabond.* 1819.
A book with pictures of bulls, dogs, bears and wolves. Another nature book.

Grainger, Arthur M. *Aunt's Plot; or, the Stolen Heir.* New York: Frank Starr Co., 1871.

_____. *Beautiful Jewess; or, the Young Sailor's Triumph.* New York: Frank Starr Co., 1870.

Hall, Sam S. *Big Foot Wallace, the King of the Lariat; or, Wild Wolf, the Waco.* New York: Beadle's Dime Library, 1882.
Big Foot was an early Texan and reveals a tale of San Antonio at that time.

Hall, William Jared. *Slave Sculptor; or, the Prophetess of the Secret Chambers.* New York: Beadle's Dime Novels, 1860.

Halsey, Harlan Page. *Old Sleuth, the Detective; or, the Bay Ridge Mystery.* New York: Norman Munro, 1885.
"Sleuth" was a detective first appearing in *The Family Story Paper.* One of many fictional detectives to appear in the late 1800s. Munro used court action to prevent other publishers from using Sleuth in any title. This is the first appearance of Old Sleuth in book form.

Hamilton, J. Stanley. *Twin Scouts; a Story of the Old French War.* New York: Beadle's Dime Novels, 1866.
Pseudonym of Charles Clark. This is an adventure story about young boys as scouts during the war with the French.

_____. *Two Trails; or, Sam Grinter's Search.* New York: Beadle's Dime Novels, 1868.
An adventure story of American traders in Durango and Chihuahua, Mexico, before the war with the United States.

Hamilton, William J. *Barden, the Ranger; or, the Flower of the Uchees.* New York: Beadle and Adams, 1867.
Costello's attempt to incite the Georgia Indians against the settlers.

_____. *Big Foot, the Guide; or, the Surveyors.* New York: Beadle's Dime Novels, 1866.
Big Foot was the name of Jared Tomlinson, a Tuscarora Indian of North Carolina.

_____. *Border Vengeance; or, the Night Hawk's Daughter.* New York: Beadle and Adams, 1873.
A gang of outlaws and a search for a father's murderer in Kansas.

_____. *Despard, the Spy; or, the Fall of Montreal.* New York: Beadle's Dime Novels, 1869.
A story of the fall of Montreal in 1760 and the breaking of the power of the French in America.

_____. *Eagle Eye; or, Ralph Warren and His Red Friend.* New York: Beadle's Dime Novels, 1865.
A story of the French and Indian war.

_____. *Giant Pete, the Patriot; or, the Champion of the Swamps.* New York: Beadle's Dime Novels, 1869.
This story takes place in South Carolina during the Revolutionary War. It covers the guerilla warfare between the Whigs and the English Tories.

_____. *Gulch Miners; or, the Queen of the Secret Valley.* New York: Beadle's Dime Novels, 1867.
Life in the gold diggings in 1852.

_____. *Hunchback; or, the Cave Castle.* New York: Beadle and Adams, 1867.
A tale of the American Revolution when Johnson, Claus and Brant were wreaking havoc among the frontier towns.

_____. *Indian Avenger.* New York: Beadle and Adams, 1868.
A tale of horse stealing and a Native American's vengeance.

_____. *Maid of the Mountains; or, the Brothers of the League.* New York: Beadle and Adams, 1868.
Gold seekers in California with vigilantes, outlaws and another Yankee, Josh.

_____. *Mossfoot, the Brave; or, the Fat Scout of Oneida Lake.* New York: Beadle's Dime Novels, 1874.
A Native American tale of the Mohawk Valley, New York, during the Revolutionary War.

_____. *Mountain Ned; or, the Flying Scout.* New York: Beadle's Dime Novels, 1874.
A Native American tale of New Mexico concerning an early parachutist-bomber. The story is made interesting by a Yankee Manchausen.

_____. *Peddler Spy; or, Dutchman and Yankees.* New York: Beadle and Adams, 1866.
Early days of the first Dutch settlement in Connecticut. The fort, known as "The House of Good Hope," was built to protect the colony against the English or Plymouth and against the Native Americans.

_____. *Plymouth Scout; or, Eutawan, the Slayer.* New York: Beadle's Dime Novels, 1871.
A story of the early days in the Plymouth colony.

_____. *Prairie Queen; or, Tom Western, the Texas Ranger.* New York: Beadle's Dime Novels, 1871.

A story of horse thieves, rangers and the Comanche in Texas.

_____. *Red Lightning; or, the Black League.* New York: Beadle's Dime Novels, 1872.

A tale of Pontiac and the Detroit settlements.

_____. *Shawnees' Foe; or, the Hunter of the Juniata.* New York: Beadle and Adams, 1866.

The youthful Major General George Washington, in the war between the French and English, is prominent in this story. Colonial days in Pennsylvania.

_____. *Sons of Liberty; or, the Maid of Tyron.* New York: Beadle and Adams, 1867.

A tale of the Stamp Act and its effect on the people of New York.

_____. *Warrior Princess; or, the Pride of the Everglades.* New York: Beadle's Dime Novels, 1873.

A Spanish and Native American tale of the Tampa Bay country, Florida, in 1539.

_____. *Wenona, the Giant Chief of St. Regis; or, the Forest Flower.* New York: Beadle's Dime Novels, 1868.

A story of the French and Native American atrocities in New York.

_____. *White Hermit; or, the Unknown Foe.* New York: Beadle's Dime Novels, 1870.

The story of an Iroquois of central New York at the end of the seventeenth century.

Hammett, Dashiell. *Red Harvest.* New York: Knopf, 1929.

Hammett wrote for *Black Mask* magazine. *Red Harvest* was his first book. He is best known for *The Maltese Falcon.*

Harbaugh, Thomas. *Kiowa Charley, the White Mustanger; or, Rocky Mountain Kit's Last Scalp Hunt.* New York: Beadle and Adams, 1879.

An adventure story of the Kiowa and Kit Carson along the Wichita River at Fort Sill.

Hazeltine, Lieut. Col. *California Joe; or, the Angel of the Wilderness.* New York: Starr's American Novels, 1865.

The adventures of Joseph Milner, although he is called Joseph Ledlie in this story.

_____. *Quindaro; or, the Heroine of Fort Laramie.* New York: Beadle's Dime Novels, 1865.

A tale of the Far West.

_____. *Schuylkill Rangers; or, the Bride of Valley Forge.* New York: Beadle's Dime Novels, 1865.

George Washington at Valley Forge in 1777. At one time he is saved from the scaffold.

Henderson, J. Stanley. *Karaibe; or, the Other Fate.* New York: Beadle's Dime Novels, 1866.

A tale of Native Americans, Mexicans, outlaws and gold seekers in California and New Mexico in the early days after these states were taken from Mexico.

_____. *Kidnapped; or, the Free Rangers of the Coosaw.* New York: Beadle and Adams, 1866.

The free rangers were a set of semibandits who afflicted South Carolina during the Revolutionary War.

_____. *Man in Green; or, the Siege of Bexar.* New York: Beadle and Adams, 1866.

San Antonio de Bexar and vicinity in 1835, during its struggle with Mexico for independence. Capture of the Alamo.

_____. *Ned Sterling; or, the Marauder's Island.* New York: Beadle and Adams, 1867.

A tale of John A. Murrell's gang of highwaymen and life in the wilds of Arkansas and Tennessee and along the Mississippi in 1835.

_____. *Salouch, the Cherokee; or, the White Rose of the Saluda.* New York: Beadle and Adams, 1867.

A tale of the conflict between Native Americans and colonists in South Carolina from 1756 to 1761.

_____. *Trader Spy; or, the Victim of the Fire Raft.* New York: Beadle and Adams, 1869.

A story that takes place on the Detroit River, near the fort, in 1764. It involves Pontiac.

_____. *Unseen Hand; or, the Four Scouts of the Waccamaw.* New York: Beadle's Dime Novels, 1868.
A story that takes place in the Waccamaw Valley on the eastern shore of South Carolina in 1781, involving the Tories, the British and the patriots.

Henty, G. A. *Out on the Pampas; or, the Young Settlers.* London: Griffith and Farrar, 1871.
Henty's first book for boys. He wrote many more.

Hoffman, J. Milton. *Gunpowder Jim; or, the Mystery of Demon Hollow.* New York: Beadle's Frontier Series, 1908.

Holt, Joseph. *Captain Kyd; or, the Wizard of the Sea, a Romance.* New York: Harper, 1839.

Howard, Adam M. *Cora Clifford; or, Bound by an Oath to the Dead.* New York: Norman Munro, 1880.
One of several stories connecting marriage with death and experiences of frustration or imprisonment, considering the restricted nature of women's roles in marriage.

Howland, William Henry. *Quakeress Spy.* New York: Beadle and Adams, 1883.
This story takes place in Philadelphia in 1868. One of the few stories where women are heroines.

Hunter, Ned. *Scalp King; or, the Squaw Wife of the White Avenger.* New York: Starr's American Novels, 1875.
A story of Native American warfare and vengeance in a western state.

Ingraham, Prentiss. *Actor Detective in Chicago; or, Dick Doom's Flush Hand.* New York: Beadle and Adams, 1893.
Justin finds a body in his trunk and contacts Dick Doom, the detective. He along with his helpers capture the murderer.

_____. *Adventures of Buffalo Bill from Boyhood to Manhood.* New York: Beadle and Adams, 1882.
"Deeds of daring and romantic incidents in Buffalo Bill's early life."

_____. *Buck Taylor, King of the Cowboys; or, the Raiders and the Rangers.* New York: Beadle's Half Dime Library, Feb. 1, 1887.
The author is an ex-soldier and adventurer, a son of Joseph Holt. He wrote many Buffalo Bill stories, but this is one of his non–Buffalo Bill tales.

_____. *Buffalo Bill's Tangled Trail; or, Gentleman Jack.* New York: Beadle and Adams, 1896.

_____. *California Joe, the Mysterious Plainsman: The Strange Adventures of an Unknown Man.* New York: Beadle and Adams.
Joe's real identity, like that of the "Man in the Iron Mask," is still unsolved. Even if the real name of California Joe is unknown, some say it was Joseph Milmer; others that it was Joseph Hawkins; and some others that he was a distant relative of Daniel Boone. His service was to Reynold's wagon train; he captured 200 mustangs and in the end was assassinated.

_____. *Cowboy Clan; or, the Tigress of Texas.* New York: Beadle's Dime Library, 1891.
A true example of cowboy life in Texas.

_____. *Cuban Conspirators; or, the Island League.* New York: Beadle's Dime Novels, 1874.
An account of one of the many unsuccessful revolutions by Cubans against the Spanish rulers.

_____. *Darkie Dan, the Colored Detective; or, the Mississippi Mystery.* New York: Beadle's Dime Library, 1881.
A story of Mississippi River gamblers including high stakes and marked cards.

_____. *Hussar Captain; or, the Hermit of Hell-Gate.* New York: Beadle's Dime Novels, 1873.
General Howe is in New York City and the adjacent waters in 1776.

_____. *Masked Avenger; or, Death on the Trail.* New York: Beadle's Dime Novels, 1873.

A band of a hundred outlaws, Native Americans, Mexicans and Americans with a Santa Fe train in southwest Texas.

_____. *Rival Lieutenants; or, the Twin Cruiser*. New York: Beadle's Dime Novels, 1874.

A story whose setting is Maine, New Jersey and the sea in 1812.

_____. *Wild Bill, the Pistol Dead Shot; or, Dagger Don's Double*. New York: Beadle's New York Dime Library, 1882.

Wild Bill Hickok in Kansas; there are duels, shootings, hangings, treachery plus ghosts, secret mines and pack horses "that can shoot."

Ingraham, Rev. J. H. *Annie Temple; or, the Bankrupt's Heiress*. New York: Frank Starr Co., 1870.

A count and countess living in a shabby New York house.

Iron, Nathaniel C. *Gideon Goldbold; or, the Faithful and the Unfaithful of 1780*. New York: Beadle and Adams, 1862.

A narrative of Arnold's marriage, some secret plotting and treason. Major Andre's life is explained.

_____. *Hearts Forever; or, the Old Dominion Battle-Ground*. New York: Beadle and Adams, 1882.

A tale of 1782. Washington and Cornwallis are characters in the story.

James, Mrs. Orrin. *Old Jupe; or, a Woman's Art*. New York: Beadle and Adams, 1867.

A story of a sister's jealousy. Also continues to California and its first fire.

_____. *Wrecker's Daughter*. New York: Beadle and Adams, 1867.

There is trouble between a young wife and her husband. He dies and leaves her nothing. their daughter Myra is adopted by a wealthy couple.

Jenardo, Don. *True Life of Billy the Kid*. New York: Frank Tousey's Wide Awake Library, Aug. 29, 1881.

Johnson, Francis. *Doomed Guide; or, the Hunter's Trail*. New York: Frank Starr Co., 1871.

_____. *Giant Trailer; or, the Lost Scalp*. New York: Frank Starr Co., 1875.

A tale of gold seekers in Mexico, California and the whole southwest.

_____. *Pepe, the Scout; or, the Rangers of Sonora*. New York: Frank Starr Co., 1875.

_____. *Ranger Rifle; or, the Wolf on the War Path*. New York: Frank Starr Co., 1871.

_____. *War-Axe; or, the Trapper's Revenge*. New York: Frank Starr Co., 1871.

Jones, Hannah Maria (1784–1854). *Emily Moreland; or, the Maid of the Valley*. London: Sherwood, 1829.

Third-person narrative, taking place in Cambridge, France and Venice. Theme is the disinheritance of women, women's work and illegitimacy.

Jones, L. A. *Mexican Joe, the Snake Charmer*. New York: Munro's Ten Cent Novels, 1865.

Kellogg, Elijah. *Burying the Hatchet; or, the Young Braves of the Delaware*. Boston: Lothrop, Lee and Shepard, 1906.

_____. *Good Old Times*. Boston: Lothrop, Lee and Shepard, 1867.

Kelly, George. *Tracked to Chicago; or, Thad Burr's Great Trunk Mystery*. New York: Beadle and Adams, 1894.

A trunk with a decomposed body is found. Thad Burr, a New York detective, is in town and is pressed into service.

Kennedy, Rose. *Emerald Necklace; or, Mrs. Butterby's Boarder*. New York: Beadle's Dime Novels, 1861.

An emerald necklace is found in an old well and is supposed to have potential evil, but all turns out well.

_____. *Myrtle, the Child of the Prairie*. New York: Beadle's Half Dime Novelettes, 1860.

A child, abandoned on the prairie, is found by Hugh Fielding. The girl eventually finds her widowed mother, and all ends happily when Fielding marries her mother.

Kenward, Philip. *Bowery Detective*. New York: George Munro.

One of the first dime-novel, detective stories with the main character, Old Sleuth, appearing in continuing titles.

Kingston, William Henry Giles. *Peter the Whaler, His Early Life and Adventures in the Arctic Regions*. London: Sydney, Griffith Farrar, Okeden and Welsh, 1851.

Peter is bound on a ship where he is maltreated but escapes and after many adventures returns to his home and family.

_____. *Snow Shoes and Canoes*. 1876.

_____. *Three Midshipmen*. London: Sydney, Griffith Farrar, Okeden and Welsh, 1873.

Klapp, H. Milnor. *Cruiser of the Bay*. New York: Irwin Beadle, 1866.

Lager, Fetrick. *Abler Holders' Bound Boy; or, the Poor Relation*. 1871.

LaSalle, Charles E. *Forest Monster; or, Lamora, the Maid of the Canon*. New York: Beadle's Dime Novels, 1870.

A story about an emigrant train and gold seekers. There are Native American encounters in the Black Hills country.

LeGrand, Louis. *Hunter's Vow*. New York: Beadle's Dime Novels, March 3, 1864.

A tale of Ohio in the 1790s, after Harner's defeat and the retreat of St. Clair's army.

Lewis, Leon. *Daredeath Dick, King of the Cowboys; or, in the Wild West with Buffalo Bill*. New York: Beadle and Adams, 1890.

Buffalo Bill and Nat Salsburg in show business. Also a tale of the Jay Hawk gang in the cattle country.

_____. *Kit's Last Trail*. New York: R. Bonner's Sons, 1891.

Pseudonym of George Blakelee. There were many Kit Carson authors; he is but one.

Libbey, Laura Jean. *Heiress of Cameron Hall*. New York: George Munro, 1889.

_____. *Ione, a Broken Love Dream*. New York: R. Bonner's Sons, 1890.

_____. *Junie's Love-Test*. New York: George Munro, 1889.

_____. *Leonie Locke; or, the Romance of a Beautiful New York Working Girl*. New York: Munro's *Fireside Companion*, 1884.

_____. *Little Leafy, the Cloakmaker's Beautiful Daughter*. New York: Ogilvie Publishing Co., 1886.

A romantic story of a lovely working girl in the city of New York.

_____. *Little Rosebud's Lovers; or, a Cruel Revenge*. New York: George Munro, 1886.

_____. *Lyndall's Temptation; or, Blinded by Love*. New York: Norman Munro, 1892.

_____. *Mad Betrothal; or, Nadine's Vow*. New York: R. Bonner's Sons, 1890.

_____. *Madolin Rivers*. New York: George Munro, 1889.

_____. *Miss Middleton's Lover*. New York: American News Co., 1888.

_____. *Parted at the Altar*. New York: R. Bonner's Sons, 1893.

_____. *Pretty Madcap Dorothy; or, How She Won a Lover*. Cleveland: Arthur Westbrook Co., 1892.

Libbey's first book was *Fatal Wooing* (New York: Munro, 1883). She wrote many, many more. Most of her stories were about women of the day and their plight.

_____. *Struggle for a Heart*. New York: George Munro, 1889.

Lippard, George. *Quaker City; or, the Monks of Monk Hall*. Pennsylvania: Zieber, 1844–1845.

A romance of Philadelphia life, mystery and crime. This book sold over 100,000 copies.

Madden, Billy. *John L., Jr., the Young Knocker-Outer; or, Fighting for a Fortune.* New York: Five Cent Library, Aug. 13, 1892.
A story based on the real John Lawrence Sullivan, even though the main character is called John Lawrence, Jr. The real Sullivan was sometimes called "the Great Knocker Out." Billy Madden was the pseudonym for Alfred B. Tozer, who ghost wrote this series.

Marryat, Frederick. *Masterman Ready; or, the Wreck of the Pacific.* London: Longman, Orm, 1841–1842.
The Masterman family were ship owners and builders. The story gives descriptions of Africa, northward from the Cape of Good Hope: lions rhinoceroses, and lots of adventure. The first children's novel written by Marryat. Based, roughly, on *Swiss Family Robinson.*

_____. *Settlers in Canada.* London: Longman, Brown, 1844.
Story of an English family who emigrate to Canada in 1794. It details pioneer life and the lives of Martin Suoer, the trapper, Malachi Bone, the hunger, and John, the boy who was born a backwoodsman.

Marshall, John J. *Outlaw Brothers; or the Captive of the Harpes.* New York: Beadle and Adams, 1879.

Martin, Eugene. *Randy Starr After an Air Prize.* Philadelphia: Altemus, 1931.
Randy Starr flies as a test and acrobatic pilot. The fourth book in this series is *Randy Starr Tracing the Air Spy* (1933).

Martine, Max. *Old Bear-Paw, the Trapper King; or, the Love of a Blackfoot Queen.* New York: Beadle's Dime Novels, 1873.
Gold seekers and Native Americans in the Black Hills.

McKenna, Charlotte Stanley. *Bound for Life; or, Death-Bed Marriage.* New York: Norman Munro, 1881.
Another one of several stories connecting marriage with death and experiences of frustration or imprisonment.

Meredith, C. Leon. *Kit Carson, the Border Boy.* New York: Nickel Library Co., N.D.
There are many Kit Carson authors and stories; this is but one.

Miller, Alex M. *Senator's Bride.* New York: Street and Smith, 1887.

_____. *Dreadful Temptation.* New York: Street and Smith, 1883.

Miller, Alexandria McVeigh. *Bride of the Tomb; or, Lancelot Darling's Betrothed.* New York: Norman Munro, 1883.
Other titles are *An Old Man's Darling* (1881) and *Bonne Dora.* A Gothic horror story.

Millett, Edward. *Black Eyes; or, the Three Captives.* New York: Beadle's Dime Novels, 1867.
Life in New Mexico during the attempted uprising of 1848.

Mogridge, George. *Sergeant Bell and His Raree-Show.* London: Thomas Tegg, 1829.
The first edition of this book is often ascribed to Charles Dickens. Woodcuts are by George Cruikshank.

Monstery, Thomas Hoyer. *Czar's Spy; or, the Nihilist League.* New York: Beadle's Half Dime Library, 1897.
Alexander II was czar of Russia. This story covers the recovery of the Orloff diamond by Olaf Svenson, the sword master.

_____. *El Rubio Bravo, King of the Swordsmen; or, the Terrible Brothers of Tabasco.* New York: Beadle's Half Dime Library, 1881.
A story of Honduras when Guartiola was president.

_____. *Iron Wrist, the Sword Master.* New York: Beadle's Half Dime Library, 1879.

Morris, Anthony Paschel. *Electro Pete, the Man of Fire; or, the Wharf Rats of Locust Point.* Cleveland: Arthur Westbrook Co., 1884.

Murray, Captain. *White Brave; or, the Flower of the Lenape Lodge.* New York: Beadle and Adams, 1881.

_____. *Wingenund, the Young Trail-Hunter; or, the Death of War Eagle.* New York: Beadle's Half Dime Library, 1872.

A sequel to *The White Brave.* A continuing story of the Delaware Wingenund.

Musick, John Roy. *Train Robbers; or, a Story of the James Boys.* New York: Frank Tousey, 1881.

Jesse Woodson James (1847–1882) and Alexander Franklin James (1843–1915) are the James brothers. The first story in the New York Detective Library is "Chasing the James Boys; or, a Detective's Dangerous Case (1889). The first Street and Smith story is "Jesse the Outlaw, a Narrative of the James Boys" (1882). The last Westbrook story is "Jesse James' Fate; or, the End of the Crimson Trail (1910).

Myers, P. Hamilton. *Ellen Welles; or, the Siege of Fort Stanwix.* New York: W. O. M'Clure, 1848.

A Native American invasion of the Mohawk Valley.

_____. *Nick Doyle, the Gold Hunter.* New York: Beadle's Dime Novels, 1871.

A tale of California and its gold fields.

North, Ingoldsby. *Job Dean, the Trapper.* New York: Beadle and Adams, 1868.

Native American warfare and adventures at the frontier posts of the Kansas-Nebraska border in 1860.

"An Old Scout." *Boy Rifle Rangers; or, Kit Carson's Three Young Scouts.* New York: Frank Tousey, 1917.

"Old Sleuth." *Dutch Detective; or, The Mystery of the Black Pool.* New York: George Munro, 1870.

Old Sleuth dons his favorite disguise to assist three colleagues investigating the case of a missing woman.

Patten, William George. *Cowboy Steve, the Ranch Mascot; or, the Bond of Blood.* New York: Beadle's Half Dime Library, Jan. 3, 1893.

A bad woman and bad blood on a cattle ranch out west.

_____. *Hurricane Hal, the Cowboy Hotspur; or, Old True Blue's Pilgrimage in Satan's Section.* New York: Beadle's Half Dime Novels, 1891.

_____. *Old True Blue the Trusty; or, the Marauder of the Membres.* New York: Beadle's Dime Novels, 1891.

A tale of New Mexico, Geronimo and his band, gamblers, soldiers and cowboys.

Penne, Agile. *Detective's Ward; or, the Fortunes of the Bowery Girl.* New York: Beadle and Adams.

Periodical. *Liberty Boys of '76.* New York: Frank Tousey, 1901–1925.

A group of 100 young men won the war against Britain and helped the colonies with their independence. Considered one of the "big six."

Periodical. *Pluck and Luck.* New York: Frank Tousey, 1898–1929.

One of the "big six," this one is an adventure story. "Big Six" is what collectors call these major publications. This was the longest-running, dime-novel series. A weekly magazine featuring Fred Fearnot, a young man who travels around the world doing good deeds. There are also other short stories, current events and advertising.

Periodical. *Secret Service.* New York: Frank Tousey, 1899–1928.

The third of the "Big Six" from Tousey. It is about the detectives par excellence, the Bradys.

Periodical. *Wild West Weekly.* New York: Street and Smith, 1902–1927.

The fifth of the "Big Six," where the heroic "Young Wild West" tamed the West.

Porter, Ann E. *Guilty or Not Guilty; or, the Ordeal of Fire.* New York: Beadle's Dime Novels, 1966.

A tale of false accusation of murder.

Prentice, George Henry. *Marked Bullet; or, the Squaw's Reprieve.* New York: Beadle's Dime Novels, 1864.

This book includes excerpts from *The Outlaw Brothers* by John J. Marshall.

Prest, Thomas Peckett. *Almira's Curse; or, the Black Tower of Bransdorf; a Romance.* London: Edward Lloyd, 1842.

An example of the type of books read by youngsters in the early 1800s.

_____. *Demon of the Hartz; or, the Three Charcoal Burners*. London, 1835.

_____. *Geralda the Demon Nun*. London: Edward Lloyd. N.D.

_____. *Maniac Father; or, the Victim of Seduction*. London: Edward Lloyd, 1850.

_____. *Sweeney Todd; the Demon Barber of Fleet Street* (also known as *The String of Pearls*). London: Fox, 1878.

Preston, Percy. *Café Detection; or, Roy Kennedy's Big Score*. New York: Beadle's Dime Novels, 1890.

The result of buying a second-hand phonograph involves a wicked uncle and a falsely accused clerk.

Rede, William Leman. *Sixteen-String Jack, a Romantic Drama*. London: G. H. Davidson, 1891.

The hero is known as Sixteen-String Jack because he wears eight decorative tags at each knee. His henchman is Kit Clayton. (J. B. Barrie went by this nickname in his schooldays.)

Reed, Abner. *Love Triumphant; or, Constancy Rewarded*. New York: Luther Pratt, 1797.

A romance between star-crossed lovers who are separated by the girl's parents.

Reid, Mayne. *Castaways*. New York: Beadle and Adams, 1871.

_____. *Rifle-Rangers; or, Adventures in Southern Mexico*. New York: Carleton, 1870.

_____. *Scalp Hunters, a Romance of the Plains*. New York: Beadle's Dime Library, 1868.

A story of a journey with the trader St. Vrin, from St. Louis to Santa Fe and on to Mexico. Describes the flora and fauna encountered while adventurous brothers search for a white buffalo on the American prairie.

_____. *White Squaw*. New York: Beadle and Adams, 1868.

A story of Florida during the Seminole War. Whites fight for conquest; Seminoles try to retain their own. A stockade; death at the stake; and a white captive is saved.

Reynolds, George William McArthur. *Mysteries of the Court of London*. London: J. Dicks, 1850.

Reynolds was a member of the 1848 Chartist movement. He was a radical populist and a respected author. This story depicts many courtroom scenes.

Robins, Seelin. *Trappers of the Gila; or, Life and Adventures in the Far Southwest*. New York: Beadle's Dime Novels, 1867.

A Yankee with a drove of sheep from Santa Fe is on his way to Lower California to establish his "Institute for the Education of Youths of Both Sexes."

Robinson, J. H. *Adopted Daughter; or, the Half-Brother's Snare*. New York: Frank Starr Co., 1870.

An adopted daughter stands in the way of a half-brother's inheritance. A substituted dead body is buried.

_____. *Artist's Bride; or, Noll Darker's Protégé*. New York: Frank Starr Co., 1871.

_____. *Fair Schemer; or, the Dread Secret*. New York: Frank Starr Co., 1871.

_____. *Milrose, the Heiress; or, the Step-Father's Plot*. New York: Frank Starr Co., 1871.

_____. *Uncle's Crime; or, the Doctor's Beautiful Ward*. New York: Frank Starr Co., 1870.

A melodramatic story of a man walled up alive; yellow fever in New Orleans; a girl who feigns death and a useless murder for an inheritance.

Rockwood, Roy. *Five Thousand Miles Underground; or, the Mystery of the Center of the Earth*. New York: Cupples and Leon, 1908.

A tale of murderous plots, subterranean giants, weird animals, and the Lost Race's Temple of Treasure.

_____. *Jack North's Treasure Hunt; or,*

Daring Adventures in South America. Cleveland: Goldsmith, 1907.
Fantastic adventure revisiting the island of Robinson Crusoe, including jungle adventures of quicksand, encounters with jaguars, ocelots and enormous snakes and a hidden treasure of the Boiling Lake.

_____. *Through the Air to the North Pole; or, the Wonderful Cruise of the Electric Monarch.* New York: Cupples and Leon, 1906.
A story of flying ships over mountain lakes and polar tribes attacking these aircraft.

Rodman, Emerson. *Mad Captain.* New York: Street and Smith, Nov. 1, 1866.

Rymer, James Malcolm. *Varney, the Vampire; or, the Feast of Blood.* London: Edward Lloyd, 1847.
"Variously attributed to T. P. Prest or James Malcolm Rymer. Among the first of the "gothic" novels.

St. George, Harry. *Daring Davy, the Young Bear Killer; or, the Trail of the Border Wolf.* New York: Beadle's Half Dime Library, Aug. 19, 1879.
A story of Davy Crockett in Tennessee.

St. John, Percy B. *Blackhawk, the Bandit; or the Indian Scout.* New York: Beadle's Dime Novels, 1872.
Bandits and Native Americans in Texas, shortly after it had declared itself independent of Mexico.

_____. *Queen of the Woods; or, the Shawnee Captive.* New York: Beadle's Dime Novels, 1869.
A tale of Daniel Boone and Girty in Kentucky from 1769 to 1770, when the Native Americans were on the warpath.

Sala, George Augustus. *Strange Adventures of Captain Dangerous; a Narrative in Plain English.* Boston: T. O. H. P. Burnham, 1863.
Captain Dangerous is a soldier, a pirate, a merchant, a spy, and so on. Sala also rewrote Prest's novels for Charles Cox.

Sawyer, Eugene T. *Maltese Cross; or, the Detective's Quest.* New York: Street and Smith, 1888.

Scott, J. R. *Red River Bill, the Prince of Scouts.* New York: Frank Tousey's Wide Awake Library, Mar. 19, 1897.

Senarens, Luis. *Ashtray in the Selvas; or, the Wild Experiences of Frank Reade, Jr.* New York: Frank Tousey, 1895.

_____. *Beyond the Gold Coast; or, Frank Reade Jr.'s Overland Trip with His Electric Phaeton.* New York: Frank Tousey, 1896.

_____. *Young Frank Reade and His Electric Air Ship; or, a 10,000-Mile Search for a Missing Man.* New York: Frank Tousey, 1899.

Sherman, John. *Daniel Boone's Best Shot; or, the Perils of the Kentucky Pioneers.* New York: Frank Tousey's Wide Awake Library, Dec. 3, 1892.

Sherwood, Scott R. *Veiled Benefactress; or, the Rocking Stone Mystery.* New York: Beadle and Adams, 1867.
A rocking stone tests the innocence or guilt of women suspected by their lovers or husbands. A cruel trick is played on an innocent girl.

Smith, Elizabeth Oakes. *Bald Eagle; or, the Last of the Ramapaughs.* New York: Beadle and Adams, 1867.
Struggle of the American patriots against the British in the Ramapo Valley from 1781 to 1784. The cowboys were marauders who preyed upon settlers but did not belong to the army.

Southworth, Arabella. *Her Hidden Foes; or, Love at All Odds.* New York: Beadle and Adams.

Southworth, Emma D. E. N. *Deserted Wife.* New York: Appleton and Co., 1855.
Popular novel about women who are deserted by their husbands. Southworth was a Washington school teacher and wrote many other books about women.

Sproat, Nancy. *Ditties for Children.* Philadelphia: Benjamin Warner, 1818.
A chapbook of moral poems with sixteen woodcuts.

Starbuck, Roger. *Blue Clipper; or, the Smuggler Spy*. New York: Beadle's Dime Novels, 1871.

This story covers the events in the Gulf of Mexico near Vera Cruz and west of Tampico.

_____. *Foul-Weather; or, the Double Wreck*. New York: Beadle's Dime Novels, 1867.

A story that takes place off the coast of Chile, at Honolulu and in the Okhotsk Sea.

_____. *Ice Fiend; or, the Hunted Whalemen*. New York: Beadle's Dime Novels, 1871.

A tale of the Arctic Ocean and fishermen.

_____. *Lost Ship; or, the Cruise for a Shadow*. New York: Beadle and Adams, 1866.

A long search in the Kamchatka Sea for the wreck of a whaling vessel and one of its officers.

_____. *Phantom Ship; or, the Island Cairn*. New York: Beadle's Dime Novels, 1869.

A story of a castaway in Honolulu, through the Straits of Magellan and Tierra del Fuego.

_____. *Port at Last; or, a Cruise of Honor*. New York: Beadle and Adams, 1867.

Cape Cod seafaring in 1815. 'Round the world in the trader *Watchfire*. Around the Horn to the Navigator Islands for copra and to the Moluccas for spices.

_____. *Rival Rovers; or, the Flying Wake*. New York: Beadle's Dime Novels, 1873.

A story that takes place on an island near the Fijis and adjacent seas in the early nineteenth century.

_____. *Shadow Jack; or, the Spotted Cruiser*. New York: Beadle's Dime Novels, 1868.

A story of the Algerine War of 1814.

_____. *Sheet-Anchor Tom; or, the Sunken Treasure*. New York: Beadle and Adams, 1867.

The voyage of the *Meteor* from New York to Rio de Janeiro. Wreck of the ship on a reef, the loss of the cargo and a chest of jewels, and the final salvaging of the wreck under difficulties.

_____. *Specter Shipper; or, the Sunken Will*. New York: Beadle and Adams, 1869.

A brig, one of Commodore Porter's fleet, is bound for the West Indies in 1832 to suppress piracy.

Stephens, Ann Sophia Winterbotham. *Malaeska: The Indian Wife of the White Hunter*. New York: Beadle's Dime Novels, June 9, 1860.

A tragic tale of a beautiful Native American maiden who follows her heart and marries a white settler. This is Stephens's most famous book, although she wrote many others.

_____. *Myra, the Child of Adoption*. New York: Beadle's Dime Novels, 1860.

False friends make trouble between a young wife and her husband. He dies and leaves none of his wealth to his wife or daughter, Myra. The latter is adopted by a wealthy Philadelphia couple and eventually marries. Her husband dies of yellow fever, and Myra marries General Gaines. At the end of the story, the suit is not yet settled.

Steuart, Andrew. *Royal Old Song: Containing the Life and Tragical End of Fair Rosamund*. Philadelphia: Andrew Steuart, 1763.

"...[W]ho was concubine to King Henry the Second and put to death by Queen Eleanor in the famous bower of Woodstock near Oxford to which is added The Northern Lass."

Stratemeyer, Edward. *Dash Dare on His Mettle; or, Clearing Up a Double Tragedy*. New York: Edward Stratemeyer, 1892.

Stratemeyer wrote under James A. Cooper, Julia Edwards, Robert Hamilton and Winfield. This is a rewrote of the Lizzie Borden case, published two months after the murder. A coverage of Lizzie Borden with Ellen Canby in the role of Lizzie. The role is not true to the facts.

Thomas, Mrs. Henry J. *Prairie Bride; or, the Squatter's Triumph*. New York: Beadle's Dime Novels, 1869.

A story about covered wagons on the plains of Iowa. There is a fight for a claim, a prairie fire and a St. Louis housewarming.

_____. *Prairie Rifles; or, the Captives of New Mexico.* New York: Beadle's Dime Novels, 1869.

A story of Texas after it separated from Mexico in 1834. Also takes place in New Mexico.

Turner, William Mason. *Red Belt, the Tuscarora; or, the Death Trail.* New York: Beadle's Dime Novels, 1870.

A tale of the Kanawha in 1774 during the Dunmore War, when Ohio and West Virginia were frontiers.

Tuthill, Louisa Caroline. *Love of Admiration; or, Mary's Visit to Boston.* New Haven: A. H. Maltby, 1828.

_____. *Mirror of Life.* Philadelphia: Lindsay and Blakeston, 1847.

Unknown. *William and Eliza; or, the Visit.* New York: R. L. Underhill, 1841.

A chapbook with illustrations about a visit to the country.

Urban, Septimus R. *Wronged Wife; or, the Heart of Hate.* New York: Frank Starr Co., 1870.

An English love story. This book is sometimes attributed to the author Margaret Blount, but this is in error.

Victor, Metta. *Alice, Wilde, the Raftsman's Daughter.* New York: Beadle's Dime Novels, 1860.

A young man, rejected by his girl because he loses his fortune, goes west to work in a sawmill owned by the Wildes.

_____. *Maum Guinea and Her Plantation Children.* New York: Beadle's Dime Novels, N.D.

Viles, Edward. *Black Bess; or, the Knight of the Road.* London: E. Harrison, 1866.

Based on the real Richard Turpin, who was hanged for horse stealing. A famous fictional character. He lived under the name John Almer. He appears in several books. Black Bess was Turpin's horse.

_____. *Gentleman Jack; or, Life on the Road.* London: Edward Lloyd, 1852.

A series issued at a penny a week. Volume 1: *Vileroy; or, the Horrors of Zindorf Castle.* Bloodthirsty stories suitable for penny dreadfuls. Part of the Claude Duval series.

Wheeler, Edward L. *Hurricane Nell, the Girl Dead-Shot; or, the Queen of the Saddle and Lasso.* New York: Frank Starr Co., 1877.

The adventures of outlaws and bad men in Colorado.

_____. *Wild Ivan, the Boy Claude Duval; or the Brotherhood of Death.* New York: Beadle and Adams, 1878.

Whittaker, Frederick. *Boone, the Hunter; or, the Backwoods Belle.* New York: Beadle's Dime Library, March 25, 1873.

An episode in the life of Daniel Boone, when he goes west to find a landed estate so that his brother may marry a planter's daughter with whom he was in love.

_____. *Jaspar Ray, the Journeyman Carpenter; or, One Man as Good as Another in America.* New York: Beadle's Dime Novels, 1883.

A story of how a carpenter makes his way in the world.

_____. *John Armstrong, Mechanic; or, from the Bottom to the Top of the Ladder.* New York: Beadle's Dime Novels, 1886.

A story of how a man rises above his humble beginnings in America.

_____. *Knight of Labor; or, Job Many's Rise in Life.* New York: Beadle's Dime Novels, 1884.

A story of a young man's move from the country to the city.

_____. *Larry Locke, the Man of Iron; or, a Fight for Fortune.* New York: Beadle's Dime Novels, 1883.

A story of labor, capital and the troubles between the two.

_____. *Marshal of Satanstown; or, the League of Cattle Lifters.* New York: Beadle's Dime Novels, 1884.

_____. *Mustang Hunters; or, the Beautiful Amazon of the Hidden Valley.* New York: Beadle's Dime Novels, 1871.

The business of rounding up and breeding mustang horses in Texas.

_____. *Nemo, King of the Tramps; or, the Romany Girl's Vengeance.* New York: Beadle's Dime Novels, 1881.

A story of the great railroad riots.

_____. *Old Cross Eye, the Maverick Hunter; or, the Night Riders of Satantown County.* New York: Beadle's Dime Novels, 1884.

A story about Texas cowboys, Native Americans, night riders and trouble with fences on the range.

_____. *Parson Jim, King of the Cowboys; or, the Gentle Shepard's Big "Clean Out."* New York: Beadle's Dime Novels, 1882.

_____. *Red Prince; or, Last of the Aztecs.* New York: Beadle's Dime Novels, 1871.

A story that takes place in the Sierra Madre in eastern Sonora in 1865.

_____. *Top Notch Tom, the Cowboy Outlaw; or, the Satantown Election.* New York: Beadle's Dime Novels, 1884.

The villain of this story is an English nobleman. Describes a murder and many courtroom scenes.

_____. *White Gladiator; or, Manola, the Sun-Child.* New York: Beadle's Dime Novels, 1872.

A story of the Spanish conquistadors of Mexico in 1519.

Willett, Edward. *Black Arrow, the Avenger; or, Judge Lynch on the Border.* New York: Beadle's Dime Novels, 1871.

A story of Texas about 1830, shortly before its admission as a state. There are outlaws and a vigilance committee.

_____. *Border Foes; or, the Perils of a Night.* New York: Beadle and Adams, 1867.

A story that tells of Kentucky at the headwaters of the Kentucky River, trouble with Native Americans, the famous "dark night" of 1781.

_____. *Five Champions; or, the Backwoods Belle.* New York: Beadle and Adams, 1867.

A tale of old Kentucky. A shooting match and its results.

_____. *Forest Specter; or, the Young Hunter's Foe.* New York: Beadle's Dime Novels, 1871.

A story of the time when men wore knee breeches, wigs and cocked hats.

_____. *Gray Scalp; or, the Blackfoot Brave.* New York: Beadle's Dime Novels, 1870.

A story of the Blackfoot along the Oregon trail in the early part of the nineteenth century.

_____. *Hidden Home; or, the Backwoods Bandit.* New York: Beadle and Adams, 1866.

Bandits, trappers and Native Americans west of the Rockies about 1850.

_____. *Hunted Life; or, the Outcasts of the Border.* New York: Beadle's Dime Novels, June 4, 1867.

A Native American tale of Kentucky in 1780.

_____. *Mountaineer; or, Lost in the Depths.* New York: Beadle and Adams, 1868.

A story of the Grand Canyon of Arizona.

_____. *Old Honesty; or, Guests of the Beehalt Tavern.* New York: Beadle's Dime Novels, 1867.

A story of a pack train on the Wilderness Road in Kentucky.

_____. *Tonkawa Spy; or, the Comanche Foray.* New York: Beadle's Dime Novels, 1873.

A tale of northwestern Texas in 1835. Battles with Native Americans. Grant, Burleson, Johnson, Houston, Fannin, and Caldwell are mentioned in this story.

_____. *Twin Trailers; or, the Gamecock of El Paso.* New York: Beadle's Dime Novels, 1872.

Apache raids in Texas; life in the missions and haciendas in the vicinity of El Paso, Texas.

______. *White Apache; or, the Lifted Trail.* New York: Beadle's Dime Novels, 1872.

A story of the Native Americans of the Santa Fe trail and the San Juan River country in northwestern New Mexico.

Wilton, Mark. *Big Brave, Scout of the Mohawk.* New York: Norman Munro, 1873.

Winthrop, Theodore (1828–1861). *John Brent, a Western Romance, Set in the Rockies.* Boston: Ticknor and Fields, 1862.

As the title indicates, this is a Western tale of life in the Rocky Mountain region of the West.

Woodworth, Francis. *Jack Mason, the Old Sailor.* New York: Clark, Austin and Co., 1850.

A look-alike of the Peter Parley books. This one covers whaling, Egypt, Inuits and morality.

Worcester, J. R. *Yankee Eph; or, the Thwarted Plot.* New York: Beadle and Adams, 1867.

The Revolutionary War in South Carolina from 1780 to 1781. Francis, Marion, Summer and Tarleton are characters in this story.

Appendix C: List of Series Books

Listed by series name and individual titles. The numbering does not in all cases reflect the actual published number of titles.

Air Combat Series. Author: Thomson Burtis (1–4), Eustace Adams (5–7). Publisher: Grosset and Dunlap.
1. *Daredevil of the Air* (1932). 2. *Four Aces* (1932). 3. *Wind for Wings.* (1932). 4. *Flying Blackbirds* (1932). 5. *Doomed Demons* (1935). 6. *Wings of the Navy* (1936). 7. *War Wings* (1937).

Air Mail Series. Author: Lewis Theiss. Publisher: W. A. Wilde.
1. *Piloting the United States Mail; or, Flying for Uncle Sam* (1927). 2. *Search for the Lost Mail Plane* (1928). 3. *Trailing the Air Mail Bandits* (1929). 4. *Pursuit of the Flying Smugglers* (1930). *Flying Reporter* (1931). 6. *Wings of the Coast Guard* (1932).

Airplane Boys Series. Author: Edith Janice Craine. Publisher: World Syndicate.
1. *Airplane Boys on the Border Line* (1930). 2. *Airplane Boys at Cap Rock* (1930). 3. *Airplane Boys Discover the Secrets of Cuzco* (1930). 4. *Airplane Boys Flying to Amy-Ran Fastness* (1930). 5. *Airplane Boys at Platinum River* (1930). 6. *Airplane Boys with the Revolutionists in Bolivia* (1931). 7. *Airplane Boys at Black Woods* (1932). 8. *Airplane Boys at Belize* (1932).

Airplane Girl Series. Author: Edith Janice Craine. Publisher: World Syndicate.
1. *Lurtiss Field Mystery* (1930). 2. *Roberta's Flying Courage* (1930). 3. *Mystery Ship* (1931). 4. *Mystery of Seal Islands* (1931).

Airship Boys Series. Author: Harry Lincoln Sayler. Publisher: Reilly and Britton.
1. *Airship Boys* (1909). 2. *Airship Boys Adrift* (1909). 3. *Airship Boys Due North* (1910). 4. *Airship Boys in the Barrel Lands* (1910). 5. *Airship Boys in Finance* (1911). 6. *Airship Boys' Ocean Flyer* (1911). 7. *Airship Boys as Detectives* (1913). 8. *Airship Boys in the Great War* (1913).

All Aboard Series. Author: Edward Augustus Rand. Publisher: Fairbanks and Palmer.
1. *All Aboard for Sunrise Lands* (1881). 2. *All Aboard for the Lakes and Mountains* (1883).

All-Over-the World Series. Author: Oliver Optic. Publisher: Lee and Shepard.

1. *Missing Million; or, Adventures of Louis Belgrave* (1891). 2. *Millionaire at Sixteen; or, the Cruise of the Guardian-Mother* (1892). 3. *Young Knight-Errant* (1893). 4. *Strange Sights Abroad; or, a Voyage in European Waters* (1893). 5. *American Boys Afloat; or, Cruising in the Orient* (1893).

Allan Quartermain Series. Author: H. Rider Haggard. Publisher: McKinley, Stone and Mackenzie.

1. *Marie* (1912). 2. *Allan's Wife* (1887). 3. *Child of Storm* (1913). 4. *Tales of Three Lions* (1887). 5. *Maiwa's Revenge* (1888). 6. *Allan the Hunter.* (1898). 7. *Holy Flower* (1915). 8. *Heu-Heu* (1924). 9. *She and Allan* (1921). 10. *Treasure of the Lake* (1926). 11. Haggard, H. Rider. *Ivory Child* (1916). 12. *Finished* (1917). 13. *King Solomon's Mines* (1885). 14. *Ancient Allan* (1920). 15. *Allan and the Ice Gods* (1927). 16. *Allan Quartermain* (1887).

Andy Blake Series. Author: Leo Edwards. Publisher: Grosset and Dunlap except where noted.

1. *Andy Blake in Advertising* (Publisher: D. Appleton) 1922. 2. *Andy Blake's Comet Coaster* (1928). 3. *Andy Blake* (1928). 4. *Andy Blake's Secret Service* (1929). 5. *Andy Blake and the Pot of Gold* (1930).

Andy Lane Series. Author: Eustace Adams. Publisher: Grosset and Dunlap.

1. *Fifteen Days in the Air* (1928). 2. *Over the Polar Ice* (1928). 3. *Racing around the World* (1928). 4. *Runaway Airship* (1929). 5. *Pirates of the Air* (1929). 6. *On the Wings of Flame* (1930). 7. *Mysterious Monoplane* (1930). 8. *Flying Windmill* (1930). 9. *Plane without a Pilot* (1931). 10. *Wings of Adventure* (1931). *Across the Top of the World* (1932). 12. *Prisoners of the Clouds* (1933). 13. *Doomed Demons* (1936). 14. *Wings of the Navy* (1937). 15. *War Wings* (1937).

Army and Navy Stories Series. Author: William Taylor Adams (Oliver Optic). Publisher: Lee and Shepard.

1. *Soldier Boy; or, Tom Sommers in the Army* (1863). 2. *Sailor Boy; or, Jack Sommers in the Navy* (1863). 3. *Young Lieutenant; or, the Adventures of an Army Officer* (1865). 4. *Yankee Middy; or, the Adventures of a Naval Officer* (1866). 5. *Fighting Joe; or, the Fortunes of a Staff Officer* (1866). 6. *Brave Old Salt; or, Story of a Great Rebellion* (1865).

Atlantic Series. Author: Horatio Alger. Publisher: Altemus.

1. *Young Circus Rider; or, the Mystery of Robert Rudd* (1883). 2. *Do and Dare* (1884). 3. *Hector's Inheritance; or, the Boys of Smith Institute* (1885). 4. *Helping Himself* (1886).

Aviation Series. Author: John Prentice Langley. Publisher: Barse.

1. *Trail Blazers of the Skies* (1927). 2. *Spanning the Pacific; or, A Non-Stop Hop to Japan* (1927). 3. *Masters of the Airlines* (1928). 4. *Pathfinder's Great Flight* (1928). 5. *Air Voyages of the Arctic* (1929). 6. *Desert Hawks on the Wing* (1928). 7. *Chasing the Setting Sun* (1930). 8. *Bridging the Seven Seas* (1930). 9. *Staircase of the Wind* (1931).

Betty Leicester Series. Author: Sarah Orne Jewett. Publisher: Houghton and Mifflin.

1. *Betty Leicester* (1890). 2. *Betty Leicester's Christmas* (1899).

Betty Wales Series. Author: Margaret Warde. Publisher: Penn.

1. *Betty Wales, Freshman* (1904). 2. *Betty Wales, Sophomore* (1905). 3. *Betty Wales, Junior* (1906). 4. *Betty Wales, Senior* (1907). 5. *Betty Wales, B.A.* (1908). 6. *Betty Wales and Com-*

pany (1909). 7. *Betty Wales on the Campus* (1910). 8. *Betty Wales Decides* (1911). 9. *Betty Wales' Girls and Mr. Kidd* (1912). 10. *Betty Wales, Business Woman* (1917).

Bill Bolton Series. Author: Noel Sainsbury. Publisher: Goldsmith.
1. *Bill Bolton, Flying Midshipman* (1933). 2. *Bill Bolton and the Flying Fish* (1933). 3. *Bill Bolton and the Hidden Danger* (1933). 4. *Bill Bolton and the Winged Cartwheels* (1933).

Bill Bruce Series. Author: Henry "Hap" Arnold. Publisher: Dodd, Mead.
1. *Bill Bruce and the Pioneer Aviators* (1928). 2. *Bill Bruce and the Flying Cadet* (1928). 3. *Bill Bruce Becomes an Ace* (1928). 4. *Bill Bruce on the Border Patrol* (1928). 5. *Bill Bruce and the Transcontinental Race* (1928). 6. *Bill Bruce on Forest Patrol* (1928).

Billy Smith Series. Author: Noel Sainsbury. Publisher: McBride.
1. *Billy Smith, Exploring Ace* (1928). 2. *Billy Smith, Secret Service Ace* (1932). 3. *Billy Smith, Mystery Ace* (1932). 4. *Billy Smith, Trail Eater Ace* (1933). 5. *Billy Smith, Shanghaied Ace* (1934).

Blythe Girls Series. Author: Laura Lee Hope. Publisher: Grosset and Dunlap.
1. *Helen, Margy and Rose* (1925). 2. *Margy's Queer Inheritance* (1925). 3. *Rosie's Great Problem* (1925). 4. *Helen's Strange Boarder* (1925). 5. *Three on Vacation* (1925). 6. *Margy's Secret Mission* (1926). 7. *Rosie's Odd Discovery* (1927). 8. *Disappearance of Helen* (1928). 9. *Snowbound in Camp* (1929). 10. *Margy's Mysterious Visitor* (1930). 11. *Rosie's Hidden Talent* (1931). 12. *Helen's Wonderful Mistake* (1932).

Boat Club Series. Author: William Taylor Adams (Oliver Optic). Publisher: Lee and Shepard.
1. *Boat Club; or, the Bunkers of Rippleton* (1855). 2. *All Aboard; or, Life on the Lake* (1856). 3. *Now or Never; or, the Adventures of Bobby Bright*. Boston (1857). 4. *Try Again; or, the Trials and Triumphs of Harry West* (1858). 5. *Poor and Proud; or, the Fortunes of Katy Redburn* (1858). 6. *Little by Little; or, the Cruise of the Flyaway* (1861).

Bomba Series. Author: Roy Rockwood. Publisher: Edward Stratemeyer.
1. *Bomba the Jungle Boy* (1926). 2. *Bomba the Jungle Boy at the Moving Mountains* (1926). 3. *Bomba the Jungle Boy and the Giant Cataract* (1926). 4. *Bomba the Jungle Boy on Jaguar Island* (1927). 5. *Bomba the Jungle Boy in the Abandoned City* (1927). 6. *Bomba the Jungle Boy on Terror Trail* (1928). 7. *Bomba the Jungle Boy in the Swamp of Death* (1929). 8. *Bomba the Jungle Boy Among the Slaves* (1929). 9. *Bomba the Jungle Boy on the Underground River* (1930). 10. *Bomba the Jungle Boy and the Lost Explorers* (1930). 11. *Bomba the Jungle Boy in a Strange Land* (1931). 12. *Bomba the Jungle Boy Among the Pygmies* (1931). 13. *Bomba the Jungle Boy and the Cannibals* (1932). 14. *Bomba the Jungle Boy and the Painted Hunters* (1932). 15. *Bomba the Jungle Boy and the River Demons* (1933). 16. *Bomba the Jungle Boy and the Hostile Chieftain* (1934). 17. *Bomba the Jungle Boy Trapped by the Cyclone* (1935). 18. *Bomba the Jungle Boy in the Land of Burning Lava* (1936). 19. *Bomba the Jungle Boy in the Perilous Kingdom* (1937). 20. *Bomba the Jungle Boy in the Steaming Grotto* (1938).

Bound to Succeed Series. Author: Edward Stratemeyer. Publisher: Merriam.
1. *Richard Dare's Venture* (1894). 2. *Oliver Bright's Search* (1895). 3. *To Alaska for Gold* (1899).

Bound to Win Series. Author: Edward Stratemeyer (1, 4, 7, 10), Arthur M. Winfield (2, 5, 8, 11), Ralph Bonehill (3, 6, 9, 12). Publisher: W. L. Allison.

1. *Bound to Be an Electrician* (1897). 2. *Schooldays of Fred Harley* (1897). 3. *Gun and Sled* (1897). 4. *Shorthand Tom* (1897). 5. *Missing Tin Box* (1897). 6. *Young Oarsman of Lakeview* (1897). 7. *Young Auctioneers* (1897). 8. *Poor but Plucky* (1897). 9. *Rival Bicyclists* (1897). 10. *Fighting for His Own* (1897). 11. *By Pluck, Not Luck* (1897). 12. *Leo, the Circus Boy* (1897).

Bound to Win Trilogy. Author: Edward Sylvester Ellis. Publisher: John C. Winston.

1. *Brave Billy* (1897). 2. *Plucky Dick* (1897). 3. *Tam* (1897).

Boy Hunter Series. Author: Mayne Reid. Publisher: G. Putnam's Sons.

1. *Boy Hunters; or, Adventure sin Search of a White Buffalo* (1854).

Boy Hunters Series. Author: Ralph Bonehill (1, 3, 4, 5), Mayne Reid (2). Publisher: Edward Stratemeyer except where noted.

1. *Four Boy Hunters* (1906). 2. *Young Voyageurs; or, Boy Hunters in the North.* (Publisher: Hurst and Co.) 1899. 3. *Guns and Snowshoes* (1907). 4. *Young Hunters of the Lake* (1908). 5. *Out with Guns and Cameras* (1910).

Boy Trapper Series. Author: Harry Castlemon. Publisher: Porter and Coates.

1. *Boy Trapper* (1878). 2. *Mail Carrier* (1879).

Brave and Bold Series. Author: Horatio Alger. Publisher: Loring.

1. *Brave and Bold; or, the Fortunes of a Factory Boy.* Boston (1874). 2. *Jack's Ward* (1875). 3. *Shifting for Himself* (1876). 4. *Wait and Hope* (1877).

Bright and Bold Series. Author: Arthur M. Winfield. Publisher: Edward Stratemeyer.

1. *Poor but Plucky* (1905). 2. *By Pluck, Not Luck* (1905). 3. *Missing Tin Box* (1905).

Buffalo Bill Series. Author: Ned Buntline. Publisher: Street and Smith.

1. *Buffalo Bill, King of the Bordermen* (1881). 2. *Buffalo Bill's First Trail.* (1888). 3. *Buffalo Bill's Best Shot* (1890). 4. *Buffalo Bill's Last Victory* (1890).

Bunny Brown and His Sister Sue Series. Author: Laura Lee Hope. Publisher: Grosset & Dunlap.

1. *Bunny Brown and His Sister Sue* (1916). 2. *Bunny Brown and His Sister Sue on Grandpa's Farm* (1916). 3. *Bunny Brown and His Sister Sue Playing Circus* (1916). 4. *Bunny Brown and His Sister Sue at Camp Rest-a-While* (1916). 5. *Bunny Brown and His Sister Sue at Aunt Lou's City Home* (1916). 6. *Bunny Brown and His Sister Sue in the Big Woods* (1917). 7. *Bunny Brown and His Sister Sue on an Auto Tour* (1917). 8. *Bunny Brown and His Sister Sue and Their Shetland Pony* (1918). 9. *Bunny Brown and His Sister Sue Giving a Show* (1919). 10. *Bunny Brown and His Sister Sue at Christmas Tree Cove* (1920). 11. *Bunny Brown and His Sister Sue in the Sunny South* (1921). 12. *Bunny Brown and His Sister Sue Keeping Store* (1922). 13. *Bunny Brown and His Sister Sue and Their Trick Dog* (1923). 14. *Bunny Brown and His Sister Sue at a Sugar Camp* (1924). 15. *Bunny Brown and His Sister Sue on a Rolling Ocean* (1925). 16. *Bunny Brown and His Sister Sue on Jack Frost Island* (1927). 17. *Bunny Brown and His Sister Sue at Shore Acres* (1927). 18. *Bunny Brown and His Sister Sue at Berry Hill* (1929). 19. *Bunny Brown*

and His Sister Sue at Sky Top (1930). 20. *Bunny Brown and His Sister Sue at the Summer Carnival* (1931).

Campaign Trilogy. Author: Horatio Alger. Publisher: Loring.

1. *Frank's Campaign; or, What boys Can Do on the Farm for the Camp* (1864). 2. *Paul Prescott's Charge* (1865). 3. *Charlie Cadman's Cruise* (1866).

Camping Out Series. Author: Charles Asbury Stephens. Publisher: *Youth's Companion.*

1. *Camping Out, as Recorded by Kit* (1867). 2. *Left on Labrador* (1872). 3. *Off to the Geysers* (1872). 4. *Lynx Hunting* (1872). 5. *Fox Hunting, as Recorded by Raid* (1872). 6. *On the Amazon* (1872).

Cap'n Abe Series. Author: W. Bert Foster. Publisher: Sully and Kleinteich.

1. *Cap'n Abe* (1917). 2. *Sheila; or, Big Wreck Cove* (1922). 3. *Tobias o' the Light; a Story of Cape Cod* (1920).

Castlemon's War Series. Author: Harry Castlemon. Publisher: Porter and Coates except where noted.

1. *True to His Colors* (1889). 2. *Rodney the Partisan* 1890. 3. *Marcy, the Blockade-Runner* (1891). 4. *Rodney, the Overseer* (1892). 5. *Marcy, the Refugee* (John C. Winston) 1892. 6. *Sailor Jack, the Trader* (1893).

Clint Webb Series. Author: Walter Bertram Foster. Publisher: M. A. Donohue.

1. *Swept Out to Sea* (1913). 2. *Frozen Ship; or, Clint Webb Among the Sealers* (1913). 3. *From Seat to Sea* (1914). 4. *Sea Express* (1914).

Cloud Patrol Series. Author: Irving Crump (1, 2, 5), Harold Morrow Sherman (3), Percy Kees Fitzhugh (4, 6, 7). Publisher: Grosset & Dunlap.

1. *Cloud Patrol* (1929). 2. *Pilot of the Cloud Patrol* (1929). 3. *Ding Palmer, Air Detective* (1930). 4. *Mark Gilmore, Scout of the Air* (1930). 5. *Craig of the Cloud Patrol* (1931). 6. *Mark Gilmore, Speed Flyer* (1931). 7. *Mark Gilmore's Lucky Landing* (1931).

Colonial Series. Author: Edward Stratemeyer. Publisher: Lothrop, Lee, Shepard.

1. *With Washington in the West* (1901). 2. *Marching on Niagara* (1902). 3. *At the Fall of Montreal* (1903). 4. *On the Trail of Pontiac* (1904). 5. *Fort in the Wilderness* (1906). 6. *Trail and Trading Post* (1906).

Conquest of the United States Series. Author: H. Irving Hancock. Publisher: Altemus.

1. *Invasion of the United States; or, Uncle Sam's Boys at the Capture of Boston* (1916). 2. *At the Defense of Pittsburgh* (1916). 3. *In the Battle for New York* (1916). 4. *Making the Stand for Old Glory* (1916).

Dalton Boys Series. Author: W. B. Lawson. Publisher: Street and Smith.

1. *Dalton Boys in California, or a Bold Holdup at Ceres* (1893). 2. *Dalton Boys and the MK and T Robbery* (1899).

Dave Darrin Series. Author: H. Irving Hancock. Publisher: Altemus.

1. *Dave Darrin at Vera Cruz; or, Fighting with the U.S. Navy in Mexico* (1914). 2. *Dave Darrin on Mediterranean Service* (1914). 3. *Dave Darrin's South American* (1919). 4. *Dave Darrin on the Asiatic Station* (1919). 5. *Dave Darrin and the German Submarines* (1919). 6. *Dave Darrin after the Mine Layers* (1919).

Dave Dashaway Series. Author: Roy Rockwood. Publisher: Cupples.

1. *Dave Dashaway, the Young Aviator*

(1913). 2. *Dave Dashaway and His Hydroplane* (1913). 3. *Dave Dashaway and His Giant Airship* (1913). 4. *Dave Dashaway around the World* (1913). 5. *Dave Dashaway, Air Champion* (1915).

Dave Fearless Series. Author: Roy Rockwood. Publisher: Garden City Pub.

1. *Dave Fearless after a Sunken Treasure* (1905). 2. *Dave Fearless on a Floating Island* (1907). 3. *Dave Fearless and the Cave of Mystery* (1908). 4. *Dave Fearless Among the Icebergs* (1926). 5. *Dave Fearless Wrecked Among Savages* (1926). 6. *Dave Fearless and His Big Raft* (1926). 7. *Dave Fearless on Volcano Island* (1926). 8. *Dave Fearless Captured by Apes* (1926). 9. *Dave Fearless and the Mutineers* (1926). 10. *Dave Fearless under the Ocean* (1926). 11. *Dave Fearless in the Black Jungle* (1926). 12. *Dave Fearless Near the South Pole* (1926). 13. *Dave Fearless Caught by Malay Pirates* (1926). 14. *Dave Fearless on the Ship of Mystery* (1927). 15. *Dave Fearless on the Lost Brig* (1927). 16. *Dave Fearless at Whirlpool Point* (1927). 17. *Dave Fearless Among the Cannibals* (1927).

Dave Porter Series. Author: Edward Stratemeyer. Publisher: Lothrop, Lee, Shepard.

1. *Dave Porter at Oak Hall.* (1905). 2. *Dave Porter in the Far North* (1906). 3. *Dave's Return to School* (1907). 4. *Dave Porter in the Far North* (1908). 5. *Dave Porter and His Classmates* (1909). 6. *Dave Porter at Star Ranch* (1910). 7. *Dave Porter and His Rivals* (1911). 8. *Dave Porter on Oak Island* (1912). 9. *Dave Porter and the Runaways* (1913). 10. *Dave Porter in the Gold Fields* (1914). 11. *Dave Porter at Bear Camp* (1915). 12. *Dave Porter and His Double* (1916). 13. *Dave Porter's Great Search* (1917). 14. *Dave Porter under Fire* (1918). 15. *Dave Porter's War Honors* (1919).

Deadwood Dick Series. Author: Edward L. Wheeler. Publisher: Beadle's Half Dime Library.

1. *Deadwood Dick's Death Plant.* 2. *Double Daggers; or, Deadwood Dick's Defiance* (1899). 3. *Deadwood Dick, the Outlaw of the Black Hills.* 4. *Deadwood Dick of Deadwood; or, the Picked Party* (1880). 5. *Buffalo Bed, the Prince of the Pistol; or, Deadwood Dick in Disguise* (1878). 6. *Phantom Miner; or, Deadwood Dick's Bonanza* (1878). 7. *Deadwood Dick's Eagles; or, the Pards of Flood Bar* (1878). 8. *Deadwood Dick on Deck; or Calamity Jane the Heroine of Whoop-Up* (1878). 9. *Omaha Oll, the Masked Terror; or, Deadwood Dick in Danger* (1879). 10. *Deadwood Dick in Leadville; or, Strange Strokes for Liberty* (1879). 11. *Deadwood Dick's Device; or, the Sign of the Double Cross* (1879). 12. *Deadwood Dick as Detective* (1879). 13. *Deadwood Dick's Double; or, the Ghost of Gordon's Gulch* (1880). 14. *Blond Bill; or, Deadwood Dick's Home Base* (1880). 15. *Game of Gold; or, Deadwood Dick's Big Strike* (1880). 16. *Deadwood Dick's Dream; or, Rivals of the Road* (1881). 17. *Black Hills Jezebel; or, Deadwood Dick's Ward* (1881). 18. *Deadwood Dick's Doom; or, Calamity Jane's Last Adventure* (1881). 19. *Gold Dust Dick* (1882). 20. *Deadwood Dick's Divide, or the Spirit of Swamp Lake* (1882). 21. *Deadwood Dick's Death Trail; or, From Ocean to Ocean* (1882). 22. *Deadwood Dick's Ten Strike* (1883). 23. *Deadwood Dick's Big Deal; or, the Gold Brick of Oregon* (1883). 24. *Deadwood Dick's Dozen; or, Fakir of Phantom Flats* (1883). 25. *Deadwood Dick, the Prince of the Road; or, the Black Rider of the Black Hills* (1884). 26. *Deadwood Dick's Ducats; or, Rainy Days in the Diggings* (1884). 27. *Deadwood Dick Sentenced; or, the Terrible Vendetta* (1884). 28. *Deadwood Dick's Claim; or, the Fairy Face of Faro Flats* (1884). 29. *Corduroy Charlie, the Boy Hero; or, Deadwood Dick's Last Act* (1885). 30. *Deadwood Dick in Dead City* (1885).

31. *Deadwood Dick's Diamonds; or, Mystery of Jane Porter* (1885). 32. *Deadwood Dick in New York, or, a Cute Case* (1885). 33. *Deadwood Dick's Dust* (1885). 34. *Sunflower Sam of Shasta; or, Deadwood Dick's Full Hand* (1886). 35. *Deadwood Dick's Death Hunt; or the Way of the Transgressor* (1887). 36. *Deadwood Dick's Deliverance; or, Fatal Footsteps* (1887). 37. *Deadwood Dick's Mission; or, Cavic, the Kidnapped Boy* (1889). 38. *Deadwood Dick's Kidnapper Knock Out* (1893). 39. *Deadwood Dick, the Artist Detective* (1886). 40. *Deadwood Dick Trapped; or, Roxey Ralph's Ruse* (1899). 41. *Deadwood Dick's Demand.*

Deerfoot Series. Author: Edward Sylvester Ellis. Publisher: John C. Winston.

1. *Hunters of the Ozark* (1887). 2. *Camp in the Mountains* (1887). 3. *Last War Trail* (1887).

Diamond Dick Series. Author: W. B. Lawson. Publisher: Street and Smith.

1. *Diamond Dick's Dead Head; or, the Pirates of Pend d'Oreille* (1899). 2. *Diamond Dick's Deuce-Ace; or, the Freebooters of Flathead Lake* (1899). 3. *Diamond Doom List; or, the White Wolves of Umatilla* (1899). 4. *Diamond Dick's Drag-Net; or, the Killers of Kootenai* (1899). 5. *Diamond Dick's Dummy; or, the Yellers of Yuba* (1899). 6. *Diamond Dick at Secret Pass; or, Handing Out Stern Justice.* 7. *Diamond Dick and the Gold Bugs; or, a Fight for a Mine* (1901). 8. *Diamond Dick's Split-Trick; or, the Dashing Dup and the Circus Crooks* (1901). 9. *Diamond Dick's Daring Deeds* (1901–2). 10. *Diamond Dick and the Black Dwarf; or, Hot Work for Uncle Sam* (1902). 11. *Diamond Dick in Old Mexico; or, The Gold Bugs of Guanajay* (1903). 12. *Diamond Dick in the Field; or, Handsome Harry's Peril* (1903). 13. *Diamond Dick Missing; or, the Veteran's Unknown Pard* (1903). 14. *Diamond Dick's Farewell Performance; or, a Warm Go for the Gate Money* (1903). 15. *Diamond Dick's Treasure-Trove; or, the Secret of the Great Stone Idol* (1903). 16. *Diamond Dick in Old Santa Fe; or, the League of the Montezumas* (1904). 17. *Diamond Dick in the land of Gold; or, the Bald Hornets of Crimson Bar* (1904). 18. *Diamond Dick's Red Trailer; or, a Hairbreadth Escape* (1904). 19. *Diamond Dick's Signal; or, the Sympathy Strike at Skiplap* (1904). 20. *Diamond Dick's Signal; or, the Boldest Move on Record* (1904). 21. *Diamond Dick in the Desert of Death; or, the Cryptogram of the Cliff Dwellers* (1904). 22. *Diamond Dick's Black Hazard; or, the Feud at Roaring Water* (1905). 23. *Diamond Dick's Darkest Trail; or, Secret of the Haunted Mine* (1905). 24. *Diamond Dick's Center Shot; or, the Hoorah at the Golden Gate* (1905). 25. *Diamond Dick's Cool Trust; or, the Trail of the Silent Three* (1905). 26. *Diamond Dick's Secret Foe; or, Nightwolf, the Red Terror* (1905). 27. *Diamond Dick in the Desert; or, the Shot-Gun Messenger from Fargo* (1905). 28. *Diamond Dick's Blind Lead; or, the Rustlers of Sandy Gulch* (1905). 29. *Diamond Dick's Deadly Peril; or, a Fight for Life in the Rapids* (1905). 30. *Diamond Dick's Swiftest Ride; or, Won by the Pony Express* (1905). 31. *Handsome Harry's Fierce Games; or, the Moonshiner's Oath* (1905). 32. *Diamond Dick's Steeplechase; or, the Leap That Won the Race* (1905). 33. *Handsome Harry's Trump Card; or, the Bad Man from Texas* (1905). 34. *Diamond Dick's Red Foe; or, the Renegades of the Cascades* (1906). 35. *Diamond Dick's Secret Scent; or, the Doom of the Three Masked Men* (1906). 36. *Diamond Dick in the Breakers; or, the Life-Savers of Vancouver* (1906). 37. *Diamond Dick's Lucky Ace; or, Turning the Trump in a Hard Game* (1906). 38. *Diamond Dick's Death Chase; or, Running a Weasel to Earth* (1906). 39. *Diamond*

Dick on the Dead Line; or, Battle for Canyon Creek (1906). 40. *Diamond Dick's Vampire Trail; or, the Mad Horseman of Thunder Mountain* (1906). 41. *Diamond Dick's Long Leap; or, Single-Handed against a Giant* (1906). 42. *Diamond Dick Below the Line; or, an American against Big Odds* (1907). 43. *Diamond Dick in the Deep Snows; or, Close Call on the Yukon* (1907). 44. *Diamond Dick on Shipboard; or, Blocking a Slick Game* (1907). 45. *Diamond Dick's College Scrap; or, a Battle for His Alma Mater* (1907). 46. *Diamond Dick's Inferno; or, the Madman of the Great Black Tunnel* (1907). 47. *Diamond Dick's Merciless Trail; or, the Two Rascals of White Horse* (1907). 48. *Diamond Dick's Royal Foe; or, the Strange Passage of the Santa Cruz* (1907). 49. *Diamond Dick's Shower of Gold; or, the Princess of the Montezumas* (1907). 50. *Diamond Dick's Steel Heart; or, the Fire Train of the Sierras* (1907). 51. *Diamond Dick's Wide Loop; or, Roping Five at One Throw* (1907). 52. *Diamond Dick and the Coast Indians; or, Handsome Harry's Closest Call* (1908). 53. *Diamond Dick and the Filibusters; or, the Pirates of Curacoa* (1908). 54. *Diamond Dick in the Canal Zone; or, Varola, the Voodoo King* (1908). 55. *Diamond Dick on Hard Luck; or, Playing a Game with Death* (1908). 56. *Diamond Dick's Alkali Trail; or, Run to Earth in the Bad Lands* (1908). 57. *Diamond Dick's Close Shave; or, Knife to Knife with the Yellow Peril* (1908). 58. *Diamond Dick's Death Notice; or, the Star That Fell from the Sky* (1908). 59. *Diamond Dick's Decoration; or, the King of the Lonesome Islands* (1908). 60. *Diamond Dick's Great Find; or, the Tigers of the High Divide* (1908). 61. *Diamond Dick's Great Railroad Feat; or, Putting Her Through on Time* (1908). 62. *Diamond Dick's High Sign; or, the Secret of the Adobe Castle* (1908). 63. *Diamond Dick's Master Stroke; or, the Unmasking of Seattle Sim* (1908). 64. *Diamond Dick's Maverick; or, Running a New Brand in Arizona* (1908). 65. *Diamond Dick's Scarlet Enemy; or, the Foxy Role of Foggy Ike* (1908). 66. *Diamond Dick's Slashing Blow; or, a Close Call in the Big Ditch* (1908). 67. *Diamond Dick's Solid Shot; or, the Spies of the Pacific Fleet* (1908). 68. *Diamond Dick's Sure Scent; or, the Marked Man from Chicago* (1908). 69. *Diamond Wireless Signal, or the Lone Traitor of the Sierras* (1908). 70. *Diamond Dick, the Lariat King, or, Silver Sam's Silver* (1908). 71. *Diamond Dick's Lost Trail; or, a Queer Hunt in Oregon* (1908). 72. *Diamond Dick's Gift Horse; or, the Man with the Metal Head* (1908). 73. *Diamond Dick's Decoy Duck; or, How Handsome Harry Played the Game* (1908). 74. *Diamond Dick's Greenroom Raid; or, Bucking the Insurance Gamblers* (1908). 75. *Diamond Dick's Desperate Detail; or, the Hounds of Orinoco* (1908). 76. *Diamond Dick and the Dakota Dazzler; or, Up against the Land Thieves* (1908). 77. *Diamond Dick and the White Hawk Boomers; or, What Caused the Raid of Kicking Bird* (1908). 78. *Diamond Dick's River Rats; or, the Rubber-Hunters of La Paz* (1908). 79. *Diamond Dick's Vengeance; or, the Defeat of the Destroying Angel* (1908). 80. *Diamond Dick's Voyage of Mystery; or, the Shadows of the Amazon* (1908). 81. *Diamond Dick's Boldest Move; or, the Wedding Bells of Buck Price* (1908). 82. *Diamond Dick and the Black Owl; or, the Fight with the Fortune-Tellers* (1908). 83. *Diamond Dick on the Timber Trail; or, the Ordeal of Fire* (1908). 84. *Diamond Dick's High-Water Mark; or, the Flood That Paralyzed Pumpkinville* (1908). 85. *Diamond Dick and the Mounted Police; or, Duke Dashaway's Dash* (1908). 86. *Diamond Dick and "Pard Jimmy"; or, the Mystery of Cranberry Cove* (1909). 87. *Diamond Dick's Tennessee Mission; or, the Perils of a "Moonshine."* New York: Street and Smith, 1909). 88. *Diamond Dick's Double Chase; or, the Warm Welcome of the West* (1909). 89. *Diamond*

Dick and the Wildcat Syndicate; or, Silver Will's Strange Scheme (1909). 90. *Diamond Dick in the Adirondacks; or, the Man with the Scarred Face* (1909). 91. *Diamond Dick's Last Eastern Trail; or, the Chase after Craig* (1909). 92. *Diamond Dick and the Dummy Deacon; or, on a Silent Trail* (1909). 93. *Diamond Dick at Craven Creek; or, a Still Hunt in the Land of the Sky* (1909). 94. *Diamond Dick's Power; or, the Affair on the Road from Flagstaff* (1909). 95. *Diamond Dick's Strategy; or, the Final Stand of the Moonshiners* (1909). 96. *Diamond Dick on the Farm; or, the Mission of the Strangers* (1909). 97. *Diamond Dick's Chase; or, On the Track of Charlie* (1909). 98. *Diamond Dick's Young Partner; or, Jimmy Lang's Western Tour* (1909). 99. *Diamond Dick's Sagacity; or, a Clever Scheme Disclosed* (1909). 100. *Diamond Dick and the Land-Sharks; or, the Hoodoo of Number Thirteen* (1909). 101. *Heart of Diamond Dick; or, the Trail of an Ancient Enemy* (1909). 102. *Diamond Dick's Pledge; or, the Giant Poacher of Loon Lake* (1909). 103. *Diamond Dick and the Red Desert Land; or, the Misfortune of Handsome Harry* (1909).

Dick Daresome Series. Author: Frank Forrest. Publisher: Frank Tousey.

1. *Dick Daresome's Champion Pitching; or, Saving the Day for Merrivale* (1909). 2. *Dick Daresome's Summer Baseball Nine; or, New Victories for Merrivale.* (1909). 3. *Dick Daresome's Mistake; or, Losing a Game to Belleville* (1909). 4. *Dick Daresome's Quarrel; or, Showing Up a Coward* (1909). 5. *Dick Daresome's Fight for Honor; or, Clearing a School Suspicion* (1909). 6. *Dick Daresome's Canoe Race* (1909).

Dick Doom Series. Author: Prentiss Ingraham. Publisher: Beadle's Half Dime Library.

1. *Dick Doom's Death Grip* (1892). 2. *Dick Doom's Destiny* (1892). 3. *Dick Doom, the Death-Grip Detective* (1892). 4. *Dick Doom in Boston,* (1892). 5. *Dick Doom in Chicago; or, the Ferret of the Golden Fetters* (1892). 6. *Dick Doom in the Wild West* (1892). 7. *Dick Doom's Clean Sweep* (1892). 8. *Dick Doom's Diamond Deal* (1893). 9. *Dick Doom's Girl Mascot* (1893). 10. *Dick Doom's Shadow Hunt* (1893). 11. *Gentleman Crook in Chicago; or, Nick Norcross, the Pier Rat, Dick Doom's Shadow Hunt* (1893). 12. *Dick Doom's Big Haul; or, the Rogue Round-Up in Chicago* (1893). 13. *Actor Detective in Chicago; or, Dick Doom's Flush Hand* (1893). 14. *Dick Doom's Ten Strike; or, the Top Floor Club's Exposé* (1893).

Don Kirk Series. Author: Gilbert Patten. Publisher: McKay.

1. *Boy Cattle King* (1895). 2. *Boy from the West* (1895). 3. *Don Kirk's Mine* (1895).

Don Sturdy Series. Author: Victor Appleton. Publisher: Grosset and Dunlap.

1. *Don Sturdy in the Desert of Mystery* (1925). 2. *Don Sturdy with the Big Snake Hunters* (1925). 3. *Don Sturdy in the Tombs of Gold* (1925). 4. *Don Sturdy across the North Pole* (1925). 5. *Don Sturdy in the Land of Volcanoes* (1925). 6. *Don Sturdy in the Port of Lost Ships* (1926). 7. *Don Sturdy Among the Gorillas* (1927). 8. *Don Sturdy Captured by Headhunters* (1928). 9. *Don Sturdy in Lion Land* (1929). 10. *Don Sturdy in the Land of Giants* (1930). 11. *Don Sturdy on the Ocean Bottom* (1931). 12. *Don Sturdy in the Temples of Fear* (1932). 13. *Don Sturdy in Glacier Bay* (1933). 14. *Don Sturdy Trapped in the Flaming Wilderness* (1934). 15. *Don Sturdy with Harpoon Hunters* (1935).

Dora Darling Series. Author: Jane Goodwin Austin. Publisher: J. E. Tilton.

1. *Dora Darling* (1865). 2. *Outpost.* (1867).

Dorothy Dale Series. Author: Margaret Penrose. Publisher: Cupples and Leon.

1. *Dorothy Dale, a Girl of Today* (1908). 2. *Dorothy Dale at Glenwood School* (1908). 3. *Dorothy Dale's Great Secret* (1909). 4. *Dorothy Dale and Her Chums* (1909). 5. *Dorothy Dale's Queer Holidays* (1910). 6. *Dorothy Dale's Camping Days* (1911). 7. *Dorothy Dale's School Rivals* (1912). 8. *Dorothy Dale in the City* (1913). 9. *Dorothy Dale's Promise* (1914). 10. *Dorothy Dale in the West* (1915). 11. *Dorothy Dale's Strange Discovery* (1916). 12. *Dorothy Dale's Engagement* (1917). 13. *Dorothy Dale to the Rescue* (1924).

Dorothy Dixon Series. Author: Dorothy Wayne. Publisher: Goldsmith Pub.

1. *Dorothy Dixon and the Double Cousin* (1933). 2. *Dorothy Dixon and the Mysterious Plane* (1933). 3. *Dorothy Dixon Solves the Conway Case* 1933. 4. *Dorothy Dixon Wins Her Wings* (1933).

Dorothy Draycott Series. Author: Virginia Frances Townsend. Publisher: Lee and Shepard.

1. *Sirs, Only Seventeen* (1894). 2. *Dorothy Draycott's Tomorrow* (1897).

Drumthacty Series. Author: Ian Maclaren. Publisher: Dodd, Mead.

1. *Beside the Bonnie Briar Bush* (1894). 2. *Days of Auld Lang Syne* (1895). 3. *Kate Carnegie and Those Ministers* (1896).

Elsie Dinsmore Series. Author: Martha Farquharson Finley. Publisher: Dodd, Mead.

1. *Elsie Dinsmore* (1867). 2. *Elsie's Holiday at Roselands* (1868). 3. *Elsie's Girlhood* (1872). 4. *Elsie's Womanhood* (1875). 5. *Elsie's Motherhood* (1876). 6. *Elsie's Children* (1877). 7. *Elsie's Widowhood* (1880). 8. *Grandmother Elsie* (1882). 9. *Elsie's New Relations* (1883). 10. *Elsie at Nantucket* (1884). 11. *Two Elsies* (1885). 12. *Elsie's Kith and Kin* (1886). 13. *Elsie's Friends at Woodburn* (1887). 14. *Christmas with Grandma Elsie* (1888). 15. *Elsie and the Raymonds* (1889). 16. *Elsie Yachting with the Raymonds* (1890). 17. *Elsie's Vacation and After Events* (1891). 18. *Elsie at Viamede* (1892). 19. *Elsie at Ion* (1893). 20. *Elsie at the World's Fair* (1894). 21. *Elsie's Journey on Inland Waters* (1895). 22. *Elsie at Home* (1897). 23. *Elsie on the Hudson and Elsewhere* (1898). 24. *Elsie in the South* (1899). 25. *Elsie's Young Folks in Peace and War* (1900). 26. *Elsie's Winter Trip* (1902). 27. *Elsie and Her Loved Ones* (1903). 28. *Elsie and Her Namesakes* (1905).

Flag and Frontier Series. Author: Ralph Bonehill. Publisher: Edward Stratemeyer.

1. *Pioneer Boys with Boone on the Frontier* (1903). 2. *Pioneer Boys at the Great Northwest* (1912). 3. *Pioneer Boys of the Gold Fields* (1912). 4. *Pioneer Boys with Custer in the Black Hills* (1912). 5. *Pioneer Boys at the Fort* (1912). 6. *Young Bandmaster* (1900). 7. *Pioneer Boys Off for Hawaii* (1912). 8. *Sailor Boy with Dewey* (1899). 9. *When Santiago Fell* (1899).

Flag of Freedom Series. Author: Ralph Bonehill. Publisher: Edward Stratemeyer.

1. *When Santiago Fell* (1899). 2. *Sailor Boy with Dewey* (1912). 3. *Off for Hawaii* (1905). 4. *Young Bandmaster* (1912). 5. *At the Fort* (1912). 6. *With Custer in the Black Hills* (1902).

Flash Gordon Series. Author: Alex Raymond (1), Con Steffanson (2-5), Carson Bingham (6-7), Arthur Byron Cover (8), David Hagberg (9-14). Publisher: Grosset and Dunlap.

1. *Flash Gordon in the Caverns of Mongo* (1937–40), paperback edition (1974–84). 2. *Lion Man of Mongo* (1974). 3. *Plague of Sound* (1974). 4. *Space Circus* (1974). 5. *Time Trap of Ming XIII* (1974). 6. *Witch Queen of Mongo* (1974). 7. *War of the Cybernauts* (1975). 8. *Flash Gordon* (1980). 9. *Massacre in the Twenty-second Century* (1980). 10. *War of the Citadels* (1980). 11. *Crisis on Citadel II* (1980). 12. *Forces from the Federation* (1981). 13. *Citadel under Attack* (1981). 14. *Citadels on Earth* (1981).

Flying Boys Series. Author: Edward Sylvester Ellis. Publisher: John C. Winston.

1. *Flying Boys in the Sky* (1911). 2. *Flying Boys to the Rescue* (1911).

Frank and Fearless Series. Author: Horatio Alger. Publisher: H. T. Coates.

1. *Frank Hunter's Peril* (1896). 2. *Frank and Fearless* (1897). 3. *Young Salesman* (1896).

Frank Reade Jr. Series. Author: Harry Enton. Publisher: Tousey Wide Awake Library.

1. *Frank Reader Jr. in the Far West* (1884). 2. *Frank Reader Jr. and His Adventures with His Latest Invention* (1884). 3. *Frank Reader Jr. and His Electric Boat* (1884). 4. *Frank Reader Jr. and His Electric Coach* (1884). 5. *Frank Reader Jr.'s Great Electric Tricycle* (1885). 6. *Across the Continent on Wings; or Frank Reader Jr.'s Greatest Flight* (1886). 7. *Frank Reader Jr. and His Electric Team* (1888). 8. *Frank Reader Jr. Exploring a River of Mystery* (1890). 9. *Frank Reader Jr.'s Electric Ice Boat* (1892). 10. *Frank Reader Jr. and His Queen Clipper on the Clouds* (1892). 11. *Black Range; or Frank Reade Jr. Among the cowboys with His New Electric Caravan* (1892). 12. *Chase of a Comet; or, Frank Reade Jr.'s Aerial Trip with the Flash* (1895). 13. *Frank Reader Jr.'s Electric Van* (1903). 14. *Frank Reader Jr. Chased across the Sahara* (1903). 15. *Frank Reader Jr.'s Electric Air Canoe* (1903). 16. *Frank Reader Jr. in the Clouds; or, Chased around the World in the Sky* (1903). 17. *Frank Reader Jr.'s Electric Invention, the Warrier* (1903). 18. *Frank Reader Jr. in Central Africa* (1903).

Frank Reade Series. Author: Harry Enton. Publisher: Tousey Wide Awake Library.

1. *Frank Reader and His Steam Man of the Plains* (1876). 2. *Electric Horse* (1887). 3. *Frank Reader and His Steam Horse* (1883). 4. *Frank Reader and His Steam Team* (1884). 5. *Silent Band* (1893). 6. *Six Weeks in the Clouds* (1903).

Fred Fearnot Series. Author: Hal (Harvey King Shackleford) Standish. Publisher: Street and Smith except where noted.

1. *Fred Fearnot's Great Peril* (Feb. 10, 1899). 2. *Fred Fearnot's Double Victory* (Feb. 17, 1899). 3. *Fred Fearnot's Great Run; or, an Engineer for a Week* (March 3, 1899). 4. *Fred Fearnot's Twenty Rounds; or, His Fight to Save His Honor* (March 10, 1899). 5. *Fred Fearnot's Good Work* (March 24, 1899). 6. *Fred Fearnot's Luck; or, Fighting an Unseen Foe* (April 7, 1899). 7. *Fred Fearnot's Defeat; or , A Fight Against Great Odds* (April 14, 1899). 8. *Fred Fearnot's Own Show; or, On the Road with a Combination* (April 21, 1899). 9. *Fred Fearnot in Chicago; or, The Abduction of Evelyn* (April 28, 1899). 10. *Fred Fearnot Out West; or, Adventures with the Cowboys*. 11. *Fred Fearnot's Mettle; or, Hot Work Against Enemies* (Oct. 27, 1899). 12. *Fred Fearnot's Great Mystery* (Nov. 17, 1899). 13. *Fred Fearnot's Skate for Life; or, Winning the "Ice Flyers" Pennant* (Dec. 8, 1899). 14. *Fred Fearnot as Actor; or, Fame Before the Footlights* (Dec. 20, 1899). 15. *Fred*

Fearnot and Oom Paul; or, Battling for the Boers (Jan. 16, 1900). 16. *Fred Fearnot in the South; or, Out with Old Bill Bland* (April 30, 1900). 17. *Fred Fearnot's Moose-Head; or, Adventures in the Maine Woods* (July 20, 1900). 18. *Fred Fearnot's Deadly Peril; or, His Narrow Escape from Ruin* (Aug. 24, 1900). 19. *Fred Fearnot's Long Chase; or, Trailing a Cunning Woman* (Sept. 7, 1900). 20. *Fred Fearnot's Common Sense; or, the Best Way Out of Trouble* (Sept. 21, 1900). 21. *Fred Fearnot's Great Find; or, Saving Terry Olcott's Fortune* (Sept. 28, 1900). 22. *Fred Fearnot's Strategy; or, Outwitting a Troublesome Couple* (Oct. 19, 1900). 23. *Fred Fearnot and the Duelist; or, The Man Who Wanted to Fight* (Dec. 5, 1900). 24. *Fred Fearnot at St. Simons; or, The Mystery of a Georgia Island* (Dec. 7, 1900). 25. *Fred Fearnot Deceived; or, After the Wrong Man* (Dec. 14, 1900). 26. *Fred Fearnot's Charity; or, Teaching Others a Lesson* (Dec. 21, 1900). 27. *Fred Fearnot as the Judge; or, Heading Off the Lynchers* (Dec. 28, 1900). 28. *Fred Fearnot's Round Up; or, A Lively Time on the Ranche* (Jan. 25, 1901). 29. *Fred Fearnot and the Giant; or, A Hot Time in Cheyenne* (Feb. 1, 1901). 30. *Fred Fearnot's Way; or, Doing Up a Sharper* (Feb. 15, 1901). 31. *Fred Fearnot and His Mascot; or, Evelyn's Fearless Ride* (Mar. 8, 1901). 32. *Fred Fearnot Captured; or, In the Hands of His Enemies* (Mar. 29, 1901). 33. *Fred Fearnot and the Banker; or, A Schemer's Trap to Ruin Him* (April 5, 1901). 34. *Fred Fearnot's Great Feat; or, Winning a Fortune on Skates* (April 12, 1901). 35. *Fred Fearnot at West Point; or, Having Fun with the Hazers* (May 24, 1901). 36. *Fred Fearnot and the Gambler; or, The Trouble on the Lake Front* (June 7, 1901). 37. *Fred Fearnot in Atlanta; or, The Black Fiend of Dark Town* (June 28, 1901). 38. *Fred Fearnot's Camp Hunt; or, The White Deer of the Adirondacks* (Aug. 9, 1901). 39. *Fred Fearnot and the Baron; or, Calling Down a Nobleman* (Sept. 13, 1901). 40. *Fred Fearnot and the Brokers; or, Ten Days in Wall Street* (Sept. 20, 1901). 41. *Fred Fearnot's Greatest Danger; or, Ten Days with the Moonshiners* (Oct. 4, 1901). 42. *Fred Fearnot and the Kidnappers; or, Trailing a Stolen Child* (Oct. 11, 1901). 43. *Fred Fearnot Cornered; or, Evelyn and the Widow* (Tousey). 44. *Fred Fearnot's Quick Work; or, The Hold Up at Eagle Pass* (Oct. 18, 1901). 45. *Fred Fearnot Lost; or, Missing for Thirty Days* (Nov. 15, 1901). 46. *Fred Fearnot's Fine Work; or, Up Against a Crank* (Dec. 11, 1901). 47. *Fred Fearnot Fined; or, The Judge's Mistake* (Dec. 27, 1901). 48. *Fred Fearnot and the Man Who Wanted to Fight* (Feb.5, 1902). 49. *Fred Fearnot in Turkey; or, Defying the Sultan* (Feb. 7, 1902). 50. *Fred Fearnot and the Kaiser; or, In the Royal Palace at Berlin* (Feb. 21, 1902). 51. *Fred Fearnot's Justice; or, The Champion of the School Marm* (March 14, 1902). 52. *Fred Fearnot's Big Day; or, Harvard and Yale at New Era* (April 4, 1902). 53. *Fred Fearnot and the Lynchers; or, Saving a Girl Horse Thief* (April 18, 1902). 54. *Fred Fearnot's Wonderful Feat; or, The Taming of Black Beauty* (April 25, 1902). 55. *Fred Fearnot and the Rioters; or, Backing Up the Sheriff* (May 23, 2902). 56. *Fred Fearnot in New Mexico; or, Saved by Terry Olcott* (June 20, 1902. 57. *Fred Fearnot in Montana; or, The Dispute at Rocky Hill* (July 4, 1902). 58. *Fred Fearnot and the Raiders; or, Fighting for His Belt* (Sept. 12, 1902). 59. *Fred Fearnot and the Amazon; or, The Wild Woman of the Plains* (Oct. 24, 1902). 60. *Fred Fearnot's Training School; or, How to Make a Living* (Oct. 31, 1902). 61. *Fred Fearnot and the Old Trapper; or, Searching for a Lost Cavern* (Nov. 14, 1902). 62. *Fred Fearnot on the Stump; or, Backing an Old Veteran* (Dec. 12, 1902). 63. *Fred Fearnot's New Trouble; or, Up Against a Monopoly* (Dec. 19, 1902). 64. *Fred Fearnot as Marshal; or, Commanding the Peace* (Dec. 26,

1902). 65. *Fred Fearnot and the Miners; or, the Trouble at Coppertown* (Jan. 9, 1903). 66. *Fred Fearnot and the "Blind Tigers"; or, More Ways Than One* (Jan. 16, 1903). 67. *Fred Fearnot's Great Fire Fight; or, Rescuing a Prairie School* (Feb. 6, 1903). 68. *Fred Fearnot in New Orleans; or, Up Against the Mafia* (Feb. 13, 1903). 69. *Fred Fearnot and the Haunted House; or, Unraveling a Great Mystery* (Feb. 20, 1903). 70. *Fred Fearnot's Wolf Hunt; or, A Battle for Life in the Dark* (March 6, 1903). 71. *Fred Fearnot and the Grave Digger; or, the Mystery of the Cemetery* (April 3, 1903). 72. *Fred Fearnot and "Mr. Jones"; or, The Insurance Man in Trouble* (April 17, 1903). 73. *Fred Fearnot's Big Gift: or, A Week at Old Avon* (April 24, 1903). 74. *Fred Fearnot and the "Witch"; or, Exploring an Old Fraud* (May 1, 1903). 75. *Fred Fearnot at Canyon Castle; or, Entertaining His Friends* (May 29, 1903). 76. *Fred Fearnot and the Commanche; or, Teaching a Red-Skin a Lesson* (June 5, 1903). 77. *Fred Fearnot Suspected; or, Trailed by a Treasure Sleuth* (June 12, 1903). 78. *Fred Fearnot in Tennessee; or, the Demon of the Mountains* (June 17, 1903). 79. *Fred Fearnot in West Virginia; or, Helping the Revenue Agents* (July 31, 1903). 80. *Fred Fearnot's Strange Adventure; or, The Queer Old Man of the Mountain* (Aug. 14, 1903). 81. *Fred Fearnot and the Wrestler; or, Throwing a Great Champion* (Sept. 4, 1903). 82. *Fred Fearnot and the "Greenhorn"; or, Fooled for Once in His Life* (Sept. 25, 1903). 83. *Fred Fearnot's Boy Scouts; or, Hot Time in the Rockies* (Oct. 9, 1903). 84. *Fred Fearnot and the Promoter; or, Breaking Up a Big Scheme* (Tousey). 85. *Fred Fearnot and the Mill Boy; or, a Desperate Dash for Life* (Oct. 30, 1903). 86. *Fred Fearnot and the Sheep Herders; or, Trapping the Ranch Robbers* (Feb. 19, 1904). 87. *Fred Fearnot and His Dog; or, The Boy Who Ran for Congress* (April 1, 1904). 88. *Fred Fearnot and the Boy Teamster; or, The Lad Who Bluffed Him* (June 17, 1904). 89. *Fred Fearnot and the Oil King; or, the Tough Gang of the Wells* (July 15, 1904). 90. *Fred Fearnot's Wonderful Courage* (Aug. 5, 1904). 91. *Fred Fearnot and the Poor Widow; or, Making a Mean Man Do Right* (Aug. 19, 1904). 92. *Fred Fearnot and the Money Lenders; or, Breaking Up a Swindling Gang* (Sept. 2, 1904). 93. *Fred Fearnot's Gun Club; or, Shooting for a Diamond Cup* (Sept. 9, 1904). 94. *Fred Fearnot and the Braggart; or, Having Fun with an Egoist* (Sept. 16, 1904). 95. *Fred Fearnot and the Wall Street Broker; or, Helping the Widows and Orphans* (Nov. 11, 1904). 96. *Fred Fearnot and "Red Pete"; or, The Wickedest Man in Arizona* (Dec. 9, 1904). 97. *Fred Fearnot and "Red Pete"; or, A Slick Chap from Warsaw* (Dec. 23, 1904). 98. *Fred Fearnot and "Uncle Pike"; or, A Slick Chap from Warsaw* (Dec. 23, 1904). 99. *Fred Fearnot's Change of Front; or, Staggering the Wall Street Brokers* (July 28, 1905). 100. *Fred Fearnot and the Railroad Gant; or, A Desperate Fight for Life* (Sept. 15, 1905). 101. *Fred Fearnot and the Indian Guide; or, the Abduction of a Beautiful Girl* (Tousey) Oct. 27, 1905. 102. *Fred Fearnot's Daring Deed; or, Saving Terry from the Lynchers* (Jan. 5, 1906). 103. *Fred Fearnot's Game Teamster; or, A Hot Time on the Plains* (Jan. 5, 1906). 104. *Fred Fearnot and the Diamond Queen; or, Helping the Treasury Department* (March 9, 1906). 105. *Fred Fearnot and the Snake-Charmer; or, Out with the Circus Fakirs* (April 6, 1906). 106. *Fred Fearnot's Promise; or, Helping a Drunkard's Boy* (May 11, 1906). 107. *Fred Fearnot and the Silver Syndicate; or, Beating the Wall Street Sharks* (June 22, 1906). 108. *Fred Fearnot and His No-Hit Game; or, Striking Out the Champions* (July 27, 1906). 109. *Fred Fearnot and the Farmer's Boy; or, A Greenhorn from the Country* (Aug. 31, 1906). 110. *Fred Fearnot and the White Moose; or, Out on a Strange Hunt* (Sept.

7, 1908). 111. *Fred Fearnot's Football Boys; or, Winning on the Gridiron* (Oct. 12, 1906). 112. *Fred Fearnot and the Broker's Game; or, Downing a Wall Street Gang* (Oct. 19, 1906). 113. *Fred Fearnot and the Temperance Boy; or, Driving Out the Home Wreckers* (Nov. 16, 1906). 114. *Fred Fearnot and the Mill Girl; or, The Factory Gang of Fairdale* (Dec. 7, 1906). 115. *Fred Fearnot and the Boy Who Tried; or, Bound to Rise in the World* (Dec. 28, 1906). 116. *Fred Fearnot and the Ice King; or, Beating the Champion* (Dec. 6, 1907). 117. *Fred Fearnot's Revenge; or, Defeating the Congressman* (Jan. 2, 1914).

Good Fortune Trilogy. Author: Horatio Alger. Publisher: H. T. Coates.

1. *Walter Sherwood's Probation; or, Cool Head and Warm Heart* (1897). 2. *Young Bank Messenger* (1898). 3. *Boys' Fortune* (1898).

Gun Boat Series. Author: Harry Castlemon. Publisher: R. W. Carroll except where noted.

1. *Frank, the Young Naturalist* (1865). 2. *Frank Before Vicksburg* (John C. Winston), 1892.

Hit the Big League Series. Author: Burt L. Standish. Publisher: Barse & Hopkins.

1. *Brick King, Backstop* (1914). 2. *Making of a Big Leaguer* (1915). 3. *Courtney of the Center Garden* (1915). 4. *Covering the Look on Corner* (1915). 5. *Crossed Signals* (1928). 6. *Guarding the Keystone Sack* (1917). 7. *Man on First* (1920). 8. *Lego Lamb, Southpaw* (1923). 9. *Grip of the Game* (1924).

How to Rise Trilogy. Author: Horatio Alger. Publisher: John C. Winston.

1. *Jed, the Poorhouse Boy* (1899). 2. *Rupert's Ambition* (1899). 3. *Lester's Lunch* (1901).

Hunniwell Boys Series. Author: Levi Parker Wyman. Publisher: A. L. Burt.

1. *Hunniwell Boys in the Air* (1928). 2. *Hunniwell Boys' Victory* (1928). 3. *Hunniwell Boys in the Secret Service* (1928). 4. *Hunniwell Boys End the Platinum Mystery* (1928). 5. *Hunniwell Boys' Longest Flight* (1928). 6. *Hunniwell Boys in the Gobi Desert* (1930). 7. *Hunniwell Boys in the Caribbean* (1930). 8. *Hunniwell Boys' Non-Stop Flight around the World* (1931).

Jack Harkaway Series. Author: Bracebridge Hemyng. Publisher: Street and Smith except where noted.

1. *Jack Harkaway Stories*. 2. *Jack Harkaway in Search of the Mountain of Gold* (Hogarth House), 1870. 3. *Jack Harkaway Out West Amongst the Indians* (1880). 4. *Jack Harkaway and His Son's Adventures in Greece* (M. A. Donohue), 1896. 5. *Jack Harkaway and His Son's Adventures in China* (M. A. Donohue), 1900. 6. *Jack Harkaway's Boy Tinker Among the Turks* (M. A. Donohue), 1900. 7. *Jack Harkaway in New York; or, the Adventures of the Traveler's Club* (1904). 8. *Jack Harkaway's Adventures in America* (M. A. Donohue), 1904. 9. *Jack Harkaway's Battle with the Turks* (1904). 10. *Jack Harkaway's Confidence* (Federal Book Co.), 1904. 11. *Jack Harkaway's Struggles* (1904). 12. *Young Jack Harkaway in Search of His Father* (1904). 13. *Jack Harkaway on the Isle of Pines* (1904). 14. *Jack Harkaway Afloat and Ashore* (1906). 15. *Jack Harkaway in Australia* (1925). 16. *Jack Harkaway after Schooldays* (1925). 17. *Jack Harkaway Among the Brigands* (1925). 18. *Jack Harkaway Among the Indians* (1925). 19. *Jack Harkaway Among the Pirates* (1925). 20. *Jack Harkaway and the Bushrangers* (1925). 21. *Jack Harkaway and the Red Dragon* (1925). 22. *Jack Harkaway and the Turks* (1925).

23. *Jack Harkaway around the World* (1925). 24. *Jack Harkaway at Oxford* (1925). 25. *Jack Harkaway in America* (1925). 26. *Jack Harkaway in China* (1925). 27. *Jack Harkaway in the Black Hills* (1925). 28. *Jack Harkaway in the Toils* (1925). 29. *Jack Harkaway Out West* (1925). 30. *Jack Harkaway's Escape from the Turks* (1925). 31. *Jack Harkaway and the Sacred Serpent* (1926). 32. *Jack Harkaway's School-days* (1926). 33. *Jack Harkaway, Missing* (1926). 34. *Adventures of Young Jack Harkaway and His Boy Tinker* (M. A. Donohue), 1929. 35. *Jack Harkaway's Capture* (Federal Book Co.), 1940. 36. *Jack Harkaway's Escape from the Brigands of Greece* (M. A. Donohue).

Jack Hazard Series. Author: John Townsend Trowbridge. Publisher: H. T. Coates.
1. *Jack Hazard and His Fortunes* (1871). 2. *Chance for Himself* (1872). 3. *Jack Hazard Doing His Best* (1873). 4. *Jack Hazard's Fast Friends* (1874). 5. *Young Surveyor* (1875).

Jack Lightfoot Series. Author: Maxwell Stevens. Publisher: Street and Smith.
1. *Jack Lightfoot Down in Dixie; or, the Voyage of the Single-Hand Cruisers* (1905). 2. *Jack Lightfoot in Camp; or, the Appearance of an Old Enemy* (1905). 3. *Jack Lightfoot the Athlete; or, Clean Sport* (1905). 4. *Trapped; or, Caught by His Enemies* (1905). 5. *Jack Lightfoot's Challenge; or, the Winning of the Wager* (1905). 6. *Jack Lightfoot's Blind; or, with Rod and Gun* (1905). 7. *Jack Lightfoot's Iron Arm; or, the Trick That Did Not Work* (1905). 8. *Jack Lightfoot's Rival; or, a Jockey for a Day* (1905). 9. *Jack Lightfoot's Canoe Trip; or, Making a Name* (1905). 10. *Jack Lightfoot's Gun Club; or, On to Victory* (1905). 11. *Jack Lightfoot's Hoodoo; or, the New Shortstop* (1905). 12. *Jack Lightfoot's Decision; or, Bound in Honor* (1905). 13. *Jack Lightfoot on Snow Shoes; or, Chase of the Great Moose* (1906). 14. *Jack Lightfoot's Wisdom; or, Working His Own Salvation* (1906). 15. *Jack Lightfoot's Headwork; or, How He Won* (1906). 16. *Jack Lightfoot's Capture; or, In the Hands of His Foes* (1906).

Jane Allen Series. Author: Edith Bancroft. Publisher: Cupples.
1. *Jane Allen of the Sub Team* (1917). 2. *Jane Allen, Right Guard* (1918). 3. *Jane Allen, Center* (1920). 4. *Jane Allen, Junior* (1921). 5. *Jane Allen, Senior* (1922).

Jerry Todd Series. Author: Leo Edwards. Publisher: Grosset and Dunlap.
1. *Jerry Todd and the Whispering Mummy* (1924). 2. *Jerry Todd and the Rose-Colored Cat* (1924). 3. *Jerry Todd and the Oak Island Treasure* (1925). 4. *Jerry Todd and the Waltzing Hen* (1924). 5. *Jerry Todd and the Talking Frog* (1924). 6. *Jerry Todd and the Purring Egg* (1926). 7. *Jerry Todd and the Whispering Cave* (1927). 8. *Jerry Todd, Pirate* (1928). 9. *Jerry Todd and the Bob-Tailed Elephant* (1929). 10. *Jerry Todd, Editor-in-Chief* (1930). 11. *Jerry Todd, Caveman* (1932). 12. *Jerry Todd and the Flying Flapdoodle* (1934). 13. *Jerry Todd and the Buffalo Bill Bathtub* (1936). 14. *Jerry Todd's Up-the-Ladder Club* (1927). 15. *Jerry Todd's Poodle Parlor* (1935). 16. *Jerry Todd Cockoo Camp* (1940).

Jesse James Series. Author: W. B. Lawson (1-a2, b5, c1-d1), D. W. Stevens (b1-b4, b6, d2) Publisher: Street and Smith except where noted.
1. *Jesse James at Coney Island* (1898). 2. *Jesse James at Long Beach* (1898). 3. *Jesse James's Double* (1898). 4. *Jesse James in New York* (1899). 5. *Jesse James' Oath* (1898). 6. *Jesse James in St. Louis* (1898). 7. *Bob Ford, the Slayer of Jesse James* (1892). a1. *Jesse,*

the Outlaw: A Narrative of the James Boys (1882). a2. *Jesse James in Chicago* (1898). b1. *James Boys in a Trap* (Frank Tousey), 1901. b2. *James Boys' Dash for Life or Death* (Frank Tousey), 1902. b3. *James Boys' Fight for $100,000* (Frank Tousey), 1902. b4. *James Boys' Missouri Raid* (Frank Tousey), 1902. b5. *Jesse James' Death Sentence* (Frank Tousey), 1903. b6. *James Boys at Cracker Neck* (Frank Tousey), n.d. c1. *Jesse James' Daring Joke; or, the Kidnapping of a Bank President* (Arthur Westbrook), 1909. c2. *Jesse James' Narrow Escape; or, Ensnared by a Woman Detective* (Arthur Westbrook), 1909. c3. *Jesse James' Fate; or, the End of the Crimson Trail* (Arthur Westbrook), 1910. c4. *Jesse James' Midnight Raid; or, the Fight at Battle Mountain* (Arthur Westbrook), 1920. d1. *Chasing the James Boys; or, a Detective's Dangerous Case* (New York Detective Library), 1889. d2. *James Boys in No Man's Land; or, the Bandit King's Last Ride* (New York Detective Library), 1891.

Khaki Boys Series. Author: Gordon Bates. Publisher: Cupples and Leon.

1. *Khaki Boys at Camp Sterling* (1918). 2. *Khaki Boys on the Way* (1918). 3. *Khaki Boys at the Front* (1918). 4. *Khaki Boys over the Top* (1919). 5. *Khaki Boys Fighting to Win* (1919). 6. *Khaki Boys along the Rhine* (1920).

Khaki Girls Series. Author: Edna Brooks. Publisher: Cupples and Leon.

1. *Khaki Girls of the Motor Corps* (1918). 2. *Khaki Girls behind the Lines* (1918). 3. *Khaki Girls at Windsor Barracks* (1919). 4. *Khaki Girls in Victory* (1920).

Knockabout Club Series. Author: Charles Asbury Stephens. Publisher: *Youth's Companion.*

1. *Knockabout Club in the Woods* (1881). 2. *Knockabout Club along Shore* (1882). 3. *Knockabout Club in the Tropics* (1883). 4. *Knockabout Club in the Everglades* (1887). 5. *Knockabout Club in the Antilles and Thereabouts* (1888). 6. *Knockabout Club in Spain* (1889). 7. *Knockabout Club in North Africa* (1890). 8. *Knockabout Club on the Spanish Main* (1891). 9. *Knockabout Club in Search of Treasures* (1892).

Lake Shore Series. Author: William Taylor Adams (Oliver Optic). Publisher: Lee and Shepard.

1. *Through the Daylight; or, the Young Engineer of the Lake Shore Railroad* (1869). 2. *Lightning Express; or, the Rival Academies* (1870). 3. *One Time; or, the Young Captain of the Ucaygo Steamer* (1870). 4. *Switch Off; or, the Way to the Students* (1870). 5. *Break Up; or, the Young Peacemakers* (1869). 6. *Bear and Forbear; or, the Young Skipper of Lake Ucaygo* (1871).

Lakeport Series. Author: Edward Stratemeyer. Publisher: Lothrop, Lee and Shepard.

1. *Gun Club Boys at Lakeport* (1908). 2. *Baseball Boys of Lakeport* (1908). 3. *Boat Club Boys of Lakeport* (1908). 4. *Football Boys of Lakeport* (1909). 5. *Automobile Boys of Lakeport* (1910). 6. *Aircraft Boys at Lakeport* (1912).

Launch Boys Series. Author: Edward Sylvester Ellis. Publisher: John C. Winston.

1. *Launch Boys' Adventure in Northern Waters* (1912). 2. *Launch Boys' Cruise in Deerfoot* (1912).

Lefty Locke Series. Author: Burt L. Standish. Publisher: Barse and Hopkins.

1. *Lefty o' the Training Camp* (1914). 2. *Lefty o' the Blue Stockings* (1914). 3.

Lefty o' the Bush (1914). 4. *Lefty o' the Big League* (1914). 5. *Lefty Locke, Pitcher-Manager* (1916).

Linda Carlton Series. Author: Edith Lavell. Publisher: A. L. Burt.

1. *Linda Carlton, Air Pilot* (1930).2. *Island Adventure* (1931). 3. *Linda Carlton's Ocean Flight* (1931). 4. *Linda Carlton's Perilous Summer* (1932). 5. *Linda Carlton's Hollywood Flight* (1932).

Link Rover Series. Author: Gale Richards. Publisher: Street and Smith.

1. *Link Rover at School Abroad; or, Lively Times at Old Swindon* (1904). 2. *Link Rover Among the Calists* (1904). 3. *Link Rover in Algiers; or, Waking Up a Sleepy Oriental City* (1904). 4. *Link Rover in America; or, In Search of Fun at the Golden Gate* (1904). 5. *Link Rover in Chicago; or, Making Things Fairly Hum* (1905). 6. *Link Rover in Florida; or, Hilarious Times under the Palmettoes* (1905). 7. *Link Rover's Flying Wedge; or, Football Tactics on a Mississippi Steamboat* (1905). 8. *Link Rover's Triumph; or, Whooping Things Up along the Road* (1905). 9. *Link Rover Stranded; or, Finding Fun on the Road* (1905). 10. *Link Rover and the Money Makers; or, Something Not Down on the Bills* (1905). 11. *Link Rover Among the Fire Worshippers; or, Yankee Joker in the Land of Diaz* (1905). 12. *Link Rover Afloat and Ashore; or, Not So Simple as He Seemed* (1905).

Little Colonel Series. Author: Annie Fellows Johnston. Publisher: J. Knight.

1. *Little Colonel* (1896). 2. *Gate of the Giant Scissors* (1898). 3. *Little Colonel's House Party* (1900). 4. *Two Little Knights of Kentucky* (1901). 5. *Little Colonel's Holiday* (1901). 6. *Little Colonel's Hero* (1902). 7. *Little Colonel at Boarding School* (1903). 8. *Little Colonel in Arizona* (1904). 9. *Little Colonel's Christmas Vacation* (1905). 10. *Little Colonel, Maid of Honor* (1906). 11. *Little Colonel's Knight Comes Riding* (1907). 12. *Mary Ware, the Little Colonel's Chum* (1908). 13. *Mary Ware in Texas* (1910). 14. *Little Colonel's Good Times Book* (1910). 15. *Little Colonel's Doll Book* (1910). 16. *Mary Ware's Promised Land* (1912). 17. *Mary Ware Doll Book* (1914).

Log Cabin Series. Author: Edward Sylvester Ellis. Publisher: Porter and Coates.

1. *Lost Trail* (1884). 2. *Campfire and Wigman* (1885). 3. *Footprints in the Forest* (1886).

Luck and Pluck Series. Author: Horatio Alger. Publisher: Loring.

1. *Luck and Pluck; or, John Oakley's Inheritance* (1869). 2. *Sink or Swim* (1870). 3. *Strong and Steady* (1871). 4. *Strive and Succeed* (1872). 5. *Try and Trust* (1873). 6. *Bound to Rise* (1873). 7. *Risen from the Ranks* (1874). 8. *Herbert Carter's Legacy* (1875).

Lucky Terrell Flying Series. Author: Canfield Cook. Publisher: Grosset and Dunlap.

1. *Spitfire Pilot* (1942). 2. *Sky Attack* (1942). 3. *Secret Mission* (1943). 4. *Lost Squadron* (1943). 5. *Springboard to Tokyo* (1943). 6. *Wings over Japan* (1944). 7. *Flying Jet* (1945). 8. *Flying Wing* (1946).

Mexican War Series. Author: Ralph Bonehill. Publisher: Edward Stratemeyer.

1. *For the Liberty of Texas* (1900). 2. *With Taylor on the Rio Grande* (1901). 3. *Under Scott in Mexico* (1902).

Minute Boys Series. Author: Edward Stratemeyer. Publisher: Dana Estes and Co.

1. *Minute Boys at Lexington* (1898).

2. *Minute Boys of Bunker Hill* (1899). 3. *Minute Boys of the Green Mountains* (1904). 4. *Minute Boys of the Mohawk Valley* (1905). 5. *Minute Boys of the Wyoming Valley* (1906). 6. *Minute Boys of South Carolina* (1907). 7. *Minute Boys of Long Island* (1908). 8. *Minute Boys of New York* (1909). 9. *Minute Boys of Boston* (1910). 10. *Minute Boys of Yorktown* (1912).

Motor Boat Club Series. Author: H. Irving Hancock. Publisher: Altemus.

1. *Motor Boat Club of the Kennebec* (1909). 2. *Motor Boat Club at Nantucket* (1909). 3. *Motor Boat Club off Long Island; or, a Daring Marine Game at Racing Speed* (1909). 4. *Motor Boat Club and the Wireless* (1909). 5. *Motor Boat Club in Florida* (1909). 6. *Motor Boat Club on the Golden Gate* (1909). 7. *Motor Boat Club on the Great Lakes* (1912).

Motor Girls Series. Author: Penrose, Margaret. Publisher: Cupples.

1. *Motor Girls* (1910). 2. *Motor Girls on the Town* (1910). 3. *Motor Girls at Lookout Beach* (1911). 4. *Motor Girls through New England* (1911). 5. *Motor Girls on Cedar Lake* (1912). 6. *Motor Girls on the Coast* (1913). 7. *Motor Girls on Crystal Bay* (1914). 8. *Motor Girls on Waters Blue* (1915). 9. *Motor Girls at Camp Sunrise* (1916). 10. *Motor Girls in the Mountains* (1917).

Moving Picture Girls Series. Author: Laura Lee Hope. Publisher: Grosset and Dunlap.

1. *Moving Picture Girls* (1914). 2. *Moving Picture Girls at Oakfarm* (1914). 3. *Moving Picture Girls Snowbound* (1914). 4. *Moving Picture Girls under the Palms; or, Lost in the Wilds of Florida* (1914). 5. *Moving Picture Girls at Rocky Ranch* (1914). 6. *Moving Picture Girls at Sea* (1915). 7. *Moving Picture Girls in War Plays* (1916).

New World Trilogy. Author: Horatio Alger. Publisher: Collier Books.

1. *Digging for Gold: A Story of California* (1892). 2. *Facing the World; or, the Haps and Mishaps of Harry Vane* (1893). 3. *In a New World* (1893).

Oakdale Series. Author: Morgan Scott. Publisher: Hurst and Co.

1. *Ben Stone at Oakdale* (1911). 2. *Great Oakdale Mystery* (1912).

Old Glory Series. Author: Edward Stratemeyer. Publisher: Lothrop, Lee and Shepard.

1. *Under Dewey at Manila* (1898). 2. *Young Volunteer in Cuba* (1898). 3. *Fighting in Cuban Waters* (1899). 4. *Under Otis in the Philippines* (1899). 5. *Campaign of the Jungle* (1900). 6. *Under MacArthur at Luzon* (1901).

Oriole Series. Author: Amy Bell Marlowe. Publisher: Grosset and Dunlap.

1. *When Oriole Came to Harbor Light* (1920). 2. *When Oriole Traveled Westward* (1921). 3. *When Oriole Went to Boarding School* (1927).

Outdoor Girls Series. Author: Laura Lee Hope. Publisher: Grosset and Dunlap.

1. *Outdoor Girls of Deepdale* (1913). 2. *Outdoor Girls at Rainbow Lake* (1913). 3. *Outdoor Girls in a Motor Car* (1913). 4. *Outdoor Girls in a Winter Camp* (1913). 5. *Outdoor Girls in Florida* (1913). 6. *Outdoor Girls at Ocean View* (1915). 7. *Outdoor Girls on Pine Island* (1916). 8. *Outdoor Girls in Army Service* (1918). 9. *Outdoor Girls at the Hostess House* (1919). 10. *Outdoor Girls at Bluff Point* (1920). 11. *Outdoor Girls at Wild Rose Lodge* (1921). 12. *Outdoor Girls in the Saddle* (1922). 13. *Outdoor Girls around the Campfire* (1923). 14. *Outdoor Girls at Cape Cod* (1924). 15. *Outdoor Girls at*

Foaming Falls (1925). 16. *Outdoor Girls along the Coast* (1926). 17. *Outdoor Girls at Spring Hill Farm* (1927). 18. *Outdoor Girls at New Moon Ranch* (1928). 19. *Outdoor Girls on a Hike* (1929). 20. *Outdoor Girls on a Canoe Trip* (1930). 21. *Outdoor Girls at Cedar Ridge* (1931). 22. *Outdoor Girls in the Air* (1932). 23. *Outdoor Girls in Desert Valley* (1933).

Pacific Series. Author: Horatio Alger. Publisher: John C. Winston.
1. *Young Adventure; or, Tom's Trip across the Plain* (1878). 2. *Young Miner; or, Tom Nelson in California* (1879). 3. *Young Explorer; or, Among the Sierras* (1880). 4. *Ben's Nuggets; or, a Boy's Search for Fortune* (1882).

Pan American Series. Author: Edward Stratemeyer. Publisher: Lee and Shepard.
1. *Lost in the Orinoco* (1902). 2. *Young Volcano Explorers* (1902). 3. *Young Explorers of the Isthmus* (1903). 4. *Young Explorers of the Amazon* (1904). 5. *Treasure Seekers of the Andes* (1907). 6. *Chased across the Pampas* (1911).

Poppy Ott Series. Author: Leo Edwards. Publisher: Grosset and Dunlap.
1. *Poppy Ott and the Stuttering Parrot* (1926). 2. *Poppy Ott's Seven-League Stilts* (1926). 3. *Poppy Ott and the Galloping Snail* (1927). 4. *Poppy Ott's Pedigreed Pickles* (1927). 5. *Poppy Ott and the Freckled Goldfish* (1928). 6. *Poppy Ott and the Tittering Totem* (1929). 7. *Poppy Ott and the Prancing Pancake* (1930). 8. *Poppy Ott Hits the Trail* (1933). 9. *Poppy Ott & Co., Inferior Decorators* (1937). 10. *Monkey's Paw* (1938). 11. *Hidden Hand* (1939).

Putnam Hall Series. Author: Arthur M. Winfield. Publisher: Edward Stratemeyer.
1. *Putnam Hall Cadets* (1901). 2. *Putnam Hall Rivals* (1906). 3. *Putnam Hall Champions* (1908). 4. *Putnam Hall Rebellion* (1909). 5. *Putnam Hall Encampment* (1910). 6. *Putnam Hall Mystery* (1911).

Ragged Dick Series. Author: Horatio Alger. Publisher: Loring.
1. *Ragged Dick; or, Street Life in New York* (1868). 2. *Fame and Fortune; or, the Progress of Richard Hunter* (1868). 3. *Mark, the Match Boy; or, Richard Hunter's Ward* (1869). 4. *Rough and Ready; or, Life Among the New York Newsboys* (1869). 5. *Ben, the Luggage Boy; or, Among the Wharves* (1870). 6. *Rufus and Rose* (1870).

Randy Starr Series. Author: Eugene Martin. Publisher: Altemus.
1. *Randy Starr above Stormy Seas* (1931). 2. *Randy Starr Leading the Air Circus* (1932).

Red Randall Series. Author: Robert Sidney Bowen. Publisher: Grosset and Dunlap.
1. *Red Randall at Midway* (1944). 2. *Red Randall on New Guinea* (1942). 3. *Red Randall at Pearl Harbor* (1944). 4. *Red Randall in Burma* (1945). 5. *Red Randall in the Aleutians* (1945). 6. *Red Randall's One-Man War* (1946).

Rex Kingdom Series. Author: Gordon Braddock. Publisher: Hurst and Co..
1. *Rex Kingdom in the North Woods* (1914). 2. *Rex Kingdom at Wolcott Hall.* (1915).

Rex Lee Series. Author: Thomson Burtis. Publisher: Grosset and Dunlap.
1. *Rex Lee, Gypsy Flyer* (1928). 2. *Rex Lee in the Border Patrol* (1928). 3. *Rex Lee, Ranger of the Sky* (1928). 4. *Rex Lee, Sky Trailer* (1929). 5. *Rex Lee, Ace of the Air Mail* (1927). 6. *Rex Lee, Night Flyer* (1929). 7. *Rex Lee's Mysterious Flight* (1930). 8. *Rex Lee, Rough*

Rider (1930). 9. *Rex Lee, Aerial Acrobat* (1930). 10. *Rex Lee Trailing Air Bandits* (1931). 11. *Rex Lee, Flying Detective* (1932).

Rise in Life Series. Author: Horatio Alger. Publisher: Cupples.
1. *Out for Business* (1900). 2. *Falling In with Fortune* (1900). 3. *Young Captain Jack* (1901). 4. *Nelson, the Newsboy* (1901). 5. *Jerry, the Backwoods Boy* (1904). 6. *Lost at Sea* (1904). 7. *From Farm to Fortune* (1905). 8. *Young Book Agent* (1905). 9. *Randy of the River* (1906). 10. *Joe, the Hotel Boy* (1912). 11. *Ben Logan Triumph* (1912).

Riverdale Series. Author: William Taylor Adams (Oliver Optic). Publisher: Lee and Shepard.
1. *Little Merchant; a Story for Little Folks* (1863). 2. *Young Voyagers; a Story for Little Folks* (1863). 3. *Christmas Gift; a Story for Little Folks* (1863). 4. *Dolly and I; a Story for Little Folks* (1863). 5. *Uncle Ben; a Story for Little Folks* (1863). 6. *Birthday Party; a Story for Little Folks* (1865). 7. *Proud and Lazy; a Story for Little Folks* (1863). 8. *Careless Kate; a Story for Little Folks* (1863). 9. *Robinson Crusoe, Jr.; a Story for Little Folks* (1863). 10. *Picnic Party; a Story for Little Folks* (1863). 11. *Gold Thimble; a Story for Little Folks* (1863). 12. *Do-Somethings; a Story for Little Folks* (1863).

Rocky Mountain Series. Author: Harry Castlemon. Publisher: Porter and Coates except where noted.
1. *Frank at Don Carlos Rancho* (1871). 2. *Frank Among the Rancheros* (John C. Winston), 1896.

Rod and Gun Club Series. Author: Harry Castlemon. Publisher: Porter and Coates.
1. *Rod and Gun Club* (1883). 2. *Don Gordon's Shooting Box* (1883).

Rollo Series. Author: Jacob Abbott. Publisher: Harper.
1. *Rollo Learning to Talk* (1835). 2. *Rollo Learning to Read* (1835). 3. *Rollo at Work* (1838). 4. *Rollo at Play* (1838). 5. *Rollo at School* (1839). 6. *Rollo's Vacation* (1839). 7. *Rollo's Experiments* (1839). 8. *Rollo's Museum* (1839). 9. *Rollo's Travels* (1840). 10. *Rollo's Correspondence* (1840). 11. *Rollo's Philosophy, Water* (1841). 12. *Rollo's Philosophy, Air* (1841). 13. *Rollo's Philosophy, Fire* (1842). 14. *Rollo's Philosophy, Sky* (1842).

Rollo's Tour in Europe. Author: Jacob Abbott. Publisher: Harper.
1. *Rollo on the Atlantic* (1853). 2. *Rollo in Paris* (1854). 3. *Rollo in Switzerland* (1855). 4. *Rollo in London* (1855). 5. *Rollo on the Rhine* (1855). 6. *Rollo in Scotland* (1856). 7. *Rollo in Geneva* (1857). 8. *Rollo in Holland* (1857). 9. *Rollo in Naples* (1858). 10. *Rollo in Rome* (18580.

Roughing It Series. Author: Harry Castlemon. Publisher: Porter and Coates.
1. *George in Camp; or, Life on the Plains* (1879). 2. *George at the Wheel; or, Life in the Pilot House* (1881). 3. *George at the Fort; or, Life Among the Soldiers* (1882.

Rover Boys Series. Author: Arthur M. Winfield. Publisher: Mershon Co.
1. *Rover Boys at School* (1899). 2. *Rover Boys on the Ocean* (1899). 3. *Rover Boys in the Jungle* (1899). 4. *Rover Boys Out West* (1900). 5. *Rover Boys on the Great Lakes* (1901). 6. *Rover Boys in the Mountains* (1902). 7. *Rover Boys on Land and Sea* (1903). 8. *Rover Boys in Camp* (1904). 9. *Rover Boys on the River* (1905). 10. *Rover Boys on the Plains* (1906). 11. *Rover Boys in Southern Waters* (1907). 12. *Rover Boys on the Farm* (1908). 13. *Rover Boys on Treasure Isle* (1909). 14.

Rover Boys at College (1910). 15. *Rover Boys Down East* (1911). 16. *Rover Boys in the Air* (1912). 17. *Rover Boys in New York* (1913). 18. *Rover Boys in Alaska* (1914). 19. *Rover Boys in Business* (1915). 20. *Rover Boys on a Tour* (1916). 21. *Rover Boys at Colby Hall* (1917). 22. *Rover Boys on Snowshoe Island* (1918). 23. *Rover Boys under Canvas* (1919). 24. *Rover Boys on a Hunt* (1920). 25. *Rover Boys in the Land of Luck* (1921). 26. *Rover Boys at Big Horn Ranch* (1922). 27. *Rover Boys at Big Bear Lake* (1923). 28. *Rover Boys Shipwrecked* (1924). 29. *Rover Boys at Sunset Trail* (1925). 30. *Rover Boys Winning a Fortune* (1926).

Roy Blakely Series. Author: Percy Keese Fitzhugh. Publisher: Grosset and Dunlap.

1. *Roy Blakely* (1920). 2. *Roy Blakely's Adventure in Camp* (1920). 3. *Roy Blakely's Camp on Wheels* (1920). 4. *Roy Blakely, Pathfinder* (1920). 5. *Roy Blakely's Silver Fox Patrol* (1920). 6. *Roy Blakely's Motor Caravan* (1921). 7. *Roy Blakely, Lost, Strayed or Stolen* (1921). 8. *Roy Blakely's Bee-Line Hike* (1922). 9. *Roy Blakely at the Haunted Camp* (1922). 10. *Roy Blakely's Funny Bone Hike* (1923). 11. *Roy Blakely's Tangled Trail* (1924). 12. *Roy Blakely on the Mohawk Trail* (1925). 13. *Roy Blakely's Elastic Hike* (1926). 14. *Roy Blakely's Roundabout Hike* (1927). 15. *Roy Blakely's Happy-Go-Lucky Hike* (1928). 16. *Roy Blakely's Go-as-You-Please Hike* (1929). 17. *Roy Blakely's Wild Goose Chase* (1930). 18. *Roy Blakely Up in the Air* (1931).

Ruth Darrow Series. Author: Mildred Wirt. Publisher: Barse and Co..

1. *Ruth Darrow in the Air Derby* (1930). 2. *Ruth Darrow in the Fire Patrol* (1930). 3. *Ruth Darrow in the Yucatan* (1931). 4. *Ruth Darrow in the Coast Guard* (1931).

Ruth Fielding Series. Author: Alice B. Emerson. Publisher: Cupples.

1. *Ruth Fielding of the Red Mill* (1913). 2. *Ruth Fielding at Briarwood Hall* (1913). 3. *Ruth Fielding at Snow Camp* (1913). 4. *Ruth Fielding at Lighthouse Point* (1913). 5. *Ruth Fielding at Silver Ranch* (1913). 6. *Ruth Fielding on Cliff Island* (1915). 7. *Ruth Fielding at Sunrise Farm* (1915). 8. *Ruth Fielding and the Gypsies* (1915). 9. *Ruth Fielding in Moving Pictures* (1916). 10. *Ruth Fielding Down in Dixie* (1916). 11. *Ruth Fielding at College* (1917). 12. *Ruth Fielding in the Saddle* (1917). 13. *Ruth Fielding in the Red Cross* (1918). 14. *Ruth Fielding at the War Front* (1918). 15. *Ruth Fielding Homeward Bound* (1919). 16. *Ruth Fielding Down East* (1920). 17. *Ruth Fielding in the Great Northwest* (1921). 18. *Ruth Fielding on the Saint Lawrence* (1922). 19. *Ruth Fielding Treasure Hunting* (1923). 20. *Ruth Fielding in the Far North* (1924). 21. *Ruth Fielding at Golden Pass* (1925). 22. *Ruth Fielding in Alaska* (1926). 23. *Ruth Fielding and Her Great Scenario* (1927). 24. *Ruth Fielding at Cameron Hall* (1928). 25. *Ruth Fielding Clearing Her Name* (1929). 26. *Ruth Fielding in Talking Pictures* (1930). 27. *Ruth Fielding and Baby Jane* (1931). 28. *Ruth Fielding and Her Double* (1932). 29. *Ruth Fielding and Her Greatest Triumph* (1933). 30. *Ruth Fielding and Her Crowning Victory* (1934).

Sam Spade Series. Author: Hammett, Dashiel. Publisher: Dell.

1. *Maltese Falcon* (1930). 2. *Adventures of Sam Spade* (1944). 3. *Man Called Spade* (1945).

Ship and Shore Series. Author: Edward Stratemeyer. Publisher: Street and Smith.

1. *Last Cruise of the Spitfire* (1894). 2. *Rueben Stone's Discovery* (1895). 3. *True to Himself* (1900).

Slim Tyler Series. Author: Robert Henry Stone. Publisher: Cupples and Leon.

1. *Sky Riders of the Atlantic; or, Tyler's First Trip in the Clouds* (1930). 2. *Lost over Greenland* (1930). 3. *Air Cargo of Gold* (1930). 4. *Adrift over Hudson Bay* (1931). 5. *Airplane Mystery* (1931). 6. *Secret Sky Express* (1932).

Soldiers of Fortune Series. Author: Edward Stratemeyer. Publisher: Edward Stratemeyer.

1. *On to Peking* (1900). 2. *Under the Mikado's Flag* (1900). 3. *At the Fall of Port Arthur* (1904). 4. *Under Togo for Japan* (1905).

Starry Flag Series. Author: William Taylor Adams (Oliver Optic). Publisher: Lee and Shepard.

1. *Starry Flag; or, the Young Fisherman* (1867). 2. *Breaking Away; or, Fortunes of a Student* (1867). 3. *Seek and Find; or, the Adventures of a Smart Boy* (1868). 4. *Make or Break; or, Rich Man's Daughter* (1868). 5. *Freaks or Fortune; or, Half around the World* (1869). 6. *Down the River; or, Buck Bradford and His Tyrants* (1869).

Tattered Tom Series. Author: Horatio Alger. Publisher: John C. Winston.

1. *Tattered Tom; or, the Story of a Street Arab* (1871). 2. *Paul, the Peddler; or, the Fortunes of a Young Street Merchant* (1871). 3. *Phil, the Fiddler; or, the Story of a Young Street Musician* (1872). 4. *Slow and Sure* (1872). 5. *Julius* (1874). 6. *Young Outlaw* (1875). 7. *Sam's Chance and How He Improved It* (1876). 8. *Telegraph Boy; or, Making His Way in New York* (1879).

Ted Scott Flying Series. Author: Franklin W. Dixon. Publisher: Grosset and Dunlap.

1. *Over the Ocean to Paris* (1927). 2. *Rescued in the Clouds* (1927). 3. *Over the Rockies with the Air Mail* (1927). 4. *First Stop Honolulu* (1927). 5. *Search for the Lost Flyers* (1928). 6. *South of the Rio Grande* (1928). 7. *Across the Pacific* (1928). 8. *Lone Eagle of the Border* (1929). 9. *Flying against Time* (1929). 10. *Over the Jungle Trails* (1929). 11. *Lost at the South Pole* (1930). 12. *Through the Air to Alaska* (1930). 13. *Flying to the Rescue* (1930). 14. *Danger Trails of the Sky* (1931). 15. *Following the Sun Shadow* (1932). 16. *Battling the Wind* (1933). 17. *Brushing the Mountain Top* (1934). 18. *Castaways of the Stratosphere* (1935). 19. *Hunting the Sky Spies* (1941). 20. *Pursuit Patrol* (1943).

Ted Strong Series. Author: Edward C. Taylor. Publisher: Street and Smith.

1. *Ted Strong in Montana; or, With Lariat and Spur* (1904). 2. *Ted Strong Among the Cattlemen; or, a Firm and Steady Hand* (1904). 3. *Ted Strong and the Last of the Herd; or, Big Contract Well Filled* (1904). 4. *Ted Strong and the Rival Miners; or, On the Trail* (1904). 5. *Ted Strong Fighting the Rustlers; or, a Race with Death* (1904). 6. *Ted Strong in Kansas City; or, the Last of the Herd* (1904). 7. *Ted Strong in Montana; or, Trouble at Blackfoot Agency* (1904). 8. *Ted Strong in Nebraska; or, the Trail to Fremont* (1904). 9. *Ted Strong in the Chaparral; or, the Hunt at Las Animas* (1904). 10. *Ted Strong in the Land of Little Rain; or, Bud Morgan's Vengeance* (1904). 11. *Ted Strong Lost in the Desert; or, Merciful Toward His Enemy* (1904). 12. *Ted Strong on the Trail; or, the Cattle Men of Salt Licks* (1904). 13. *Ted Strong with Rifle and Lasso; or, a Triumph of the Right* (1904). 14. *Ted Strong, Cowboy; or, Bound to Succeed* (1904). 15. *Ted Strong's Rough Riders; or, the Boys of Black Mountain* (1904). 16. *Ted Strong's Nerve; or, Wild West Sport at Black Mountain* (1904). 17. *Ted Strong's Rival; or, the Cowboys at Sunset Ranch*

(1904). 18. *Ted Strong across the Prairie; or, a Hard Game to Play* (1905). 19. *Ted Strong Challenged; or, a Fight for Right* (1905). 20. *Ted Strong in Colorado; or, on a Dangerous Mission* (1905). 21. *Ted Strong on a Mountain Trail; or, a Redskin Foe* (1905). 22. *Ted Strong Out for Big Game; or, the Land of the Setting Sun* (1905). 23. *Ted Strong, King of the Wild West; or, Winning a Town by a Ride* (1905). 24. *Ted Strong, Manager; or, a Business Proposition* (1906). 25. *Ted Strong, Manager; or, a Hard Job to Hold* (1906). 26. *Ted Strong and the Cattle Raider; or, a Border Drama* (1927). 27. *Ted Strong and the Sagebrush Kid; or, a Pard Worth Having* (1927). 28. *Ted Strong and the Sioux Players; or, a Real Indian Trail* (1927). 29. *Ted Strong and the Two-Gun Men; or, with Lasso and Rifle* (1927). 30. *Ted Strong at Los Gulch; or, a Private War* (1927). 31. *Ted Strong at Z-Bar Ranch; or, a New Pard* (1927). 32. *Ted Strong in Bandit Canyon; or, on a Merciless Trail* (1927). 33. *Ted Strong on U.P. Duty; or, the Trail That Ran West* (1927). 34. *Ted Strong Tries Prospecting; or, a Try for Nature's Treasure* (1927).

Tom Slade Series. Author: Percy Keese Fitzhugh. Publisher: Grosset and Dunlap.

1. *Tom Slade, Boy Scout* (1915). 2. *Tom Slade at Temple Camp* (1917). 3. *Tom Slade on the River* (1917). 4. *Tom Slade with the Colors* (1918). 5. *Tom Slade on a Transport* (1918). 6. *Tom Slade with the Boys Over There* (1918). 7. *Tom Slade, Motorcycle Dispatch Bearer* (1918). 8. *Tom Slade with the Flying Corps* (1919). 9. *Tom Slade Back Home* (1920). 10. *Tom Slade, Scout Master* (1920). 11. *Tom Slade at Black Lake* (1921). 12. *Tom Slade on Mystery Trail* (1921). 13. *Tom Slade's Double Dare* (1922). 14. *Tom Slade on Overlook Mountain* (1923). 15. *Tom Slade Picks a Winner* (1924). 16. *Tom Slade at Bear Mountain* (1925). 17. *Tom Slade, Forest Ranger* (1926). 18. *Tom Slade in the North Woods* (1927). 19. *Tom Slade at Shadow Isle* (1928). 20. *Tom Slade in the Haunted Cavern* (1929). 21. *Parachute Jumper* (1930).

Tom Swift Series. Author: Victor Appleton. Publisher: Grosset and Dunlap.

1. *Tom Swift and His Motor Cycle* (1910). 2. *Tom Swift and His Motor Boat* (1910). 3. *Tom Swift and His Airship* (1910). 4. *Tom Swift and His Submarine Boat* (1910). 5. *Tom Swift and His Electric Runabout* (1910). 6. *Tom Swift and His Wireless Message* (1910). 7. *Tom Swift Among the Diamond Makers* (1911). 8. *Tom Swift in the Caves of Ice* (1911). 9. *Tom Swift and His Sky Racer* (1911). 10. *Tom Swift and His Electric Rifle* (1911). 11. *Tom Swift in the City of Gold* (1912). 12. *Tom Swift and His Air Glider* (1912). 13. *Tom Swift in Captivity* (1912). 14. *Tom Swift and His Wizard Camera* (1912). 15. *Tom Swift and His Great Searchlight* (1912). 16. *Tom Swift and His Giant Cannon* (1913). 17. *Tom Swift and His Photo Telephone* (1914). 18. *Tom Swift and His Aerial Warship* (1915). 19. *Tom Swift and His Big Tunnel* (1916). 20. *Tom Swift in the Land of Wonders* (1917). 21. *Tom Swift and His War Tank* (1918). 22. *Tom Swift and His Air Scout* (1919). 23. *Tom Swift and His Undersea Search* (1920). 24. *Tom Swift Among the Fire Fighters* (1921). 25. *Tom Swift and His Electric Locomotive* (1922). 26. *Tom Swift and His Flying Boat* (1923). 27. *Tom Swift and His Great Oil Gusher* (1924). 28. *Tom Swift and His Chest of Secrets* (1925). 29. *Tom Swift and His Airline Express* (1926). 30. *Tom Swift Circling the Globe* (1927). 31. *Tom Swift and His Talking Pictures* (1928). 32. *Tom Swift and His House on Wheels* (1929). 33. *Tom Swift and His Big Dirigible* (1930). 34. *Tom Swift and His Sky Train* (1931). 35. *Tom Swift and His Giant Magnet* (1932). 36. *Tom Swift and His*

Television Detector (1933). 37. *Tom Swift and His Ocean Airport* (1934). 38. *Tom Swift and His Planet Stone* (1935). 39. *Tom Swift and His Space Solatron* (1939). 40. *Tom Swift and His Triphibian Atomicar* (1941).

Trigger Berg Series. Author: Leo Edwards. Publisher: Grosset and Dunlap.

1. *Trigger Berg and the Treasure Tree* (1930). 2. *Trigger Berg and His 700 Mouse Traps* (1930). 3. *Trigger Berg and the Sacred Pig* (1931). 4. *Trigger Berg and the Cockeyed Ghost* (1933).

Tuffy Bean Series. Author: Leo Edwards. Publisher: Grosset and Dunlap.

1. *Tuffy Bean's Puppy Days* (1931). 2. *Tuffy Bean's One-Ring Circus* (1931). 3. *Tuffy Bean at Funny Bone Farm* (1931). 4. *Tuffy Bean and the Lost Fortune* (1932).

Uncle Sam's Boys Series. Author: H. Irving Hancock. Publisher: Altemus.

1. *Uncle Sam's Boys in the Ranks* (1910). 2. *Uncle Sam's Boys on Field Duty* (1911). 3. *Uncle Sam's Boys as Sergeants* (1911). 4. *Uncle Sam's Boys in the Philippines* (1912). 5. *Uncle Sam's Boys on Their Mettle* (1916). 6. *Uncle Sam's Boys as Lieutenants* (1919). 7. *Uncle Sam's Boys with Pershing* (1919). 8. *Uncle Sam's Boys Smash the Germans* (1919).

Upward and Onward Series. Author: William Taylor Adams (Oliver Optic). Publisher: Lee and Shepard.

1. *Field and Forest; or, the Fortunes of a Farmer.* (1871). 2. *Plane and Plank; or, the Mishaps of a Mechanic* (1871). 3. *Desk and Debit; or, the Catastrophes of a Clerk* (1871). 4.*Cringle and Cross-Fire; or, the Sea Swashes of a Sailor* (1870). 5. *Bivouac and Battle; or, the Struggles of a Soldier* (1871). 6. *Sea and Shore; or, the Tramps of a Traveler* (1872).

Vicki Barr Series. Author: Helen Wells (1-4, 8-16), Julie Tatham (5-7). Publisher: Grosset and Dunlap.

1. *Silver Wings for Vicki* (1947). 2. Wells, Helen. *Vicki Finds the Answer* (1948). 3. *Hidden Valley Mystery* (1949). 4. *Secret of Magnolia Manor* (1949). 5. *Clue of the Broken Blossom* (1950). 6. *Behind the White Veil* (1951). 7. *Mystery at Hartwood House* (1952). 8. *Peril over the Airport* (1953). 9. *Mystery of the Vanishing Lady* (1954). 10. *Search for the Missing Twin* (1954). 11. *Ghost at the Waterfall* (1956). 12. *Clue of the Golden Coin* (1958). 13. *Silver Ring Mystery* (1960). 14. *Clue of the Carved Ruby* (1961). 15. *Mystery of Flight 908* (1962). 16. *Mystery of the Brass Idol* (1964).

Victory Trilogy. Author: Alger, Horatio. Publisher: John C. Winston.

1. *Only an Irish Boy; or, Andy Burke's Fortune* (1894). 2. *Victor Vane* (1894). 3. *Adrift in the City* (1895).

War Eagle Series. Author: Ned Buntline. Publisher: George H. Williams.

1. *Ice King; or, the Fate of the Lost Steamer, a Fanciful Tale of the Far North* (1848). 2. *War Eagle* (1869).

Way to Success Series. Author: Horatio Alger. Publisher: Porter and Coates.

1. *Store Boy; or, the Fortunes of Ben Barclay* (1887). 2. *Bob Burton; or, the Young Ranchman of Missouri* (1888). 3. *Luke Walton; or, the Chicago Newsboy* (1889).

Wood Rangers Series. Author: Mayne Reid. Publisher: Routledge.

1. *Wood Rangers* (1860). 2. *Wood Rangers; from the French of Bellamare* (*sic*) (1860). 3. *Wood Rangers; or, the*

Trappers of Sonora (1860). 4. *Wood Rangers, a Tale of the Ohio* (1865).

Woodville Series. Author: William Taylor Adams (Oliver Optic). Publisher: Lee and Shepard.

1. *Rich and Humble; or, the Mission of Bertha Grant* (1864). 2. *In School and Out; or, the Conquest of Richard Grant* (1864). 3. *Watch and Wait* (1864). 4. *Work and Win; or, Noddy Newman on a Cruise* (1864). 5. *Hope and Have; or, Fanny Grant Among the Indians* (1866). 6. *Haste and Waste; or, the Young Pilot of Lake Champlain* (1866).

Working Upward Series. Author: Edward Stratemeyer. Publisher: Street and Smith.

1. *Richard Dare's Venture; or, Striking Out for Himself* (1903). 2. *Young Auctioneers* (1903). 3. *Bound to Be an Electrician* (1903). 4. *Shorthand Tom, the Reporter* (1903). 5. *Fighting for His Own* (1903). 6. *Oliver Bright's Search; or, the Mystery of the Mine* (1903).

Yacht Club Series. Author: William Taylor Adams (Oliver Optic). Publisher: Lee and Shepard.

1. *Little Bobtail; or, the Wreck of the Penobscot Club* (1874). 2. *Yacht Club; or, the Young Boat Builder* (1874). 3. *Money-Maker; or, the Victory of the Basilisk* (1874). 4. *Coming Wave; or, the Hidden Treasure of High Road* (1875). 5. *Dorcas Club; or, Girls Afloat* (1875). 6. *Ocean Born; or, the Cruise of the Clubs* (1875).

Yankee Flier Series. Author: Rutherford George Montgomery. Publisher: Grosset and Dunlap.

1. *Yankee Flier with the R.A.F.* (1941). 2. *Yankee Flier in the Far East* (1942). 3. *Yankee Flier in the South Pacific* (1943). 4. *Yankee Flier in North Africa* (1943). 5. *Yankee Flier in Italy* (1944). 6. *Yankee Flier over Berlin* (1944). 7. *Yankee Flier in Normandy* (1945). 8. *Yankee Flier on a Rescue Mission* (1945). 9. *Yankee Flier under Secret Orders* (1945).

Young Americans Abroad Series. Author: William Taylor Adams (Oliver Optic). Publisher: Lee and Shepard.

1. *Outward Bound; or, Young America Afloat* (1867). 2. *Shamrock and Thistle; or, Young Americans in Ireland and Scotland* (1868). 3. *Red Cross; or, Young Americans in England and Wales* (1868). 4. *Dikes and Ditches; or, Young Americans in Holland Belgium* (1868). 5. *Palace and Cottage; or, Young Americans in France and Switzerland* (1872). 6. *Down the Rhine; or, Young Americans in Germany* (1868). 7. *Up the Baltic; or, Young Americans in Norway, Sweden and Denmark* (1869). 8. *Northern Lands; or, Young Americans in Russia and Prussia* (1871). 9. *Cross and Crescent; or, Young Americans in Turkey and Greece* (1872). 10. *Sunny Shores; or, Young Americans in Italy and Austria* (1875). 11. *Vine and Olive; or, Young Americans in Spain and Portugal* (1876). 12. *Isles of the Sea; or, Young Americans Homeward Bound* (1877).

Young Engineers Series. Author: H. Irving Hancock. Publisher: Altemus.

1. *Young Engineers in Colorado* (1912). 2. *Young Engineers in Arizona* (1912). 3. *Young Engineers in Nevada; or, Seeking Fortune on the Turn of a Pick* (1913). 4. *Young Engineers in Mexico* (1913). 5. *Young Engineers in the Gulf* (1920).

Young Wide Awake Series. Author: Robert Lennox. Publisher: Frank Tousey.

1. *Young Wide-Awake's Axe Brigade; or, Hewing His Way to a Fire's Heart* (1907). 2. *Young Wide-Awake's Cascade of Flame; or, Within an Inch of a Fiery Death* (1907). 3. *Young Wide-Awake's General Alarm; or, Meeting the Neptunes on Their Own Ground* (1907).

4. *Young Wide-Awake's Powder Mill Blaze; or, Breaking through a Wall of Flame* (1907). 5. *Young Wide-Awake Saving a Million Dollars; or, the Mystery of the Bank Blaze* (1908). 6. *Young Wide-Awake's Trumpet Call; or, a Bold Fight to Save a Life* (1908).

Appendix D: Periodicals (Story Papers)

These publications were books passing themselves off as periodicals to save on postage.

Adventure Series. Arthur Westbrook, 1908–1933.
All Sports Library. Street and Smith, 1905–1906.
All Story Magazine. Frank Munsey, 1905–1914.
American Union. Thomes and Talbot, 1840–1877.
Banner Weekly. Beadle and Adams, 1888–1895.
Beadle's Half-Dime Library. Beadle and Adams, 1877–1905.
Boys' Home Weekly. Arthur Westbrook, 1911–1912.
Boys' and Girls' Weekly. Frank Leslie, 1866–1884.
Boys of America. Street and Smith, 1874–1900.
Boys of England. Brett, Edwin John, 1866–1899.
Boys of New York. Frank Tousey, 1875–1894.
Boys of the Empire. Brett, Edwin John, 1888–1906.
Boys' Star Library. Tousey, 1800s.
Boys' Comic Journal. Brett, Edwin John, 1883–1898.
Brave and Bold. Street and Smith, 1902–1911.
Brother Jonathan Weekly. Park Benjamin, 1839–1843.
Buffalo Bill Border Stories. Street and Smith, 1917–1925.
Buffalo Bill Stories. Street and Smith, 1902-1912.
Day's Doing. Frank Leslie, 1885–1890.
Deadwood Dick Library. Beadle and Adams, 1878–1883.
Detective Story Magazine. Street and Smith, 1915–1927.
Diamond Dick Jr. Street and Smith, 1896–1911.
Fame and Fortune Weekly. Frank Tousey, 1908–1928.
Family Story Paper. Norman Munro, 1873–1921.
Far West Library. Street and Smith, 1907–1915.
Fireside Companion. George Munro, 1867–1903.
Flag of Our Union. Elliott, Thomes and Talbot, 1846–1870.
Frank Leslie's Illustrated Newspaper. Frank Leslie, 1855–1922.
Frank Leslie's Pleasant Hours. Frank Leslie, 1866–1885.
Frank Manley. Frank Tousey, 1906.

Frank Reade Library. Frank Tousey, 1892–1898.
Franklin Square Library. Harper, 1878.
Golden Argosy. Frank Munsey, 1882–1888.
Golden Days. James Elverson, 1880–1907.
Golden Hours. Norman Munro, 1889–1904.
Golden Weekly. Frank Tousey, 1889–1892.
Good News. Street and Smith, 1890–1898.
Great Western Library. Street and Smith, 1927–1932.
Happy Days. Frank Tousey, 1894–1924.
Harper's Weekly. Harpers, 1957–1916.
James Boys Weekly. Frank Tousey, 1900–1903.
Jesse James Stories. Street and Smith, 1901–1903.
Lakeside Library. Donnelley, Lloyd and Co., 1874–1879.
Liberty Boys of '76. Frank Tousey, 1901–1925.
Live Girl Stories. Street and Smith, 1914–1928.
Log Cabin Library. Street and Smith, 1889–1897.
Love Story Magazine. Street and Smith, 1905.
Lovell's Library. John Lovell, 1882–1889.
Magnet Detective Library. Street and Smith, 1897.
Medal Library. Street and Smith, 1898–1917.
Monthly Story Magazine. Story Press, 1904–1907.
Munro's Library. Norman Munro, 1883–1888.
New Buffalo Bill Weekly. Street and Smith, 1912–1919.
New Magnet Library. Street and Smith, 1933.
New Medal Library. Street and Smith, 1908–1917.
New Nick Carter Weekly. Street and Smith, 1912–1915.
New Tip Top Weekly. Street and Smith, 1912–1915.
New York Boys' Library. Norman Munro.
New York Detective Library. Frank Tousey, 1883–1898.
New York Dime Library. Beadle and Adams, 1878–1898.
New York Fashion Bazar. George Munro, 1879–1890.
New York Five-Cent Library. Street and Smith, 1892–1896.
New York Ledger. Robert Bonner, 1847–1903.
New York Mercury. Cauldwell, Southworth and Whitney, 1835–1870.
New York Weekly. Street and Smith, 1897–1912.
New York Weekly Story Teller. Norman Munro, 1875–1877.
New York Weekly Welcome. Street and Smith, 1858–1915.
Nick Carter Detective Library. Street and Smith, 1891–1896.
Nick Carter Library. Street and Smith, 1891–1897.
Nick Carter Stories. Street and Smith, 1912–1915.
Nick Carter Weekly. Street and Smith, 1897–1903.
Old Cap Collier Library. Norman Munro, 1883–1899.
Old Sleuth Library. Norman Munro, 1885–1905.
Oliver Optic's Magazine for Boys and Girls. Lee and Shepard, 1871–1875.
People's Literary Companion. E. Allen, 1869–1907.
Pluck and Luck. Frank Tousey, 1898–1929.
Popular Magazine, Street and Smith, 1903–1927.
Rover Boy Library. Street and Smith, 1904.
Rovers of the Sea. Brett, Edwin John, 1872–1873.
Saturday Star Journal. Beadle and Adams, 1870–1882.
Seaside Library. George Munro, 1877–1890.
Secret Service. Frank Tousey, 1898–1925.

Smith's Magazine. Street and Smith, 1905–1922.

Tip Top Weekly. Street and Smith, 1896–1912.

Uncle Sam. Edward, Henry and George Williams, 1841–1850?

Western Story Magazine. Street and Smith, 1919–1950.

Wide Awake Library. Frank Tousey, 1878–1898.

Wild West Weekly. Frank Tousey, 1902–1927.

Women's Stories. Street and Smith, 1913–1925.

Work and Win Weekly. Frank Tousey, 1898–1925.

Young Men of America. Frank Tousey, 1877–1889.

Young Men of Great Britain. Brett, Edwin John, 1868–1889.

Youth's Companion. Nathaniel Willis, 1827–1929.

Appendix E: Children's Literature Year by Year: A Chronological Listing of Significant Publications

This list of books traces the development of children's reading material in England and America from 1484 to the early 1900s. These titles are mentioned in the text. They are listed by date, author and title.

Herodotus. *Aesop's Fables*. London: Caxton, 1484.

A collection of tales with a moral. It is said that Aesop really did exist (mid-sixth century B.C.) and that Herodotus collected the tales. This is the first English edition.

Malory, Thomas. *Le Morte d'Arthur*. London: Caxton, 1485.

See *Boy's King Arthur*.

Anon. *Gest of Robyn Hode*. London: Wynkyn de Worde, 1492/1534.

A narrative about outlaws. This one is based on a shorter ballad. It was reprinted a number of times before 1600.

Anon. *Guy of Warwick, Seven Champions*, etc. London: Wynkyn de Worde, ca. 1500.

Appeared in Steele's *Tattler*. The broadside and chapbook retellings reduced the length. The children's editions include one by C. Sheppard (1780) and G. H. Gerould (1912), "containing a full and true account of his many famous and valiant actions, remarkable and brave exploits and noble and renowned victories."

Anon. *A. B. C. for Children*. W. Powell, 1561.

Early in the seventeenth century alphabet books were available in English. This one is one of the survivors of these pamphlets.

Feyerabend, Sigmund. *Kunst und Lehrbüchlein* (*Little Book of Art and Instruction for Young People*). Germany: Frankfurt am Main, 1580.

The earliest known picture book for children. "A book of art and instruction for young people. Herein may be discovered all manner of merry and agreeable drawings." It contained the first printed pictures of a student using a horn book.

Johnson, Richard. *Seven Champions of Christendom.* London: Hodgson and Co., 1596–1597.

"Printed by J. B. for Andrew Crook ca. 1660." At least ten editions appeared in the century after its release. It appeared as broadsides and chapbooks in abridged form. A modern publication is by Harvey Darton (1913).

Basile, Giambattista. *Pentamerone; or, the Tale of Tales.* London: Henry and Co., 1634–1636.

Contains versions of several of the best-known fairy stories. It was translated into English by Richard Burton in 1893.

Comenius, Johann Amos. *Orbis Sensualium Pictus* (*Visible World*). Nuremberg: unknown, 1658.

First translated into English in 1658 by Charles Hoole. The earliest instructional picture book. A picture book showing pictures and the related words. This is Hoole's translation.

Chear, Abraham. *Looking-Glass for Children.* London: R. Boulten, 1672.

A book of poems, written while Chear was in prison for his unpopular beliefs. Contains the often-quoted "Tis pity, such a pretty maid/ As I should go to Hell."

Janeway, James. *Token for Children.* London: Dorman Newman, 1672.

The earliest copy extant is dated 1676, including a 1673 edition of part 2. Bodleian Library, Oxford.

Erasmus, Desiderious. "The Child's Piety" in *Colloquies.* London: Wynkyn de Worde, 1673.

Translated by N. Bailey; edited by E. Johnson. Dialogue between Erasmus and Gaspar, a boy, presumably of St. Paul's, as he refers to "that honestest of men, John Colet, who instructed me when I was young in these Precepts."

Halliwell, James O. *History of Thomas Hickathrift.* London: J. R. Smith, 1675?

A popular chapbook in the late-seventeenth century. It later appeared in *Popular Rhymes and Nursery Tales* (1849) and in Joseph Jacob's *More English Fairy Tales* (1894).

Tom Hickathrift is a hero and a mythical strong man. The story tells how he, armed with an axle-tree and cartwheel, killed a giant who dwelled in a marsh at Tilney (Norfolk). As a reward he was knighted and made a governor of Thanet.

Bunyan, John. *Books for Boys and Girls, or, Country Rhymes for Children.* London: Nathaniel Ponder, 1686.

The first edition was in 1686, but the 1701 edition had 25 of the original 74 meditations omitted and bore the subtitle "book for boys and girls; or Temporal things spiritualized." The ninth and later editions were titled "Divine emblems; or, Temporal things spiritualized."

A facsimile of the first edition, with an introduction by John Brown, was published in 1889 by Elliot Stock.

Bunyan, John. *Pilgrim's Progress.* London: Nathaniel Ponder, 1686.

Although not written for children, this has become a basic book in children's literature collections. Christian, in a dream, travels and learns about life's trials and tribulations. The first edition was not illustrated; the first one that was was in 1707.

Anon. *New England Primer.* Boston: B. Harris, 1690.

Exact date of the first edition is not known. Generally believed to have been published between 1687 and 1690 but may have been printed earlier.

Anon. *Sir Bevis of Southampton.* London: Wynkyn de Worde, sixteenth century.

A hero who, with his faithful horse, Arundel, slew sixty heathens and won the king's daughter. There are retellings by Laura Hibbard (1911), W. S. Durrant (1914) and Aylwin Sampson (1963).

Anon. *History of the Two Children in the Wood.* London: Dean and Munday, 1700.

A tale of humor. Includes many woodcuts. Possible authorship is R. S. Sharpe and Mrs. Person.

Janeway, James/Cotton Mather. *A Token for Children/A Token for Children of New England.* Boston:

Nicholas Boone/London: Dorman Newman, 1700/1672.

This is the first American edition. It contains both parts of Janeway's *Token* with the supplementary part, which was written by Cotton Mather. The earliest copy extant is dated 1676, including a 1673 edition of part 2. Bodleian Library, Oxford.

Johnson, Richard. *History of Sir Richard Whittington, thrice Lord-Mayor of London.* London, 1700s.

A popular and widely read chapbook. There are many editions of *Dick Whittington and His Cat.*

White, Thomas. *Little Book for Little Children.* London, 1702 or 1712.

The first known book for children to contain traditional nursery rhymes. Illustrated with woodcuts. Another book by the same title was published in 1660; it is by Thomas White; this 1702 edition is by "T. W."

Aulnoy, Marie Catherine. *Tales of the Fairies* (in three parts). New York: Garland, 1707.

A collection of fairy tales, translated by J. R. Planche. Was also published by McKay of Philadelphia. It includes twenty-two stories from the late-seventeenth century.

Anon. *Jack and the Gyants, Tom Thumb, etc.* Unknown, 1708.

Chapbooks mentioned these folk tales in *The Weekly Comedy.*

Lauron, M. *Cries and Habits of the City of London.* London: H. Overton, 1709.

Phrases called out in the streets to sell food and other items and offer various trades.

Watts, Isaac. *Divine Songs; Attempted in Easy Language for the Use of Children.* London: M. Lawrence, 1715.

Contents: Twenty-eight religious songs; the Ten Commandments and Our Savior's Golden Rule. Pierpont Morgan was one of the only two known perfect copies of the first edition.

Defoe, Daniel. *Life and Strange Surprising Adventures of Robinson Crusoe, Mariner.* London: W. Taylor, 1719.

This is one of four editions that appeared within four months during the year of first publication.

Aulnoy, Marie Catherine. *Collection of Novels and Tales.* London: W. Taylor and W. Chetwood, 1721.

Translated from the original French. First edition of this important translation.

Bunyan, John. *Book for Boys and Girls; or, Temporal Things Spiritualized.* London: Blackie, 1724.

A shortened version of *A Book for Boys and Girls, or, Country Rhymes for Children* (1686).

Swift, Jonathan. *Gulliver's Travels.* London: Benjamin Motte, 1726.

Published as a satire for adults in 1726, "Gulliver" is now also read as a tale by boys and girls. An account of four voyages: one to Lilliput, one to Brobdingnag; one to Laputa and one to Houhnhnms.

Perrault, Charles. *Histories or Tales of Past Times, with Morals* (*Histories ou Contes de Temps Passés*). New York: Garland (Paris: a publisher in Paris) 1729/1697.

Once thought to be issued in 1729, but the discovery of a 1719 copy proves this incorrect. There is an eleventh edition in 1719. First date is undetermined.

Boreman, Thomas. *Gigantic History of the Two Famous Giants.* London: Thomas Boreman, 1741.

A publisher of children's books. Miniature guide books to the sights of eighteenth-century London, both in stories and in poems. Boreman was also the owner of the book store Boot and Crown. Completes the *History of the Guildhall* (London). The second of Boreman's miniature works.

Anon. *Little Master's Miscellany.* Unknown, 1743.

A collection of songs and verses meant especially for children, moral dialogues such as "On Lying," "On Death," etc. "Little Jack" was among the stories presented, probably written by Thomas Day.

Cooper, Mary. *Tommy Thumb's Pretty Song Book*, Vols. 1 and 2. Massachusetts: Isaiah Thomas, 1744.

A successor to *Tommy Thumb's Song*

Book. The only surviving copy is in the British Library. Contains "Baa, Baa Black Sheep." Printed from copperplates.

Nurse Lovechild. *Tommy Thumb's Song Book*. London: Mary Cooper, 1744.

No copy has survived, but a book with the same title was published in 1788 by Isaiah Thomas of Worchester, Mass.

Anon. *Circle of the Sciences, or Compendious Library*. London: John Newbery, 1745–1748.

Six volumes: *Grammar*, *Arithmetic*, *Rhetoric*, *Poetry*, *Logic*, and *Geography*. The commencement of this publication dates from about 1755. It includes manuals on all sorts of subjects, from a spelling dictionary to a polite letter writer. It was written in a question-and-answer format.

Fielding, Sarah. *Governess; or the Little Female Academy*. London: A. Millar, 1749?

This was called "the first full-length novel for children in which the plot has a contemporary setting and characters drawn from life."

Goldsmith, Oliver (?) *Lilliputian Magazine*. London: John Newbery, 1751.

A year or so later this manuscript was put in book form and went into several editions. The first periodical for children.

Newbery, John? *Pretty Book of Pictures for Little Masters and Misses; or Tommy Trop's History of Birds and Beasts*. London: John Newbery, 1752.

A book mostly of animal and bird woodcuts with short verses and prose descriptions.

Anon. *Top Book of All for Little Masters and Misses*. London: R. Baldwin, S. Crowder and B. Collins, 1760.

One of the earliest English books to contain nursery rhymes.

Collins, Benjamin? *Royal Primer; or an Easy and Pleasant Guide to the Art of Reading*. London: John Newbery, 1762.

The first rhymed alphabet books were published in Boston in 1690. They preceded the *New England Primer* and were called *Royal Primers*. They were used as textbooks, and over five million were sold during the years they were in use.

Wesley, Charles. *Hymns for Children*. Bristol: E. Farley, 1763.

Later named *Hymns for Children and Others of Riper Years*. Charles's brother, John, wrote the introduction.

Goldsmith, Oliver, or John Newbery. *Renowned History of Giles Gingerbread; a Little Boy Who Lived upon Learning*. London: John Newbery, 1764.

Giles rose from a poor errand boy to become partner and then heir to his benefactor's business. The author could be Oliver Goldsmith or John Newbery of the Jones Brothers, Giles and Griffith. A story of how Giles, a bad boy, turns into a good boy.

Goldsmith, Oliver (?). *History of Little Goody Two-Shoes*. London: John Newbery, 1765.

A reproduction of the 1766 edition was published in 1881 by Griffith, a publisher of London. Margery is an orphan; she is befriended by a charitable gentleman. She stays with a local clergyman who buys her her first pair of shoes.

Goldsmith, Oliver (?). *Mother Goose Melodies; or, Sonnets for the Cradle*. London: John Newbery, 1765.

A reproduction of this edition with introductory notes by W. H. Whitmore was published in 1889 by Munsell. A reproduction of the earliest-known English edition, with introduction and notes by W. F. Prideaux, was published in 1904 by Bullen. Isaiah Thomas of Worchester, Mass., reprinted the English edition in 1785. Second part contains songs from Shakespeare.

Newbery, John? *Little Pretty Pocket-Book*. London: John Newbery, 1767.

No copy from before 1760 exists. Contains the alphabet, verses about games and pastimes, nursery rhymes and fables. "Intended for the instruction and amusement of Little Master Tommy and Pretty Miss Polly. With two letters from Jack the giant-killer; ... ; the use of which will infallibly make Tommy a good boy and Polly a good girl. To which is added, A Little Song-Book, being a new attempt to teach children the use of the English alphabet, by way of diversion" (from the subtitle). Reprinted by Isaiah Thomas of Massachusetts in 1787.

Anon. *Most Delightful History of the King and the Cobbler.* Boston: Thomas Fleet, 1770.

"Shewing how the king first came acquainted with the cobbler and the pleasant humorous [events] which happened thereupon."

Basedow, Johann. *Elementar Werke für Jugend und Ihrer Freunde.* Unknown, 1774.

Copperplate engravings by Daniel Chodowiecki. His illustrations depict middle-class, everyday life. Contains over thirty different children's games, including the teen game of billiards played on a slate-bedded table.

Goldsmith, Oliver. *History of the Earth, and Animated Nature.* London: John Newbery, 1774.

This was the last of Goldsmith's works. It went through many editions and was a favorite until the second half of the nineteenth century.

Barbauld, Anna Letitia. *Hymns in Prose for Children.* London: J. Johnson, 1781.

Subtitled "by the author of Lessons for Children." Barbauld was the sister of John Aikin and helped him write *Evenings at Home* (1792). Charles Lamb, who criticized her heavily, called her work dull.

Berquin, Arnaud. *L'ami des Enfants* (*Children's Friend*). London: Elizabeth Newbery, 1782–1783.

First translated into English as *The Children's Friend* and later as *The Looking Glass of the Mind or Intellectual Mirror.*

Kilner, Dorothy. *Life and Perambulations of a Mouse.* London: John Marshall, 1783.

Perhaps the first English story where animals are given distinct personalities (i.e., as people). A story of Nimble, the mouse, and his adventures in the great world. Pseudo. Mary Pelham. John Bewick did the woodcuts for this edition.

Day, Thomas. *History of Sandford and Merton.* London: J. Stockdale, 1783–1789.

Merton is a spoiled child. One day Sandford rescues him from a snake. From then on they face many important situations, sharing theories and beliefs. One story seems to rise from the subject of the previous story, and it was this "linking" that made the book so popular.

An example of Rousseau's theories at work. Children were to learn from direct experience with nature through instincts and feelings.

Genlis, Stephanie Félicité Ducrest de Saint-Aubin. *Adelaide and Theodore; or, Letters on Education.* London: Bathurst and Cadell, 1784.

Subtitled "containing all the principles relative to three different plans of education, to that of princes, and to those of young persons of both sexes, translated from the French."

Genlis, Stephanie Félicité Ducrest de Saint-Aubin. *Tales of the Castle; or, Stories of Instruction and Delight.* Paris: Libraries Associes, 1785.

Translated from the French by Thomas Holcroft (9th ed. Vermont: Fessenden, 1813).

Raspe, Rudolph Erich. *Adventures of Baron Munchausen.* Oxford: Smith, 1786.

Although Raspe's stories were exaggerated and improbable, the children of the day read them with gusto. A printer named Smith, of Oxford, collected these stories and built tales around Hieronymus Munchausen, a German nobleman. A series of tall tales. It is thought that this book inspired Jonathan Swift's *Gulliver's Travels.*

Trimmer, Sarah. *Fabulous Histories; designed for the Instruction of Children, Respecting their Treatment of animals* (*History of the Robins*). London: Longman, 1786.

A book about kindness to animals. Now published as *History of the Robins* (1819).

Berquin, Arnaud. *Looking-Glass for the Mind; or Intellectual Mirror.* London: Elizabeth Newbery, 1787.

First published in 1787; second edition

in 1789 and third edition in 1792. Translated by Richard Johnson from *L'Ami des Enfants* (*Children's Friend*).

Day, Thomas. *History of Little Jack*. London: John Stockdale, 1788.

The woodcuts are said to be by John Bewick, a very famous carver of the time, and the cover is an example of flowered Dutch paper.

Wollstonecraft, Mary. *Original Stories from Real Life, with Conversations Calculated to Regulate the Affections and Form the Mind to Truth and Goodness*. London: J. Johnson, 1788.

The first illustrated edition was published in 1791 by J. Johnson.

Cooper, W. D. *Blossoms of Morality*. London: Elizabeth Newbery, 1789.

Theophilus is a reader and lover of books and gives credit to his father and the St. Paul's churchyard (Newbery's Bible and Sun) bookstore.

Wyss, Johann David. *Swiss Family Robinson*. London: John Stockdale, 1792.

A Swiss family—a pastor, his wife and four children—are shipwrecked on an uninhabited island.

Aikin, John. *Evenings at Home; or the Juvenile Budget Opened*. London: J. Johnson, 1792–1796.

"Consisting of a variety of miscellaneous pieces for the instruction and amusement of young persons." Anna Barbauld contributed fourteen selections.

Edgeworth, Maria. *Parent's Assistant; or, Stories for Children*. London: Routledge, 1796.

A collection of short stories: "Little Dog Trusty"; "Orange Man"; "Tarlton"; "Lazy Lawrence"; "False Key"; and others. Released in three volumes; some from *Early Lessons* and eight new ones.

Mavor, William Fordyce. *Historical Account of the Most Celebrated Voyages*. London: Elizabeth Newbery, 1796.

An early work on travel and exploration. The full set contains twenty-five volumes, issued five and ten at a time.

Salzmann, Christian G. *Elements of Morality for the Use of Children*. Philadelphia: J. Hoff, 1796.

A book of ethics and conduct of life. Moral tales which earlier formed the basis of Mary Wollstonecraft's *Elements of Morality* (1790).

Anon. *Death and Burial of Cock Robin*. Boston: S. Hall, 1798.

It is rumored that this story refers to the downfall of Robert Walpole's ministry. It was issued as a chapbook.

Edgeworth, Maria. *Practical Education*. London: J. Johnson, 1798.

Gives insight into the theories underlying Edgeworth's writings.

Genlis, Stephanie Félicité Ducrest de Saint-Aubin. *Young Exiles; or Correspondence of Some Juvenile Emigrants*. London: V. Dowling and J. Stockdale, 1799.

In the "epistle dedicatory" to her grandchildren, the author says, "I have copied from nature all the portraits of my virtuous characters."

Edgeworth, Maria. *Early Lessons*. London: J. Johnson, 1801.

A series of storybooks with simple reading matter and practical information. Two parts of Harry and Lucy; three parts of Rosamond; four parts of Frank. See sequels *Frank*; *Harry and Lucy*; and *Rosamond*.

Mavor, William Fordyce. *English Spelling Book*. London: Routledge, 1801.

The book begins with an illustrated alphabet, followed by a syllabary. It includes history, geography and moral lessons. It is said to have had 241 editions.

Taylor, Ann and Jane. *Original Poems, for Infant Minds*. London: Darton and Harvey, 1804.

A book of poems, many of which became widely known. Easy poetry for young children. Considered a landmark in children's literature.

Lamb, Charles. *King and Queen of Hearts*. London: Thomas Hodgkins, 1805.

The first children's book written by Charles Lamb. Based on an earlier nursery rhyme called "Queen of Hearts," about kings, queens and knaves. A comic version of the original.

King, Samuel. *Young Child's ABC; or, First Book*. Unknown, 1806.
American publisher. King offered at least 160 titles.

Taylor, Ann. *Rhymes for the Nursery*. London: Darton and Harvey, 1806.
Contains "Twinkle, Twinkle, Little Star" by Jane Taylor.

Dorset, Catherine Ann. *Lion's Masquerade*. London: John Harris, 1807.
A sequel to *The Peacock "at Home."*

Dorset, Catherine Ann. *Peacock "at Home."*
A sequel to *The Butterfly's Ball* (Roscoe). A story of why the birds, because they were envious of the butterflies, had a ball of their own. Dorset was one of many imitators of Roscoe's earlier work.

Lamb, Charles. *Tales from Shakespeare*. London: T. Hodgkins, 1807.
Charles Lamb wrote the seven tragedies. Mary Lamb wrote the rest.

Turner, Elizabeth. *Daisy; or Cautionary Stories in Verse*. London: John Harris, 1807.
Illustrated by Samuel Williams. The Library of Congress has a copy published by Samuel Babcock of New Haven. It is undated and has sixteen pages.

Lamb, Charles. *Adventures of Ulysses*. London: M. J. Godwin, 1808.
The suggestion for this book seems to have come from William Godwin and was probably due to the success of *Tales from Shakespeare*. Based on George Chapman's translation of the *Odyssey* of Homer.

Lamb, Charles. *Mrs. Leicester's School*. London: M. J. Godwin, 1808.
Written with Mary Lamb. Three stories are by Charles; ten by Mary. The stories are drawn from their own childhood.

Roscoe, William. *Butterfly's Ball and the Grasshopper's Feast*. London: John Harris, 1808.
This poem first appeared in *The Gentlemen's Magazine*, November 1803, and the following year became first in the Harris Cabinet series. Roscoe was "the first author to write sheer nonsense" for the enjoyment of boys and girls.

Lamb, Charles. *Poetry for Children*. London: M. J. Godwin, 1809.
With Mary Lamb as coauthor. Described as "entirely original. By the author of *Mrs. Leicester's School*."

Lamb, Charles (?). *Beauty and the Beast; or a Rough Outside with a Gentle Heart*. London: M. J. Godwin, 1811.
It is not clearly established that the Lambs wrote this book.

Turner, Elizabeth. *Cowslip; or More Cautionary Stories in Verse*. London: John Harris, 1811.
Some of the poems were written by her brother, Thomas. Verses about good and bad behavior and its rewards. Her first book was *The Daisy* (1807), another collection of verses of "cautionary stories."

Grimm, Jacob and Wilhelm. *Fairy Tales*. London: C. Baldwyn, 1812–1815.
Titled *Kinder- und Haumärchen* but is widely known as *Grimm's Fairy Tales: A Collection of Folk Tales and Fairy Stories Collected by Word of Mouth from Country Folk*. The first English edition, *German Popular Stories*, appeared between 1823 and 1826. Translated by Edgar Taylor.

Sherwood, Mary Martha. *History of Little Henry and His Bearer*. London: Wellington, Salop, 1815.
A popular toy book. The book was accompanied by a series of painted figures, each with a slot at the back to take the movable head.
Boosy is Henry's bearer and loves him; he is an orphan who has been neglected and needs love.
A missionary story for children; written in India.

Taylor, Isaac. *Scenes in Europe*. London: John Harris, 1818.
"For the amusement and instruction of little tarry-at-home travelers."

Sherwood, Mary Martha. *History of the Fairchild Family*. London: J. Hatchard and Son, 1818–1847.

This book was still being published in 1931. One of the first "family stories" subtitled "for the child's manual, being a collection of stories calculated to show the importance and effects of a religious education."

Edgeworth, Maria. *Rosamond*. London: R. Hunter, 1821.

A sequel to *Early Lessons*. Contains twelve stories about Rosamund.

Edgeworth, Maria. *Frank: A Sequel to Early Lessons*. London: R. Hunter, 1822.

A sequel to *Early Lessons*. This contains the four stories of Frank.

Cooper, James Fenimore. *Leather-Stocking Tales*. New York: Pantheon, 1823.

Five novels about Natty Bumppo and Chingachgook. The stories take place in the American frontier between 1740 and 1804. *The Pioneers* (1823); *Last of the Mohicans* (1826); *The Prairie* (1827); *Pathfinder* (Bentley) (1840); and *Deerslayer* (Lea and Blanchard) (1841).

Uncertain. *Dame Wiggins of Lee and Her Seven Wonderful Cats*. London: Dean and Munday, 1823.

A tale of humor including many woodcuts. Possible authors are R. S. Sharpe and Mrs. Person. This story has been in publication for many years before this date.

Grimm, Jacob. *German Popular Stories*. London: C. Baldwyn, 1823–1826.

Illustrated by George Cruikshank. Translated from the German by Edgar Taylor.

Edgeworth, Maria. *Harry and Lucy Concluded, Being the Last Part of* Early Lessons. London: R. Hunter, 1825.

Concluding stories of Harry and Lucy.

Goodrich, Samuel Griswold. Peter Parley Series. *Tales of Peter Parley about America*. Boston: T. H. Carter; London: Thomas Tegg, 1827.

The *Tales of Peter Parley about America* was the first book in this series. Popular geography and travel books; fictionalized travelogues. The Library of Congress has one of the four known copies.

Scott, Walter. *Tales of a Grandfather*. Edinburgh: Cadell, 1827–1830.

Stories taken from Scottish history from the earliest period to the close of the reign of James the Fifth. This was the only book Scott wrote specifically for children. It is a history of Scotland and France.

Hale, Sarah Josepha. *Mary's Lamb*. Boston: Marsh, Capes and Lyon, 1830.

There is some controversy about who really wrote *Mary's Lamb* ("Mary had a little lamb"), but the accepted author seems to be Hale.

Child, Lydia Maria. *Little Girl's Own Book*. Boston: Carter, Hendee and Babcock, 1832.

A book of games. Includes illustrations and songs with music. The bibliography included in the collection of Child's letters gives the publication date as 1831; in other lists this date is given as 1832. Copyrighted in 1833.

Schmid, Christoph von. *Basket of Flowers; or, Piety and Truth Triumphant*. Halifax: W. Nicholson, 1833.

A translation of *Das Blumenkörbchen*. A story of a gardener and his daughter, Mary. A Reward Book in the nineteenth century. A Sunday school book.

Abbott, Jacob. Rollo Series. New York: Harper, 1834.

Abbott wrote about 200 books, including Franconia stories. The first was *Rollo Learning to Talk* (1834). Of the 200 books he wrote, some were biographies. Twenty-eight titles in this series of instructive books. A picture of New England life at the time they were written (1835). Some titles are *Rollo's Experiments* (1841) and *Rollo in London* (1855). The Library of Congress has the only surviving copy of *A Picture Book of Rollo* (1835).

Bowring, John. *Minor Morals for Young People*. London: Whittaker and Company, 1834, 1835, 1839.

This was Bowring's only children's book; released in three volumes. Mostly tales of travels, but it also has some fairy tales translated into English for the first time.

Callcott, Maria. *Little Arthur's History of England.* London: Murray, 1835.

A popular children's history book. The author had no children of her own but in her introduction said, "This little history was written for a real Arthur, and I have endeavored to write it nearly as I would tell it to an intelligent child."

Howitt, William. *Boy's Country Book.* London: Religious Tract Society, 1839.

A story that tells what childhood was like in Derbyshire; based roughly on Howitt's own childhood. It also contains a ghost story and some fairy tales. He also wrote *A Boy's Adventures in the Wilds of Australia* (1854).

Sinclair, Catherine. *Holiday House: A Book for the Young.* Edinburgh: William Whyte and Co., 1839.

This controversial book describes the adventures of Laura and Harry, with their older brother Frank. Laura and Harry are unbelievably naughty, but Frank has little control of them. The introduction humorously protests against the prevailing type of informational books for children.

Howitt, Mary. *Strive and Thrive.* London: Tegg, 1840.

Howitt is also the author of the poem "'Will you walk into my parlor?' said the Spider to the Fly," collected in her *Sketches of Natural History* (1834).

Hawthorne, Nathaniel. *Famous Old People; Being the Second Epoch of Grandfather's Chair.* Boston: E. P. Peabody, 1841.

A follow-up book to *Grandfather's Chair.* This was book two, followed by *Liberty Tree* and preceded by *Famous Old People,* and these three books were later issued together as *The Whole History of Grandfather's Chair.*

Hawthorne, Nathaniel. *Grandfather's Chair; a History for Youth.* Boston: E. P. Peabody, 1841.

One of Hawthorne's earlier books, written while he worked with S. G. Goodrich. This was book one, followed by *Famous Old People* and *Liberty Tree.* These three books were later issued together as *The Whole History of Grandfather's Chair.*

Hawthorne, Nathaniel. *Liberty Tree, with the Last Words of Grandfather's Chair.* Boston: E. P. Peabody, 1841.

A follow-up book to *Grandfather's Chair.* This was book three, preceded by *Famous Old People* and *Liberty Tree.*

Marryat, Frederick. *Masterman Ready; or, the Wreck of the Pacific.* London: Longman, Orm, 1841–1842.

The Masterman family were shipowners and builders. The story gives descriptions of Africa, northward from the Cape of Good Hope: lions, rhinoceroses, and lots of adventure.

The first children's novel written by Marrat. Based, roughly, on *Swiss Family Robinson.*

Summerly, Felix (Cole, Sir Henry). *Home Treasury of Books.* London: John Stockdale, 1843.

A series of children's books, mostly reprints of earlier suppressed books: *Beauty and the Beast* and *Little Red Riding Hood.*

Anon. *Reynard the Fox.* London: Percy Society (reprint), 1844.

Caxton of England was the first to have printed this story in 1481.

Child, Lydia Marie. *Flowers for Children* (3 vols.). New York: C. S. Francis and Co., 1844–1855.

Selections from "The Juvenile Miscellany" and other articles. Includes what is now known as "Over the River and Through the Woods." This is book two of a series of three books. The three volumes were for (1) children age eight or nine years; (2) children age four to six years; (3) children of eleven or twelve years.

Andersen, Hans Christian. *Fairy Tales.* London: Chapman and Hall, 1846.

Wonderful Stories for Children (1846) was translated into English: "Emperor's New Clothes"; "Little Mermaid"; "Snow Queen"; "Ugly Duckling"; and others. Translated by Mary Howitt. "Nobody ever caught the spirit of Andersen as she (Mrs. Howitt) has done, and she is loyally literal or fearlessly free as the occasion demands it." R. N. Bain.

Lear, Edward. *Book of Nonsense.* London: Thomas McLean, 1846.

A popular collection of limericks. First

published in America in 1863 by Willis P. Hazard.

Howitt, Mary. *Children's Year*. London: Longman, Brown, 1847.

A chronicle of one year of the voluntary occupations, plays and pleasures of the author's two youngest children. A story about one year in the life of two young children, Herbert and Meggy.

Marryat, Frederick. *Children of the New Forest*. London: H. Hurst, 1847.

Marryat's last book. Story of the English Civil War; it is a historical novel for children.

Moore, Clement Clarke. *Visit from Santa Claus*. New York: Onderdonck, 1848.

The first, independent publication of this poem. The woodcuts, by Theodore Boyd, show a recognizable Santa Claus.

Warner, Susan Bogert. *Wide, Wide World*. New York: Putnam, 1850.

A story of Ellen Montgomery. She is sent to the home of her aunt, where she is befriended by Alice and her brother John. She is sent to live in the backwoods of New York state and is later sent to Scotland, but she always remembers her friends from New York, Alice and John Humphreys. Alice dies, but Ellen's friendship with John continues. Pseudo. Elizabeth Wetherell.

Gatty, Margaret. *Fairy Godmothers and Other Tales*. London: G. Bell, 1851.

Other tales: "Joachim, the Mimic"; "Darkness and Light"; "The Love of god"; and "Parables from Nature" (1855).

Gatty was the mother of Juliana Horatio Ewing.

Hawthorne, Nathaniel. *Wonder-Book for Girls and Boys*. Boston: Ticknor, 1851.

A retelling of twelve Greek legends. They are told by a young student to a group of children named Primrose, Periwinkle, Sweet Fern and others. Contents: "The Gordon's Head"; "The Golden Touch"; "The Paradise of Children"; "The Three Golden Apples"; "The Miraculous Pitcher"; "The Chimera."

Ruskin, John. *King of the Golden River; of The Black Brothers, a Legend of Stiria*. London: Smith and Elder, 1851.

Three brothers, two mean and nasty and one the opposite. An early fantasy written specifically for children.

The first illustrator was Richard Doyle. Subtitle: *A tale for young folks and their elders*.

Abbott, Jacob. *Franconia Stories*. New York: Harper, 1851–1854.

More popular in England than in America. *Mary Bell, a Franconia Story* (1859) and *Malleville: A Franconia Story* (1850). This series represents Abbott at his best. These ten volumes were published between 1851 and 1854, when he gave up teaching to devote himself to writing, and at the beginning of his twenty years of greatest literary activity.

Stowe, Harriet Beecher. *Uncle Tom's Cabin; or, Life among the Lowly*. Boston: J. P. Jewett, 1852.

A story of plantation life before the Civil War. Although Stowe wrote many other children's stories, she is remembered for this slavery story which left deep impressions on children, although the book was not intended for them. She also wrote three series book: *Harry Henderson* (two titles, 1871; 1875); *Old Town* (two titles, 1869; 1872); and *Uncle Tom* (two titles, 1852; 1853).

Warner, Susan Bogert. *Queechy*. New York: Putnam, 1852.

A sentimental novel similar to the *Wide, Wide World*.

Dickens, Charles. *Child's History of England*. London: Bradbuy and Evans, 1852–1854.

Serialized in three volumes in *Household Words* from January 1851 to December 1853.

Hawthorne, Nathaniel. *Tanglewood Tales for Girls and Boys; Being a Second Wonder-Book*. Boston: Ticknor, 1853.

A sequel to *Wonder Book*. Contents: "The Minotaur"; "The Pygmies"; "The Dragon's Teeth"; "Circe's Palace"; "The Pomegranate Seeds"; "The Golden Fleece."

Cruikshank, George. *George Cruikshank's Fairy Library*. London: Routledge, 1853–1854.

Cruikshank was a great illustrator of the time who chose to illustrate children's books.

Yonge, Charlotte Mary. *Heir of Redclyffe*. London: J. W. Parker, 1853–1854.

A "classic of a period."—Arnole Bennett.

A romantic novel that was popular with older girls. Guy Morville's reputation is marred by his cousin, Philip, who does not confess until on his death bed.

Charlesworth, Maria Louisa. *Ministering to Children; a Tale Dedicated to Childhood*. New York: Garland, 1854.

A story of the good works of the Clifford family, whose father was a country squire. Followed by a sequel, *Ministering Children, a Sequel* (1867).

Alcott, Louisa May. *Flower Fables*. Boston: Briggs, 1855.

Contains a short story of the conduct and life of fairies. This was Alcott's first book. It is a collection of her own short stories about birds, fields and flowers.

Lippincott, Sara Jane (Clarke). *Merrie England: Travels, Descriptions, Tales and Historical Sketches*. Boston: Ticknor, Reed and Fields, 1855.

Pseudo. Grace Greenwood. Stories about Sherwood Forest, Nottingham Castle, Warwick Castle, Yorkminster, London Tower, Robin Hood and many more.

Longfellow, Henry Wadsworth. *Song of Hiawatha*. Boston: Ticknor and Fields, 1855.

This poem relates Native American myths and legends surrounding the epic figure of Hiawatha. An American epic.

Thackeray, William. *Rose and the Ring: or, the History of Prince Giglio and Prince Bulbo*. London: Smith and Elder, 1855.

A satire that is devoid of sentimentality of morality and is still funny today.

Kingsley, Charles. *Heroes; or Greek Fairy Tales*. London: Macmillan, 1856.

Written for Kingsley's children, Rose, Maurice and Mary. Three of the stories are "Perseus," "Argonauts" and "Theseus." These were different versions from those in Nathaniel Hawthorne's *Wonder Book*.

Yonge, Charlotte Mary. *Daisy Chain; or, Aspirations, a Family Chronicle*. London: J. W. Parker, 1856.

The life of the May family, especially Ethel. Portrays the mid-nineteenth century family life. *The Trial; or, More Links of the Daisy Chain* is a sequel.

Hughes, Thomas. *Tom Brown's School Days*. Cambridge: Macmillan, 1857.

A sequel to this is *Tom Brown at Oxford* (1861).

Set in an 1830s' private school. Tom is the son of a country squire.

Tucker, Charlotte Maria. *Rambles of a Rat*. Edinburgh: Thomas Nelson and Sons, 1857.

The rat's name is Oddity; he has seven brothers and lives in a large warehouse. They are mischievous rats, and the stories were gladly read by children even though there was a bit of moralizing.

Alexander, Cecil Francis Humphreys. *Hymns for Little Children*. London: Joseph Masters, 1858.

First published in 1848 with a prefatory note by John Keble, author of *The Child's Christian Year*, a book written for children.

Farrar, Frederick William. *Eric or Little by Little, a Tale of Roslyn School*. Edinburgh: Adam and Charles Black, 1858.

A school story and Eric's role there, including his foolishness and mischief. A "morality, a fierce, uncompromising, blood and thunderous, lightning literature tossed, doom-dealing morality." Appeared in *The Spectator* (1871).

Gatty, Margaret. *Aunt Judy's Tales*. London: Bell and Daldy, 1858.

Contains "Little Victims"; "Vegetables Out of Place"; "Cook Stories"; "Rabbits' Tails"; "Out of the Way"; "Nothing to Do." Gatty founded *Aunt Judy's Magazine*.

Ballantyne, Robert Michael. *Martin Rattler; or a Boy's Adventure in the Forests of Brazil*. Edinburgh: Thomas Nelson and Sons, 1860.

An adventure in the forests of Brazil which teaches geography and history.

Lippincott, Sarah Jane (Clarke). *Bonny Scotland: Tales of Her History, Heroes and Poets*. Boston: Ticknor, 1860.

Pseudo. Grace Greenwood. Stories about Glasgow and Edinburgh.

Andrews, Jane. *Seven Little Sisters Who Lived on the Round Ball That Floats in the Air*. Boston: Ticknor, 1861.

Andrews was a school teacher who wrote a series of books teaching geography, history and natural history by means of stories. She also wrote *The Stories Mother Nature Told Her Children* (1888) and *Ten Boys Who Lived on the Road from Long Ago to Now* (1885).

Ewing, Juliana Horatia. *Melchior's Dream and Other Tales*. London: Bell and Daldy, 1862.

This is the first of her many books for children.

Whitney, Adeline Dutton (Train). *Faith Gartney's Girlhood*. Boston: Loring, 1862.

This was followed by *The Gayworthys* (1865). By the author of *Boys at Chequasset*.

Kingsley, Charles. *Water Babies: A Fairy Tale for a Land Baby*. London: Macmillan, 1863.

This appeared as a serialization in *Macmillan's Magazine* from August 1862 to March 1863. A satire as well as a fairy story with imaginative writing and a lot of moralizing. A standard among children's early books.

In 1886 Macmillan reprinted this with 100 illustrations. (The original had only one illustration.)

Carroll, Lewis. *Alice's Adventures in Wonderland*. London: Macmillan, 1865.

Forty-four illustrations by John Tenniel. Second edition was in 1866. Carroll didn't like the first edition.

Although Alice is real she is in a fantasy world. It is the juxtaposition of realism and fantasy that makes this book a literary classic.

Dodge, Mary Mapes. *Hans Brinker or The Silver Skates: A Story of Life in Holland*. New York: James O'Kane, 1865.

A boy encourages his sisters to enter a skating contest because of the prize involved. Their family needs help. A story including a skating contest with a brother and sister; an attempt to get a great doctor to cure a father; a description of Dutch life, customs and history; and a tale of the boy who puts his finger in the dam.

Crane, Walter. *Picture Books*. London: Warne, 1865–1876.

A series of toy books with the help of Edmond Evans, the famous color printer.

Yonge, Charlotte Mary. *Dove in the Eagle's Nest*. New York: Appleton, 1866.

Intended for older readers, this book describes the life of a young girl among robber barons near Ulm in the days of Kaiser Maximilian.

Laboulaye, Edouard. *Fairy Tales of All Nations*. New York: Harper, 1867.

Translated by M. L. Booth. A collection of tales in Hebrew, Russian, Sanskrit, Icelandic and other languages.

MacDonald, George. *Dealing with the Fairies*. London: Strahan, 1867.

Five stories illustrated by Arthur Hughes. Contents: "The Light Princess"; "The Giant's Heart"; "The Shadows"; "Cross-Purposes"; "Golden Boy."

Stowe, Harriet Beecher. *Queer Little People*. Boston: Ticknor and Fields, 1867.

Legends and stories of animals.

Stretton, Hesba (Smith, Sarah). *Jessica's First Prayer*. New York: Garland, 1867.

A story of the religious education of a poor London girl. There is a sequel, *Jessica's Mother* (1867).

Finley, Martha. *Elsie Dinsmore*. New York: Dodd, 1868.

Pseudo. Martha Farquharson. Farquharson is a Gaelic for of Finley. She wrote about 100 children's books, more than 25 of which were Elsie titles: *Elsie's Girlhood* on to *Grandmother Elsie*. She also wrote a Mildred series beginning with *Mildred Keith* (New York: Dodd, 1876). This is an autobiographical novel.

Alcott, Louisa May. *Little Women.* Boston: Roberts, 1868–1869.

A book that describes a few months in the lives of the March sisters, Meg (16), Jo (15), Beth (13), and Amy (12). Amy, Joe, Beth and Meg recall their childhood. This is a story of the process of growing up in difficult times.

Ingelow, Jean. *Mopsa, the Fairy.* London: Longman, Green, 1869.

Jack finds a nest of fairies and is carried off to fairyland. There he meets Mopsa, a small girl fairy.

Kingsley, Charles. *Madam How and Lady Why, or, First Lessons in Earth Lore for Children.* London: Bell and Daldy, 1869.

In the preface, Kingsley expresses his indebtedness to the story "Eyes and No Eyes" by John Aikin. This was serialized in *Good Words for the Young* from November 1868 to October 1869.

Lang, Andrew. *In Fairyland; Pictures from the Elf World.* London: Longman, 1869.

Contains, among others, "The Princess Nobody," "Lang's first fairy tale. Illustrations by Richard Doyle.

Alcott, Louisa May. *Old-Fashioned Girl.* Boston: Roberts, 1870.

This was serialized in *Merry's Museum* from July to December 1870.

Aldrich, Thomas Bailey. *Story of a Bad Boy.* Boston: Fields, 1870.

Originally published in twelve installments in *Our Young Folk* in 1869. Based on the childhood of the author in Portsmouth, New Hampshire.

Diaz, Abby (Morton). *William Henry's Letters to His Grandmother.* Boston: Fields, 1870.

Appeared in *Our Young Folks* 1867–1870. One of Diaz's other books is *Cats' Arabian Nights* (1881).

Alcott, Louisa May. *Little Men.* Boston: Roberts, 1871.

Life at Blumfield with Jo's boys; a sequel to *Little Women.*

Dodgson, Charles Lutwidge (Carroll, Lewis). *Through the Looking Glass.* New York: Macmillan, 1871.

A sequel to *Alice's Adventures in Wonderland.* This edition has fifty illustrations by John Tenniel.

Eggleston, Edward. *Hoosier School Master; a Story of Backwoods Life in Indiana.* New York: Scribner, 1871.

A story based on the experiences of Eggleston's brother as a teacher. This was followed by *The Hoosier Schoolboy* (1883). A school story told from the point of view of the student. Ralph Harsock, a teacher in Flat Creek, is a hero in conflict with a school bully, Bud Means.

Hemyng, Bracebridge. *Jack Harkaway's Schooldays.* London: Edwin Brett, 1871.

In the eighteen Harkaway stories Jack goes to sea, to Oxford, lives among pirates, goes out West, tries gold-prospecting, and more.

MacDonald, George. *At the Back of the North Wind.* London: Strahan, 1871.

Little Diamond, son of a coachman, has two parallel lives: one of harsh reality in working-class London; the other a dream life in which he travels with the north wind. Diamond is awakened by the North Wind, who takes him across London and "back of the north wind." This experience gives Diamond inner calm and a gift of poetry.

Coolidge, Susan. *What Katy Did; a Story.* Boston: Roberts, 1872.

Pseudo: Sarah Chauncey Woolsey. The Katy stories are based on Coolidge's own sisters, Jane, Elizabeth and Theodora. This is followed by *What Katy Did in School* (1873) and *What Katy Did Next* (1886). A series of books about family and school life in New England.

Cowper, William. *Diverting History of John Gilpin.* London: Warne, 1872.

A ballad about John Gilpin, whose horse took him past his intended destination and then took him back home again.

Randolph Caldecott's first illustrated book, to be followed by many more.

Ewing, Juliana Horatia. *Flat Iron for a Farthing; or, Some Passages in the Life of an Only Son.* London: Bell and Daldy, 1872.

The childhood reminiscences of the only son of a widowed father in Yorkshire, England.

MacDonald, George. *Princess and the Goblin.* London: Chatto and Windus, 1872.

Princess Irene lives in a castle. Above her lives her mysterious grandmother and below her live the malicious goblins. A miner's son, Curdie, saves her and her grandmother. A sequel is *Princess and Curdie* (1883).

Rossetti, Christina. *Sing-Song; a Nursery Rhyme Book.* London: Routledge, 1872.

A book of nonsense verse illustrated by Arthur Hughes.

Stephens, Charles Asbury. *Camping Out; as Recorded by "Kit."* Boston: Osgood, 1872.

American writer of boys' stories. Stephens may have written 3,000 short stories and 100 serials. Wrote the Camping Out Series (five titles) and Knockabout Club Series (three titles), both published in Boston in 1883.

Cary, Alice, and Cary, Phoebe (1820–1871). *Ballads for Little Folks.* Boston: Hurd and Houghton, 1873.

Edited by Mary Clemmer. First publication under this title. Her better-known book is *Girl's Own Book* (1831). Cary also wrote a series called *Clovernook Children* (Boston: Ticknor and Fields, 1854).

Ewing, Juliana Horatia. *Lob Lie-by-the-Fire, and Other Tales.* London: Bell and Daldy, 1873.

Subtitled "or the Luck of Lingborough, and other tales." Illustrated by George Cruikshank. The title comes from a short story of an abandoned gypsy child who is adopted by two spinsters who name him John Broom. He is told the tales of Lob, a brownielike creature. He runs away, and after some tough times he repents and returns disguised as a farmhand and helps the two spinsters.

Beecher, Henry Ward. *Norwood; or Village Life in New England.* New York: J. B. Ford, 1874.

Henry Ward was a brother of and assistant to Harriet Beecher Stowe. He was also a writer himself.

Craik, Dinah. *Little Lame Prince and His Traveling Cloak.* London: Daldy, Isbister, 1875.

Prince Dolor, imprisoned in a tower and unable to use his legs, escapes with the help of his magic traveling cloak.

Scudder, Horace Elisha. *Doings of the Bodley Family in Town and Country.* Boston: Hurd and Houghton, 1875.

Scudder's Bodley series of books began in 1875. He was the author of the first real travel stories for children. He was editor of *Hurd and Houghton* and the *Atlantic Monthly*. Other titles are *Bodleys Telling Stories* and *Bodleys on Wheels*.

Walton, O. F. (Amy Catherine). *Christie's Old Organ; or "Home Sweet, Home."* New York: Robert Cater, 1875.

The friendship between Treffy, a barrel organist, and Christie, an orphan.

Clemens, Samuel. *Adventures of Tom Sawyer.* San Francisco: A. Roman, 1876.

Tom, with two friends, Joe Harper and Huckleberry Finn, play "pirates," disappear and are presumed dead.

The author recalls his past as the "bad boy" of a small Missouri town in pre–Civil War days.

A boy's childhood in a Mississippi River village.

Crane, Walter. *Baby's Opera: A Book of Old Rhyme with New Dresses.* London: Routledge, 1876.

A collection of nursery songs illustrated by Walter Crane. One of the songs, "I Saw Three Ships Come Sailing By" required five color blocks. A lavish and innovative combination of color and music printing.

Ewing, Juliana Horatia. *Jan of the Windmill: Story of the Plains.*

Published in *Aunt Judy's Magazine*, November 1872 to October 1873, under the title "The Miller's Thumb." A story of a foundling raised by a miller and his wife. He goes on to become a famous painter.

Habberton, John. *Helen's Babies.* Boston: Loring, 1876.

An account of a vacation spent by a young uncle in charge of his sister's nieces and nephews.

Molesworth, Mary Louisa. *Carrots: Just a Little Boy*. London: Macmillan, 1876.

Ennis Graham is a pseudonym Molesworth uses. She is said to have the "ability to enter into the personalities of her children." *Carrots* was her first children's novel, a story of the youngest boy in a family who finds it hard to learn the ways of the adult world.

Alcott, Louisa May. *Under the Lilacs*. Boston: Roberts.

This book was serialized in *St. Nicholas* 1877–1878.

Caldecott, Randolph (illus.). *Diverting History of John Gilpin*. London: Warne, 1877.

Caldecott's first illustrated book, to be followed by many more, "showing how he [Gilpin] went further than he intended and came safe home again."

Sewell, Anna. *Black Beauty*. Boston: Lothrop, 1877.

An account of a horse's experience at the hands of many owners.

Andrews, Jane. *Each and All: The Seven Little Sisters Prove their Sisterhood*. Boston: Ginn and Co., 1878.

A story describing the life of the inhabitants of the seven continents. A companion book to *Seven Little Sisters Who Live on the Round Ball That Floats in the Air* and *Ten Boys Who Lived on the Road from Long Ago to Now*.

Caldecott, Randolph. *R. Caldecott's Picture Books*. London: Routledge, 1878–1885.

An outstanding illustrator. The Caldecott Medal Award is named for this man. Nursery rhymes with colorful illustrations; these loose, humorous illustrations were never seen before in children's books and made a name for Caldecott.

Church, Alfred. *Stories from the Greek Tragedians*. New York: Dodd, 1879.

Author of *The Story of the* Iliad *and the Story of the* Odyssey (1892).

Greenaway, Kate. *Under the Window; Pictures and Rhymes for Children*. London: Edmond Evans, 1879.

Greenaway's first picture book for children. It contains her own verses and illustrations.

Hutchinson, George Andrew (ed.). *Boy's Own Paper*. London: Religious Tract Society, 1879.

The society's answer to the penny dreadfuls so popular at the time.

Anon. *Girl's Own Paper*. London: Religious Tract Society, 1880.

A companion to *Boy's Own Annual*. Contains stories of elopement and reconciliation, some fashions, articles on sewing and cooking, and, of course good behavior.

Hale, Lucretia Peabody. *Peterkin Papers*. Boston: Osgood, 1880.

A collection of comic stories about the Peterkin family—Mrs. Peterkin and her children, especially her son, Agamemnon. These stories are partly a satire on Boston society.

Lucretia was the sister of Edward E. Hale (*Man Without a Country*). She wrote magazine articles for twenty years before she wrote the *Peterkin Papers*.

Malory, Thomas. *Boy's King Arthur*. New York: Scribner, 1880.

All the tales of Arthur, Lancelot, Tristram, Gareth, Galahad, Percival and the Holy Grail.

A limited facsimile version of Caxton's 1485 edition. This is "the most famous version and the first time in English prose of all the legends which have collected about King Arthur. It is the only true English epic."

Diaz, Abby (Morton). *Polly Cologne*. Boston: Lothrop, 1881.

Appeared in *Wide, Wide World* Jan.–Dec. 1881. Earlier Diaz wrote *William Henry's Letters to His Grandmother* (1870), a story of life at boarding school.

Harris, Joel Chandler. *Uncle Remus: His Songs and His Sayings*. Boston: Houghton, 1881.

This is the collection upon which Harris's fame is based. He also wrote *Little Mr. Thimblefinger and His Queer Country* (1894); *Wally Wanderoom and His Story-Telling Machine* (1903), among others.

Stockton, Frank Richard. *Floating Prince, and Other Fairy Tales*. New York: Scribner, 1881.

Stories collected from *St. Nicholas*; one of Stockton's best collections.

Dodge, Mary Mapes. *Donald and Dorothy*. New York: Century, 1883.

Eggleston, Edward. *Hoosier School-Boy*. New York: Orange Judd, 1883.

Sequel to *The Hoosier School-Master*, the author's best-known book.

Pyle, Howard. *Merry Adventures of Robin Hood*. New York: Scribner, 1883.

This book, written two years after Pyle's marriage, established him as a leading American author for children. The book was well illustrated by the author. Robin Hood robs the rich in the name of evil Prince John. He supports Richard the Lionhearted and has many adventures. An American edition of the Robin Hood of Sherwood Forest stories so popular in England.

Stevenson, Robert Louis. *Treasure Island*. London: Cassell, 1883.

The familiar adventures of Long John Silver and Jim Hawkins.

Blake, William. *Songs of Innocence*. London: J. Pearson, 1884.

Twenty-three poems with illustrations. Ironically only twenty-three copies are known to exist. These books were produced on demand, and each one was slightly different. Known for "Little Lamb, who made thee" and "Tyger, Tyger, burning bright."

Reproduced from the volume that Blake gave to Flaxman.

Carryl, Charles Edward. *Davy and the Goblins*. Boston: Ticknor, 1884.

Carryl was a New York stockbroker. He turned to writing for his daughter. This edition appeared in *St. Nicholas*, vol. 12, Dec. 1884–Mar. 1885. This is thought to be his best work. The continuing title is *Or, what followed reading* Alice's Adventures in Wonderland.

Ewing, Juliana Horatia. *Jackanapes*. London: S.P.C.K., 1884.

Illustrated by Randolph Caldecott. A story of an orphaned boy who is brought up by an aunt and who serves in the army, where he dies while saving a friend's life.

Ross, Clarke. *Ally Sloper's Half Holiday*. London: *Judy Magazine* (A take-off of *Punch Magazine*), 1884.

From 1884 until the 1920s Ally Sloper was a weekly comic strip character in England. Ally was the hero in this first British comic strip. He was very likely today's Andy Capp, a drinking, rather disreputable character.

Andrews, Jane. *Ten Boys Who Lived on the Road from Long Ago to Now*. Boston: Lee and Shepard, 1885.

A school teacher who wrote a series of books teaching geography, history and natural history by means of stories. She also wrote *The Stories Mother Nature Told Her Children* (1888) and *Seven Little Sisters Who Live on the Round Ball That Floats in the Air* (1861).

Burnett, Frances Hodgson. *Little Lord Fauntleroy*. London: Warne, 1885.

First published in *St. Nicholas*. Burnett also wrote *Secret Garden* (1910). This is one of the author's best-known stories. It is frequently dramatized, and many editions were released.

Clemens, Samuel. *Adventures of Huckleberry Finn*. New York: Charles Webster, 1885.

This is an important American novel. Huckleberry Finn is Tom Sawyer's friend. Official publication date Dec. 1884 but not ready for delivery until Feb. 1885. A sequel to *Adventures of Tom Sawyer* (1876). The story of both Tom and Huck and their daily lives as they cope with restrictions they opposed. Pseudo. Mark Twain.

Greenaway, Kate. *Marigold Garden: Pictures and Rhymes*. London: Routledge, 1885.

A picture book of verses by the author. This book was engraved and printed by Edmond Evans. It is Greenaway's own verses, with nursery rhymes, humor and nonsense.

Stevenson, Robert Louis. *Child's Garden of Verses*. London: Longman, 1885.

A collection of poems, describing childhood as seen by an adult.

Hale, Lucretia Peabody. *Last of the*

Peterkins, with Others of Their Kin. Boston: Roberts, 1886.

A continuation of the Peterkin family stories. Although a funny set of stories about the "stupid" family of Peterkins, it is actually a satire on Boston society.

Crane, Walter. *Baby's Own Aesop.* London: Routledge, 1887.

Crane, in collaboration with Edmond Evans, designed three small, square picture books: *Baby's Opera*; *Baby's Bouquet* and *Baby's Own Aesop.*

"Fables condensed in rhyme, with portable morals pictorially painted by Walter Crane."

Crane illustrated a toy book series between 1867 and 1876 such as *Absurd ABC* and *Sleeping Beauty.*

Stockton, Frank Richard. *Bee-Man of Orn and Other Fanciful Tales.* New York: Scribner, 1887.

A comic short story about an old beekeeper, who, because he was granted the ability, decides to be a baby. Maurice Sendak illustrated a 1964 edition of this book. One of Stockton's best.

Wiggin, Kate Douglas (Riggs). *Bird's Christmas Carol.* Boston: Houghton, 1887.

A story of Carol Bird, an invalid girl so named because she was born at Christmas, but the author's greatest success is *Rebecca of Sunnybrook Farm* (1903).

Page, Thomas Nelson. *Two Little Confederates.* New York: Scribner, 1888.

Appeared in *St. Nicholas*, vol. 15, May–Oct. 1888. A story about the Civil War as seen through Southern eyes, especially those of Frank and Willy. Page also wrote *Among the Camps* (1891) and *Pastime Stories* (1894).

The author's best-known book for children, written to broaden sympathy and understanding.

Pyle, Howard. *Otto of the Silver Hand.* New York: Scribner, 1888.

A historical novel set in medieval Germany about a boy who is heir to Castle Drachenhausen. An adventure story about the kidnapping of Otto and his time spent among soldiers and robber barons. One day the son of one of the robber barons is kidnapped. Robber barons were cruel leaders of feudal Germany. The monks were peaceful and scholarly.

Lang, Andrew. *Fairy Books.* London: Longman, 1889–1910.

The Blue, Red, Green, Yellow, Pink, Gray, Violet, Crimson, Brown, Orange, Olive and Lilac—all these are collections of fairy tales from all over the world.

Jewett, Sarah Orne. *Betty Leicester: A Story for Girls.* Boston: Houghton, 1890.

A teen-age novel set in Maine. Followed by *Betty Leicester's English Christmas* (1894).

Foote, Mary Hallock. *Chosen Valley.* Boston: Houghton, Mifflin, 1892.

Mary Hallock Foote achieved national attention with *The Chosen Valley*, a Western written from a woman's point of view.

Pyle, Howard. *Men of Iron.* New York: Harper, 1892.

A historical romance set in England in the early fifteenth century. It concerns a son's mission to restore the name of his father. A story of England between the years 1066 and 1485. A literary standard about the bravery of knights in England.

Kipling, Rudyard. *Jungle Book.* New York: Macmillan, 1894.

A story where a human baby is given shelter by a family of wolves. The boy is called Mowgli, which in the wolf's language means Frog.

Johnston, Annie Fellows. *Little Colonel.* Boston: L. C. Page, 1895.

Story of a girl living in the South (Kentucky) after the Civil War; a girl with a temper. The first of a successful series.

Kipling, Rudyard. *Second Jungle Book.* New York: Doubleday, 1895.

Most of the stories are set in India, and all concern animals; also, the boy Mowgli and his relationship with animals.

Upton, Florence K. *Golliwog.* London: Longman, 1895.

Hair-raising adventures of the Golliwog family. A golliwog is a type of doll.

Stead, W. T. (ed.). *Book for the Bairns.* London: Stead, W. T., 1896.

An illustrated booklet of fairy tales and folk tales, sixty-two pages long.

Bennett, John. *Master Skylark; a Story of Shakespeare's Time*. New York: Century, 1897.

Appeared in *St. Nicholas*, vol. 24, Nov. 1896–Oct. 1897. This is a historical novel taking place in London during Shakespeare's time. An outstanding example of historical fiction set in the Elizabethan period.

Kipling, Rudyard. *Captain Courageous; a Story of Grand Banks*. New York: Century, 1897.

A story set in Newfoundland. Harvey Cheyne, a millionaire's son, is washed overboard; he is rescued by a crew member of a fishing schooner. His summer in Glouster toughens him and changes his spoiled ways. This experienced changes him from a selfish boy into a self-disciplined young man.

Bannerman, Helen. *Story of Little Black Sambo*. London: Grant Richards, 1898.

A little black boy who outwits three lions. This is the fourth title in the Dumpy books for children. This one was followed by *The Adventures of Little Black Mingo* (1901).

Falkner, John Meade. *Moonfleet*. London: Edward Arnold, 1898.

A story of fifteen-year-old John Trenchard is involved with smugglers in the Dorset village of Moonfleet. Elzevir Block is one of the memorable characters in the book.

Kipling, Rudyard. *Stalky & Co.* New York: Macmillan, 1899.

A story of a boys' boarding school. The boys are Beetle, M'Turk and Corkran, who is nicknamed Stalky, a word meaning sly, clever or wily. Kipling wrote four more Stalky stories.

A school story with strong autobiographical elements. McTurk was George Beresford, who wrote about Rudyard Kipling in *Schooldays with Kipling* (1936).

Nesbit, Edith (Bland). *Story of the Treasure Seekers*. London: T. Fisher Unwin, 1899.

A story of Oswald Bastable and his six children: Dora, Oswald, Dicky, the twins Alice and Noel and Horace Octavius, known as H.O. The first book about the Bastables.

Baum, Lyman Frank. *Wonderful Wizard of Oz*. Chicago: George M. Hill, 1900.

Dorothy is transported to the land of Oz and must find a way to get back home. Also in the story are the Tin Woodman, the Cowardly Lion and the Scarecrow. This went on to become a very well-known work. It was later made into a popular movie.

Potter, Beatrix. *Tale of Peter Rabbit*. London: Frederick Warne, 1902.

The first Beatrix Potter book. It was based on her own pet rabbit, Peter.

Anstey, F. (Thomas Anstey Guthrie). *Only Toys!* London: Grant Richards, 1903.

A collection of short stories for children.

Nesbit, Edith (Bland). *Railway Children*. London: Wells Gardner, 1906.

Roberta, Peter and Phyllis lose their father mysteriously, the mother becomes ill and they save a train wreck and are rewarded.

Pseudo. E. Nesbit.

Grahame, Kenneth. *Wind in the Willows*. New York: Scribner, 1908.

Toad, Mole, Rat and Badger live along a river and are close, visiting friends. A children's classic.

Porter, Gene Stratton. *Girl of the Limberlost*. New York: Doubleday, 1909.

Elnora's life in the Limberlost Swamp in Indiana. She collects moths to sell for money to pay for her education. This book has never been out of print.

Barrie, James Matthew. *Peter and Wendy*. Oxford: University Press, 1911.

A retelling of the story of Peter Pan in book form. Tells how Wendy and her brothers knew Peter Pan.

Burnett, Frances Hodgson. *Secret Garden*. New York: Phillips, 1911.

Mary and Colin's lives are changed as they work together to rebuilt a hidden garden. Based on Burnett's own recollection of her childhood and her youth.

Burroughs, Edgar Rice. *Tarzan of the Apes*. New York: A. L. Burt, 1914.

A British boy is abandoned in the African jungle in childhood and is raised by apes. Some sequels are *Return of Tarzan* (1915) and *Beasts of Tarzan* (1911). In 1918 the first Tarzan film was made, and in 1929 he appeared in comic strips.

Tarkington, Booth. *Penrod*. New York: Doubleday, 1914.

A novel about "the Worst Boy in Town." He was friends with two Black brothers, Herman and Verman, and a dog named Duke. He actually begins to write a dime novel in this book.

Lamburn, Richmal Crompton. *Just William*. London: G. Newnes, 1922 (1965).

The first of a long series of William books. Thirty-six stories were published including *More William* (1922), *William Again* (1923) and *William the Fourth* (1924).

Kastner, Erich. *Emil and the Detectives*. New York: Doubleday, 1929.

Emil, after being robbed, decides to find the culprits himself rather than call the police. The first English edition was in 1931. Kastner followed this with *Emil and the Three Twins* (1934).

Ransome, Arthur. *Swallows and Amazons*. New York: Lippincott, 1930.

John, Susan, Titty and Roger Walker are on vacation and go sailing on the *Swallow*. This is the first of twelve novels by Ransome.

Appendix F: List of Pseudonyms

Agile, Penne—Crowell, Mary Reed
Anstey, F.—Guthrie, Thomas Anstey
Bardwell, Harrison—Craine, Edith J.
Barnard, A. M.—Alcott, Louisa May
Bell, Emerson—Stratemeyer, Edward
Braddock, Gordon—Patten, William George
Buntline, Ned—Judson, Edward Zane Carroll
Collingwood, Harry—Lancaster, W. J. Z.
Coolidge, Susan—Woolsey, Sarah Chauncey
Cooper, James A.—Foster, W. Bert
Crompton, Richmal—Lamburn, Richmal Crompton
Cushman, Corinne—Crowell, Mary Reed
Daly, Jim—Stratemeyer, Edward
Dangerfield, Harry—Patten, William George
Dixon, Franklin W.—Stratemeyer, Edward
Edwards, Leo—Lees, Edward Edson
Emerson, Alice—Foster, W. Bert
Farquharson, Martha—Finley, Martha Farquharson
Faulkner, Frank—Ellis, Edward Sylvester
Harkaway, Hal—Stratemeyer, Edward
Harkaway, Jack—Hemyng, Bracebridge
Hill, Grace—Foster, W. Bert
Holding, Ephraim—Mogridge, George
James, Lewis—Stratemeyer, Edward
James, Stephanie—Krentz, Jayne Ann
Keene, Carolyn—Benson, Mildred Wirt
Kennedy, Rose—Crowell, Mary Reed
Madden, Billy—Tozer, Alfred B.
Old Humphrey—Mogridge, George
Optic, Oliver—Adams, William Taylor
Parley, Peter—Martin, William
Parley, Peter—Mogridge, George
Parley, Peter—Goodrich, Samuel G.
Preston, Percy—This is known as a pseudonym but the real author's name is unknown.
Rann, Jack—Rede, William Leman
Scot, Morgan—Patten, William George
Sixteen String Jack—Rede, William Leman
Standish, Bert L.—Patten, William George
Stretton, Hesba—Smith, Sarah
Twain, Mark—Clemens, Samuel L.
Uncle Harry—Habberton, John
Ward, Tom—Stratemeyer, Edward
Wilson, Rev. T.—Clark, Samuel
Zimmy—Stratemeyer, Edward

Appendix G: List of Character Names

Names of characters identified with both series books and individual titles, listed by CHARACTER, author and *individual or series title.*

ALICE LEIGHTON	Cupples, Anne Jane	*Alice Leighton; or, a Good Name Is Rather to Be Chosen Than Riches*
ALLAN QUARTERMAIN	Haggard, H. Rider	*Allan Quartermain Series*
ANDY LANE	Adams, Eustace	*Andy Lane Series*
AYESHA	Haggard, H. Rider	*She*
BERT HOWARD	Hancock, H. Irving	*Conquest of the United States Series*
BETTY GORDON	Emerson, Alice B.	*Betty Gordon and Her School Chums*
BETTY WALES	Warde, Margaret	*Betty Wales Series*
BILL BOLTON	Sainsbury, Noel	*Bill Bolton Series*
BILL BRUCE	Arnold, Hap	*Bill Bruce Series*
BILL BRUCE	Patten, William George	*Bill Bruce Series*
BILLY SMITH	Sainsbury, Noel	*Billy Smith Series*
BOB GORDON	Dean, Graham	*Bob Gordon, Cub Reporter*
BOB TERRELL	Cook, Canfield	*Lucky Terrell Flying Series*
BRENDEN JACKOROWSKY	Floyd, C. J.	*Assault #1: Sands Run Red*
BUNNY BROWN	Hope, Laura Lee	*Bunny Brown and His Sister Sue Series*
C. J. MAHONEY	David, G.	*Sergeant #9: Hammerhead*

CLAUDE DUVAL	Errym, Malcolm J.	*Duval at Bay; or, Claude's Career Closed*
CLAUDE DUVAL	Taylor, Tom	*Claude Duval*
CLINT WEBB	Foster, W. Bert	*Clint Webb Series*
DAN DALZELL	Hancock, H. Irving	*Dan Dalzell at Vera Cruz*
DARESOME DICK	Forrest, Frank (house name)	*Schooldays; or, the Victory of the New Boy*
DASH DARE	Stratemeyer, Edward	*Dash Dare on His Mettle; or, Clearing Up a Double Tragedy*
DAVE DARRIN	Hancock, H. Irving	*Conquest of the United States Series*
DAVE DAWSON	Bowen, R. Sidney	*Dave Dawson Series*
DAVE PORTER	Patten, William George	*Dave Porter Series*
DEADWOOD DICK	Wheeler, Edward L.	*Deadwood Dick Series*
DEL ADAM	Webb, A.	*Decker's Demons #1: Decker's Demons*
DICK PRESCOTT	Hancock, H. Irving	*Dick Prescott Series*
DICK TURPIN	Ainsworth, William Harrison	*Dick Turpin, the Highwayman*
DON STURDY	Appleton, Victor	*Don Sturdy Series*
DOROTHY DALE	Penrose, Margaret	*Dorothy Dale Series*
DOROTHY DIXON	Wayne, Dorothy	*Dorothy Dixon Series*
ELLEN CANBY	Stratemeyer, Edward	*Dash Dare on His Mettle; or, Clearing Up a Double Tragedy*
ELSIE DINSMORE	Finley, Martha	*Elsie Dinsmore Series*
ERNESTO COLON	Rovin, J.	*Force Five #1: Destination Algiers*
FLASH GORDON	Raymond, Alex	*Flash Gordon Series*
FRANK MERRIWELL	Patten, William George	*Frank Merriwell Series*
FRANK MERRIWELL	Standish, Burt L. (William George)	*Frank Merriwell Series*
FRANK READE	Enton, Harry	*Frank Reade Series*
FRANKIE LABARBARA	Mackie, J.	*Rat Bastards #1: Hit the Beach*
FRED FEARNOT	Patten, William George	*Fred Fearnot Series*
FREDDY FARMER	Bowen, R. Sidney	*Dave Dawson Series*

Gentleman Jack	Daly, Jim	*Gentleman Jack's Big Hit; or, Downing the Rise Ring Fakirs*
Glinda	Baum, Lyman Frank	*Glinda of Oz*
Grace Harlowe	Flowers, Jessie Graham	*Grace Harlowe's Return to Overton Campus*
Greg Homes	Hancock, H. Irving	*Uncle Sam's Boys' Series*
Guy of Warwick	Unknown	*History of Guy, Earl of Warwick*
Hapworth, Walter	Dixon, Franklin W.	*Across the Ocean to Paris*
Harlan Halsey	Old Sleuth	*Flyaway Ned; or, the Old Detective's Pupil*
Harry Hazleton	Hancock, H. Irving	*Young Engineers Series*
Homer Gladley	Mackie, J.	*Rat Bastards #1: Hit the Beach*
Jack Lightfoot	Stevens, Maurice	*Jack Lightfoot Series*
Jack Maynard	Daly, Jim (ghostwriter of Edward Stratemeyer)	*Gentleman Jack's Debut; or, the Ring Champion on the Stage*
Jack Sheppard	Ainsworth, William Harrison	*Jack Sheppard: A Romance*
Jack Standfast	Not identified	*Jack Standfast at School; or, the Arrival of a Champion*
Jane Allen	Bancroft, Edith	*Jane Allen Series*
Jerry Todd	Lees, Edward Edson	*Jerry Todd Series*
Jimmy Donnelly	Theiss, Lewis	*Air Mail Series*
Jimmy Joyce	Bowen, R. Sidney	*Red Randall Series*
Jo March	Alcott, Louisa May	*Little Women*
John Butsko	Mackie, J.	*Rat Bastards #1: Hit the Beach*
John L., Jr.	Madden, Billy	*John L., Jr. at Coney Island; or, the Plot to Keep a Fighter Down*
Linda Carlton	Lavell, Edith	*Linda Carlton Series*
Link Rover	Richards, G.	*Link Rover Series*
Lucky Terrell	Cook, Canfield	*Lucky Terrell Flying Series*
Mac McLeane	Darby, John	*McLeane's Rangers #4: Saipan Slaughter*
Mac Wingate	Swift, Byron	*Mac Wingate #1: Mission Code Symbol*

Mark Gilmore	Fitzhugh, Percy Keese	*Cloud Patrol Series*
Mathilde Arnheim	Alcott, Louisa May	*Skeleton in the Closet*
Morris Shilansky	Mackie, J.	*Rat Bastards #1: Hit the Beach*
Nancy Drew	Wirt, Mildred Benson (Keene, Carolyn)	*Secret of the Old Clock*
Nick Carter	Coryell, John Russell	*Old Detective's Pupil; or, the Mysterious Crime of Madison Square*
Nick Chase	Cort, Ned	*Boxer Unit OSS #1: French Entrapment*
O'Conner	Darby, John	*McLeane's Rangers #1: The Bougainville Breakout*
Old Cap Collier	No named author	*On to Washington: or, Old Cap Collier with the Coxey Army*
Old King Brady	Doughty, Francis	*Old King Brady, the Sleuth-Hound*
Old Sleuth	Coryell, John Russell	*Old Detective's Pupil; or, the Mysterious Crime of Madison Square*
Old Sleuth, the Detective	Halsey, Harlan	*Dutch Detective; or, the Mystery of the Black Pool*
Patty Fairfield	Wells, Carolyn	*Patty Fairfield*
Phil Rushington	Norms, Stanley	*Phil Rushington; or, the Sophs of Spring Vale Academy*
Poppy Otts	Edwards, Leo (Edward Edson Lees)	*Poppy Otts Series*
Randy Starrs	Martin, Eugene	*Randy Starr Series*
Red Randall	Bowen, R. Sidney	*Red Randall Series*
Renfrew	Erskine, Laurie York	*Renfrew Flies Again*
Rex Kingdom	Patten, William George	*Rex Kingdom Series*
Rex Lee	Burtis, Thomson	*Rex Lee Series*
Roy Blakeley	Fitzhugh, Percy Keese	*Roy Blakeley Series*
Ruth Fielding	Foster, W. Bert	*Ruth Fielding Series*
Sam Spade	Hammett, Dashiell	*Sam Spade Series*
Slim Evans	Burtis, Thomson	*Slim Evans, Air Ranger*
Slim Tyler	Stone, Robert Henry	*Slim Tyler Series*
Stan Wilson	Avery, Al	*Yankee with the R.A.F.*
Steve Knight	Copp, Ted	*Steve Knight Flying Stories*

TED STRONG	Taylor, Edward C.	*Ted Strong Series*
TIM MURPHY	Dean, Graham	*Treasure Hunt of the S18*
TOM READE	Hancock, H. Irving	*Young Engineers Series*
TOM SLADE	Fitzhugh, Percy Keese	*Tom Slade Series*
TOM SWIFT	Appleton, Victor	*Tom Swift Series*
TOM WILDRAKE	Emmett, George	*Tom Wildrake's Schooldays*
VICKI BARR	Wells, Helen	*Vicki Barr Series*
VINCE CONTARDO	Darby, John	*Sergeant #4: The Liberation of Paris*
WILD WEST YOUNG	Shea, Cornelius	*Young Wild West, the Prince of the Saddle*
WILKINS, RAYMOND	Darby, John	*McLeane's Rangers #2: Target Rabaul*
WILL HARRISON	Decker, John	*Tac One #1: Assignment North Africa*

Appendix H: Biographical Dictionary

These are the authors, printers, publishers, illustrators, and others who are mentioned in this book.

Abbott, Jacob (1803–1879). Abbott was the sole or joint author of nearly 200 books, some of which were biographies. He was the author of the Franconia stories, which were more popular in England than in America. The first two Rollo books appeared in America in 1835. There were 28 titles in the series.

Adams, Harriet (Stratemeyer) (1892–1982). She was the daughter of Edward Stratemeyer and a senior officer of the Stratemeyer Syndicate. She also wrote under the pseudonyms of Victor Appleton, Mary Hollis and many others.

Adams, William Taylor (1822–1897). W. T. Adams wrote under the pseudonym of Oliver Optic and was the author of the Army and Navy Series; the Boat Club Series; the Great Western Series; the Lake Shore Series; the Riverdale Series; Starry Flat Series; Upward and Onward Series; Yacht Series; and the Young Americans Abroad Series. From 1850 to 1890 he published about 1,000 stories. Also 116 full-length books.

Aelfric (955–1020). Wrote a Latin grammar book that could be understood by "you little boys of tender years." The format was one of the boys asking questions, especially about occupations (ploughboy, shepherd, oxherd, etc.) and the master's giving the answers. The master also teaches the boys to behave themselves and forgives their sins.

Aikin, John (1747–1822). Aikin and his sister, Anna Barbauld, coauthored *Evenings at Home* (1792–1796), a collection of stories, poems and dialogues. He also wrote a few books on his own, for example, *Calendar of Nature* (1784).

Alcock, John (1892–1919). An aviator who flew the Atlantic, upon whom many of Stratemeyer's flying books were based.

Alcott, Louisa May (1832–1888). Her best-known book is *Little Women*, which reflects her own home life. It has been translated into many languages and is now a children's classic. She also wrote novels, short stories and poems. She was a teacher, a seamstress and a domestic servant. She edited the *Merry's Museum*, a children's magazine. She wrote at least 33 books; some of them are less known but considered part of the dime-novel era. She wrote these titles under the name A. M. Barnard.

Alcuin (735–804). Alcuin used the question-and-answer form of writing in his lesson books, mainly about grammar. He was the teacher of Charlemagne. This is an example of an early book written for children; true to tradition it was informative, not entertaining.

Aldrich, Thomas Bailey (1836–1907). Aldrich and Lucy Larcom were joint editors of *Our Young Folks*, in which the *Peterkin Papers* appeared. His *Story of a Bad Boy* reflects New England village life; his short stories are his best work.

Alger, Horatio (1832–1899). His stories concern poor boys who succeed by hard work, thrift and resisting temptation. His first rags-to-riches book is *Ragged Dick; or Street Life in New York with the Boot-Blacks*, which was published in 1868. He wrote popular books that were badly written and repetitive.

Allingham, J. W. A London Fleet Street publisher. He was a competitor of the Brett Publishing House and a contemporary of Bracebridge Hemyng, in the mid- and late 1800s.

Allison, W. L. Company of New York. In 1897 Allison reissued E. J. Brett's stories of Jack Harkaway in fifteen uniform hardcover volumes.

Altemus, Henry. A Philadelphia publisher; published *History of Tom Thumb*. He was also the publisher of H. I. Hancock's *Uncle Sam's Boys* series in the early 1900s. A popular publisher of the time.

Andersen, Hans Christian (1805–1875). Andersen wrote 156 fairy tales and stories. The first of these (1835) was published in Denmark; they were translated into English in 1846.

Anderson, William (1952–). A biographer who advises museums based on his experience with early books.

Bailey and Noyes (1800–1870). Publishers in Portland, Maine. Printed readers and other children's stories: *Two Goats and the Sick Monkey*; *Shepherd Boy*; and *Sailor Boy, or, the First and Last Voyage of Little Andrew.*

Ballantyne, Robert Michael (1825–1894). Ballantyne published well over 100 books. A popular prolific writer of books for boys. The settings were the South Seas, Africa, the Arctic and the Rocky Mountains.

Barbauld, Anna Letitia (1743–1825). She helped her brother, John Aikin, in his writing of *Evenings at Home* (1792–1796). She was a critic of children's reading material; she was heavily criticized by Charles Lamb, who called her work dull and too instructive as compared to books for amusement.

Beadle, Irwin and Erastus (1821–1894). Editors, authors and publishers. They and Robert Adams formed a publishing company. They advertised "a dollar book for a dime." their first book was *Maleaska*, which sold 600,000 copies and was published in at least six languages. They also published the works of Reid, Buntline, Ingraham and Wheeler.

Beaumont, Marie le Prince de (1711–1780). In 1757 her work was translated into English under the title *The Young Misses' Magazine.*

Belarski, Rudolph (1900–1983). Noted for pulp fiction and paperback detective images, Belanski was said to be "the perfect paperback artist" by art editor Ken Stuart of the *Saturday Evening Post.*

Voluptuous dames in distress and

square-jawed thugs. As his illustrations soared alongside the growth of our history of popular culture, so does the nostalgic trend that he spawned.

Bergey, Earle K. (1901–1952). Cover artist for pulps and paperbacks. He has had exhibits in several American museums. His work has appeared in many auctions. Bergey created a distinctive style for Popular Library, one of his best-selling lines of paperbacks. His specialty was the lush human female figure wearing suggestive ladies' garments that later became known as the "brass brassiere" school of art.

Berquin, Arnaud (1749–1791). Author of *The Looking Glass for the Mind.* He also translated the Sandford and Merton books into French.

Birch, Reginald (1856–1943). An illustrator who did the art work for *Little Lord Fauntleroy.*

Blake, William (1757–1827). William Blake was an engraver, a poet, a painter and a mystic. *Songs of Innocence* (1789) and *Songs of Experience* (1794) are his best works.

Bonner, Robert (1824–1899). Proprietor of the *New York Ledger*, a story paper. A publisher of Laura Jean Libbey's work. Bonner paid well for Libbey's work, and she profited from it.

Boreman, Thomas (1623–?). A publisher of children's books. Miniature guide books to the sights of eighteenth-century London, both in stores and in poems. He is also the owner of the well-known Boot and Crown bookstore.

Bunyan, John (1628–1688). Author and poet. His most famous work is *Pilgrim's Progress*, but he also wrote his autobiography, *Grace Abounding to the Chief of Sinners* (1666). Also a book specifically for children, *A Book for Boys and Girls*, a collection of verses, published in 1686.

Burnett, Frances Hodgson (1849–1924). Burnett wrote many adult novels with a mixture of romance and reality. Her first story was published in *Godey's Lady's Book* in 1868. Her most successful book was the juvenile *Little Lord Fauntleroy* (1886). She also wrote *Little Princess* (1905) and *Secret Garden* (1911).

Castlemon, Harry (1824–1915). This is a pseudonym for Charles Austin Fosdick. He wrote over sixty adventure stories for boys. His best-known books about Frank Nelson were based on his own experience during the Civil War. Considered by many as the inventor of the "boy thriller."

Caxton, William (1422–1491). Caxton introduced fictional printing to England. The first books printed in English were *Reynard the Fox* (1481), *Aesop* (1484) and *Morte d'Arthur* (1485).

Clemens, Samuel Langhorne (1835–1910). *Tom Sawyer* and *Huckleberry Finn* are based on Clemens's personal experiences in Hannibal, Missouri. Wrote under the name of Mark Twain. These two books are American classics.

Collins, Benjamin (1770). Printer and bookseller. A business associate of John Newbery. Possibly the inventor of the battledore. A writer of sensational stories but also a serious author. Alleged to be the author of *Royal Primer; or an Essay and Pleasant Guide to the Art of Reading.*

Comstock, Anthony (1844–1915). A strong critic of the dime novels and story papers with the warning: "Your Child is in danger of having its pure mind cursed for life." Author of *Traps for the Young* (1883).

Cotton, John (1584–1652). He authored *Milk for Babes* (1646). This book had many editions printed in both America and England. It was a 64-page book catechism.

Craik, Dinah Mulock (1826–1887). *Adventures of a Brownie* (1872) and *Little Lame Prince* (1875) are examples of her writings for children and are still favorites.

Dalziel, Gilbert (1815–1902). The first British comic to appear regularly was "Ally Sloper's Half Holiday" (Clarke Ross, 1884), which was published in London by the Dalziel brothers; it features the adventures of a hard-drinking ne'er-do-well. (Andy Capp of today?) It was meant to entertain boys and young men.

Dana, John Cotton (1856–1929). Librarian of the Newark Free Library. Although dime novels were forbidden, he read them as a youngster.

Day, Mahlon (1790–1854). American printer. Published the *New York Cries*. He referred to his little books as toys, taken from the term "toy-book" used in England.

Day, Thomas (1748–1789). The author of the very popular Sandford and Merton books (1783–1789). He also wrote *History of Little Jack* (1788).

De Soto, Raphael (1661–1731). Artist of the pulps (actually the beginning of today's paperback books). With other great pulp artists such as Rudolph Belarski and Earle Bergey, they made pulp artistry an art form in its own right.

Defoe, Daniel (1661–1731). *Robinson Crusoe* is his greatest work and was widely read by children; it is still read today by youngsters and adults alike.

DeWitt, Robert M. (1827–1877). A publisher of "DeWitt's Ten-Cent Romances" (1867–1873). Jack Sheppard is one of his stock-in-trade characters. He became known for his publishing of sensational literature, mostly pirated from British sources.

Dirks, Rudolph (1877–1968). Artist of comic strips. He was both a painter and engraver as well as a cartoonist. He founded the American comics with the "Katzenjammer Kids" in 1897.

Dodge, Mary Mapes (1838–1905). Dodge's *Hans Brinker* (1865) originated as a continued story which she told her sons. It has become a children's classic and has been translated into many languages. Dodge was also the first editor of the famous *St. Nicholas Magazine*. She began to write after she passed her thirtieth birthday.

Elliott, James R. (1820–1890). Of the Elliott, Thomes and Talbot publishing firm. Connected with Louisa May Alcott's *Flag of Our Union* and three of her "thrillers." *V.V.*, *Skeleton in the Closet* and *Mysterious Key*. He was in business in the early and mid–1850s.

Elliott, Thomes and Talbot. Boston publishers: James R. Elliott (1820–1890), William Henry Thomes (1824–1895) and Newton Talbot (1815–1904). Competed with Beadle and Adams with the publication of the ten-cent novelette series.

Ellis, Edward Sylvester (1840–1916). Ellis was an educator, novelist, poet, editor and historian. One of his pseudonyms, E. S. St. Mox is but an example of the many pseudonyms he used. Ellis wrote over thirty series and ten trilogies from the Arizona trilogy to *Wyoming Valley Trial*.

Emmett, George. British publisher of boys' story papers: *Tom Wildrake's Schooldays*. Emmett had taken part in the Charge of the Light Brigade. He wrote many stories but was not as successful as Edwin Brett. He and Brett were serious publishing enemies during the latter half of the nineteenth century.

Everette, William (1839–1910). He wrote for the *New York Ledger*. He was a former president of Harvard, former governor of Massachusetts and former United States senator. He wrote fifty-two weekly columns in 1858 and 1859 in return for a substantial contribution to the Mount Vernon fund, from Bonner. He wrote for the *North American Review*, where he favorably reviewed "Beadle Dime Books."

Feyerabend, Sigmund (1580). The earliest-known picture book for children. "A book of art and instruction for young people. Herein may be discovered all manner of merry and agreeable drawings." It contains the first printed pictures of a student using a horn book.

Fleet, Thomas and John (1685–1758). Prominent American colonial printers and publishers. From 1731 until death they published a weekly paper called *Weekly Rehearsal*; in 1735 the name was changed to the *Boston Evening Post*.

Fosdick, Charles Austin (1842–1915). Under the pseudonym of Castlemon he wrote post–Civil War stories for boys. He wrote nearly seventy books, nine of which were the Gun Boat series, featuring Frank.

Gatty, Margaret Scott (1809–1873). Used the name of Aunt Judy. She started and edited *Aunt Judy's Magazine*. She wrote for the magazine and published *Parables from Nature*.

Genlis, Madame de Stephanie (1746–1830). She attacked fairy stories as containing "ridiculous ideas" and lacking any "moral tendency." Her own work was *Moral Tales*, translated into English as *Tales of the Castle* (1785).

Gilpen, Thomas (1776). A businessman from Brandywine, Delaware, who is credited with the development of paper-making techniques.

Gleason, Frederick (1816–1896). Publisher in Boston. Published the first story paper, *The Flag of Our Union*. They also published the works of Ned Buntline and Edgar Allan Poe.

Goldsmith, Alfred F. (1881–1947). Book dealer. Author of a Walt Whitman biography. He is also quoted as having read dime novels as a youngster, even though it was forbidden.

Goodrich, Samuel Griswold (1783–1860). Author of the original Peter Parley Series, a different type of instruction books for children. They were widely popular in America and pirated by England, who used the name freely.

Green, S. S. In 1897 Green defended fiction books for the young, including those by Oliver Optic and Horatio Alger.

Haggard, Henry Rider (1856–1925). Among other important titles Haggard wrote nine series starting with the Allan Quartermain Series and ending with the Zulu Series.

Hale, Lucretia P. (1820–1900). Author of the Peterkin papers. Although she wrote for the *Atlantic* magazine for twenty years, she became successful only with the Peterkin Paper series, including *Last of the Peterkins*, with *Others of Their Kin*.

Halliwell, James Orchard (1820–1889). He published the first scholarly study of English nursery rhymes: *Nursery Rhymes of England* (1842) and *Popular Rhymes and Nursery Tales* (1849). He is also credited with the publication of *The History of Thomas Hickathrift*.

Hancock, Irving (1868–1922). The author of the Conquest of the United States Series, the Annapolis Series, the Dave Darrin Series, the Uncle Sam's Boys Series, the West Point Series and the Young Engineer Series.

Harmsworth, Alfred (1865–1922). In May of 1890 Alfred Harmsworth, a British newspaper proprietor, launched "Comic Cuts" and "Chips," which were intended to catch the penny dreadful market; like other early comics, they contained many one-picture jokes as well as comic strips.

Harris, Benjamin (1673–1716). Compiler of the *New England Primer.* He came to America from England in 1686, where he had printed pamphlets and broadsides, but it was the *New England Primer* that became very popular in both England and America.

Harris, Joel Chandler (1848–1908). Author of the Uncle Remus stories (1880). This was his most famous work, but he also wrote for children: *Little Mr. Thimblefinger and His Queer Country* (1894), *Wally Walderoom and His Story-Telling Machine* (1903).

Hawthorne, Nathaniel (1804–1864). Samuel G. Goodrich, who published the Peter Parley series, brought attention to Hawthorne, who later went on to write two American children's classics, *Wonder Book for Boys and Girls* (1851) and *Tanglewood Tales* (1853). He is the author of many children's books.

Hess, George H. (1873–1954). A Saint Paul businessman. In 1954 he gave the University of Minnesota Library over fifty thousand dime novels, story papers and children's series books.

Hoe, Richard (1812–1886). Pressman. Inventor of the rotary printing press, which revolutionized newspaper printing.

Hogarth, William of England (1796–1764). During the eighteenth century William Hogarth of England printed a series of satirical drawings telling various stories. One of the best known is "A Rake's Progress."

Hood, Thomas (1799–1845). In England, *The Comic Annual* (1830–1839), edited by Thomas Hood, although primarily aimed at the adult market, was very popular with the young. His technique was highly successful and widely imitated.

Howitt, Mary Botham (1799–1888). Mary and her husband, William, were both writers for children. Together they wrote about 180 books. Mary was mainly a poet and wrote the famous "'Will you walk into my parlour?' said the Spider to the Fly." She also wrote novels: *Sowing and Reaping; or, What Will Come of It?* William wrote the *Boy's Country Book* (1839).

Ingraham, Prentiss (1843–1904). Ingraham wrote about 600 novels (in longhand). These include 130 Buffalo Bill titles. He, like so many dime novel authors, wrote under many pseudonyms. He wrote the Dick Doom Series.

Jewett, Sarah Orne (1849–1909). Her *Betty Leicester* (1890) is still read today. It is a realistic story based in Maine and covers customs and manners.

Johnson, Jacob. American publisher based in Philadelphia; published *Daisy; or, Cautionary Stories in Verse* by Elizabeth Turner. Also a thirty-two page *History of Whittington and His Cat.*

Johnston, Annie F. (1863–1931). Author of the Little Colonel series, which began with *Little Colonel* (1895). It ran for at least seventeen titles.

Judson, E. Z. C. (1832–1886). Wrote under the pseudonym of Ned Buntline. A journalist, publisher, lecturer, novelist and entrepreneur. Best known for his frontier and Western stories and creating the persona of Buffalo Bill.

Knight, Charles (1791–1873). Nineteenth-century publisher of chapbooks. He published the Playfellow Series by Harriet Martineau in 1841.

La Fontaine, Jean de (1621–1695). He wrote *Fables*, which was published between 1668 and 1694. It contains 125 fables; later 100 more were added. In 1693 he added another 24. They were translated into English in 1734.

Lamb, Charles (1776–1834). Charles wrote many poems; *Rosamund Gray* (1798), a tragic story; *Adventures of Ulysses* (1808) and two plays. With his sister Mary he wrote *Tales from Shakespeare.*

Lamb, Mary Anne (1764–1847). Author of *Mrs. Leicester's School* (1809). With Charles she wrote *Tales from Shakespeare.* She was outproduced by her brother, Charles. Both brother and sister were never well, and both had several mental breakdowns.

LeBlanc, Edward (1920–). Editor of the *Dime Novel Round-Up*, the main periodical dealing with popular fiction of the nineteenth century. This is the foundation for any scholarly or critical examination of bibliographic work of the dime novels.

Leslie, Frank (1821–1880). Publisher of *Frank Leslie's Boys of America* and *Frank Leslie's Boys' and Girls' Weekly.* Much of the content was reprinted from English publications without author identification.

Libbey's, Laura Jean (1862–1924). Wrote over eighty novels in the late-nineteenth century. She wrote melodramatic romances. She appeared weekly as a serial in the family story papers. She was very successful financially and was very popular.

Lovecraft, Howard Phillip (1890–1937). A pulp fiction writer; wrote at least seventy-five books.

Mathiews, Franklin K. (1873–1950). A strong critic of series books, especially the Frank Merriwell nickel novel series and Edward Stratemeyer.

McCormack, William. Wrote an article titled "The Dime Novel Nuisance" in a magazine called *Lend a Hand*, edited by Edward Everett Hale. Although he didn't praise the dime novels, he objected to the Sunday school libraries.

More, Hannah (1745–1833). British writer of religious and moral tracts. Her *Thoughts on the Importance of the Manners o the Great to General Society* (1788) was widely read. She was credited with creating a literary genre, the tracts, which influenced young people's reading. Though not strictly a writer for children, she wrote, in chapbook fashion, moral stories for them. Basically she was against the widespread distribution of children's books.

Munro, George (1825–1896). Brother of Norman Munro, with whom he shared a publishing business. they published 39 different series. Published one of the first dime-novel, detective stories, *The Bowery Detective* by Kenward Philip, the first series story with a continuing hero (Old Sleuth) and established the Seaside Library. Published *Munro's Ten-Cent Novels* (1863–1877). He was formerly a foreman with the Beadle Publishing Company. Also published the Old Sleuth Library (1885–1905).

Munro, Norman (1844–1894). Publisher of the Jack Harkaway Series; also the Munro's Library, Munro's Ten-Cent Library and Old Cap Collier Library (1883–1899). Munro began publishing *The New York Fireside Companion* as a family paper (1867). Norman Munro, having departed from his brother's firm in 1873, begins publishing *The Boy's Own Story Teller*, a series of novels with adolescent heroes (1875).

Munsey, Frank A. (1854–1925). Publisher of *Argosy* magazine. He published many of W. Bert Foster's books under seven different pseudonyms. He changed the *Argosy* to the *Golden Argosy* for young people in 1882.

Newbery, John (1713–1767). The first English publisher of children's books. An early book was *The Circle of the Sciences* (1745–1745). His more famous ones were *A Pretty Book of Pictures for Little Masters and Misses* (1750?) and *Little Pretty Pocket-Book* (1744). Many of his books were pirated and imitated in America, usually by Isaiah Thomas of Worchester, Mass.

O'Brien, Frank P. He had a large collection of Beadle's dime novels, part of which was auctioned to the public in 1920, but most of it was donated to the New York Public Library. He did not refer to them as dime novels but as American pioneer life. The New York Public Library catalogs them as dime novels. There were 1,500 Beadle publications, plus original manuscripts, copyrights and correspondence.

Outcault, Richard Felton (1863–1928). Comic strip writer. Began the first colored comic strip. It was the "Great Show Dog in M'Googon's Avenue" for *New York World.*

Perrault, Charles (1628–1703). A collector of fairy tales. He was the first to put in writing *Bluebeard, Cinderella, Diamonds* and *Toads* and many more.

Preiss, Byron. An author of books on pulps; gave his opinion this way: "The old American pulps were filled with adventure, ambitious plots, and taut dramatic stories. At times they were also filled with hack writing, racism, and titillation. They were products of their times and, as such, remain an accurate portrait of tastes and attitudes of America in the first forty years of the nineteenth century."

Prentiss, C. A former teacher who turned to begin a chapbook publisher. He published Chapman Whitcomb's work out of Leominster, Mass.

Priest, Josiah (1788–1851). Historical writer of chapbooks about the colonial and Revolutionary War period. He also wrote about Native American captivities.

Putnam, Herbert (1861–1955). American librarian; son of George Palmer Putnam, a noted publisher. In 1895, after practicing law in Boston, Putnam became librarian of the Boston Public Library, and in 1899 he began his 40 years of service as librarian of Congress. He built the collection of the Library of Congress into one of the finest in the world, reorganizing and introducing important procedures and establishing a classification system that has come into wide use.

Pyle, Howard (1853–1911). An American author and illustrator. His list of books contains *Merry Adventures of Robin Hood, Pepper and Salt* (1886), *Wonder Clock* (1888), *Otto of the Silver Hand* (1888), *Men of Iron* (1892), and others. He was also an illustrator; he illustrated his own books and those of many other writers.

Raymond, Alex (1909–1956). Artist. Responsible for the comic strip stories of Tillie the Toiler, Flash Gordon, Secret Agent X9 and others. Many of his comic strips were collected and made into books.

Reynolds, George William McArthur (1814–1879). Reynolds and Edwin Brett were members of the 1848 Chartist movement. Reynolds was a radical populist and British novelist. Author of *Youthful Impostor* (1835), *Drunkard's Progress* (1841) and *Mary Price* (1852).

Richards, Laura E. Howe (1850–1943). Richards was a poet; her most well known poem is "Eletelephony." She also wrote stories for children: "Joyous Story of Toto" (1885) and "Captain January" (1890).

Roscoe, William P. (1753–1831). Roscoe was a historian, botanist and poet. His *Butterfly's Ball* (1807) was one of the earliest books for children that didn't have a moral attached.

Scudder, Horace E. (1838–1902). His Bodley series of books began in 1875. He was editor at Hurd and Houghton ad for the *Atlantic Monthly.*

Steeger, Henry (1903–1990). Associated with Popular Publications: *Argosy, Black Mask, Spider* and *Dime Detective.*

Stephens, Ann Sophia Winterbotham (1810–1886). The original author of what became *Malaeska: The Indian Wife of the White Hunter.* It was resurrected by the Beadle Company. Stephens was paid $250 for her serialized story of twenty years earlier.

Stockton, Frank Richard (1834–1902). A humorist writer who wrote the *Bee Man of Orn* and other fantasies but later wrote only adult books. Maurice Sendak illustrated editions of *The Bee Man of Orn* (1964).

Stonehill, C. A. (1677–1707). Publisher of English newspapers (1641–1665). He also wrote *Child's Bible of the Fifteenth Century.*

Stowe, Harriet Beecher (1811–1896). Author of *Uncle Tom's Cabin.* It is often cited as one of the causes of the start of the Civil War, and although not meant for children it was read by and impressed children. She wrote several children's books: *Queer Little People* (1867) and *Pussy Willow.*

Stratemeyer, Edward (1862–1930). He formed Stratemeyer Syndicate and began to formulate plots and characters for many children's series: Nancy Drew and Rover Boys (under the name Arthur Winfield), Motor Boys (under the name Clarence Young), Tom Swift by "Victor Appleton," Outdoor Girls and Bobbsey Twins by "Laura Lee Hope" and many more. He wrote about fifty books under his own name.

Street, Francis Scott, and Smith, Francis Shubael. New York publisher of Edward S. Ellis's *White Mustang.* Francis Street began as a clerk in different publishing houses. They were the publishing houses of the Jack Harkaway series, the New York Five-Cent Library, the *Tip-Top Weekly* among many others. This house also published Devil Dog Comics and Red Dragon Comics.

Swift, Jonathan (1667–1745). The author of *Gulliver's Travels* (1726), a fantasy of strange animals and people met on a journey to remote nations of the world. Although meant as an adult satire, it is read by youngsters as a humorous tale.

Swinnerton, James (1875–1974). The first comic strip artist. He worked for the *San Francisco Examiner* in 1892. He was responsible for "Little Jimmy" and "The Little Bears and Tigers."

Talbot, Newton (1815–1909). Of the Elliott, Thomes and Talbot publishing firm. Connected with Louisa May Alcott's *Flag of Our Union* and three of her "thrillers": *V.V., Skeleton in the Closet* and *Mysterious Key.*

Thomas, Isaiah (1750–1831). American printer of books for children, including chapbooks. Among the more than one hundred titles are *Goody Two Shoes, Mother Goose Melody* and the *New England Primer.*

Topffer, Rudolph (1799–1846). The first cartoon strip in Europe was seen in the early 1800s. Rudolph Topffer, a Swiss artist, offered a strip which divided stories into individual pictures frames and the continuous narrative printed beneath the pictures.

Tozer, Alfred B. (1847–1916). One of the many pseudonyms for the Nick Carter series. He wrote 27 Nick Carter novelettes.

Trimmer, Sarah Kirby (1741–1810). Her best-known book is *History of the*

Robins. She was active in the Sunday school movement and had concerns about morals.

Trowbridge, John Townsend (1827–1916). He wrote novels as well as poetry. His *Jack Hazard and His Fortunes* (1871) is one of his best; there were several sequels. It was serialized in *Our Young Folks*.

Twain, Mark (1835–1910). Best known among children readers are *The Adventures of Tom Sawyer* and the *Adventures of Huckleberry Finn*. He also wrote *Prince and the Pauper* (1882), which is a children's favorite. See Clemens, Samuel Langhorne.

Vallely, Henry (1881–1950). Henry Vallely was an American comic artist, and the books illustrated by him are valuable regardless of text context. *Gang Busters*, *Jack Armstrong*, and *Lone Ranger* are among the favorites.

Venerable Bede (673–735). Wrote a book consisting of several hundred Latin words arranged under letters of the alphabet; each word was the subject of a comment. He also wrote a book on writing Latin verse.

Victor, Orville J. (1827–1910). In 1861 Orville Victor became the editor for Beadle publications and remained a powerful influence on the material produced until 1898. He was known for his moral and literary standards. He was a graduate of the Seminary and Theological Institute of Norwalk, Ohio.

Walters and Norman. A Philadelphia publishers in 1779. Published *Whittington and His Cat* and *World Turned Upside Down*, among others.

Watson, John W. (1850–1907). "Ian Maclaren" is the pseudonym used for fiction writing by John Watson. He published a number of religious works under his own name, but as Ian Maclaren he was a leading member of the Kailyard School of Scottish fiction, which came into being toward the end of the nineteenth century.

Weems, Mason Locke (1759–1825). A parson who was also a chapman. He worked along the East coast from New York to Georgia. He wrote and sold many of his own works. Many titles start with "God's Revenge Against..." dueling, adultery, drinking, gambling, murder, etc.

Westbrook, Arthur (1876–1911). Publisher of the Adventure Series (139 volumes), the Hart Series (187 volumes), the All-Star Series (100 volumes) and the Deadwood Dick Library (64 volumes).

Whitman, Albert (1933–). Owner of Whitman Publishing Company. Introduced the Big Little Books. Also published some of the Nick Carter books.

Wiggin, Kate Douglas (1856–1923). Her first book was *The Story of Patsy* (1883). Then she wrote *The Birds' Christmas Carol*, but her great success is *Rebecca of Sunnybrook Farm* (1903).

Wilder, Salmon. American printer. In 1814 he printed the *New Hieroglyphical Bible*. "For the amusement & instruction of children; Being A Selection of the most useful Lessons and most interesting Narratives; (Scripturally arranged) From Genesis to the Revelations. Embellished with Familiar Figures, and Striking Emblems. To the whole is added a sketch of the life of Our Blessed Saviour."

Wilson, John James. In 1832 he argued that dime novels were the origin of all youthful crimes.

Worde, Wynkyn de (?–1543). An early printer and bookseller in London. He succeeded Caxton. His first books were *Bevis of Hampton*, *Guy of Warwick* and *Robin Hood*.

References

Allen, Frederick L. "Horatio Alger Jr.: A Critical Commentary." *Saturday Review* 18 (Sept. 17, 1938): 3–4, 16–17.

Anglo, Michael. *Penny Dreadfuls and Other Victorian Horrors*. London: Jupiter, 1977.

Arbuthnot, May Hill. *Children and Books*. Glenview: Scott, Foreman, 1957.

Arnold, Arnold. *Pictures and Stories from Forgotten Children's Books*. New York: Dover, 1969.

Ashton, John. *Chapbooks of the Eighteenth Century*. New York: Kelley, 1970.

Avery, Gillian. *Nineteenth-Century Children: Heroes and Heroines in English Children's Stories, 1780–1900*. London: Hodder and Stoughton, 1965.

Axe, John. *Secret of Collecting Girls' Series Books, 1840–1991*. Grantsville, Md.: Hobby House Press, 2000.

Barrier, Michael. "Novel Kind of Business." *Nation's Business* 85 (8) (Aug. 1997): 64.

Barry, Florence. *Century of Children's Books*. London: Methuen and Co., 1922.

Bennett, Charles Henry. *Shadows*. London: David Bogue, 1856.

Bingham, Jane. *Fifteen Centuries of Children's Literature*. Westport, Conn.: Greenwood Press, 1980.

Bishop, Barbara. *American Boys' Series Books, 1900 to 1980*. Tampa: University of South Florida Library Associates, 1987.

Bishop, W. H. "Story-Paper Literature." *Atlantic Monthly* (Sept. 1879): 383–393.

Blanck, Jacob. *Harry Castlemon, Boys' Own Author*. New York: Bowker, 1941.

Bleiler, E. F. *Eight Dime Novels*. New York: Dover, 1974.

Borden, Bill. *Big Book of Big Little Books*. San Francisco: Chronicle Books, 1997.

Bragin, Charles. *Bibliography of Dime Novels, 1860–1928*. New York: C. Bragin, 1938.

_____. *Dime Novels, 1860–1864*. New York: C. Bragin, 1964.

Branch, E. D. *Sentimental Years, 1836–1860*. New York: Appleton-Century/Hill and Wang, 1834/1965.

Brant, Sandra. *Small Folk: A Celebration of Childhood in America*. New York: Dutton, 1980.

Brett, E. J. *Young Jack Harkaway and His Boy Tinker among the Turks*. London: Boys of England Office, 1876.

Britt, George. *Forty Years—Forty Millions*. New York: Kennikat Press, 1935.

Brown, Bill, ed. *Reading the West*. Boston: Bedford Books, 1997.

Brown, Herbert Ross. *Sentimental*

Novel in America, 1789–1860. Durham: Duke Univ. Press, 1940.

Burgess, Gelett. "Confessions of a Dime Novelist." *Bookman* (Aug. 1902): 528–533.

Carney, Carol Ruth. *Constructive Narratives of American Culture and Identity: Beadle's Dime Novels by and about Women, 1860–1870*. Ann Arbor: University of Michigan Press, 1995.

Carpenter, Humphrey. *Oxford Companion to Children's Literature*. London: Oxford University Press, 1995.

Castlemon, Harry. "Inventor of the Boy Thriller." *Literary Digest* **50** (Sept. 11, 1915): 558–560.

"Cheap Libraries" Question. *Publishers Weekly*, April 14, 1888: 634–635.

Clark, Thomas. "Virgins, Villains and Varmints." *American Heritage* (Spring 1952): 42–72.

Commire, Anne, ed. *Yesterday's Authors of Books for Children*. Detroit: Gale Research, 1960/1977.

Comstock, Anthony. "Vampire Literature." *North American Review* (1891): 160–171.

_____. *Traps for the Young*. New York: Funk and Wagnalls, 1883/1967.

Cook, Michael L. *Dime Novel Roundup: Annotated Index, 1931–1981*. Ohio: Bowling Green University Press, 1983.

Cowie, Alexander. "Vogue of the Domestic Novel 1850–1870." *Southern Atlantic Quarterly* **41** (Oct. 1942): 416–432.

Cox, J. Randolph. *Dime Novel Companion: A Source Book*. Westport, Conn.: Greenwood Press, 2000.

Cummings, R. F. *Ralph F. Cummings, Standard Dime and Nickel Novel Catalogue of Old Weeklies*. Grafton, Mass.: R. F. Cummings, 1936.

Curti, Merle. "Dime Novel in the American Tradition." *Yale Review* **26** (Summer 1937): 761–778.

Cutler, John Levi. "Gilbert Patten and His Frank Merriwell Saga; a Study in Sub-Literary Fiction, 1896–1913." *Maine Bulletin* **36** (10) (May 1934).

Daly, Jim. "Gentleman Jack; or, from Student to Pugilist." *New York Five-Cent Library* **14** (Nov. 12, 1892).

Dalziel, Margaret. *Popular Fiction One Hundred Year Ago: An Unexplored Tract of Literary History*. London: Cohan and West, 1957.

Darling, R. L. "Authors vs. Critics; Children's Books in the 1870s." *Publishers Weekly* **192** (Oct. 16, 1967): 25–27.

Dawson, Michael. "The Mountie from Dime Novel to Disney." *Beaver* (Apr./May 1999): 47–48.

De Vinne, Theodore Low. *Chap-Book and Its Outgrowths*. New York: Literary Collector, 1902.

Deane, Paul. *Mirrors of American Culture*. Metuchen, N.J.: Scarecrow Press, 1991.

Denning, Michael. *Mechanic Accents: Dime Novels and Working-Class Culture in America*. London: Verso, 1987.

Donelson, K. "Censorship and Early Adolescent Literature." *Dime Novel Roundup* **47** (1978): 119–121.

Droter, Kirsten. *English Children and Their Magazines, 1751–1945*. New Haven: Yale University Press, 1988.

Dunae, Patrick. "Penny Dreadfuls: Late Nineteenth-Century Boys' Literature and Crime." *Victorian Studies* **22** (1979): 133–150.

Durham, Phillip. "Dime Novels: An American Heritage." *Western Humanities Review* **9** (Winter 1954–1955): 33–43.

_____. "General Classification of 1,531 Dime Novels." *Huntington Library Quarterly* **17** (May 1954): 287–291.

Eaton, Anne Thaxter. *Treasure for the Taking*. New York: Viking, 1957.

Edgeworth, Maria. *Practical Education*. London: J. Johnson, 1798.

Egoff, Shelia. *Only Connect*. London: Oxford University Press, 1969/1996.

Eisgruber, Frank. *Gangland's Doom: Shadow of the Pulps*. Mercer Island, Wash.: Starmount House, 1985.

Elliot, Jeffrey M. *Pulp Voices: Interviews with Pulp Magazine Writers and Editors*. San Bernardino: Borgo Press, 1982.

Ellsworth, William W. *Golden Age of Authors*. Boston: Houghton Mifflin, 1919.

Erickson, Paul J. "Judging Books by Their Covers: Format, the Implied Reader and the 'Degenerations.'" *ATQ* **12** (3) (Sept. 1998): 247.

Everett, William. "Critical Notices: Dime Books." *North American Review* **24** (1864): 303–309.

Fiedler, Leslie. *Love and Death in the American Novel*. New York: Stein and Day, 1966.

Floyd, Bianca. "Bookmark." *Chronicle of Higher Education* **46** (16) (Dec. 10, 1999): 48.

Fraser, C. Lovat. *Old Broadside Ballads*. Reprint of the 1920 ed. Norwood, Penn.: Norwood Editions, 1974.

Frolich, Karl. *Frolich's with Scissors and Pen*. New York: R. Worthingham, 1879.

_____. *Spectropia; or, Surprising Special Illusions*. Brighton: J. H. Brown, 1864.

"From Penny Dreadfuls to Harlequin." *Wilson Library Bulletin*, June 1995: 20.

Gleason, Gene. "From Penny Dreadfuls to Harlequin." *Wilson Library Bulletin* (May 1975): 647–656.

Grade, Arnold. *Merrill Guide to Early Juvenile Literature*. Columbus, Ohio: C. E. Merrill, 1970.

Green, S. S. "Sensational Fiction in Public Libraries." *Library Journal* 4 (9–10) (Sept./Oct. 1879): 345–355.

Haining, Peter. *Art of Horror Stories*. Secaucus, N.J.: Chartwell Books, 1986.

Hall, G. Stanley. "Children's Reading as a Factor in Their Education." *Library Journal* (1908): 123–124.

Harvey, Charles M. "Dime Novel in American Life." *Atlantic Monthly* (July 1907): 37–45.

Haviland, Virginia. *Yankee Doodle's Literary Sampler*. New York: Crowell, 1974.

Hazard, Paul. *Books, Children and Men*. Boston: Horn Book, 1960.

Helbig, Alethea K. *Dictionary of American Children's Fiction 1859–1959*. Westport, Conn.: Greenwood Press, 1985.

Herman, Gertrude B. "Chapbooks, 'Star Wars,' and Other Entertainments." *School Library Journal* (March 1980): 87–90.

Hersey, H. B. *Pulpwood Editor*. New York: Fred Stokes, 1937.

Hewins, Caroline M. *Caroline M. Hewins. Her Book: Containing a Mid-Century Child and Her Books*. Boston: Horn Book, 1954.

_____. "Yearly Report on Boys' and Girls' Reading." *Library Journal* **33** (1908): 123–124.

Hoppenstand, Gary, ed. *Dime Novel Detective*. Ohio: Bowling Green University Press, 1982.

_____, ed. *Defective Detective in the Pulps*. Ohio: Bowling Green University Press, 1983.

Hudson, H. *Bibliography of Hard-Cover Boys Books*. Tampa: Data Print, 1977.

Jakubowski, Maxim. *Mammoth Book of Pulp Fiction*. New York: Carroll and Graf, 1996.

James, Elizabeth. *Penny Dreadful and Boys' Adventures*. London: British Library, 1998.

James, Philip. *Children's Books of Yesterday*. Reprinted by Gale Research in 1933. London: Studio Ltd., 1976.

Jencks, George. "Dime Novel Makers." *Bookman* (Oct. 1904): 198–214.

Johannsen, Albert. *House of Beadle and Its Dime and Nickel Novel*. Norman: University of Oklahoma Press, 1950.

Johnson, Clifton. *Old-Time Schools and School-Books*. New York: Dover, 1963.

Johnson, Deidre A. *Edward Stratemeyer and the Stratemeyer Syndicate*.

New York: Twayne Publishers, 1993.
_____. *Girls' Series Books: A Checklist of Titles Published 1840–1991.* Minneapolis: Children's Literature Research Collections, University of Minnesota, 1992.
Johnson, Edna. *Anthology of Children's Literature.* Boston: Houghton Mifflin, 1935.
Jones, Daryl E. "Clenched Teeth and Curses." *Journal of Popular Culture* 7 (Winter 1973): 652–665.
_____. *Dime Novel Western.* Ohio: Bowling Green University Press, 1978.
Jones, Robert Kennedy. *Lure of Adventure.* Mercer Island, Wash.: Starmount House, 1989.
Judson, Edward. "Buffalo Bill's Best Shot." *New York Weekly* (Mar. 3–July 17, 1872): 27.
_____. "Buffalo Bill's Last Victory." *New York Weekly* (Aug. 7–Nov. 13, 1872): 27.
_____. "Buffalo Bill, King of the Border." *New York Weekly* (Dec. 23, 1869–Mar. 10, 1870): 25.
Keifer, Monica. *American Children through Their books.* Philadelphia: University of Pennsylvania, 1948.
Kent, Thomas. *Interpretation and Genre.* Lewisburg, Penn.: Bucknell University, 1986.
Landells, Ebenezer. *Boy's Own Toy-Maker.* New York: Appleton and Co., 1860.
Landers, Ann. "History Lesson on Hearts and Flowers." *Chicago Tribune* (Feb. 14, 1998).
Lanes, Selma. *Down the Rabbit Hole.* New York: Atheneum, 1971.
LeBlanc, Edward T. *Bibliography of Four Tousey Dime Novel Stories.* New York: Garland, 1979.
Leithead, J. Edward. "Klondike Stampede." *American Book Collector* (May-June 1973): 23–29.
_____. "Now They're Collector's Items." *Dime Novel Roundup* (June 15, 1966): 58–60.
_____. "Pulp King W. Bert Foster." *Relics* 2 (Summer 1968): 10–12.
Lewis, Leon. *Daredeath Dick, King of the Cowboys; or, in the Wild West with Buffalo Bill.* New York: Beadle's Banner Weekly, 1890.
Lonsdale, Bernard. *Children Experience Literature.* New York: Random House, 1972.
Ludlam, Charles. "Mystery of Irma Vep." *Washington Post* (Feb. 8, 2000): 1.
Lund, Michael. *America's Continuing Story.* Detroit: Wayne State University Press, 1993.
Lyons, Donald. "Theater: Pastiches Inventively Funny and Just Plain Odd." *Wall Street Journal* (Oct. 13, 1998): A20.
Machen, Arthur. *Grande Trouvaille: A Legend of Pentonville.* London: First Edition Bookshop, 1923.
MacLeod, Anne Scott. *American Childhood: Essays on Children's Literature of the Nineteenth and Twentieth Century.* Athens: University of Georgia Press, 1994.
_____. *Moral Tale: Children's Fiction and American Culture, 1820–1860.* Hamden, Conn.: Archon Books, 1975.
Maryles, Daisy. "Venerable Young Sleuths Find New Home." *Publishers Weekly* (March 5, 1979): 22.
Mathiews, Franklin K. "Blowing Out the Boys' Brains." *Outlook* **18** (Nov. 1914): 652–654.
Matter, Darryl E. "Oliver Optic (William T. Adams)." *Antiques & Collecting Hobbies* (Sept. 1986): 52–55.
Meggendorfer, Lothar. *Comic Actors.* London: H. Grevel & Co., 1891.
Meigs, Cornelia. *Critical History of Children's Literature.* New York: Macmillan, 1953.
Miller, William C. *Dime Novel Authors 1860–1900.* Grafton, Mass.: R. F. Cummings, 1933.
Mott, Frank Luther. *Golden Multitudes: Story of Best Sellers in the*

United States. New York: Bowker, 1947/1960.
Muller, Bill. "Bill Muller on Film." *Arizona Republic* (2001).
Nasaw, D. "Children and Commercial Culture." *Small Worlds: Children and Adolescents in America* (1992): 14–25.
Neuburg, Victor. *Chapbooks, a Guide to Reference Material in England, Scotland and America*. London: Waburn Press, 1972.
_____. *Penny Histories*. New York: Harcourt Brace, 1969.
Nilsen, Richard. "Comics Reveal Yesterday's Heroes." *Arizona Republic* (2001).
Noel, Mary. "Dime Novels." *American Heritage* (Feb. 1956): 112–113.
_____. *Villains Galore: The Hay-Day of the Popular Story Weekly*.
Norris, Curtis B. "Where Have You Gone, Frank Merriwell?" *Yankee* (Feb. 1970): 63–96ff.
Olcott, Frances Jenkins. *Children's Reading*. Boston: Houghton Mifflin, 1927.
Opie, Iona and Peter. *Lore and Language of School Children*. New York: Oxford University Press, 1959.
Pearson, Edmond. *Dime Novels, or Following an Old Trail in Popular Literature*. New York: Little, Brown, 1929.
Pyle, Howard. "Chapbook Heroes." *Harpers New Monthly Magazine* 81 (1890): 123–128.
Quayle, Eric. *Collector's Book of Children's Books*. New York: Clarkson N. Potter, 1971.
_____. "Juvenile Incunabula." *Wilson Library Bulletin* (Dec. 1971): 326–334.
Rapson, Richard L. "American Child as Seen by British Travelers, 1845–1935." *American Quarterly* (Fall 1965): 520–534.
Reynolds, Quentin. *Fiction Factory: From Pulp Row to Quality Street*. New York: Random House, 1955.
Rittenhouse, Jack D. *Dime Novels on Early Oil*. Sierra Madre, Calif.: Stagecoach Press, 1951.
Roberts, Gary. *Old Sleuth's Freaky Female Detectives*. Ohio: Bowling Green University Press, 1990.
Rogers, Denis. *Munro's Ten-Cent Novels*. Mass.: E. T. Le Blanc, 1958.
Rosenbach, Abraham S. Wolf. *Early American Children's Books*. New York: Dover, 1833/1971.
Ruhm, Herbert. *Hard-Boiled Detective: Stories from* Black Mask Magazine, *1920–1951*. New York: Vintage, 1977.
St. John, Judith, ed. *Osbourne Collection of Early Children's Books 1566–1910*. Toronto: Toronto Public Library, 1958.
Saltman, Judith. *Riverside Anthology of Children's Literature*, 6th ed. Boston: Houghton Mifflin, 1975.
Scarfe, Laurence. *History of Children's Books and Juvenile Graphic Art: Introduction*. New York: Visual Publications, 1975.
_____. *History of Children's Books and Juvenile Graphic Art: Part 2*. New York: Visual Publications, 1975.
Schurman, Lydia Cushman. *Scorned Literature: Essays on the History and Criticism of Popular Mass-Produced Fiction in America*. Westport, Conn.: Greenwood Press, 2002.
Scoville, Samuel. "Rescue, Robbery and Escapes." *Forum* (July 1925): 83–91.
Settle, William. "Literature as History: The Dime Novel as a Historian's Tool." *Literature & History* (1970): 9–20.
Shepard, Leslie. *History of the Horn Book*. London: Rampart Lion for the Broadsheet King, 1977.
Simmons, Michael. "Dime Novel and the American Mind." *Mankind* 2 (Oct. 1969): 58–63.
Smith, Elva Sophronia. *History of Children's Literature*. Chicago: American Library Association, 1980.
Smith, Henry Nash. *Virgin Land*.

Cambridge: Harvard University Press, 1950, pp. 99–135.

Speaight, George. *History of the English Toy Theatre*. London: Studio Vista, 1969.

Springhall, John. "A Life Story for the People?" *Victorian Studies* 33 (Winter 1990): 227–232.

_____. "Boys of Bircham School." *History of Education* 20 (1991): 77–94.

_____. "Disseminating Impure Literature: The 'Penny Dreadful' Publishing Business since 1860." *Economic History Review* 47 (1994): 567–584.

Sullivan, Larry E. "Cheap Books and Nineteenth-Century Libraries." *AB Bookman's Weekly* (March 29, 1982): 2410–2428.

_____. *Pioneers, Passionate Ladies and Private Eyes*. New York: Howarth Press, 1996.

Thomas, James Stewart. *Big Little Book Price Guide*. Des Moines: Wallace-Homestead, 1983.

Thwaite, Mary. *From Primer to Pleasure in Reading*. Boston: Horn Book, 1963.

Ticklecheek, Timothy. *Cries of London*. London: John Fairborn, 1797.

Townsend, John Rowe. *Written for Children*. Boston: Horn Book, 1974.

Travis, Thomas. *Young Malefactor: A Study in Juvenile Delinquency, Its Causes and Treatment*. New York: Crowell, 1908.

Tuer, Andrew W. *History of the Horn Book*. New York: Benjamin Blom, 1968.

Turner, E. S. *Boys Will Be Boys*. London: Joseph Michael, 1957.

Watt, William Whyte. *Shilling Shockers of the Gothic School*. Cambridge: Harvard University Press, 1932.

Weiss, Harry B. *Book about Chapbooks*. Ann Arbor: Edwards Bros., 1969.

Welch, d'Alte A. *Bibliography of American Children's Books Printed prior to 1821*. Mass.: Shaw and Shoemaker, 1972.

Wells, Kate Gannett. "Responsibility of Parents in the Selection of Reading." *Library Journal* 4 (9–10) (Sept.-Oct. 1879): 325–330.

West, M. I. "Response of Children's Librarians to Dime Novels and Series Books." *Children's Literature Association Quarterly* 10 (3) (1985): 137–139.

Whalley, Joyce Irene. *Cobwebs to Catch Flies*. Berkeley: University of California Press, 1975.

Whipple, Kent L. *Cowboy Heroes/City Thugs*. Scottsdale, Ariz.: Meyer Gallery, 1990.

_____. "Dames! Thugs! Gore! Feel the Force of Pulp Art." *Arizona Republic* (1999): 1–4.

_____. *Detectives/City Thugs*. Scottsdale, Ariz.: Meyer Gallery, 1990.

Williamson, N. J. "Maimie Pinkering's Reading." *Children's Literature Association Quarterly* 9 (1) (1984): 3–6.

Willson, Meredith. *Music Man*. New York: Putnam, 1969.

Wohl, Bernard. *Class, Status and Power*. Glencoe, Ill.: Free Press, 1953.

"Year's Work in Dime Novels, Series Books and Pulp Magazines." *Dime Novel Round-Up*, 1983.

Young, William. *Study of Action-Adventure Fiction*. New York: Edwin Mellen, 1996.

Zuckerman, Michael. "Nursery Tales of Horatio Alger." *American Quarterly* 24 (May 1972): 191–209.

Index